Knights, Lords, and Ladies

THE MIDDLE AGES SERIES

Ruth Mazo Karras, Series Editor

Edward Peters, Founding Editor

A complete list of books in the series is available from the publisher.

KNIGHTS, LORDS, AND LADIES

In Search of Aristocrats in the Paris Region,
1180–1220

John W. Baldwin

Foreword by William Chester Jordan

PENN

UNIVERSITY OF PENNSYLVANIA PRESS

PHILADELPHIA

Published by
University of Pennsylvania Press
Philadelphia, Pennsylvania 19104-4112
www.upenn.edu/pennpress

Printed in the United States of America on acid-free paper
10   9   8   7   6   5   4   3   2   1

Library of Congress Cataloging-in-Publication Data
Names: Baldwin, John W., author. | Jordan, William C., writer of foreword.
Title: Knights, lords, and ladies : in search of aristocrats in the
   Paris region, 1180–1220 / John W. Baldwin ; foreword by
   William Chester Jordan.
Other titles: Middle Ages series.
Description: First edition. | Philadelphia : University of Pennsylvania Press,
   [2019] | Series: Middle Ages series | Includes bibliographical references
   and index.
Identifiers: LCCN 2019019900 | ISBN 9780812251289 (hardcover)
Subjects: LCSH: Aristocracy (Social class)—France—Paris—History—To
   1500. | Nobility—France—Paris—History—To 1500. | Paris (France)—
   History—To 1515. | France—History—Philip II Augustus, 1180–1223.
Classification: LCC HT653.F8 B35 2019 | DDC 305.5/20944361—dc23
LC record available at https://lccn.loc.gov/2019019900

To Jenny,
and to our grandchildren,
Karen, Elias, Lily, Lukas, Justin, Nell, Maude

Contents

Color plates follow page 158

Illustrations

PLATES

Foreword

William Chester Jordan

The present book, *Knights, Lords, and Ladies: In Search of Aristocrats in the Paris Region, 1180–1220*, was Professor John Baldwin's last. The distinguished Johns Hopkins University historian completed a full draft of the manuscript, which he had submitted to the University of Pennsylvania Press before his death. The readers whom the Press solicited were enthusiastic about the manuscript. Although they had suggestions for final revisions, as readers always have, they were in agreement that the manuscript was excellently argued, important substantively, clearly written, and, for all these reasons, worthy of publication. Unfortunately, Baldwin passed away before he could engage with their suggestions. Everyone concerned in the production of this volume, however, believes that even without his response to the readers' reports and what might have been his own potential recommendations for additional revisions, the manuscript was a powerful and learned exemplar of scholarship and representative of the interests and thrust of the entire corpus of Baldwin's impressive work. Careful copyediting and the verification of references and statistics rather than stylistic or organizational changes have thus guided the transition from the manuscript to the book. In its current state, the study must be very close to the volume that John Baldwin intended it to be.

Knights, Lords, and Ladies, as I have already implied, appears at the end of a series of Baldwin's scholarly interventions in the course of a very long and productive career. Indeed, even without its publication, scholars would consider his contribution to medieval studies profound. Only forty-one when his two-volume *Masters, Princes, and Merchants: The Social Views of Peter the Chanter and His Circle* appeared in 1970, Baldwin provided scholars in the first volume of that work precise and supremely intelligent reconstructions of some of the leading moral issues discussed by scholars in Catholic Europe in the late twelfth and early thirteenth centuries. In doing so, he demonstrated his impressive paleographic skills and his wide-ranging command of scholastic philosophy, theology, and canon law. The second volume made numerous excerpts of the texts that were at the center of his study available to subsequent scholars and indicated where they might find many more.

All reviewers recognized the importance of the volumes, and the criticisms, such as there were, tended to fall under two headings. First, because he had recovered Master Peter the Chanter's circle of colleagues and so enthusiastically made them known in ways in which many of them had not been known before, Baldwin, it was alleged, sometimes overestimated the master's and his students'— but especially the master's—influence and originality. But what scholar who has the good fortune to pore over a fascinating and largely unknown body of texts or group of persons and shows the cohesive bonds among them for basically the first time does not occasionally imagine their impact on a historical era as somewhat greater than it might have been. Even if the originality of the views emanating from Peter and his circle is often hard to prove and at times contestable, Baldwin's assessment has, in the main, stood the test of time very well indeed.

The second body of criticisms was, loosely speaking, "formal." Why, it was wondered, did Baldwin proceed in his first volume thematically, since doing so made getting a sense of the development of the views of any single member of Master Peter's circle difficult? Why had he set the texts apart in a separate volume? Why did he not insist on footnotes instead of endnotes, which he had also relegated to the second volume? Finally, reviewers' perennial default lament, when they have little else to criticize: why did his work cost so much? In fact, $22.50, the purchase price, does not sound like a lot even in 1970 dollars, particularly since Baldwin's study consisted of two volumes, while one-volume scholarly books were regularly selling at the time for $10.00 or $12.50.

Masters, Princes, and Merchants was not John Baldwin's first major study. That distinction goes to *Medieval Theories of the Just Price: Romanists, Canonists, and Theologians in the Twelfth and Thirteenth Centuries*, which appeared as one of the "Transactions" volumes of the American Philosophical Society in 1959. This work demonstrated Baldwin's remarkable knowledge of juristic thought and its connections with theology and in particular revealed his interest in the morality of commerce as understood by a variety of medieval commentators. When he published *Masters, Princes, and Merchants* a decade later, it came as no surprise that he devoted a substantial section of his commentary in volume 1 and of the excerpted texts in volume 2 to commerce and most especially to the problem of usury and its reckoning as a serious sin in medieval theology. Meanwhile, he continued to publish detailed technical studies on scholasticism and university culture in the late twelfth and thirteenth centuries, the discursive medium and the venue respectively for so many of the discussions he analyzed in his early works.

Undoubtedly, because Paris loomed large in all his projects up to and including *Masters, Princes, and Merchants* and because Paris was the royal city of France par excellence in his preferred period of study, John Baldwin soon turned his considerable talents to excavating the history of the monarchy and the city. He did so in a series of brilliant studies and editions that earned him the deep respect and lasting gratitude of French medievalists. His 1986 book *The Government of Philip Augustus: Foundations of French Royal Power in the Middle Ages* appeared in French translation only a few years later in 1991. Like *Masters, Princes, and Merchants*, its elaborate apparatus follows the study per se— and there are no footnotes, just endnotes, often full of tantalizing material and hints for new directions of inquiry.

Baldwin's collaborative work on editing original documents from the period of Philip II Augustus's reign is already apparent in *The Government of Philip Augustus*, but it culminated in the publication of the magisterial *Les Registres de Philippe Auguste* in 1992. More popular, but undergirded by this firsthand familiarity with the documentary records, was *Paris, 1200*, which he published in 2006 and had written primarily for a French audience. Almost immediately, however, it came out in English translation for an American scholarly public eager to read in its own language what Baldwin said about the great city on the river Seine on the eve of its medieval demographic surge. The French expressed their admiration of Baldwin and his work by his election to the vaunted Académie des Inscriptions et Belles-Lettres and making him a Chevalier de la Légion d'Honneur and a Chevalier de l'Ordre des Arts et des Lettres.

John Baldwin's work has always interested me and my graduate students, in particular what he wrote on French administration and the difficulties of reconstructing the kingdom's administrative development because of the destruction of fiscal records in the great fire at the Chambre des Comptes on the night of 26/27 October 1737. It is not possible to summarize his marvelous insights and general conclusions in this area in a few lines, but his major findings and claims are the following. The reign of Philip II Augustus, 1179/80–1223, saw a revolution in the administration and record keeping of the French kingdom. The impulse for this revolution was the continuing struggle with the Plantagenets. Possessing a kingly title, even an ideologically charged one, as Philip II did, was insufficient in and of itself to command the resources needed to hold the country's own against its rivals, let alone turn the tables on them. The hard work that made Philip II a great king was more mundane. He needed to exploit every opportunity to increase his direct influence, and this meant trying to get control over and access to resources in wide swaths of territory that were held either tenuously or tentatively by aristocratic lineages. Circumstances that made this possible might be, among others, the minority of an heir over whom Philip II could exercise guardianship or the suppression of a rebellion that permitted his men to oversee the defeated rebel's lands.

Another opportunity offered itself in the crusade. Philip II used his preparations as an opportunity to improve the operation of government by streamlining administrative offices and clarifying chains of command and administrative procedures in anticipation of his absence in the eastern Mediterranean. These measures were strengthened in the "decisive decade" following the king's brief expedition to the Holy Land, and in doing so Philip drew on the talents of the lesser nobility, especially the knights, who as a result of their service owed their increased prestige and a considerable portion of their income to him. Effectively he created a financially dependent and deeply loyal administration, whose employment allowed him largely to bypass the high aristocracy. He was not always on good terms with the church, in whatever way the word "church" is defined (the papacy, the French bishops, clerical zealots who wanted to confound the alleged heretics and their supporters in Languedoc, and so on). Yet despite very significant tensions with churchmen over his governmental policies and irregular personal life, he managed to keep his conflicts with the church from undermining his efforts to increase the power and reach of the crown.

Philip II found himself aided by the incompetency of King John of England. Of that, there can be no doubt. As long as Richard I the Lionheart lived, the Plantagenets were more than a match for the Capetians, despite all the French king's efforts. It was John's loss of Normandy in 1204 and of other territories north of the Loire soon afterward that cemented the accomplishments of France's decisive decade. The conquest stimulated an ideological revolution in France, with clear roots in the past, of course, but more pronounced from the latter part of Philip II Augustus's reign and forward into the thirteenth century: proud and challenging claims to the special sacrality of the French crown and dynasty. Nonetheless, according to John Baldwin, it would be difficult even to imagine the success Philip II enjoyed in his claims to authority and in the execution of governance in France after his conquest of Normandy in the absence of the accomplishments made during the decisive decade. In this scenario, the victories against the Plantagenets and their allies in 1214 at Bouvines and Roche-au-Moine simply sealed the king's achievement, or as John Baldwin liked to say to me and no doubt to others, "it was because of Philip Augustus that France could have a Saint Louis."

Meanwhile, Baldwin continued to produce gemlike articles on subjects on which he was already a recognized authority. At the same time, some of his newer work appeared to veer away from the history of scholastic culture and the French government. In fact, *The Language of Sex: Five Voices from Northern France Around 1200*, which appeared in 1996, and *Aristocratic Life in Medieval France:*

The Romances of Jean Renart and Gerbert de Montreuil, 1190–1230, published in 2000, had more in common with what we now know was his overall project than simply an overlap in the period covered. To scholastic culture and government, Baldwin was adding the aristocracy as one of his principal interests. In doing so, he needed to probe the moral sentiments and ethical dilemmas of the upper class and their public expression and representation. In addition, he had to determine how aristocratic culture differed from that of other social (and professional) groups, preeminently the clergy. In particular, he had to justify using fiction (romances, fabliaux, and the like) and performative practices such as tournaments to recover aristocratic culture. His goal—and the present book is the fulfillment of it—was nothing less than a comprehensive portrait of life in the heartland of the territory that Baldwin had studied his entire scholarly life, the Île-de-France. He succeeded masterfully in painting this portrait by bringing together evidence from chronicles, charters, fiscal documentation, archaeological reports, and belletristic sources, including poems and songs. The result is a multi-dimensional description and explication of the relations of kings, governmental administrators, aristocratic lineages, churchmen, and to some extent burghers in the precisely defined period of Philip II Augustus's reign, the era, as it is so often said, when France was "made."

I have said that the description offered in this book is multidimensional, but, as Baldwin had to admit and explicitly remarks, it is not a genuinely comprehensive description. The amount of space in the work devoted to the political, social, and economic interactions—indeed, interdependency—of the bourgeoisie and the aristocracy in the Île-de-France is quite limited. Moreover, there are no peasants to speak of in Baldwin's story; yet he knew the story would be far richer with their presence. No one, I think, can rationally doubt that John Baldwin had the intellectual capacity to expand the book to cover these other areas, but mastering the large number of studies of regional economies that meticulously detail the bourgeois economy and seigneurs' relations with their rustic dependents would also have taken a great deal of time, perhaps too much. He would have needed to devote another five or ten years to doing his own specialized studies to fill in gaps, as he had done in writing on scholasticism, government, and the aristocratic ethos; and he may have thought this was an unachievable undertaking at this stage in his career. Therefore, he gestured to the major standard studies but did not go further, committing himself instead to bringing together without further delay the results of the in-depth research he had already accomplished. He also intended and to all appearances succeeded in imposing on his analysis a statistical rigor that really is quite amazing. *Knights, Lords, and Ladies: In Search of Aristocrats in the Paris Region, 1180–1220* is the culmination of John Baldwin's career as a scholar—and it is a magnificent accomplishment, ranking with *Masters, Princes, and Merchants* and *The Government of Philip Augustus* and likely to have a similar enduring legacy.

One can anticipate criticisms, of course. They are by now old hat. Some readers will continue to wish for thematic integration in a chronological narrative. However, Baldwin was profoundly committed to thematic analysis. Moreover, he appears to have felt that limiting his study to Philip II Augustus's reign was not only defensible on substantive grounds but, given the span of only forty years, doing so implicitly undermined the potential criticism that his argument would be hard to reconfigure in the reader's mind as a chronological story of development. He was also determined to maintain the strict separation between the technical matter—presented in the appendixes at the end of the book—and the history he was writing with the help of this technical matter. This determination on his part will also call to mind the organization of *Masters, Princes, and Merchants* and *The Government of Philip Augustus*. As to price, it is no longer an issue. *Knights, Lords, and Ladies* is a monument to a great historian. As such, it is priceless.

Abbreviations and Short Titles

In addition to the abbreviations below, the first section of the bibliography lists abbreviations of cartularies and charter collections.

Actes	*Recueil des actes de Philippe Auguste*, ed. Delaborde et al.
Arch. dép.	Archives départementales
AN	Archives nationales, Paris
AN Supp. seals	AN, Centre de sigillographie et d'héraldique, Collection supplément à la collection des moulages des sceaux des Archives nationales
Bibl. mun.	Bibliothèque municipale
BnF	Bibliothèque nationale de France
BnF Est.	BnF, Département des estampes et de la photographie
Bouchot I/II	Bouchot, *Inventaire des dessins exécutés pour Roger de Gaignières*, vol. 1 or 2
Budget	*Le Premier Budget de la monarchie française*, ed. Lot and Fawtier
CCCM	Corpus Christianorum Continuatio Mediaevalis
com.	commune
dép.	département
Douët d'Arcq I/II	Douët d'Arcq, *Collection de sceaux*, vol. 1 or 2
INRAP	Institut national de recherches archéologiques préventives
MGH	Monumenta Germaniae Historica
PL	Patrologia Latina
Register A	MS, Bibl. Apost. Vaticana, Ottoboni lat. 2796
Register C	MS, Paris, AN JJ 7
Register E	MS, Paris, AN JJ 26
Registres	*Les Registres de Philippe Auguste*
RHF	*Recueil des historiens des Gaules et de la France*
SRA	Service régional de l'archéologie

Chapter 1

In Search of Aristocrats

At the beginning of the twelfth century the region around Paris entered history with the reputation for being the land of unruly aristocrats. Entrenched within their castles they were viewed as quarreling among themselves, terrorizing the countryside, harassing churchmen and peasants, pillaging, and committing unspeakable atrocities. There is an immediate explanation for this bad press. It is Suger, the contemporary abbot of Saint-Denis, who wrote a biography of the reigning Capetian monarch, Louis VI (1106–37). In his vivid account he pictured the king riding tirelessly throughout the region, besieging the castles (not always successfully), suppressing the disputes of aristocrats, and pacifying the region. Abetting the anarchy in the background was the unsettling presence of the powerful Anglo-Norman king Henry I, whom the Capetian was unable to defeat in pitched battle. Suger's *Vie de Louis VI le Gros* therefore has provided the master narrative for the period. Although occasionally exaggerated and infused with a royal perspective, Suger's picture of the region nonetheless is essentially correct in its broad outlines. His themes are supported by contemporary ecclesiastical charters and confirmed by similar reports from contemporary church chroniclers for the neighboring regions. Orderic Vitalis in Normandy, Guibert de Nogent in the Beauvaisis, Galbert de Bruges in Flanders, and William of Malmesbury in England at civil war depicted remarkably comparable disturbances for their regions. In fact, modern historians often depict the turn of the eleventh and twelfth centuries as the "Age of Anarchy."[1] Suger himself wrote not only as a spokesman for the Capetian monarchy, but also as a churchman who was sensitive to the endemic depredations against monasteries, beginning with his own Saint-Denis and spreading to other churches throughout the region.

When we return to the Paris region at the end of the twelfth century during the reign of Philip Augustus (1179–1223), however, the picture has changed dramatically both at the higher level of the kingdom as well as at the local level around Paris. At the higher level, Philip Augustus had created the major governmental organs of the Capetian monarchy and replaced the feudal magnates at the royal court with loyal men of lesser rank. Most important, he had taken the duchy of Normandy from the English kings and expelled them to territories south of the Loire. All of these achievements were confirmed with his stunning victories against King John of England and his allies at the battles of La Roche-aux-Moines and Bouvines in 1214.[2] At the local level the major castles were subdued; peace reigned throughout the countryside; the same aristocratic families reappeared, but they acted no longer as brigands but as *fideles* of the king, at times offering loyal service in his court. This pacification of the Paris region itself, however, had been in process since the time of his grandfather. Louis VI not only reduced the offending castles, but he began to recruit aristocratic families into his entourage. The policy of co-opting the local lords was continued by his son Louis VII, so major progress had already been accomplished before Philip Augustus's accession. The churches and monasteries were now secure from despoliation by the local castellans with the result that the usurpation of land had markedly decreased. Instead, land circulated peacefully and principally through substantial transfers of property and revenues from the aristocracy to churches, all accomplished by the instrument of written charters.

Benefiting from this condition of peace and stasis, the present study proposes an examination of the aristocracy of the Paris region exclusively during the reign of Philip Augustus. It will forgo further attention to previous or later developments that would enable establishing long-term trends. By focusing on the four decades pivoted on the year 1200 (1180–1220), it will compensate for this reduction of time span by attempting to plumb the depths of all the sources available for the period. This will involve relatively little reliance on the chroniclers' accounts and relies instead on large numbers of ecclesiastical charters and frequent statistical analyses of their contents, joined with church obituaries, tombstones, saints' lives, and royal inventories of fiefs and vassals. In addition to these traditional sources largely written in Latin will be the archaeological excavations both of castles and residences as well as of their moats and latrines, the examination of numerous aristocratic seals and of works of history and literature recited, not in Latin, but in the vernacular French, composed for the pleasure of aristocratic audiences. Sacrificing extended chronology and broad geography, this study shall attempt to provide vivid concreteness of detail as well as quantitative analysis for an important area. During the reign of Philip Augustus, Paris was undoubtedly the dynamic center of the Capetian realm, and the local aristocrats contributed not only to Philip Augustus's military victories but also to the creation of the Capetian monarchy that dominated western Europe in the thirteenth century.

À la recherche of aristocrats . . . When called upon, our aristocrats identified themselves by the concrete terms of "knight," "lord," and "lady." (The two or three who qualified used the title of "count.") To designate themselves in the aggregate they did not use the qualification of "noble" (*nobilis, noble*), which was employed exclusively by the clergy when they addressed the lay aristocracy. "Nobility" as a generic term did not come into common parlance until later in the thirteenth century. The term "aristocrat" (of Greek etymology), however, originated in the late medieval period and is currently employed by historians in a sociological sense to identify the free, dominant class of the medieval period.[3] At the turn of the twelfth and thirteenth centuries, however, our aristocrats would not have understood it; nonetheless we are obliged to use it because we lack alternatives.

Once Upon a Time There Was No Île-de-France

Nor would they have understood the term "Île-de-France." In 1913 when Marc Bloch published a trailblazing monograph on the Île-de-France, he asserted that no one had yet written a history of the region. To justify this bleak observation, he recited a litany of reasons. The name was recent and its geographical limits were never defined. Although the church archives were rich, no one had yet inventoried the unpublished manuscripts, and until modern times the region contained no archives produced by laymen. Undoubtedly Bloch would further agree that the national interests of the king and his capital at Paris have continually overshadowed attention to local affairs. And he concluded that not only has the history never been written, but it should not be written because the region lacks social and political cohesion unlike Champagne or Burgundy.[4] A century after Marc Bloch's appraisal, the history of the Île-de-France has remained unwritten for the medieval period. The present volume is an attempt to meet his challenge for the period from 1180 to 1220, a period that roughly corresponds to the reign of Philip II Augustus.

Personal Choices

Like most historical enterprises, studies of medieval local aristocracies are conditioned by two underlying sets of criteria, the personal choices of the researcher and the availability of sources. My personal choices affect the present project both longitudinally in time and laterally in space. Recent and successful studies of the aristocracies in medieval France such as those of the Mâconnais, the Vendômois, Anjou, and Champagne have extended their scope over more than a century to explain change in society over time.[5] This approach became less feasible for me in 2006 with the appearance of Nicolas Civel's noteworthy study *La Fleur de France: Les Seigneurs d'Île-de-France au XIIe siècle*. Concentrating primarily on the first half of the twelfth century, he has written a penetrating examination of seigneurial society in the Île-de-France and has raised many of the questions that I had already posed for the period of Philip Augustus. Drawing primarily on the chronicles and charter sources from the twelfth century, he has come close to exhausting the available evidence. Since I could hardly hope to improve on his work, I have gladly welcomed his study as a benefit that freed me to limit my study to the later period of 1180 to 1220. Eschewing the longitudinal approach, therefore, I have made a personal choice to limit my research to a brief half century comprising little more than two or three generations conveniently delimited by the reign of Philip Augustus. It is the period with which I am most familiar and constitutes a pendant to a previous study, *Paris, 1200*, which was likewise focused tightly in time and place.[6] Making a virtue of this restriction I propose a sharply focused snapshot of the period—hopefully with the precision of MRI imaging—that offers more in detail than in broad scope in pursuit of evolving trends.

Like Bloch I have sought to limit my study spatially to the region around Paris, but I have abstained from the modern terms Île-de-France or Francilien, which, as Bloch pointed out, were not known in the twelfth and thirteenth centuries.[7] It is nonetheless true that in the early Middle Ages the West Franks had long distinguished a small *Francia* that was centered on Paris from a large *Francia* that encompassed the western half of the empire. For example, in my period, Pierre the Chanter, the celebrated Parisian theologian, echoed this distinction when he noted in glossing the Bible that just as there was a particular Judea as distinct from a general Judea in the Holy Land, there is also "a particular *francia* around Paris and a general *francia*."[8] Moreover, the smaller category of "castellany of Paris" that emerged in thirteenth-century royal administration is too limited, but the boundaries of the royal domain, that is, land benefiting the king directly, is too large and fluid because it expanded exponentially during Philip's reign, increasing to two to three times its former size. To recreate an Île-de-France for my period, therefore, I have found it most useful to set the boundaries arbitrarily by juxtaposing two sets of sources: two surveys of fief-holders ordered by Philip Augustus and the corresponding concentration of ecclesiastical cartularies.[9] Defined by feudal surveys and church cartularies, the limits of this territory can be best envisaged in a map (Map 1). It is likewise my personal choice to remain as rigorously within the temporal and spatial limits as possible. All material before and especially after my period has been considered anachronistic, and all witnesses have been restricted as much as possible

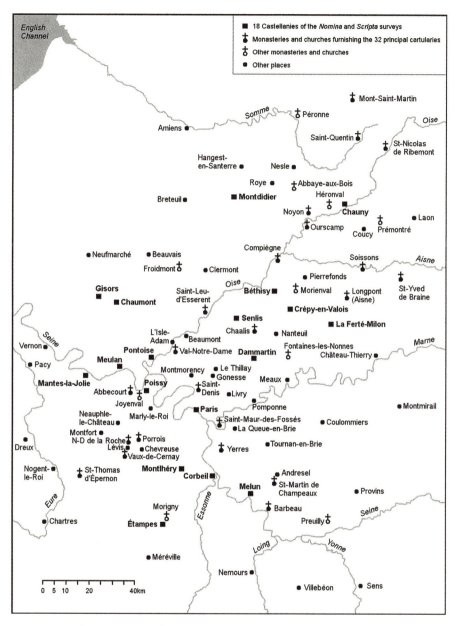

Map 1. The aristocracy of the Paris region. Eight foundations among those furnishing the thirty-two principal cartularies were located in and around Paris and are not shown on the map: Notre-Dame de Paris, the Hôtel-Dieu, Sainte-Geneviève-du-Mont, Saint-Lazare, Saint-Martin-des-Champs, Saint-Antoine, Saint-Victor, and Saint-Germain-des-Prés.

to within the geographic boundaries, although admittedly I have been occasionally tempted to include sources close to these boundaries in order to enrich the narrative with testimony unavailable within my prescribed limits. A final, but not innocent, choice has been to exclude peasants. I fully recognize the value of treating the aristocracy in symbiosis with their unfree tenants, but this option was not possible within the constraints of the present research.

Sources Are Indispensable . . . Churchmen Have
Seized the Microphone

Personal choices are arbitrary, but credible sources are supremely important for shaping any regional study.[10] Professional historians, to be sure, are fully aware of this condition, but readers of history may not always realize how much the results of research are shaped by the sources. The conclusions attained are usually determined by the nature of the sources from which they are drawn. We shall see that the sources in Latin and the vernacular produced, in fact, perspectives that were remarkably different. Careful consideration of the nature and properties of sources, therefore, is essential to evaluating the conclusions of regional studies. Each category of sources will be introduced briefly here but will be treated in greater depth for their specifics when they become relevant to the discussion. There is no doubt, however, that churchmen, both clerics and monks, contributed by far the greatest quantity of documentation on the aristocracy of the Paris region, as they did for most of the early and central Middle Ages in western Europe.

Around 1200 the local chronicles were not as numerous or as influential as they were at the beginning of the century, Suger's epoch, but the two most important for the Paris region were written by ecclesiastics like Suger in the service of the king. Rigord of Saint-Denis, who wrote the *Gesta Philippi Augusti* in Latin prose, was both a doctor of medicine and a monk at Saint-Denis, as well as the king's chronicler. His status as a royal historian is not entirely clear, but he did have access to the king's archives, and his work was later incorporated into the official history of the monarchy written by the monks of Saint-Denis. The continuation of Rigord's *Gesta*, likewise in Latin prose, was undertaken by Guillaume le Breton who was a royal cleric, active at the court, chaplain of the king, and the first "official" historian of the Capetian dynasty. Guillaume also composed a second work. As chaplain he witnessed the battle of Bouvines at first hand; Philip's victory inspired him to redraft the *Gesta Philippi* into verse as the *Philippidos*, a grandiloquent tribute to the king. His works too were incorporated into the chronicles of Saint-Denis. Rigord and Guillaume were both partial to the interests of their patron and expressed a royal perspective, but as ecclesiastics their Latin histories likewise echoed the preoccupations of churchmen.[11]

Writing in Latin, churchmen not only composed the major chronicles, but, more important, they generated an enormous quantity of charters in behalf of their churches, as well as other documents such as obituaries and saints' lives. For strategic reasons I have chosen not to consult the originals of the charters deposited in the local archives. Not only would this have been onerous, it was also not altogether necessary. In the second half of the thirteenth century the individual charters were copied into codices called cartularies in which clerics and monks preserved those charters that were of greatest interest to them. The cartularies therefore preserve more charters than have survived separately, but they naturally retained those of greatest interest to their compilers. More than sixty extant cartularies from the region have generated well over two thousand charters that contained transactions pertaining directly to the local aristocracy. From thirty-two of the most substantial of these cartularies I have selected a sample of 1,729 charters that contain transactions between churches and aristocrats.[12] After the major issues had become clear, I conducted a second and more refined survey of a sample of 610 charters that dealt in greater detail with those individuals I had identified for particular attention.[13]

In addition to the massive amount of documentation preserved in cartularies, the churches and monasteries likewise compiled obituaries consisting of names of persons of interest to the religious community with the dates of their deaths and a notice of their gifts to the church. One of the major purposes of these compilations was to keep record of the donors to the church so that prayers could be offered for their souls during the daily celebrations of the liturgy. Although most of the inscribed names were clerical or monastic, lay aristocrats were also included, especially when they had been generous in their giving. Seven of these obituaries are available from the Paris region.[14] The influence of these obituaries was further expanded through the creation of mortuary rolls that circulated throughout the region bearing the names of the donor for whose soul the recipients of the roll were invited to offer prayers. A striking example of this practice is found in the roll that was circulated for Guillaume des Barres, perhaps the most celebrated knight of his day.[15]

Finally, two saints who were active within the temporal and spatial limits of my study were canonized for their sanctity, which, in turn, generated saints' lives (*vitae*) that mirrored the environment in which they lived. Since in this period a saint was invariably born to an aristocratic family, the lives of Thibaut de Marly and Jean de Montmirail deal with their aristocratic milieu as well as with their pious exploits. Thibaut originated from one of the leading aristocratic families to the southwest of Paris,[16] but Jean was from a distinguished family not far away, within the western borders of Champagne. I have felt justified to include him not only because of his unusual life but also because of his close connections to the Paris region. He was raised at the royal court, served the king loyally in the Norman wars, and was ceremoniously buried at the Cistercian abbey of Long-pont within the limits of my region.[17]

The overwhelming importance of local churches for generating the basic sources for writing regional histories has often encouraged French historians to devote separate chapters to the leading monasteries of the region. The stud-ies of the aristocracies in the Vendômois, Haute-Marne, and now the Île-de-France, for example, have designated special chapters to the leading churches of the region. Even Georges Duby's pioneering study of the Mâconnais acknowl-edged that the local society could not have been analyzed without the charters produced by the great abbey of Cluny.[18] Following the fashion of American his-torians, however, I have not attempted such a preliminary historiography. In-stead of focusing on the leading churches of the region, I have assembled charters from an array of churches and monasteries—some prominent and many not—with the purpose of subjecting them to statistical analysis. In doing so, I have drawn on a two-part statistical study of the 1,729 charters in ecclesiastical ar-chives.[19] In the present work I have made use of the data published in these two articles, occasionally summarizing conclusions previously presented. Nonethe-less, the frequent presence of tables of statistics will underline the quantitative nature of this study.

All of the ecclesiastical documents were drafted in Latin, the official language of the church, in which clerics and most monks were expected to be competent. As such, a churchman was considered to be *litteratus*, that is, proficient in Latin. A layman, however, was *illiteratus*, or not expected to know Latin, and this included most aristocrats who were thereby forced to rely on clerics to write the charters that were issued in their names. Through the monopoly of the Latin language, therefore, churchmen produced the vast majority of the documentation avail-able for this study and thereby adapted it to their particular interests. Not only is this apparent in the saints' lives and obituaries, but also in the available chron-icles, even those composed for the king, for they were likewise composed by cler-ics. It is especially pertinent to the thousands of charters that were issued in the names of aristocrats. Undoubtedly there were preliminary discussions between the aristocrat and the churchman before an agreement was reached, but it was a cleric or monk who drafted the text in Latin and then selected those charters that would be preserved in the church's archives or copied into a cartulary according to his church's interests. Those that survived were therefore invariably favorable to the church.

The contents of these charters confirm this ecclesiastical bias. The vast majority of the surviving charters involve the transfer of property from an aristocrat to the church by gift, sale, gift-countergift, exchange, or pledge, for which the former received some form of compensation in roughly a third of the transactions (see Table 2). Of the 14 percent of charters that detailed litigation between the aristocrat and the church, nearly all naturally reported settlements favorable to the church. Altogether, the charters represent a massive transfer of property to the church. Further, although the charters were issued in the name of an aristocrat, many concerns that were important to him were virtually absent: hunting, tournaments, castle-guard, warfare, even his many horses. And finally, the geographic distribution of ecclesiastical documentation, particularly the charters, was based on the implantation of churches and monasteries which did not necessarily correspond to the distribution of the aristocracy. Although some families, like the counts of Beaumont, founded religious houses that served them as writing bureaus and archives, this was not often the case. Since the founding of churches was not systematic and did not always follow aristocratic patronage, there could be, as the map shows, areas that were devoid of ecclesiastical archives and cartularies. The coverage of aristocratic families in the charters is therefore necessarily sporadic, if not haphazard; some received full attention and others were omitted.[20]

As churchmen, clerics and monks were subject to the regime of canon law that was enforced in the courts of the diocese and of the papacy. Canon law was founded on biblical passages, opinions of the church fathers, the decrees of church councils, and, most recently, decretals of popes. By the mid-twelfth century these legal materials were collected and codified by a monk named Gratian in a book called the *Decretum*, which then inspired a group of masters at Bologna to create the legal system of canon law. Ecclesiastical law was also studied at Paris by the end of the twelfth century but not as intensively as at Bologna. The treatises of the Parisian masters like Pierre the Breton, for example, were not as influential as those of masters at Bologna, such as Bernard of Pavia.[21] Bernard was the first to collect the recent decretals of the popes in a separate volume, and between 1191 and 1198 he composed a brief textbook on canon law entitled the *Summa decretalium*. Although his *Summa* was written in Bologna, it circulated widely in numerous manuscripts that were also available to the Parisian canonists. It was a particularly useful text in assembling and summarizing the basic principles of canon law that were in effect at the time.[22] Nonetheless, it is nearly impossible to judge how well the bishops, clerics, abbots, and monks of the Paris region were instructed in the rules of canon law to which they were subject in principle. None has left evidence that he studied the subject either at Bologna or Paris. In the ecclesiastical documentation available to this study,

their formation in canon law can therefore only be judged through their actions. To compensate for this lacuna, however, I have introduced the opinions
of Bernard of Pavia's *Summa decretalium* whenever they were relevant to the
issues involved. From this comparison it will appear for the most part that the
ecclesiastics of the Paris region were, in fact, aware of the broad principles of
canon law whatever their legal training.

King Philip Augustus, the Inescapable Neighbor

In addition to the numerous churches and monasteries, the region harbored
the king at Paris and his royal residences that surrounded it. Philip Augustus
enclosed his capital with walls to protect the organs of government that he had
recently created. The archives, in particular, were installed there after 1194.
They collected and preserved his incoming correspondence in a building later
known as the Trésor des Chartes. A decade after their installation the royal
chancery began compiling books, called "registers," which resembled the
ecclesiastical cartularies and recopied not only incoming and outgoing correspondence but also abundant information useful for governing the kingdom. The initial volume (called Register A) was begun in 1204 and continued
until 1212, when it was superseded by a second volume (named Register C),
which copied the contents of the first and added material until 1220 when it,
in turn, was replaced by a third (Register E) which continued through the
reign of Louis VIII and into that of Louis IX.[23] Among the information useful
for governing the kingdom, the registers produced lists of the chief personages
of the realm that included bishops, dukes, counts, barons, castellans, and
knights (*vavassores*).[24] Another list recorded the bannerets, or those who carried a banner and led companies of knights into battle, all grouped according
to region.[25] Of particular importance to my study were the royal inventories of
fiefs and vassals. Philip Augustus was not the first to compile these surveys
but followed the example of the Anglo-Norman kings and the counts of
Champagne. After Philip took possession of Caen in Normandy in 1204, his
chancery copied the earliest of the Norman inventories into the French registers.[26] Philip completed this inventory of the fiefs and vassals for the duchy
and then continued the survey into the newly acquired Vermandois and Vexin
and also into the lands surrounding Paris. Two of these surveys are of particular importance for the aristocracy of the Paris region. The first, which may be
called the *Nomina militum*, recorded those knights who possessed annual incomes of sixty *livres* or more and whether or not they owed homage to the
king. Grouping them in districts called castellanies, it covered the lands closest to Paris.[27] The second, entitled *Scripta de feodis*, followed the Norman pat-

tern of recording fiefs and homage but added further questions of military service and landed resources.[28] Thus in eighteen castellanies the aristocracy was systematically surveyed around Paris. Although both sets of inventories were incomplete, omitted territories, and occasionally overlapped, I have nonetheless found them useful for defining the boundaries of my study. These feudal inventories compiled for the king offer three important advantages. Not only do they provide information about the aristocracy unavailable elsewhere, but this information was gathered relatively free of the ecclesiastical bias of the cartularies. Furthermore, unlike the cartularies, which were distributed sporadically, the royal surveys were undertaken rigorously and systematically. If their bias was not aristocratic but royal, they nonetheless provide an escape from the shadow of ecclesiastical documentation.

Aristocratic Archives and Landbooks

If the church cartulary and the royal register embodied the interests of ecclesiastics and the king respectively, the aristocrats of the Paris region possessed few comparable archives or books to serve their own interests. The first archives of lay lords appeared in Picardy in northern France in the second half of the thirteenth century.[29] However, in the region around Paris in our period, the counts at Beaumont-sur-Oise collected their charters at their church of Saint-Léonor. These charters survive because they were incorporated into the royal archives in 1223 when the county escheated to the crown.[30]

Archives assemble documents that not only treat the lord's personal interests but also contain transactions that deal with other lords. But the aristocrat was chiefly a landholder who exploited his lands to support himself. To facilitate this task he needed landbooks to record his holdings. Landbooks had first appeared in Carolingian times, but they did not become common in France until the second half of the thirteenth century. The first aristocratic landbook to reappear in northern France was compiled by Pierre du Thillay who came from the Croult valley north of Paris and to the west of Roissy. Pierre styled himself as "knight and lord," but his chief occupation was in the king's service. First appearing in 1200 as *prévôt* of Paris, he reappeared in 1202 at Orléans where he collaborated with the bailli Guillaume de la Chapelle, but his most permanent post was at Caen in Normandy where he was royal bailli from 1205 for at least two decades. Approaching retirement, he drew up a landbook in 1219–20 that included not only the thirteen properties that the king gave him in Normandy but also three ancestral properties to the north of Paris. It is a small volume of thirty-one folios that has remained in the archives of the Hôtel-Dieu at Gonesse to this day.[31]

Such landbooks were not unknown among monasteries, particularly in Normandy, as, for example, at the abbey of the Saint-Trinité de Caen at the end of the twelfth century. In the Paris region the Cistercians at Val-Notre-Dame to the northwest of Le Thillay devoted six pages of their cartulary in the 1190s to recording their holdings at Taverny and Montmorency.[32] The Cistercians at Chaalis drew up a cadastre for their grange at Vaulerent located nearby in the Croult valley two decades after Pierre's compilation.[33] Around 1206 the clerics in Philip Augustus's chancery included in the registers a survey called a *census* that listed the revenues or rents (*cens*) from selected lands in the royal domain.[34] In Normandy the landbooks have been called "customals" or "surveys"; around Paris they were known as *censiers* because they focused on the *cens*, which was a land rent. As a landbook, Pierre du Thillay's volume essentially compiled data on the extent of his land and revenues. Since he was well established at Caen when it was compiled, his landbook generally follows the Norman format. After noting the size of the land, it turned to the revenues—money rents, usually called *cens*, and produce in kind (*regarda*), which included grain (wheat, oats, and barley), loaves of bread, capons, hens, geese, and eggs. Its significance lies in that it is the first of its kind composed for a nonroyal layman and that it contained three chapters devoted to Gonesse, Tessonville, and Sarcelles at the heart of the Paris region. Although miniscule in size, it offers a momentary glimpse into what constituted the landed wealth of a minor aristocrat of the Paris region.

The Aristocrat Imposes His Seal

With the absence of archives and paucity of landbooks, how did the aristocrats represent themselves and their interests apart from ecclesiastical and royal documentation? It may come as a surprise that the earliest device was the wax seal that they attached to their charters. From early times the charters composed in Latin that were issued in the name of aristocrats and collected by churchmen were authenticated by witnesses who were named at the end of the charter and who testified to the veracity of the text. These witness lists, however, began to disappear at the end of the twelfth century. In their place were seals that were attached to the foot of the charter by cords or strips of parchment. In our period the charter with the appended seal became the standard instrument.[35] The seal had become so mandatory that it was recorded expressly in the charter with the phrase "so that this remains firm and established, I have strengthened the present charter with my seal," and the phrase was retained in the cartulary copy where the seal itself could not be affixed.[36] Composed of wax, many of the seals have disintegrated and disappeared from the original charters, but their presence was constantly recalled in the text. Surviving evidence shows that the usage of seals virtually exploded at the turn of the century, passing from a handful to thousands of cases.[37] Most knights and many ladies possessed their own seals. This represented a substantial economic outlay because the seal was formed by the impression of wax on a matrix that was composed usually of bronze or iron and required the intricate and doubtlessly expensive skill of an artisan.

Seals served a double purpose: they authenticated documents and they represented the person who possessed the seal. As authenticators of documents, they served not to enhance the owner's image but to constrain him. With his seal the owner guaranteed that he would perform the actions detailed in the charter. By the seal, therefore, churchmen compelled the aristocrat's compliance to the terms of the charter. Beyond an instrument of constraint, however, it also provided a mode of self-representation.[38] We shall explore in later chapters how lords and knights expressed themselves individually and collectively by means of the legends, images, and heraldry on their seals.

Vernacular French, the Aristocrat's Voice

Measuring only fifty to seventy millimeters in diameter, the seal was indeed a minute witness to aristocratic self-identity. The broader entrance into his world was his language. I keep emphasizing that the great majority of records pertaining to the aristocracy were produced in Latin for the church and the king. As *illiteratus* the knight did not participate directly in this medium of expression. His language, of course, was vernacular French, which he spoke and heard every day. Until the twelfth century very little was written in vernacular French that has survived, but during the second half of the century laymen appeared who read the vernacular and wrote in the vernacular, thus producing the *chevalier lettré*, or literate knight.[39] By 1200 a considerable body of vernacular literature had come into existence in France. Little of this literary production, however, occurred at Paris or in its immediate surroundings for reasons that remain obscure. Philip Augustus's open hostility to the profession of jongleurs perhaps contributed to this absence, but in any event, the main centers of vernacular literary production were clearly located not in Paris but in Normandy, Flanders, and, most important, in Champagne where prolific and influential writers such as Chrétien de Troyes and Jean Renart flourished. Lacking vernacular voices in my chosen place and time, I have scoured the frontiers of the Paris region to identify authors who, although residing on the perimeters, had connections with Paris and were acquainted with the region. This recruitment has produced a handful of vernacular lay authors, namely, the author of the *Histoire de Guillaume le Maréchal*, Gerbert de Montreuil, Gace Brulé, the Châtelain de Coucy,

and Raoul de Hodenc, to whom I have added two monks, Thibaut de Marly and
Hélinand de Froidmont, who likewise wrote in the vernacular.

While history by and large was composed in Latin, a notable exception appears in the *Histoire de Guillaume le Maréchal*, which was commissioned in the 1220s by one of the leading baronial families of England to recount the biography of their scion, Guillaume le Maréchal, earl of Pembroke, who rose from being a simple knight to become a great baron and regent of the realm. That Guillaume was an English baron would disqualify him for my purposes except that from boyhood he was raised in Normandy and as a young man he participated in the warfare and tournaments in the neighborhood of Paris from the 1180s to 1204 when Philip Augustus expelled the English from northern France. His biography therefore remains one of the most detailed and accurate histories of northern and western France at the end of the century.

At the turn of the twelfth and thirteenth centuries the county of Champagne was the undisputed center of vernacular romance, featuring, among many, two influential authors, Chrétien de Troyes and Jean Renart. While Chrétien's five celebrated romances framed the fictional world of King Arthur and thereby set the pattern for romance, the dominating genre of literature for the next century, Jean Renart who followed him closely in time established a new genre of romance. Although his narratives were entirely fictional like Chrétien's, he placed his *Roman de la Rose* (ca. 1209) in a setting that was historically precise and accurate. By adding "reality effects" (*effets de réel*), that is, details and episodes from actual life, he enhanced the realism of his narrative. For example, although the heroes of his romances were entirely fictional, the secondary characters were drawn from historical contemporaries whom the audience could recognize. Although Jean Renart was well acquainted with the Parisian region, he set his stories on the borders of the kingdom and in the German Empire. His principal hero in the *Rose*, for example, was not a French king, but a German emperor.

Jean found a close imitator in Gerbert de Montreuil who chose another flower, the *Roman de la Violette* (1225–31). From Montreuil located on the northern coast of the county of Ponthieu, Gerbert dedicated his *Violette* to Marie, countess of Ponthieu (d. 1251), who was married to a baron of the Paris region, Simon de Dammartin. Like Jean Renart in the *Rose*, Gerbert eschews Arthurian mythology in the *Violette*. His fine story, he proclaims, "is not about the Round Table, nor of King Arthur and his men" (vv. 34–35). Although he favors Chrétien's romance style more than his mentor Jean Renart (in addition to the *Violette*, Gerbert also wrote a sequel to Chrétien's *Conte du Graal*),[40] Gerbert follows Jean in adopting the crucial technique of the *effet de réel* by naming actual geographic settings and identifiable historical personages. At the same time, despite these affinities with Jean Renart, Gerbert makes a decisive break

with Jean's politics by shifting the stage from the empire to the Capetian heartland, from the fictional Emperor Conrad of the *Rose* to the historical King Louis
VIII, Philip Augustus's son. If the reality effects of geography and historical personages were calculated to capture the attention of an aristocratic audience
around Paris, Gerbert's work also continued to exploit the fictional characteristics of Chrétien de Troyes's romances. In a territory that was impoverished for
lack of vernacular writing, I have therefore found the *Roman de la Violette* to
be useful in sketching the ideals, dreams, and fantasies of the aristocrats surrounding Paris.

Gerbert de Montreuil shared one further innovation with Jean Renart. In
his prologue to the *Rose*, Jean drew attention to the songs in his story: "For just
as one puts red dye in cloth so that it will be admired and valued, so [the au-
thor] has added songs and melodies in this *roman de la Rose*, which is a novel
thing" (*Rose*, vv. 8–12). Once again Gerbert echoes Jean: "Now I shall begin a
work of the *Roman de la Violette*. You will hear many courtly songs before the
end of the story" (*Violette*, vv. 44–47). In addition to telling charming stories,
therefore, both romances were transformed, in fact, into anthologies of lyrics
popular at the time. Jean included forty-eight in the *Rose*; Gerbert, forty-four
in the *Violette*. Moreover, both proclaim that the lyrics were to be both read and
sung, therefore transforming their romances into musical comedies in which
music was interlaced with narrative. The lyrical insertions thereby perform the
role of the *effet de réel* by reminding the audience of the songs that were popular in their day.

The songs anthologized by the two romances covered the whole repertoire
of lyrics available at the turn of the twelfth century, but the most frequently cited
(seven lyrics) were composed by the best known of all trouvères, Gace Brulé. As
a songwriter, Gace's output was prodigious. By the end of the thirteenth century
the books of songs (*chansonniers*) had collected over eighty of his poems and
supplied the music for more than sixty, a record that placed him above all contemporary trouvères. As a historical personage, however, his figure is shadowy,
and the information that he supplied about himself is oblique. One of his songs
was placed in Brittany but suggested nostalgia for Champagne. Another suggests that he came from a place called Nanteuil, a common place-name. Others
mention friendships with the counts of Brittany and Blois, as well as the countess of Champagne. We are now aware of two other patrons whom he does not
mention. The registers of Philip Augustus's chancery recorded that he received
an annual *fief-rente* of twenty-four *livres* from the *prévôté* of Mantes, and the
household accounts of Prince Louis from the year 1213 recorded that he received
another ten *livres*, also from Mantes.[41] Moreover, one charter surviving from
1212 states that he held land at Groslières not far from Dreux to the west of

Paris.[42] Although literary historians have been inclined to include Gace within Chrétien de Troyes's Champenois orbit,[43] there is independent evidence that he also enjoyed Capetian patronage from the vicinity of Paris.

Closely allied to Gace was another trouvère, the Châtelain de Coucy, who was particularly known for his *chansons de croisade*.[44] Unlike Gace, he was well attested in the historical documents of the Paris region. A final but short text, the *Roman des Eles*, composed around 1210 for the aristocracy's instruction, is also drawn from the periphery of our region.[45] Despite its title it was not a *roman* in Chrétien's sense but a didactic poem teaching the virtues of knighthood. It was organized around the schematic figure of a bird called prowess (*proesce*) with two wings—on the right side, largess (*larguesce*), and on the left, courtesy (*cortoisie*), each possessing seven feathers. The author identifies himself as Raoul de Hodenc, which is most likely the Hodenc-en-Bray in the Beauvaisis to the north of Paris.

The above writers were laymen writing for lay aristocratic audiences in their own tongue, but, as we have seen, lay aristocratic families supplied most of the clerics and monks of the neighboring churches and monasteries. While all clerics and most monks were required to obtain proficiency in Latin, a few at the turn of the century began to write in their maternal language to convey religious instruction to their own class. Because of their aristocratic origins their writings reflected the perspectives of their native milieu. Two in particular, Thibaut de Marly and Hélinand de Froidmont, came from the Paris region or close by. Thibaut de Marly has been occasionally confused with a later homonym, Saint Thibaut of the Cistercian house of Vaux-de-Cernay, who was his great-nephew from the same distinguished family of Montmorency-Marly.[46] The present Thibaut was the uncle of Mathieu de Montmorency, who became royal constable in 1218, and the brother of Hervé, dean of Notre-Dame (1184–92). Dying early in the 1190s, he had been an influential lord from the Paris region for at least two decades before his retirement from the world.[47] Between 1182 and 1189 he wrote a poem of 850 lines, simply entitled *Les Vers*, devoted to the themes of death and contempt of the world.

Hélinand, a monk at Froidmont in the diocese of Beauvais, was the other Cistercian writer to address the aristocracy directly in their tongue. Originating from a noble Flemish family, Hélinand entered the Cistercian house of Froidmont in the Beauvaisis around 1190, where he remained until his death sometime between 1223 and 1237. He composed a chronicle, political and moral treatises, and numerous sermons in Latin, but his fame is based chiefly on a vernacular poem, *Les Vers de la mort*, that was composed between 1190 and 1197, after his monastic conversion. Drawing upon his past as a jongleur, he produced a poem that meditated on death and the abandonment of the world with such vivid imagery that it obtained wide circulation.[48]

Lacking vernacular texts composed well within the Parisian region, I am obliged to draw on texts located at the peripheries. The *Histoire de Guillaume le Maréchal* provides testimony from the life of a historical knight who was active in the region during the opening decades of the reign. The *Roman de la Violette*, written at the end of our period, offers a romance, a literary genre that sums up what aristocratic audiences expected for entertainment. The lyrics of Gace Brulé and the Châtelain de Coucy offer songs that were most popular with these audiences. Cistercian monks like Thibaut de Marly and Hélinand de Froidmont discoursed in the vernacular tongue on death within their aristocratic milieu. Through the fictions and religious messages of these vernacular texts that spoke directly to aristocratic men and women I shall attempt to penetrate the mental universe of the aristocratic audience and to ascertain the ideals, fantasies, and fears that embellished and darkened the life that they pursued.

The employment of vernacular literature raises an inevitable question that merits at least a word of comment. How can a historical project justify the use of fictional works as sources? To be sure, the *Histoire de Guillaume le Maréchal* can be treated as a Latin chronicle, despite its evident differences, but Gerbert de Montreuil, Raoul de Hodenc, and Gace Brulé wrote pure literary fictions. Even the monks Thibaut de Marly and Hélinand composed similar moralizing fictions. A generation ago the response of the historical profession was simple: literary works were excluded from the historical canon because their fictionality per se rendered them unreliable testimony. With the exception of the *Histoire* and a few other vernacular histories, medieval history was written exclusively from the Latin *veritas* of the ecclesiastical chroniclers, charters, and royal administrative documents. This strategy was uncontested when applied to the early Middle Ages, but raised difficulties for the end of the twelfth century when vernacular texts established their presence. In the 1970s the separation between history and literature was challenged by a school of the literary profession known as postmodernism. They placed particular emphasis on language, discourse, and text and summed up their approach with the label "the linguistic turn." In their view, the boundary between history and literature dissolved—all writing, history and fiction, was fictional. Writing itself was not transparent. One could not assume that it conveyed truth. Instead, it was considered reflexive, that is, self-absorbed, consisting of writing about writing. We need not rehearse the debates that this school provoked and which have since subsided, but simply observe that the postmodernists did succeed in blurring the traditional boundary between history and literature. The two spheres have now become commensurate and can legitimately interact. My personal position is that fictional literature can furnish historical data, but like all historical documents it must always be interpreted according to context, genre, and authorial strategy.[49]

Not only can the vernacular *Histoire de Guillaume le Maréchal* be treated as other Latin chronicles, but romance literature and lyric verse may also be examined for what they reveal about the emotional and affective life of the aristocrat to whom they were addressed. The monks' vernacular writings likewise addressed the concerns of the aristocrats' spiritual lives. The radical differences I have perceived between the Latin world of the ecclesiastics and the vernacular world of the lay authors is less a question of contradiction than an issue of expanding horizons. The aristocrat himself, in fact, lived in both worlds and faced the conflicts between the two.

Archaeology, Hard Evidence on the Ground

Like most historians, medievalists have privileged the written word as the basic medium of their information. The abundance of medieval documentation was produced by ecclesiastical writers who wrote in Latin and thereby transmitted their particular biases. Concurrent with these written sources are, of course, the material remains of medieval civilization that lie beyond the biases of their written interpreters. Churches naturally provide the most abundant, best preserved, and most thoroughly studied of surviving structures, but they are only tangential to the aristocracy. Next are the stone castles erected by the king and high aristocrats. From the nineteenth century, archaeologists have been interested primarily in the military features of these fortifications. The science of castellography came into being to investigate their strategic emplacement and their functional design. Particular attention was paid to the towers, turrets, fortified gates, moats, and thickness of walls that were fitted with crenellations and *hourds* at the top and were penetrated with *archères*, narrow slits for archers and crossbowmen—all created to withstand prolonged sieges. These military features remain relevant to the surviving castles in the Paris region constructed before or during the reign of Philip Augustus, but the king's pacification of the aristocracy increasingly turned the attention of the medieval builders to emphasize residence for the royalty and aristocracy. Archaeologists have begun to examine the amount of space devoted to the functions of sleeping, eating, praying, and the assembling of knights or peasants for administrative purposes. Attention has likewise turned to amenities such as kitchens, windows, fireplaces, and latrines.

Whereas in the past archaeologists concentrated on churches and existing or ruined castles, a new type of archaeology was created in 2001 with the institution of INRAP, the Institut national de recherches archéologiques préventives. With the exponential expansion of urbanization in the Parisian region that paved the area in concrete and asphalt, it was deemed essential to safeguard the material remains of the past that lay beneath the surface. It was therefore mandated by law that all further development be preceded by an archaeological survey before construction could begin. Teams of archaeologists were dispatched to investigate whatever could be found beneath the surface within brief time limits. The scope of the investigations has extended beyond determining the existence of previous structures to a panoply of collateral findings. The presence of foodstuffs has been explored by carpologists for vegetable matter and by archaeozoologists for animal remains. Pottery and cooking vessels have been studied by experts in ceramics and glass; coins and implements by metallurgists. Their preferred fields of exploration have been places of disposal, in particular moats and latrines. The most interesting discoveries have been the human bones found in cemeteries or elsewhere that not only revealed burial customs but also could cast light on health, sickness, and other physical conditions of past ages. As these remains are further studied through the rapidly advancing techniques of DNA analysis, more extraordinary findings are promised for the future.[50] Although important discoveries using these new techniques were previously made within Paris itself—around the Louvre palace, for example—INRAP's most significant findings were made largely in rural areas unencumbered by existing structures. Particularly fruitful have been the explorations for new highways and rail lines. Major discoveries, therefore, have been made of rural dwellings from antiquity and the early Middle Ages. While some of these sites pertain to aristocratic dwellings from the twelfth and thirteenth centuries, those that have been of particular interest to both archaeologists and historians are from the earlier period because they illuminate prehistory before the invention of writing. Less progress has therefore been made for the period of the present study.

Three notable exceptions, however, provide illuminating examples pertinent to the aristocracy of our period. Two come from large, previously existing castles belonging to the high aristocracy, and they are now being studied with the new techniques. The first is at Chevreuse (dép. Yvelines) and is under exploration by a team of archaeologists under the direction of the regional government and concerns a major structure occupied by the Chevreuse family, one of the leading families to the southwest of Paris. The second is the relatively well-preserved and impressive castle belonging to the powerful family of royal cousins of Dreux, located at Brie-Comte-Robert (dép. Seine-et-Marne). It is being carefully preserved and studied by a team of archaeologists sponsored by the local commune. Third, although relatively new, the teams of archaeologists provided by INRAP have made a discovery of special pertinence to our study. When a chain of hotels proposed a new building at Roissy-en-France next to the Charles de Gaulle Airport, INRAP was called to investigate the site before construction.

The archaeologists discovered two previous buildings composed of wood that were followed by a modest stone structure complete with tower. These structures were clearly the residences of local aristocracy of the middle rank. Belonging to either the Roissy or Montfermeil families, these structures and their surrounding appurtenances fortuitously illustrate the material living conditions of a modest family of knights in the time and place of our study. Other examples exist that have been less thoroughly explored, but these three provide apposite examples for the aristocracy of the Paris region during the reign of Philip Augustus.

Horses, Abounding and Missing

How determinate our sources are to results obtained is illustrated by the presence or absence of horses in the history of the aristocracy around Paris at the turn of the twelfth and thirteenth centuries. If we take the one marker that immediately identifies an aristocrat, it is certainly his seal, which depicts him astride a horse at full gallop into battle. In addition to the riders, therefore, the seals offer a gallery of magnificent horses. It was the *cheval* (horse), in effect, that bestowed on the knight his professional title of *chevalier* in his maternal language. He was more than a *cavalier* (rider). In the vernacular sources that spoke directly to the aristocracy, the horse abounds. In the *Histoire de Guillaume le Maréchal*, for example, the horse appears to compete with the Marshal himself for the center of attention—at least in Guillaume's youth and early manhood in France. Prevented from engaging in the tournament between Sainte-Jamme and Valennes because he was horseless, the young Guillaume entered his career as *tornoieor* thanks to the gift of a sturdy steed from his patron the Chamberlain of Tanquerville. The author devoted nearly a hundred lines to its qualities and harness (vv. 1224–1303). Thereafter Guillaume won his livelihood by the horses he captured. The technique was to take one's opponent's horse by the reins (*al frein*, v. 1334), and thereby he gained four and a half prizes by the end of the day (vv. 1367–70). At Eu he took twelve (v. 3372) and fifteen at Anet (vv. 420–21). Identified as palfreys and destriers in one passage, the counting of forty to sixty horses at a time may have been an exaggeration (vv. 1155–56), but afterward Guillaume went into partnership with another knight and hired a cleric to keep account of their prizes, which numbered in the hundreds (vv. 3403–24). Understandably, Guillaume was not unaware of the prices they obtained on the market, ranging from fourteen to thirty *livres* (vv. 4258, 4230, 5962–65). In the time off from the tournament, he amused himself by dicing for steeds (vv. 4178–99). As to horses, there was little to distinguish the young Marshal from the cowboy broncobuster of the American Far West.

Produced for the entertainment of the aristocracy into the thirteenth century, the romances likewise are oriented around the equestrian culture. Chrétien de Troyes's romances created the fictional figure of the solitary knight-errant on horseback wandering through the wilderness in quest of adventure for whose benefit the author places a castle conveniently each night to offer hospitality to both him and his horse. Dinner was rarely served until the steed had been properly stabled.[51] Gerbert de Montreuil's romance, the *Roman de la Violette*, sent the hero Gerart de Nevers on such a journey, but Jean Renart's *Roman de la Rose* engaged his hero in tournaments like those of Guillaume le Maréchal. At the tournament of Saint-Tronde, for example, Guillaume de Dole enters the scene on a palfrey as white as snow heading two columns of knights on destriers (vv. 2471, 2492). Guillaume unhorses a Fleming opponent whose mount he uses to pay a debt; another he bestows on Jouglet, his friend, the jongleur, winning in all seven prizes that day (vv. 2665, 2693, 2708). By nightfall the chargers strayed in the field with their reins dangling on the ground—"God, one could have made a fortune there!" (vv. 2809–13). Although Gerbert quickly summarized the tournament of Montargis in the *Violette*, the hero, Gerart de Nevers, nonetheless performs the obligatory feat of unhorsing the villain Lisïart straightaway. In the following mêlée horses that had lost their riders wandered with their reins hanging; many a fine horse was lost! (vv. 6013–16).

In the Latin charters written by and for ecclesiastics, however, horses disappear completely from sight notwithstanding that the charters were composed in the chevaliers' names. Although earlier in the eleventh century horses were occasionally mentioned as serving as countergifts, such exchanges appear to have declined in the twelfth century.[52] By the reign of Philip Augustus they disappeared altogether. Of the more than two thousand charters examined, I have found only two that mention horses. In 1200 Adam son of Gobert *de Vendulia* renounced a rent that had been usurped from Mont-Saint-Martin in exchange for a horse and two hundred *livres*.[53] Similarly in 1222 Payen Gorrez exchanged with the Cistercians of Barbeau his new tithes at Nesles-la-Gilberde for one palfrey and thirty *livres parisis*.[54] In effect, both were disposing of tainted assets, as we shall see, for more useful money and horses. Apparently, whatever horses ecclesiastics were raising did not enter the transactions with the aristocracy, nor were they interested in payments in horses.[55]

The ecclesiastical chroniclers writing in Latin likewise paid little attention in their narratives to the horses that knights rode. They rarely mentioned the *eques* (the Latin equivalent of *chevalier* in French). Only when writing of the battle of Bouvines did the royal chronicler Guillaume le Breton finally acknowledge the horse's determinative role. Convinced that the battle was largely an affair of cavalry, he noticed in his prose account the large squadrons of mounted sergeants who faced the Flemish on the left wing and the fifty knights on horseback led by Thomas de Saint-Valéry. What concerned him most were the numbers of knights who were unhorsed or whose horses were killed. Thus we encounter descriptions of the fates of the mounts of the duke of Burgundy, of Michel de Harnes, of Hugues de Malaveines, of the count of Boulogne, and even of Philip Augustus himself, who escaped from his fallen horse only through the aid of knights of his entourage. When the horse of the count of Boulogne was killed from under him, its neck had pinned another knight to the ground. As an eye-witness Guillaume was therefore convinced that Philip Augustus's victory was due to the superiority of mounted knights.[56] At the end of the reign when Guil-laume transformed his prose narrative into the verse of the *Philippidos* to cele-brate the victory at Bouvines, the horse finally assumes a stature comparable to that of the vernacular romance. Guillaume opened with, "The German fights as a footman, but you, O Frenchman, fight as a chevalier (*eques*)." The duke of Burgundy was thoroughly humiliated when his horse was killed from under him. When footmen pull the king to the ground with their hooks, he leaps upon his new charger burning with rage. Pierre Mauvoisin seizes the reins of Emperor Otto's horse, but the German bodyguards give him another to escape. At the end, the field is strewn with dead horses; those alive are booty for the victorious.[57]

Although historians have never doubted the importance of the horse for aris-tocratic society in the High Middle Ages, its material evidence is lacking. Ar-chaeologists have yet to find the skeleton of a horse in the Paris region from the reign of Philip Augustus. It is true that tournaments like those at Lagny were kept to the borders, and no major battle of Bouvines's dimensions was fought in the region. (Even the wheat fields of Bouvines in Flanders, doubtlessly scoured by scavengers, have produced no remains of the fallen horses.) Nonetheless, horses must have been stabled in and around the castles and residences where the aristocracy lived. From the early Middle Ages rare skeletons of horses have been uncovered in graves of warriors in the countryside, but our period is ap-parently devoid of their remains. One possible explanation is that horses were cut up; their remains were deposited in special depots; their skin and hair were saved and resold; and other parts were recycled or eaten. Butchers and hang-men may have specialized in the disposal of horses. It is true that archaeozo-ologists today have limited their investigations to the horses that were eaten and which can be found only in the latrines and ditches near castles and residences.[58] In this digested form, however, they constituted only a small part of the aristo-cratic diet. Stables must have existed, nonetheless, where the horses were kept both within and without the precincts of the castle or residence, buildings that would leave indelible traces of nitrates from urine in the soil.[59] Here, perhaps the crowded urban conditions have prevented the scope of excavation from extending to the stables outside the castle or residence. The castle at Chevreuse, for example, is surrounded by modern houses, as is Brie-Comte-Robert, whose courtyard, furthermore, was thoroughly cleaned in the fourteenth century. The excavations at Roissy-en-France were conducted rapidly in preparation for a hotel, which occupied only a small space in an urban setting. As yet, an aristocratic stable has not turned up in the Paris region from our period. Like the ecclesiastical charters, archaeology with all of its potential for illuminating the past suffers from another gap in the reign of Philip Augustus.

Chapter 2

Who's Who

The names of the aristocrats around Paris at the beginning of the twelfth century are more familiar to us today than they were to their descendants a century later during the reign of Philip Augustus. The explanation has already been proposed. When Suger, abbot of Saint-Denis, wrote his *Vie de Louis VI le Gros*, he portrayed a turbulent aristocracy entrenched in their castles brawling among themselves and disturbing the peace of the Paris region. His pages not only exposed dramatically the infamies of a Thomas de Marle or a Hugues du Puiset, but also the quarrels of families like the Beaumonts, the Montforts, the Montmorencys, and the Montlhérys. King Philip I had confessed to his son, Louis VI, that the castle of Montlhéry on the route to Orléans had made him old before his time. The Garlandes were depicted as intruding into the offices of the royal court. The names of these troublemakers have become familiar to historians because Suger's writings have remained the principal source for the Paris region from the first half of the twelfth century. Suger's backdrop was shared by other contemporary ecclesiastical chroniclers for their neighboring provinces: Orderic Vitalis for Normandy, Guibert de Nogent for the Beauvaisis, Galbert de Bruges for Flanders, and William of Malmesbury for England. Evidently, this pandemic of aristocratic violence posed a threat to the churchmen in the early twelfth century serious enough to be recorded in their histories.

By the turn of the century, however, the campaign of pacification of these belligerent aristocrats in the Paris region was well under way. Begun by Louis VI (1106–37), it was continued by his son Louis VII (1137–80). The more aggressive families like the Marles and the Puisets disappeared from the scene, but the Beaumonts, Montforts, Montmorencys, and Garlandes remained in the region, peacefully marrying among themselves and faithfully serving their royal suzerain. Whereas Louis VI had been occupied with besieging their castles, Philip Augustus now offered them positions at his court. His treatment of the local aristocracy fitted into a general policy of reconstituting royal government. When Philip became king in 1179 at the age of fourteen, his court was filled by the high baronage of his father's generation. The position of seneschal was occupied by Thibaut V, count of Blois, the chamberlain by Raoul, count of Clermont-en-Beauvaisis, and the position of butler by the ever-present Guys, lords of Senlis. Equally apparent, the court had become the theater of a three-cornered struggle to exercise control over the young monarch. Henry II and his sons in one corner contested the families of Flanders and of Champagne in the other two. In the end the competition was reduced to two parties, Philippe of Alsace, count of Flanders, against the brothers from the house of Champagne—Thibaut, count of Blois, Étienne, count of Sancerre, and Guillaume, archbishop of Reims. Inevitably, however, the young monarch outlived the men of his father's generation and buried the last of them in the sands of the Holy Land on the Third Crusade. Philippe of Flanders, Thibaut of Blois, and Raoul of Clermont-en-Beauvaisis all perished at the siege of Acre in 1191.

When Philip returned to France that year, he could start afresh, that is, to appoint new men who were young and of lower status. He left the influential post of seneschal vacant as he had previously left the chancery. He appointed Dreux de Mello as constable in 1193 and awarded him the castle of Loches after it was taken in 1206. When Dreux died in 1218, the post was given to Mathieu de Montmorency, from the old and bellicose family in the Paris region, for his services at Bouvines. The constables, the perennial butlers of Senlis, as well as the grand chamberlain, Mathieu, count of Beaumont, however, took little part in royal government except to be present as witnesses to the sealing of royal charters. Upon the death of the Mathieu, the grand chamberlain, in 1208, the post was awarded to Barthélemy de Roye, a young knight from the Vermandois, who was the most active lay member of the royal entourage and performed a whole portfolio of administrative and military charges throughout the remainder of the reign. Along with the court chamberlains Gautier the Young and Ours, sons of Gautier the Chamberlain, and the cleric Guérin the Hospitaler, they formed the influential core of the king's entourage. Closely associated with this core were both Guillaumes de Garlandes, father and son, from another old and troublesome family, and Aubert de Hangest from an influential family in the Vermandois. The circle of familiars also included the Guillaumes des Barres, father and son, and the royal marshals Henri and Jean Clément, father and son, whose services were more military than administrative. Philip Augustus had therefore succeeded in co-opting into court service important members of the aristocracy close to his capital.[1] The major baron who resisted this royal seduction was Renaud, count of Dammartin, along with his brother Simon. Renaud, maneuvering between the Anglo-Normans and Philip, had been enlisted by Philip with favors but nonetheless he betrayed the king twice. When he and his brother were captured at Bouvines, and Renaud was condemned for life to prison, Philip's pacification of the aristocracy of the Parisian region was brought to completion.[2]

For the most part, Rigord de Saint-Denis and Guillaume le Breton, the royal historians commissioned to chronicle Philip's reign, paid little notice to the French aristocracy, focusing their accounts on the exploits of the monarch. The chief exception was afforded by the battle of Bouvines in 1214. When Philip Augustus won his signal victory over the coalition of his enemies, Guillaume le Breton turned to those knights who were responsible for the victory.[3] At this brilliant moment in Capetian history he identified the major aristocrats of the Paris region.

The second half of the twelfth century likewise witnessed a parallel growth of royal power in the Anglo-Angevin realm, not only on the island kingdom but also on the Continent where the English kings exploited their inheritance and established their authority over much of northern France. This expansion of English royal power was accompanied by the appearance of a number of competent chroniclers whose accounts followed King Henry II and his sons Richard and John across the Channel where they defended their fiefdoms against the Capetians from the 1170s into the 1190s. In the process, writers like "Benedict of Peterborough," Roger of Howden, and Ralph de Diceto thereby caught occasional glimpses of the French aristocracy who supported Philip in the Vexin and Normandy.[4] For example, Roger of Howden listed some forty French knights whom Richard captured at the skirmish of Courcelles-lès-Gisors in 1198.[5] Likewise, the author of the *Histoire de Guillaume le Maréchal* took notice of the knights from the Paris region whom Guillaume met on the battle or tournament fields.[6] After King John was finally expelled from Normandy in 1204, however, the English chroniclers likewise lost track of the French vassals of Philip Augustus. Thus in the pages of the French and English chronicles the notoriety of aristocrats around Paris during our period declined in historical memory. Until the twentieth century historians have been content to accept the accounts of the medieval chroniclers as forming the substance of past history. Although the chroniclers were read critically and tested one against the other, they were nonetheless considered as providing the sum total of available history because they were the closest witnesses to the events.[7] Even to this day teachers of history are more likely to recount the treacheries of Thomas de Marle from the pages of Abbot Suger than to recall the faithful service of Mathieu de Montmorency who is less visible in the chronicles than in royal documents.[8]

This lack of attention from the chroniclers, however, can be compensated by the royal chancery registers, which began to survey the king's resources in men and land early in the thirteenth century. Several of the surveys introduced in Chapter 1 are particularly valuable here.[9] From 1203 to 1206 the chancery clerics added to lists of bishops, abbots, and communes inventories of dukes, counts, barons, castellans, and *vavassores* (another term for *milites*, knights) whom they arranged in hierarchic order.[10] This system of classification was apparently customary within aristocratic circles. For example, in his vernacular poem *Les Vers*, composed for an aristocratic audience, Thibaut de Marly identified the protectors of the church in the same order as "kings, counts, dukes, princes, castellans, and knights (*vavassor*)."[11] Another roster, compiled by the chancery clerics between 1204 and 1208, followed shortly afterward in the registers. It listed all the "knights who carried banners" in northern France and grouped them by region. Those who were placed under the rubrics of Vermandois and the Vexin were bannerets who flourished within the boundaries of our study.[12] Finally, toward the end of the reign (ca. 1217) the clerics drew up the *Nomina militum* inventory, which recorded the knights who enjoyed annual revenues of sixty *livres*, apparently considered a standard income.[13] Of the twenty-two castellanies surveyed in the *Nomina militum*, ten belong to the Paris region.

From these inventories—the hierarchic lists, the lists of bannerets, and the *Nomina militum*—I have sought to identify the most important lords and knights of the Paris region and thus compile a who's who of the region. In the absence of contemporary biographies and with the poverty of the contemporary chronicles, only brief sketches are offered for each figure, supplemented from the monastic cartularies and other scattered sources. (Table 1 provides a list of the principal figures I have chosen.)* Unlike Suger, I shall not be able to interweave them into a continuous narrative but merely introduce them serially to facilitate their identification. The result will be a biographical dictionary that attempts to individualize each figure briefly by his or her distinctive characteristics. Like the royal registers the selection is arranged hierarchically beginning with the counts, who were reduced to three in the Paris region by 1200: Beaumont-sur-Oise, Vermandois-Valois, and Dreux.

Counts

Of Carolingian origin, the title of count was not claimed by many around Paris at the beginning of the twelfth century. The county of Paris had been subsumed by the Capetians upon their arrival in the region in the tenth century. If the counts were more numerous in the eleventh, their numbers decreased in the following century.[14] Close by to the west were the counties of Évreux and Meulan, which were in the hands of Anglo-Norman families early in the twelfth

---

*The names of the figures listed in Table 1 of Appendix 1 are in bold below. Families accompanied by a genealogy in Appendix 2 are marked with an asterisk.

century. In 1181 the count of Évreux, Simon de Montfort (d. 1181), divided his holdings between two sons, one who took the Norman lands of Évreux and the other the French lands of Montfort, but the former was acquired by Philip Augustus in the treaty of Le Goulet in 1200.[15] Meulan remained in an Anglo-Norman family faithful to the English up to the accession of King John. Count Robert of Meulan was allied with John in 1199 but was forced to concede his lands to the Capetian by 1204.[16] Close by to the north of Paris the counts of Dammartin were also deeply embroiled in Anglo-Norman alliances.[17] At the outset, Renaud, the successor to the county, was particularly favored by the king, who in 1192 confirmed Renaud's marriage to the heiress of the county of Boulogne, overlooking Renaud's unorthodox method of abducting the bride. Despite Renaud's inveterate habit of supporting the English, joining Richard's alliance in 1197 and renewing the alliance with John in 1199, Philip continued to reward him with lands in Normandy in order to encourage his loyalty. When Renaud's final treason was revealed in 1211, the king took direct action, sentenced him in his court, and finally captured him at Bouvines, after which he was imprisoned for the rest of his life. In fact, however, regardless of the enormity of Renaud's treasons, Philip Augustus had already gained the upper hand by 1201 when he affianced Renaud's sole daughter and heiress to his own infant son, Philippe Hurepel. Whatever the count's subsequent treacheries, the county of Dammartin was destined to revert to the royal family through this marriage.[18] This maneuver left Beaumont, Vermandois-Valois, and Dreux as the only counties remaining in the Paris region.[19]

Beaumont-sur-Oise* is located on the river to the north of Paris and close by to Valois. In 1179 the count was **Mathieu**, also titular chamberlain of the royal court, although, apart from witnessing royal charters, he left few traces in the royal administration. In 1188 he was among the numerous barons who took the cross with Philip Augustus on the Third Crusade.[20] He also may have taken the cross for the Fourth Crusade, but did not make the journey. At the site of his house on the Île-de-la-Cité in Paris he founded in 1206 a church in honor of Saint Denis and endowed it with two priests. This foundation was made explicitly to recompense a journey to Jerusalem, apparently promised but never made, for at the time of the Fourth Crusade in 1201 Pope Innocent III issued a letter of protection for the count for his expenditures for holy places and his displacements (*in transfretando expendisset*). It appears therefore that at the close of his life Mathieu was compensating a crusading vow that he never fulfilled.[21] In a rare participation in royal affairs at the end of his life he joined Simon de Montfort and Mathieu de Montmorency in guaranteeing the liege homage of Gaucher de Châtillon, count of Saint-Pol.[22]

Mathieu married Aliénor, heiress to Raoul, count of Vermandois and lord of Valois. While the marriage to Aliénor lasted (her career is explored below), Mathieu styled himself not only count of Beaumont but also lord of Valois from his wife's inheritance and acted frequently with the advice of his spouse in making donations to churches. Around 1192, however, he suddenly and inexplicably replaced his spouse, Aliénor de Vermandois, with Aliénor, daughter of Raoul, count of Soissons, who because of the identical first name, has long escaped historians' notice.[23] (His motives for this move totally escape us.) Aliénor de Vermandois had not delivered her spouse an heir, as she had failed to do in her three previous marriages. Aliénor de Soissons likewise was barren in her marriage to Mathieu until his death in 1208, but the fault was probably not hers because in her succeeding marriage to Étienne de Sancerre she produced seven children. Among Mathieu's numerous beneficiaries were the count's chapel, Saint-Léonor, next to his castle at Beaumont, and the Cistercian abbey of Val-Notre-Dame downstream on the Oise.[24]

Without heirs Mathieu was succeeded by his half brother **Jean**, who, from his mother Alix, added the lordship of Luzarches to the county of Beaumont.[25] In Beaumont tradition he had first married Gertrude de Soissons, sister of Aliénor, but after annulling that marriage, he turned to Jeanne de Garlande of the prominent Garlande family that was close to the king. When Jeanne's father Guillaume died in 1216 leaving as heiresses Jeanne and her two sisters, Philip Augustus intervened in the succession, as we shall see, and divided Guillaume's succession among Jean de Beaumont and the two other sons-in-law, Henri, count of Grandpré, and Guy, butler of Senlis.[26] Jean entered the battle of Bouvines in 1214 as a banneret leading a contingent of twenty knights. He opposed Count Ferrand of Flanders with distinction on the right wing of the Capetian army under the leadership of the duke of Burgundy and in the company of Mathieu de Montmorency and others.[27] Two years later he was one of the numerous "barons of the realm" who participated in the judgment of the succession of Champagne according to the customs of France at Melun.[28] Important among his revenues were the tolls on the Oise.[29] His pattern of donations followed that of his brother, but unfortunately he also inherited the family's sterility. When it became clear that he too would die without heir, he and Countess Jeanne increased the frequency of their donations to churches. His death in 1223 gave Philip Augustus the opportunity to take control and to assign the succession to Yves d'Ully, a distant cousin. In the division of lands the king took the county and most of the property, settling on Yves only minor lands and 7,000 *livres parisis* as compensation.[30] This escheat also allowed the king to take stock of the resources he gained. The charter of settlement provided an inventory of the landed possessions of Count Jean, and the names of some ninety-two vassals were inscribed in Register E.[31] The charters that the count had collected were deposited in the royal archives at Paris, thus preserving the archives of a lay seigneur for the first and only time during the reign.[32]

If the king benefited from the infertility of the counts of Beaumont and their spouses, his ideal heiress was undoubtedly his cousin **Aliénor,*** youngest daughter of Raoul, count of Vermandois, who was equally barren.[33] In the reign of Louis VII, the county and its dependencies, Amiens and Valois, had been inherited from Raoul by Aliénor's elder sister, Elisabeth, who was married to Philippe, count of Flanders.* The marriage had advanced the frontier of Philippe's territories south, much closer to Paris. And in fact, Philippe had worked out a parallel marriage between his brother Mathieu, count of Boulogne, and Aliénor (Aliénor's third marriage). After Elisabeth received the inheritance in 1164 with her husband, she was forced to resign it to Philippe sometime in the next decade, most likely as a penalty for being unfaithful to him. Louis VII confirmed this concession to Philippe, and Philip II did likewise, probably as part of a series of complex marriage negotiations that took place when he married Isabelle de Hainaut, the niece of Philippe of Flanders. But within a few years, Philippe had lost his claim on Vermandois and Valois to Aliénor. Apparently foiled by Henry II, king of England, from manipulating the young king from within the royal court, Philippe turned to open defiance against the Philip II. Further complicating his claim to Elisabeth's territories, Elisabeth died in 1182, childless, while Aliénor was now married to Mathieu of Beaumont. Philip II at this point repudiated his confirmation of Elisabeth's concession to Philippe and defended Aliénor's claim to **Vermandois and Valois**. In a peace established between the king and Philippe in 1182, Philippe renounced his ultimate rights over Vermandois and Valois but it was agreed that he would retain possession during his lifetime. Further struggle between Philip II and Philippe in 1184 and 1185 culminated in an agreement made at Boves in 1185. The count of Flanders was permitted to hold Saint-Quentin and Péronne for his lifetime. Aliénor's rights to southern Vermandois and Valois were confirmed by the young king, while he exacted the Amienois with Montdidier and Roye as a price for himself.[34] After the death of Philippe, count of Flanders, on the Third Crusade in 1191, Philip II made a second settlement with Aliénor confirming again her rights to Vermandois and Valois, but this time taking Péronne and other territories and compensating her with 13,000 *livres* for the exchange.[35] By chance this last settlement occurred just before her sudden separation from Mathieu de Beaumont in 1192. Abandoning the title countess of Beaumont, she began to call herself **countess of Saint-Quentin** (the main fortress of Vermandois) by which title she is found in the hierarchical list of the royal registers. As for this last agreement, it made explicit what had been assumed earlier, that should Aliénor die without son or daughter, the king was to become her heir, a calculated event that occurred, in fact, in 1213.

As evidence of the king's expectation that she would die childless is the fact that he began to pay close attention to the administration of her lands after 1191. Between 1192 and 1194 the countess listed all of the alms that she had agreed to pay to her churches and promised in the future that she would make no single gift above one hundred *livres*.[36] At this point the king began the regular practice of confirming her donations with his own charters.[37] Both measures were designed to keep under control the countess's almsgiving, for which he would be responsible when he later inherited the county. In addition to founding Saint-Léonor at Beaumont with her husband Mathieu she gave to over forty churches with major preferences for the female houses of Longpré and Le Parc-aux-Dames near Crépy-en-Valois and the abbey of Sainte-Geneviève-du-Mont at Paris. In 1204 she intervened at Morienval to set the number of nuns at sixty.[38] Following her death Philip Augustus conducted at least three inquests into her resources in the forest of Retz.[39] His subsequent inventories of the feudal resources of Vermandois and Valois indicate that the countess could claim at least 170 vassals and 976 subvassals.[40] On the field at Bouvines in 1214, her contingents supplied at least 190 knights.[41] The importance of her fiefs to the king is further acknowledged by the royal chancery, which drew up a special dossier of charters concerning her inheritance in Register C.[42]

She died in 1213 at one of her favored churches, Sainte-Geneviève-du-Mont in Paris, and was buried with the Cistercians at Longpont. The anniversary of her death was noted not only in the obituary of the cathedral of Soissons but also in the psalter owned by Queen Ingeborg, which most likely was made by the same artists who worked for Countess Aliénor. The two women were distantly related, a fact that was revealed in the genealogy composed by the royal clerics in Register C in an effort to demonstrate the queen's affinity to the king and to justify his separation.[43] Two other references to Aliénor are worth noting. Toward the end of the 1180s the trouvère Huon d'Oisi identified her as the countess of Crépy in his poem *Le Tournoiement des dames* and celebrated her as leading the female participants on the field.[44] Second, she provides a rare exception among the lords and ladies around Paris, as she is recorded as having made a donation to a jongleur, in this case, a jongleur named Lambert.[45]

Of the three counts listed in the chancery registers those of **Dreux*** to the west of Paris were by far the most prestigious, enjoying a status that clearly was derived from their royal blood and that placed them in the spotlight of the chroniclers, especially of Rigord and Guillaume le Breton.[46] For that reason we are better informed about their public activities than about the other baronage around Paris. The progenitor of the family was a younger son of King Louis VI on whom was bestowed the traditional Capetian name of Robert that was retained for successive generations. Guillaume le Breton identified them as *Robertigena* or *Roberti*,[47] modern historians by numbers (I–III), but they can also be remembered by the names of their principal wives. The first Robert received his title of count from an early and brief marriage to the countess of Perche. This Robert had rebelled against his older brother Louis VII when the latter departed on the Second Crusade. When Louis returned, he nonetheless bestowed on Robert the lordship of Dreux in 1152, an act of generosity that insured the unwavering fidelity of Robert and his direct descendants thereafter. About the same time, Robert married Agnès de Baudemont-Braine and took possession of her lands, which lay to the east of Paris toward Reims. (Agnès was likewise entitled countess from an earlier marriage.) Louis may have given Dreux to this brother as a marcher bulwark against the Anglo-Normans to the west, but Braine lay in Champagne under the lordship of the counts and illustrated the characteristic dispersion of the family lands.[48] Louis VII's gamble on his younger brother, however, paid off. **Robert I-Agnès** was by the side of his young nephew King Philip Augustus in the major negotiations with the Angevins until his death in 1188.[49] In the registers the chancery clerics recorded his heir simply as count of Dreux and Braine (*comes Drocensis et Brene*).[50]

Married to Yolande de Coucy by 1184, **Robert II-Yolande** followed his father's path without missing a step. Royal charters document him in frequent attendance at the royal court, as for example, at the king's divorce proceedings against Queen Ingeborg (1193), at the treaty of Le Goulet with King John (1200), at the judgment of the succession of Champagne (1201, 1216), and at the crucial assembly of Soissons (1213).[51] He was equally careful to maintain his obligations as vassal to the count of Champagne.[52] The royal chroniclers, for their part, emphasized his military acumen. He followed the king to the Holy Land on the crusade (1190) and aided him in the sieges of the castles of Nonancourt (1196) and Les Andelys (1203) in the Norman campaign against Richard and John.[53] For these services Philip increased a *fief-rente* that had originally been granted by King Henry II from four hundred to five hundred *livres*.[54] On the field of Bouvines (1214) he was joined by his brother Philippe de Dreux, bishop of Beauvais, where they took their place on the left wing of the Capetian line against their inveterate enemy, Renaud of Dammartin, count of Boulogne. For his contribution to the victory Philip rewarded him with a hostage, Earl William of Salisbury, the half brother of John, whom Robert later exchanged for his own son, **Robert III**, then being held in England.

During festive celebrations of Pentecost at Compiègne in May 1209 Philip Augustus not only belted his eldest son, Louis, with the sword of knighthood but also his two cousins Robert III and Pierre, sons of Robert II-Yolande. During the succeeding banquet the honor of serving the first course to the king was accorded to Guy de Thouars, count/duke of Brittany, but the second course was assigned to Count Robert II-Yolande whose sons had just become knights.[55] Robert III, after his marriage in 1210 to Aliénor de Saint-Valéry from Picardy north of Paris, accompanied his father to the assembly of Soissons in 1213 and participated in the military campaign of 1214.[56] Whereas Robert II-Yolande rode with the king at Bouvines, Robert III-Aliénor and Pierre, the younger brother, joined Prince Louis to oppose King John's drive north to the Loire. As John approached Nantes, Pierre remained within the city, but Robert III sallied across the bridge and rashly engaged the English forces where he was quickly captured with fourteen of his companions. John took him back to England and placed him in captivity where he awaited the ransom that his father finally procured from Earl William, who was taken at Bouvines. Apparently Robert's imprisonment was not entirely disagreeable. The chronicler the Anonymous of Béthune noted that he was retained honorably and allowed the pleasures of hunting in the forests and fishing in the streams.[57]

When Robert II-Yolande died in 1218, Robert III-Aliénor took his father's place as the eldest son and inherited his principal lands. Always faithful to the Capetians, as were his father and grandfather, Robert III-Aliénor took an active role in Prince Louis's English expedition of 1216 and in 1224 accompanied the king's descent into Languedoc.[58] Maintaining peaceful relations with the count of Champagne as well,[59] he led a relatively uneventful life at home until his death in 1234, but the younger Pierre was already embarked on a radically independent career—in part encouraged by Philip Augustus.[60] In order to solve the complex and thorny problem of the succession to the duchy of Brittany, the king had turned to his loyal cousins of Dreux. In 1212 he offered Alix, daughter of Guy de Thouars and Constance, in marriage to Pierre de Dreux. (Through her mother, Alix was the direct heiress to the duchy.) The new duke returned his gratitude by accepting the king's conditions that were, in turn, guaranteed by his father and his uncle Philippe, the bishop of Beauvais, and he accompanied Philip in the campaign of 1213 against the count of Flanders. Although Pierre enlisted in Prince Louis's expedition to England in 1216, he did not participate, but Louis nonetheless offered him the honor of Richmond with one hundred knights' fiefs should the venture succeed. He returned to the prince's side against the Albigensians in the south in aid of Amaury de Montfort at Marmande in 1219. Once established as duke, however, Pierre began to quarrel with his Breton vassals. He encroached upon his bishops, for which he was excommunicated by the bishop of Nantes in 1218, thus earning the epithet of "Mauclerc." He also sought to regain his rights to the earldom of Richmond in

England. After the death of Louis VIII, he joined the barons who defied Blanche of Castile's regency over the infant Louis IX and conspired openly with Henry III of England to secure possession of the earldom of Richmond. Duke Pierre's subsequent career as persecutor of churchmen and rebellious agent of the English takes us beyond the scope of this study, but as a member of the Dreux family of royal cousins he nonetheless maintained a presence in our region and, as will be seen, appears most prominently in the stained-glass windows of Chartres Cathedral among the other lords of the region.

If their public life is revealed by contemporary chroniclers and royal documentation, the Dreux family's widely dispersed lands appear chiefly in the charters collected by churches and monasteries. In these documents Robert I-Agnès often styled himself "count and brother of the king," thus reflecting the origins of his claim to Dreux, but he could also be satisfied with the simple "count and lord of Dreux."[61] Robert II-Yolande most often signed himself as "count, lord of Dreux and Braine,"[62] while Robert III-Aliénor employed "count of Dreux and lord of Saint-Valéry," acknowledging his wife's inheritance.[63] The Latin inscriptions on their seals replicate these titles exactly. Although the archives from the county of Dreux have been dispersed, numerous charters in the cartulary of Saint-Yved de Braine highlight their extensive holdings in Champagne.[64] At Paris, Robert I-Agnès founded the college of Saint-Thomas du Louvre in 1186 shortly before his death and made donations to the Temple and the Hôtel-Dieu, which indicate other lands around the capital.[65] The family also had transactions with Sainte-Geneviève, Saint-Victor and Saint-Germain-des-Prés involving these lands and others in the Paris region.[66] Of highest importance to the family, of course, were their castles. The castle of Dreux, granted to Robert I-Agnès by the king in 1152, was acknowledged by his grandson Robert III-Aliénor in 1223 when he promised to render it to Philip Augustus on demand.[67] The castle of Braine inherited from Countess Agnès apparently remained in the family's hands without opposition from the king or the countess of Champagne. In 1206 Countess Blanche of Champagne granted Robert II-Yolande permission to construct a new castle at nearby Fère-en-Tardenois with the proviso of rendering it to the countess on demand.[68] On the other hand, Robert II-Yolande promised the countess of Champagne in 1209 that he would not fortify Lizy-sur-Ourcq without her permission.[69] (His son, Robert III-Aliénor, made a similar promise to Louis VIII for Bonneuil-en-Valois in 1225.)[70] At the death of Count Robert II-Yolande in 1218 his sons petitioned the countess to allow Yolande to keep the lands of Braine and Fère-en-Tardenois in her dower just as their grandmother Agnès had held them,[71] and in 1225, after the death of Yolande, Pierre, duke of Brittany, surrendered his rights to Fère to Robert III-Aliénor.[72] Even in ruins the fortifications at Fère-en-Tardenois remain impressive to this day. Of all the Dreux castles, however, that of Brie-Comte-Robert near Melun is best known today thanks to its extensive restoration. Its acquisition by the family remains obscure. Robert I-Agnès undoubtedly acquired the land early in his career. At his death in 1188 it apparently passed to a younger son, Guillaume, but later, before 1198, was acquired by his older sibling Robert II-Yolande.[73] In all probability Robert III-Aliénor enjoyed possession before his father's death in 1218, but it passed to his brother Pierre, duke of Brittany, sometime before 1227.[74] As a magnificent residential castle rivaling the royal castle of the Louvre, it remains, along with the castle at Fère, a monument to the power and prestige of the Dreux family during the reign of Philip Augustus.

Barons

The disappearance of counts around Paris perhaps encouraged the clerics in the royal chancery to avail themselves of a second category, that of "barons," to identify the most powerful lords of the realm, of which five qualified from the Paris region. These included the bellicose families from the early twelfth century now reconciled with the king. The **Montforts*** with castles at Montfort-l'Amaury and Épernon to the southwest of Paris were represented by two names, **Simon V** (d. 1218) and his son **Amaury V** (d. 1241). Stemming from an Anglo-Norman family, Simon V's grandfather Simon III (d. 1181) was both count of Évreux and lord of Montfort, but he divided the two titles between his sons Amaury (d. ca. 1191), as count of Évreux, and Simon IV (d. before 1195), as lord of Montfort.[75] Amaury (d. ca. 1213), the son of Amaury (d. ca. 1191), ceded his county to Philip Augustus in the treaty of Le Goulet in 1200,[76] thus permitting the Norman county to be absorbed into the royal domain, but Simon IV of Montfort continued to retain ties with England by marrying Amicia, heiress to the earldom of Leicester. Their son Simon V, for example, served as a pledge for his uncle Earl Robert of Leicester in 1196 and confirmed an exchange between his mother and Philip Augustus in 1206 involving lands at Breteuil.[77] After Earl Robert's death Simon V occasionally styled himself as earl of Leicester,[78] but it soon became clear that his predominant interest was in France. Early in his career, like many barons, Simon V served the king as a forest warden, investigating royal rights in the forest of Yvelines.[79] His sister, Pétronille, married Barthélemy de Roye, the leading knight at the Capetian court, while Simon took as his wife Alix de Montmorency, sister of Mathieu, the principal baron to the north of Paris. Simon's close ties with the Montmorencys were illustrated in 1208 when he negotiated an important settlement between his brother-in-law Mathieu de Montmorency and the abbey of Saint-Denis in the presence of a royal bailli.[80]

In 1201 Simon V had joined the French forces on the Fourth Crusade, but refusing to participate in the attack on Zara, he returned shortly thereafter to take part in the conquest of Normandy at the crucial siege of Château-Gaillard.[81] The dominating passion of his life was nonetheless the crusade, not only the Fourth, but also the crusade against the Albigensian heretics in the south of France. From 1209 when he answered the summons of Pope Innocent III to 1218 when he died at the siege of Toulouse he was the dynamic leader of the Albigensian Crusade. His military success was recorded in the feudal titles he collected from his conquests: duke of Narbonne, count of Toulouse, vicomte of Beziers and Carcassonne. His most stunning military achievement, however, was in 1213 at Muret where he led a company of knights recruited from the Paris region and northern France. Executing a brilliant cavalry maneuver, he won a decisive victory over the king of Aragon who lost his life and cause in the mêlée. Both the leadership of the crusade and the lordship of Montfort passed to his son Amaury V in 1218 when Simon himself was killed fortuitously by a catapult missile at the siege of Toulouse. Amaury returned from the crusade to his lands in the 1220s and set about reorganizing his fiefs, thus producing a *Scripta de feodis* akin to the king's contemporary inventory. His survey accounted for some 255 vassals grouped under six castellanies.[82] When dealing with local affairs, Simon occasionally included his wife's title, but Simon and Amaury normally preferred to style themselves simply as lords of Montfort, as they also appear in the royal registers. Montfort was not elevated to the rank of count until 1226.

The Montfort family donated extensively to churches over a wide expanse of territory reaching as far south as Saint-Benôit-sur-Loire, to the cathedral of Chartres to the southwest, to Val-Notre-Dame to the north, and to Saint-Martin-des-Champs at Paris.[83] While on the Albigensian Crusade Simon V gave Prince Louis the jawbone (*mâchoire, de osse maxille*) of Saint Vincent, which he acquired at Castres in the south and which was deposited at the church of Saint-Germain-des-Prés in Paris.[84] Naturally the family concentrated their gifts on their lands at Montfort, Épernon, and Houdan. Their biggest beneficiaries were the Cistercians at Vaux-de-Cernay who supplied the monk Pierre as the principal chronicler of the Albigensian Crusade of which Simon was the leader.[85] They also favored the female houses of Hautes-Bruyères, Yerres, and Porrois.[86] Both their wealth and influence in the Chartrain is fully displayed in the two magnificent rose windows in which Simon and Amaury portrayed themselves in the clerestories of the cathedral choir.[87]

Allied to the Montforts by marriage, the **Montmorencys*** were another family of baronial status who were descended from the troublesome vassals around Paris in the early twelfth century.[88] The Montmorencys were represented solely by **Mathieu** during his long active life (1189–1230). He married Gertrude de Soissons in 1193 from the family of the counts, after her separation from Jean, count of Beaumont.[89] His castle, which has now disappeared, was located at Montmorency to the north of Paris between Beaumont-sur-Oise and Saint-Denis. The cartulary of the abbey of Saint-Denis contains numerous disputes with the Montmorencys and the resulting settlements—so many that an elm near Épinay was designated as the traditional spot for negotiating their differences.[90] With the count of Beaumont to the north, Mathieu made an agreement regarding tolls on merchants from the Beaumont lands traveling through the lands of Montmorency.[91] The donations of the Montmorency family were distributed to the major churches in the area—Saint-Victor, Saint-Martin-des-Champs, and Saint-Martin de Pontoise—but they seemed to favor the local collegiate church at Montmorency, the Cistercians at Val-Notre-Dame, and the Benedictines at Saint-Denis, with whom they were often at odds.[92] It was the occasional military activities of Mathieu, however, that caught the attention of the royal chronicles and illustrated the baron's fidelity to the king. The king reimbursed him for losses at sea on the Third Crusade.[93] Like many, he participated in the 1203–4 siege of Château-Gaillard.[94] Like Jean, count of Beaumont, he brought twenty knights to the field at Bouvines and served on the right wing of the Capetian host alongside his neighbor.[95] In 1215, he joined Prince Louis on the crusade against the Albigensians.[96] The following year, in 1216, he too joined the barons of France at Melun to judge the settlement of the succession of Champagne.[97] His faithful service was finally recognized in 1218 when, like his grandfather, he was named constable of the royal court, in which office he remained into the reign of Louis IX. As royal constable he participated in the judgments between the king and the bishop of Paris in 1220–21 and over the escheat of Beaumont in 1223.[98] While Mathieu was simply lord of Montmorency, the legend of his seal noted only his name (*Matheus de Montemorenciaco*),[99] but after he became constable of the royal court in 1218 he did not neglect to include his title (*constabularius domini regis Francie*).[100]

The most publicized of the rebellious families of the early twelfth century, however, were the **Garlandes,*** arising from obscure origins but becoming so powerful that they were able to impose five of their members into the offices of chancellor, seneschal, and butler at the royal court of Louis VI.[101] By the end of the century two branches of the family remained prominent around Paris, although they no longer retained the former appointments to high office. One branch, which was descended from the butler Gilbert, took the first names of Guy and especially Anseau, but they were less noteworthy, although they counted among their number two bishops of Orléans and perhaps even the better-known Héloïse, abbess of the Paraclete and companion to the theologian Abélard.[102] In our period they were lords of Tournan-en-Brie to the southeast of Paris by which title they identified themselves in charters and on seals.[103] At Tournan they possessed a castle, now disappeared, and most of their lands.[104] In 1186, **Guy de Garlande**, son of the butler Gilbert, confirmed before Philip Augustus that his grandson Anseau held the castle of Tournan in liege homage from the bishop of Paris.[105] **Anseau** (d. before 1182), married to Rance, married his daughters to lords of castellan rank, such as the Andresels, the Poissys, and the Île-Adams.[106] The family gave to the local church of Saint-Denis de Tournan, but their donations to the Benedictine abbey of Saint-Maur-des-Fossés were better recorded.[107]

The major branch of the Garlandes was descended from the seneschal Guillaume whose name they invariably adopted. At the turn of the century two Guillaumes were active, one (d. before 1200) married to Idoine and especially his son (d. 1216) married to Alix de Châtillon. **Guillaume-Idoine** was noticed by the biographer of Guillaume le Maréchal as one of Philip Augustus's agents in dealing with Henry II over the castle of Gisors.[108] In 1190 he participated in the regency while Philip was on crusade. **Guillaume-Alix** devoted his entire life to serving the king whom he accompanied in the military campaigns of the 1190s. He served as a war treasurer on the marches preliminary to the invasion of Normandy and entered the battle of Bouvines in the company of the king's closest circle of knights.[109] In recompense for his earlier service, in 1193 the king had bestowed on him a wife, Alix, from a family of royal cousins of Châtillon, and in 1195 granted him the Norman fief of Neufmarché.[110] By this name and that of the seigneury of Livry (the present Livry-Gargan), which he inherited from his grandmother, Guillaume-Alix was identified as baron of Livry and Neufmarché in the chancery register. On his seal, however, he took the simple name *Willermus de Garlande*.[111] His father Guillaume-Idoine founded a church of Augustinian canons at Livry, which was supported by both the family's and royal generosity,[112] but the donations of Guillaume-Alix extended throughout the Paris region to churches such as the Hôtel-Dieu at Paris, Notre-Dame de Gournay (a priory of Saint-Martin-des-Champs at Gournay-sur-Marne), and Saint-Maur-des-Fossés.[113] The family married well. Not only was Guillaume given Alix, a royal cousin, his sister was wedded to Mathieu de Marly of the Montmorency-Marly clan, and his three daughters, Jeanne, Marie, and Isabelle, were given to prominent lords—the count of Beaumont (as has been seen), the count of Grandpré, and the butler of Senlis.[114] When Guillaume-Alix died in 1216, predeceased by his son Thibaut, his inheritance escheated without male heir. The king intervened in the settlement and distributed the lands to the husbands of the three daughters.[115] The family's possessions were of such interest to the king that they were frequently confirmed by royal charters, for which the royal chancery kept a special dossier in Register C.[116] Guillaume (d.

1216) may also have possessed literary talents. The name "Noblet" circulated occasionally among the contemporary trouvères at the turn of the century. Later in the century the chronicler Aubry de Trois-Fontaines associated it with Guillaume de Garlande, but his identification may be only conjecture.[117]

At the opening of Louis VI's reign the butler at the royal court was Guy de la Tour de Senlis, but the position was soon usurped by Gilbert de Garlande (progenitor of the branch of Garlandes at Tournan-en-Brie).[118] After the Second Crusade, however, Guy's family regained the office and remained there until the end of the reign of Philip Augustus. Without variation **three Guys**, all **butlers of Senlis**, followed in succession, numbered II to IV by genealogists. Their family supplied bishops for Châlons and Toul and chapter dignitaries for Senlis and Soissons. Within this monotony of nomenclature, which makes it difficult to distinguish one from the other, however, their most evident notoriety came from subscribing to royal charters with the same name for over seventy years.[119] Guy III (1186–1221) accompanied the king on the Third Crusade and took part in the Fifth Crusade during which he was imprisoned at Damietta.[120] He received an annual *fief-rente* of thirty *livres* from the *prévôté* of Paris.[121] His son, Guy IV, was given Isabelle de Garlande as wife but was no longer royal butler, although he retained the title as part of his family name. Their seals invariably included the title of *buticularius*.[122] (The butler's office passed to Robert de Courtenay, a favorite of Louis VIII, in 1223.) Guy III gave land for founding the abbey of Hérivaux near Luzarches, but the family's major donations went to the churches in and around Senlis. The clerics of the chancery esteemed the family important enough to include them among the *barones* around Paris.

The sole figure from Vermandois to be included among the barons in the hierarchic list was **Jean II, lord of Nesle*** and castellan of Bruges (d. 1240).[123] Descended from a family that claimed the titles count of Soissons, castellan of Bruges, and lord of Nesle, Jean received the last two from his father Jean I (d. 1197–1200). (His seal bore the inscription of "lord of Nesle" on the face and "castellan of Bruges" on the counterseal.)[124] This dual inheritance made him an important baron both in Flanders and Picardy. Shortly after his father's death he took the cross on the Fourth Crusade in 1200 in the company of the major Flemish lords[125] but returned to his lands by 1205, contributing little to the crusading cause. For the rest of his career he became Philip Augustus's major agent in the Picard-Flemish region. He represented the king in implementing the marriage between Countess Jeanne, heiress of Flanders and Ferrand of Portugal. When Ferrand revolted against Capetian exactions, Jean de Nesle took part in the king's and Prince Louis's invasion into Flanders in 1213 to punish Ferrand's defection. On the battle line of Bouvines he was one of the French champions who faced the redoubtable Renaud, count of Boulogne, but Guillaume le Breton remarked that he was more interested in capturing a rich prize than in exhibiting bravery. The chronicler nonetheless conceded that he was a handsome knight of noble appearance.[126] With Ferrand now in prison, Jean de Nesle, as castellan of Bruges, became Philip Augustus's chief agent for supervising the Capetian wardship over Countess Jeanne and for governing Flanders. By 1221 he bore the title "bailli of Flanders," although shortly thereafter he fell out of favor. In 1222 he nonetheless successfully prosecuted the countess of Flanders for *defectus iuris* in the royal court. During the succeeding reigns he accompanied Louis VIII on the Albigensian Crusade in 1226 and remained an influential figure at the royal court, residing in a palatial house on the Right Bank of Paris. Trouvères like Gace Brulé occasionally include a certain Blondel de Nesle as one of their company, which has led literary scholars to hypothesize that this referred to Jean de Nesle, but the identification, like that of "Noblet," rests on little more than the similarity of names.[127] When he died in 1240, he and his wife Eustachie, daughter of the count of Saint-Pol, like so many families, left no heirs.[128]

Although he was castellan of Bruges, which would suggest that his political career was located in Flanders, Jean's extant charters show that his true power and interests were centered on his lordship of Nesle.[129] Among the recipients of his many donations was the nunnery at La Franche-Abbaye near Beaulieu-les-Fontaines, whose cartulary recorded his numerous benevolences. Having founded the house in 1202, he was also buried there.[130] Perhaps as early as 1214 Jean submitted to the king an inventory redacted in French that listed some fifty-eight places in Picardy that he held from the king and named 149 vassals who held directly from him. In 1220 when the king surveyed his feudal resources in Vermandois in the *Scripta de feodis*, Jean de Nesle's report was copied verbatim into the royal registers.[131] This document not only reveals the extent of his wealth but also explains how he was able to bring forty knights to the field of Bouvines, the largest contingent led by a banneret.[132]

The chancery clerics allotted no special chapter to the category of vicomte (*vicecomes*); most were inserted at the rank of baron and a few as castellans. Around Paris, only two vicomtes survived into the reign of Philip Augustus, both to the south of the capital, and neither was included in the hierarchical lists. Both, however, were listed among the bannerets located in the Vexin.[133] In 1206 **Adam** (d. 1217), **vicomte of Melun**, received with the knight Simon de Poissy the gift of Beaufort in Anjou from the king, for which they owed liege homage.[134] The two of them joined Prince Louis's invasion of England in 1217 where Adam met his death.[135] The bailli Adam Héron reported that the vicomte held his domain at Melun from the king and counted sixty-eight names among his vassals.[136] Despite this impressive following Adam himself left few traces in the ecclesiastical records of the region. **Payen, vicomte of Corbeil**, left even fewer. The same bailli listed Payen's holdings of land and forest from the king in the castellany of Melun, but they brought no more than thirty *livres*.[137] Evidently he held other assets since he was included in the *Nomina* survey of the castellany of Corbeil as possessing more than sixty *livres* of annual revenue.[138] Both Adam and Payen, however, did not neglect to place the title of vicomte on their seals.[139]

Castellans

The term "castellan" (*castellanus*), of course, denotes one who held a castle (*castrum*), but among the historians of the early twelfth century it bore the negative connotation of one who profited from his stronghold to terrorize his neighbors. The counts of Champagne, we shall see, used the term administratively in a positive sense to organize fiefs in castellanies, a usage adopted by the Capetians in the thirteenth century in the *Nomina militum* inventory and later applied generally to the Paris region. In the registers of Philip Augustus it also acquired an honorific valence to designate those aristocrats ranked below barons but above *vavassores* or simple knights. Two families found on the castellan list, the Marlys and the Meulans, stemmed from the early century like the above barons.[140] Situated directly to the west of Paris, **Marly-le-Roi*** produced two castellans at the turn of the century, **Mathieu** (d. 1203) and his son **Bouchard** (d. 1226). They formed a collateral branch of Montmorencys who separated at the death of Mathieu's father, around 1160, and who likewise favored the names of Mathieu and Bouchard.[141] This naming habit, added to the practice of the Marly branch to designate themselves as Montmorency as well, has produced confusion in keeping the two families separate. The confusion is exacerbated by the practice of using the same heraldry as their cousins on several of their seals.[142] Mathieu de Marly joined Philip Augustus in the campaigns of the 1190s against King Richard and was misfortunate enough to be captured at Courcelles-lès-Gisors in 1198.[143] He joined the Fourth Crusade and proceeded to Constantinople where he died in the fighting in 1203 and was later buried at Jerusalem.[144] He married, as we have seen, Mathilde de Garlande, daughter of Guillaume-Idoine. The recipients of their benevolence included the canons of Sainte-Geneviève-du-Mont and the Cistercians of Vaux-de-Cernay. Mathieu and Mathilde also founded the nunnery of Porrois (or Port-Royal) for the safekeeping of Mathieu on the crusade.[145] Among Mathieu's siblings was Thibaut who, midlife, had departed on a pilgrimage and subsequently became a Cistercian monk at Val-Notre-Dame in 1185. As mentioned above in Chapter 1, he is notable for a meditation on death composed in French verse that castigated the behavior of his contemporaries.[146]

Mathieu and Mathilde were succeeded by their son Bouchard (d. 1226) whose career was closely associated with Simon de Montfort and the Albigensian Crusade. He took the cross in 1209, serving in Simon's inner circle of supporters, returned to the south by 1213 to fight with Simon at the battle of Muret, and met his death at Montpensier in 1226 with King Louis.[147] With his wife Mathilde de Châteaufort he reinforced his parents' establishment of the nuns of Porrois, transforming it from a priory to a full abbey.[148] In addition to Porrois, the Marlys supplied personnel for the cathedral of Notre-Dame de Paris. Hervé, brother of Mathieu, was a cleric and dean of the chapter, and Guillaume, son of Mathieu, was a canon.[149] **Thibaut**, Bouchard's eldest son, began his career as a knight in the royal entourage where he excelled in hunting and tournaments, but drew up his testament in 1226 and converted to the monastic life at Vaux-de-Cernay, long patronized by his family, where he became abbot in 1234 and later was canonized.[150] Although Bouchard had quarreled with the chapter of Chartres over jurisdiction over roads, he nonetheless donated a clerestory window in the cathedral choir that contained his portrait.[151]

When Philip Augustus annexed the Anglo-Norman county of Meulan in 1202, Count Robert of Meulan's brother, **Roger de Meulan**, had been long collaborating with the Capetians. He appears on the list of castellans as lord of **La Queue-en-Brie**, directly to the east of Paris.[152] Along with Mathieu de Marly he was also captured by King Richard at Courcelles-lès-Gisors in 1198, but he subsequently enjoyed a *fief-rente* of one hundred *livres* from King Philip drawn from Évreux.[153] Like his brother Count Robert he continued to confirm the donations that his father had made as count of Meulan.[154] As early as 1190 Roger sold to the king the woods named Grosbois (*Grossum Nemus*) near Marolles-en-Brie for two hundred *livres*,[155] and along with Simon de Montfort he was acting as Philip's agent in 1196 when he stood as surety for Robert, earl of Leicester, in Robert's concession of Pacy to Philip.[156] Later he collaborated with Guillaume de Garlande (d. 1216), a royal favorite, to determine the forest usage of the men of Roissy.[157] He married a certain Isabelle who may have been related to the Mauvoisin family, likewise Capetian supporters.[158] The legend on his seal bore simply his name.[159]

Close by Montfort to the west of Paris was the castellany of **Neauphle-le-Château**, which was in the hands of a castellan named **Simon** during Philip's reign. Little is known about this particular Simon whose family stemmed from the eleventh century and frequently used the name Simon, but Philip's chancery clerics ranked him among the castellans.[160] He was closely allied to his neighbor, Simon de Montfort, whom he accompanied on the Fourth Crusade; he received from the king an annual *fief-rente* of five *livres* from the *prévôté* of Poissy, and his family was generous in their donations to the Cistercians at the neighboring Vaux-de-Cernay, which they had founded early in the century.[161] The legend on his seal reveals only his name.[162]

The lords of **Chevreuse*** were likewise located southwest of Paris.[163] The family stemmed from the turbulent Montlhéry-Chevreuse-Rochefort clan whose castles so notoriously disturbed the peace of the region south of Paris at the beginning of the century. Among their descendants was Guy (d. 1182), who died at the threshold of our period, with his wife Cécile. They were succeeded by Simon (1182–91) who accompanied Philip Augustus on the Third Crusade and likely died on the crusade. Thereafter the family favored the name of the grandfather: **Guy**, lord of Chevreuse (1191–1209), married to Aveline, and **Guy** (1208–1263), married to Helisende. The first of these Guys was the most noteworthy and well connected by marriage. He accompanied the king on the Third Crusade, along with Simon, his uncle. With Philippe de Lévis, a fellow crusader and close follower of Simon de Montfort, he borrowed money from Genoese bankers to finance their departure on the crusade. They secured their loan by pledging their holdings with the Templars.[164] By marriage, Guy was connected to the Corbeil and Mauvoisin clans. His wife Aveline was daughter of Jean de Corbeil and Jean's wife Carcassonne, both from leading families to the south of Paris, and his sister Cécile married Robert Mauvoisin from an important family in the Vexin. After Guy's death, Aveline married Pierre de Richebourg from another prominent Vexin family. (The Lévis, Corbeil, Mauvoisin, and Richebourg families are introduced below.)

Because of the survival of numerous ecclesiastical charters, their gifts to churches are the best-known facet of the family's activities. For example, in the presence of Simon de Montfort and Mathieu de Marly, Guy and Aveline contributed to the priory of Moulineaux in 1201.[165] Most of their donations went to the Cistercians at Vaux-de-Cernay beginning in 1205 when Guy-Aveline fell seriously ill; Guy's sister Cécile gave to the same abbey.[166] After Guy's death Aveline wrote to Philip Augustus, requesting that the king execute her husband's legacy to the abbey.[167] Aveline likewise donated to the nunnery of Yerres, where Elisabeth, her husband's aunt, and Aveline herself had placed daughters.[168] Later the family's attention turned to the nearby nunnery of Porrois, which was patronized principally by Guy-Helisende.[169]

At the end of the reign it was the lands of Aveline that drew the attention of the royal bailli Adam Héron when he surveyed the fiefs around Melun. Her holdings from the king are listed as well as five vassals.[170] Her son Guy-Helisende, however, is found in the *Scriptum feodorum de Monteforti* as liege vassal of Amaury de Montfort, having nine *livres* of revenues from Montfort and the fortress of La Ferté (dép. Yvelines) as well as other properties.[171] The legends on Guy-Aveline's seals alternate between the title *dominus* and the simple *Guido de Chebrosia*.[172]

The importance of the family is fully apparent in the surviving remains of their castle at Chevreuse, which is presently being restored by archaeologists from the department of Yvelines. Perched on a hill dominating the town, the donjon is a large rectangular structure with massive walls and buttresses constructed in the archaic style of previous centuries. It was probably begun under Simon in the second half of the twelfth century and later modernized by Guy-Aveline and Guy-Helisende. Although outmoded in style, it testifies to the family's importance in the region.[173]

Close to Beaumont and Montmorency to the north of Paris was the family of **Île-Adam**,* who may be the castellans cited in the royal registers by the item *Castellanus Insule*. (The registers are ambiguous at this point.)[174] Well endowed with property and well connected in marriage, they were doubtlessly an important family, but they are inexplicably absent from other royal documentation and escaped the notice of chroniclers. Little remains of the castle that they installed on their island in the Oise River downstream from Beaumont. Since the family had a penchant for alternating the names of Adam and Anseau, it is moreover difficult to keep them separate, but those of concern to this study are **Adam** (d. 1189), **Anseau** (d. 1219), and **Anseau** (d. 1252). Adam (d. 1189) married to Aelis, sister of Jean de Corbeil, took the cross on the Third Crusade. He was succeeded as castellan by Anseau (d. 1219), his son, who married Aelis de Beaumont, sister of Mathieu, count of Beaumont. After Aelis's death, Anseau married Ève from the Garlande clan. Anseau (d. 1219), in turn, was succeeded as castellan by his son Anseau (d. 1252), who married Marie Mauvoisin.

Two charters that have survived in the Beaumont archives concern Anseau (d. 1219). In 1205 Anseau acknowledged liege homage to Mathieu, count of Beaumont, for certain fiefs that he enumerated, while reserving his fealty to the king; and in 1206 he and Mathieu came to an agreement over the rights of passage and tolls at Île-Adam.[175] With the exception of these two charters from the Beaumont archives, however, most of the family's abundant documentation comes from ecclesiastical sources that testify to their donations. For example, Adam (d. 1189) contributed to the foundation of the Cistercians at Val-Notre-Dame and with his son continued to support this house where Ève de Garlande, the wife of Anseau (d. 1219), was buried.[176] Adam also gave to Saint-Léonor at Beaumont for the soul of Aelis, Anseau's first wife.[177] With his brother Manasses, Adam was also among the families around Paris who gave to the shrine of Saint Thomas Becket in Canterbury, England.[178] The legend on the seal of Anseau (d. 1219) contained simply his name: *Anselmus de Insula*.[179]

Two figures appear on the castellan list from the French Vexin to the northwest of Paris: **Hugues de Chaumont** and Jean de Gisors. For the year 1196 Roger of Howden identified Hugues as a brave and rich knight who was a familiar of the French king and whom Richard captured and imprisoned. According to Roger, he escaped over the wall at night with the collaboration of his jailer.[180] Hugues appears in the monastic charters with his wife Pétronille giving to the churches of Saint-Germain-des-Prés and Val-Notre-Dame.[181] Around 1218 (after Hugues's death) when the bailli Guillaume de Ville-Thierri reported on the fiefs of the castellany of Chaumont in the *Scripta de feodis*, he listed Pétronille as holding four fiefs at Chaumont and elsewhere and a certain **Guillaume de Chaumont** who held six fiefs at Chaumont and elsewhere, which were worth thirty-five *livres*.[182] Evidently Guillaume, whatever his relation to Hugues and Pétronille, was the heir to the castellany. The remains of the Chaumont castle, rebuilt in the fourteenth century, are still visible. Hugues's seal bore only his name: *Hugo de Calvomonte*.[183]

Gisors* stood as a flashpoint between the French and Norman Vexin, fiercely contested by the French and Angevin kings. Not only did it contain the venerable elm, the traditional spot where the two monarchs met, but also an important castle over which they fought. Henry II had constructed a huge polygon donjon at Gisors, which incited the animosity of the young Capetian. When Philip finally acquired the castle in 1194, he added an imposing tower.[184] With Gisors in the hands of Philip Augustus, the Anglo-Norman **Jean de Gisors** defected to Philip Augustus, evidently because he held extensive lands on the French side of the Vexin.[185] This is apparent in his forty-nine vassals whose names can be found in the bailli Guillaume de Ville-Thierri's survey of the fiefs of Jean, a number elevating him to the importance of a Jean de Nesle.[186] Jean's few charters are limited to the churches of Saint-Denis, Vaux-de-Cernay, and Saint-Martin de Pontoise.[187] His seal bears only his name.[188] Jean's father and **son**, both named **Hugues** (a naming practice of many families), as well as Jean's uncle, Thibaut, are found in a few charters from the period.[189] The Hugues de Gisors whom the bailli Guillaume listed as possessing three fiefs valued at sixty *livres* in the castellany of Gisors is likely Jean's son.[190]

Two families who were assiduous in service of the royal court were also ranked among the castellans by the chancery clerics: Dreux de Mello and the chamberlains, sons of Gautier the Chamberlain, who adopted the place-names of Nemours and Méréville. Despite its frequent appearance, the name of **Dreux de Mello*** is ambiguous. It could represent one of the many Dreuxs who were well documented from Mello near Senlis to the north of Paris,[191] or it could designate Dreux de Mello, who was the royal constable between 1193 and 1218. Although it is conjectural, I shall opt that the castellan listed in the chancery register was the constable Dreux de Mello. Dreux the constable was also, in fact, the half brother of Guillaume-Idoine de Garlande and Robert Mauvoisin through the three marriages of Agnès de Toucy.[192] This relationship would explain why

Dreux the constable contributed to the Garlande-sponsored abbey of Livry[193] and why among the pledges to the king for the fealty of Dreux's son in 1212 is found Guillaume-Alix de Garlande.[194] Before being named constable, Dreux accompanied Philip Augustus on the Third Crusade and was given responsibility for guarding prisoners after the fall of Acre.[195] Unlike his predecessor, the constable Raoul, count of Clermont, he was active as envoy, custodian, and judge, for which he was rewarded the lordship of Loches in the Loire valley in 1205, after the castle was taken from King John.[196] His active service for the king generated frequent notice in the royal documentation.[197] The gift of Loches almost certainly elevated him and his descendants to the status of castellan and may thereby account for his presence on the list. His son Dreux likewise did liege homage for this and other castles in the Loire valley.[198] After the death of the constable in 1218, the son remained lord of Loches, but the court office was conferred on Mathieu de Montmorency, as has been seen. Unlike his successor, however, Dreux omitted his royal title and inscribed only his name on his seal (*Droco de Merloto*).[199]

Two castellans, the lords of **Nemours** and of **Méréville**, designate the family of **Gautier the Chamberlain**,* who clearly sired the most faithful and active members of the royal entourage.[200] Gautier and his sons were not the chamberlains of the royal court who sealed the king's charters, but those who served inside the royal household. Gautier came from a family of lower status than the counts, barons, and many of the castellans. Thus, according to a contemporary chronicler, he was nobler in deeds than in family.[201] He appeared in the king's service as early as the 1150s, drew up his testament in 1198, and died in 1204, active in the king's affairs to the end. Married to Aveline of Nemours, from whom he inherited Nemours and Méréville, Gautier had seven sons with Aveline.[202] One sure sign of Gautier the Chamberlain's favor at court was the nomination of three of these sons to the bishoprics of Noyon, Paris, and Meaux.[203] Three other sons, **Philippe** (d. 1191), **Ours** (d. 1233), and **Gautier the Young** (d. 1218), succeeded Gautier the Chamberlain (or Gautier the Father, as he came to be known) in service in the royal entourage. Philippe died prematurely at the siege of Acre on the Third Crusade. Ours began in the king's court but later transferred to the entourage of Prince Louis, with whom he fought at La Roche-aux-Moines in 1214. Gautier the Young, after the father's death, took over his father's responsibilities as the factotum of the court, eventually concentrating on Norman affairs after the conquest of the duchy. While Ours fought with Prince Louis at La Roche-aux-Moines, Gautier the Young was with the king at Bouvines.

In Gautier's testament Nemours was assigned through Philippe, now dead, to his grandson Gautier, designated as "**Gauteron**" (d. 1226) to avoid further confusion; Ours was given Méréville; and Gautier the Young was designated lord of Villebéon, a less prestigious lordship.[204] Undoubtedly to compensate, the king bestowed on him the castle of Fontaine-Guérard in Normandy and provided Adam, Gautier's son, with Isabelle de Tancarville, a major Norman heiress.[205] Two other sons, Jean and Guillaume, are mentioned in the testament with their inheritances,[206] but evidently they had not served as royal chamberlains and their fiefs were not as distinguished as the castellanies of Nemours and Méréville. The donations of the family of chamberlains, following their father, concentrated on the Cistercians at Barbeau, a house founded by Louis VII, where both the king and his chamberlain were buried.[207] The family did not neglect the Hôtel-Dieu in their mother's homeland at Nemours and extended their gifts to Saint-Victor, Saint-Denis, and the cathedral of Chartres.[208] Gautier the Father's seal identified him by his royal post: *Gauterius camerarius*.[209]

A final family selected from the castellan list is that of **Aubert de Hangest-en-Santerre** (d. 1227) and **Florence de Hangest**. Aubert held fiefs in the castellanies of Montdidier and Chauny in Vermandois.[210] He participated in the Norman campaign for which the king rewarded him with Pont-Saint-Pierre in 1204, and he was later at Bouvines.[211] His administrative service for the king consisted of conducting judgments, holding inquests into tolls and forest rights, and serving as a royal messenger, all of which made him highly visible in royal documentation.[212] His nephew, Florence de Hangest, whose holdings were also at Montdidier,[213] appears more frequently in the monastic charters, thus suggesting that he was better endowed than his uncle.[214] Florence entered the life of Guillaume le Maréchal when he was taken prisoner by the Marshal at the tournament between Anet and Sorel.[215] Aubert's seal bears only his name, but Florence's adds the title of *dominus*.[216]

Vavassores (Milites)

At the bottom rung of the hierarchic list were the *vavassores*, another term for *milites* (knights).[217] From the entire French kingdom the chancery clerics offered only forty-one names, fewer than the more influential castellans and therefore only a small sample of the thousands available. From this minute sample they included four names in the Vexin to the northwest of Paris—Robert and Simon de Poissy, Guy Mauvoisin, and Pierre de Richebourg—as well as two others from Vermandois, Philippe de Nanteuil and Aubert de Hangest.[218] During the reign of Philip Augustus **the Poissys**,* located downstream from Paris on the Seine, consisted of two major branches, each distinguished by a preferred name.[219] One was represented by a succession of Gaces. **Gace** (d. 1189) married to Jacqueline had seven children, among whom were Gace, Robert, and Amaury. **Gace** (d. before 1193) succeeded his father, but when he died in the Holy Land, the family lands passed to his brother **Robert**. Both Robert and his brother **Amaury** would later join the Albigensian Crusade, while Robert appeared on the field at Bouvines with a squadron of five knights.[220] In the inventory evaluating the fiefs of the castellany of Poissy, Robert's fiefs, naturally, were the most profitable, assessed at two thousand *livres*; his brother Amaury's at three hundred.[221] (On the eve of Bouvines Robert was called "the rich.")[222] At the end of the reign, a **Gace de Poissy**, doubtlessly of the same family, appears in the inventory of fiefs of Amaury de Montfort as vassal of the count, holding twenty *livres* from the *prévôté* of Montfort with a hostel there, and owing service of one month of castle-guard.[223] But the major source of the family's revenues stemmed from the tolls at Maisons on the Seine, which were extremely profitable. As early as 1187 Gace had negotiated with the water merchants of Paris over the distribution of these tolls.[224] The family's donations were numerous. While Gace (d. 1189) was among those who gave to the Becket shrine at Canterbury, his major interest was in the foundation and the patronage of the Premonstratensian house at Abbecourt, which became the family necropolis.[225] Examples of other houses to which the family made donations are Val-Notre-Dame, Vaux-de-Cernay, and Joyenval (all three Cistercian), and one donation was made to the Cistercian order in general.[226] This branch of the Poissys inscribed their seals simply with their names.[227]

The second branch of Poissys favored the name of Simon: **Simon** (d. before 1189) married to Mathilde, **Simon** (d. 1218) married to Agnès, and **Simon** (d. ca. 1223) married to Agnès d'Andresel. They were related (*consanguineus*) to Renaud, bishop of Chartres.[228] Like his cousin Robert, Simon-Agnès participated in the crusade against the Albigensians and appeared at Bouvines, though with three knights instead of Robert's five.[229] Simon-Agnès also joined Prince Louis on his English expedition in 1217.[230] This branch of the Poissys appears occasionally in royal documentation. In 1206 the king rewarded Simon-Agnès, Adam, vicomte of Melun, and another, with Beaufort in Anjou—a recompense for lands that Arthur of Brittany, King John's nephew, had given them.[231] In 1212, Simon-Agnès abandoned to the king his rights of forest warden at Saint-Germain-en-Laye and received in exchange similar rights in the forest of Cruye.[232] In the inventory of the fiefs of the Poissy castellany, his fiefs were valued at eight hundred *livres*, second only to his cousin Robert.[233] In 1223 the king entrusted Simon-Agnès d'Andresel with the custody of the fortress of Aigremont.[234] The family also possessed considerable interests in the city of Paris, including rights over the *crieries* in the streets, property at the Thermes, and an annual revenue of sixty *livres* on the *prévôté* of the city.[235] While the principal beneficiaries of their giving were the Cistercians at Vaux-de-Cernay,[236] the most noteworthy of their gifts was situated in Paris where they had properties on the Left Bank. In 1209, with the assent of Philip Augustus, Simon de Poissy and his wife Agnès gave to Master Jean, cleric of the king, a *cens* of sixteen *deniers* on land in front of the church Saint-Étienne-des-Grès along with its customs, domain, and justice, for the purpose of constructing a hospice (or *hôtel-dieu*) called Saint-Jacques.[237] Master Jean was undoubtedly the Jean who was a theological master at Notre-Dame and who would become dean of Saint-Quentin. He was also the subsequent founder of the Jacobin convent of Dominicans, across the rue Saint-Jacques from Saint-Étienne and within the walls of the city. The Dominicans at Saint-Jacques played an important role in the development of the university at Paris during the course of the thirteenth century.

The unusual name of **Mauvoisin**[*] identifies an influential family located at the frontiers of Normandy who, unlike most lords, adopted a surname that was not a place-name. It may be derived from an island that the family possessed above the bridge at Mantes where their possessions were concentrated, or the island may have been named after the family.[238] In any event, Mauvoisin was accepted as a cognomen[239] that could be translated literally as "bad neighbor." The negative connotation undoubtedly begged for explanation, which was provided early in the century by the monks at Notre-Dame de Coulombs near Nogent-le-Roi. A certain Guillaume Mauvoisin, an excellent knight, was gravely injured in a local war in 1133. Fearing death, he put on the monastic habit at Coulombs and promised to endow a chapel in the castle at Mantes if the monks' prayers brought about his recovery. The healing did take effect, but under the influence of perfidious friends, he moved to Chartres in search of better remedies, where he forgot his monastic robes, rearmed, and mounted his horse. Divine retribution was swift to punish the broken promise, and he died at Chartres the very day he took up again his knightly arms. It fell to his brother Samson, archbishop of Reims, to execute his unfulfilled vow to endow the chapel.[240] Thus the family earned an unsavory name whose connotations were likely forgotten by the end of the century. Like many families, the Mauvoisins were split into two major branches by Philip Augustus's reign, both of which were descended from Raoul le Barbu, the father of the above Guillaume.[241] One branch consisted of **Guillaume** (d. ca. 1185), **Manasses** (d. 1205), and **Pierre** (d. 1224). The **Guy** of the chancery register, mentioned above, was either the son or grandson of Guillaume. Guillaume was noticed by the biographer of Guillaume le Maréchal when he was among those taken at the tournament of Lagny in 1179.[242] Characteristic of the family's divided loyalties, Guillaume served with King Henry II, Manasses and Pierre with Philip Augustus. Manasses served with Philip against Richard, and Pierre fought with the Capetian army at Bouvines, accompanied by a squadron of five knights.[243] For his loyal service in the conquest of Normandy Pierre had received from the king fiefs at Nonancourt, Cergy, and Saint-André, as well as *fief-rentes* of five *livres* at Pacy and twelve *livres* at

Mantes.[244] In fact Mantes appears to be the main location of their holdings, from which they gave alms to churches like Saint-Germain-des-Prés, the abbey of Josaphat, and the cathedral of Chartres.[245] Like many in the Paris region, they also contributed to the Thomas Becket shrine at Canterbury, again from revenues at Mantes.[246] In 1204 in an agreement confirmed by the king, Guy and his wife Alix commuted their revenues at Mantes, exchanging their revenues there for an annual rent of 173 *livres* from the commune of Mantes.[247] Guy's Norman fiefs were recorded in the *Feoda Normannie* of the registers.[248]

The other branch, favoring the name Robert, descended from the Robert Mauvoisin who had married Agnès de Toucy, making his sons the half brothers of Guillaume-Idoine de Garlande and Dreux de Mello, as has been seen. The most prominent of this branch was **Robert** (d. 1217), married to Cécile de Chevreuse, whose ecclesiastical donations were concentrated on the abbey of Livry (the Garlande foundation) and the Cistercians of Vaux-de-Cernay, but he also made donations to the nuns at Porrois and to the houses of Sainte-Geneviève, Saint-Denis, and Chaalis.[249] He joined the Fourth Crusade, but like Simon de Montfort refused to besiege Zara. Returning to France, he took part in the frequent expeditions against the Albigensians (1209, 1211, 1212) and later served on diplomatic missions for the king to Rome. His eulogy from his friend Pierre, abbot of Vaux-de-Cernay and chronicler of the Albigensian Crusade, called him "the most noble knight of Christ, a man of marvelous probity, perfect knowledge, incomparable goodness, who for many years dedicated himself and his belongings to the service of Christ."[250] His seal, like his cousin Guy's, bore only his name but shared the family heraldry.[251]

Related to the Mauvoisins, **Pierre de Richebourg** held fiefs that were located in the castellanies of Paris, Mantes, and Nogent-le-Roi.[252] As with the Mauvoisins, his fief at Mantes was important. At Mantes he was lord of twenty-seven vassals and at Nogent he held four fiefs with four vassals.[253] The orientation of lands to the west of Paris is confirmed by an exchange with the abbey of Josaphat at Chartres and by his presence in the survey of fiefs of the lord of Montfort who was his liege lord.[254] Despite these important possessions, he appears rarely in the contemporary documentation. In 1200 he joined Manasses, Pierre, and Guy Mauvoisin and others as guarantors for the fidelity of Robert d'Ivry for the fortress of Ivry on the Norman borders, and in 1203 he served in the king's expedition down the Seine, operating from the castle of Gaillefontaine.[255]

Like the castellans Aubert and Florence de Hangest, **Philippe de Nanteuil-le-Haudouin** (d. 1228) was listed in the royal registers as originating from Vermandois.[256] He appears only occasionally in royal records, but he was active in royal service.[257] In 1198, he was among those captured by Richard at Courcelles, and like so many at the royal court, he too was present at Bouvines.[258] His lands were located in the castellanies of Béthisy and especially Crépy, where the royal inventory recorded houses, a fortress, forests, gardens, mills, and the homages of thirty-two men.[259] When one of these forests attracted attention, the king ordered inquests into his forest and hunting rights; Philippe was induced to concede his forest usage in the forest *de Gonbria* to the commune of Crépy.[260] As an important local lord, his donations went to abbeys like Chaalis, but the priory of Nanteuil, which became the family necropolis, was especially favored.[261]

While the chancery's hierarchic list is effective for retrieving lords at the upper echelons on the feudal scale, the token sample of *vavassores* is less useful at the levels below. We may therefore turn to the more extensive *Nomina militum*, which furnished the names of knights possessing an annual income of sixty *livres* or more and which included ten castellanies extending across the Paris region. To take the castellany of Paris as an example, the *Nomina* survey provides a total of thirty names of which only seven were duplicated in the hierarchic list. To form a portrait of any of the twenty-three new names, we can look in the ecclesiastical cartularies of the region, and, in fact, most of them do appear in the cartularies. The cartularies contain the names of three-quarters of these thirty knights or their families, a testimony of the number and richness of the cartularies in the Paris region. What is gleaned from them, however, is not of much use for forming a portrait. The charters contain transactions by which aristocrats donated or sold their properties and revenues to the churches. From the charters we learn about their families who consented to the transaction—that is, the first names of wives, children, fathers, mothers, and occasional brothers or sisters. We also learn the names of feudal lords who approved the transactions. But despite the volume of information, it remains difficult to form distinctive impressions of the knights based on the charters. At best, for example, we learn that Guillaume de Cornillon was the brother of Renaud, the royal *prévôt* of Paris (1202) and later bailli of the Cotentin in Normandy.[262] Or that the king confirmed the grant of a rent by Ferry de Massy and his wife Basilia to the canons of Saint-Victor, or that he also confirmed the transactions of Gilbert de Nesles and his wife Elisabeth with the Cistercians of Barbeau and the canons of Notre-Dame de Paris.[263] For this reason I shall limit my discussion to a few selected knights in the *Nomina* inventory for whom more distinctive characteristics can be discerned.

The *Nomina* roster for the castellany of Dammartin contains the name **Guillaume des Barres**, certainly the most celebrated knight of his day.[264] The favorite of the contemporary chroniclers, Guillaume is also featured prominently in the *Histoire de Guillaume le Maréchal*, the biography of his chief competitor for the title of the most valiant of contemporary knights. Not only was he frequently mentioned in the *Histoire*,[265] but he was singled out among the most prestigious

of the French participants at the tournament of Pleurs.[266] At the death of the
Marshal the biographer needed a spokesman to sing the praises of his English
hero before the French king. He chose Guillaume des Barres to pronounce the
epithet, "For in our time there was never a better knight (*meillor chevalier*) to
be found anywhere."[267] Guillaume des Barres himself participated with éclat in
every important military campaign of the reign. On the Third Crusade he jousted
with King Richard at Messina, eventually gaining the latter's admiration. An
English chronicler called him "a *miles strenuus* from the familiars of the king
of France."[268] Guillaume le Breton honored him with an extensive eulogy in the
Philippidos.[269] At Bouvines he rode in the company of the king's closest knights
and came to Philip's rescue when the king was unhorsed.[270] Yet despite this chivalric notoriety, Guillaume's family and holdings are difficult to discern. In
1200 his counterseal bore the inscription "Count of Chalon" (*comitis Cabi-
lonis*).[271] During the period, the name Guillaume covers both a father and a
son, but only occasionally were they separated as father and junior.[272] The wives
are also difficult to identify. In 1214 he was married to Agnès,[273] but a Guillaume
des Barres also married Amicia de Leicester after the death of Simon IV de
Montfort. His lands lay scattered around Paris and in the Auxerrois. From
the king he possessed a *fief-rente* of forty *livres* from the *prévôté* of Bapaume.[274]
He was also active in the royal entourage participating in a number of important events from 1202 to 1221.[275] His donations were distributed both in Paris
and in the surroundings, but with particular attention to Fontaines-les-Nonnes
to the northeast where he was ceremoniously buried.[276] The nuns there commissioned an elaborate *rouleau des morts* that was circulated widely throughout
northeast France.

The castellany of Dammartin also contains the name **Hugues de Pomponne**.[277] Well connected with the prominent families of the region, he was the
nephew (*nepos*) of Guillaume-Alix de Garlande,[278] and when he sold tithes to
the nuns of Chelles in 1206, the transaction was witnessed by Robert Mauvoisin,
Guillaume de Cornillon, Guillaume d'Aulnay, and Simon de Poissy among
others.[279] Appearing frequently in the charters of Chaalis, he owed liege homage to the abbot of Saint-Denis for his fiefs.[280] His brother **Renaud** was listed in
the castellany of Senlis and held a *fief-rente* of seven *livres* from the king at Pierrefonds.[281] Hugues's seal bore only his name.[282]

Guillaume Pastez, a bailli who worked on a team of baillis in Vermandois,
makes his appearance in the *Nomina* survey in the castellany of Corbeil to the
south of Paris.[283] His family origins are not clear. Although he bore the name
of a former *prévôt* of Bapaume in the service of the count of Flanders, his donations to the abbeys of Vaux-de-Cernay and Yerres suggest connections to the
south at Corbeil.[284] Yet he was also vassal to the bishop of Paris and was often

called to mediate between the abbey of Saint-Denis and powerful neighbors such as Mathieu de Montmorency, Guillaume de Mello, and Anseau de Garlande.[285] This span between the regions is exemplified in 1217 by his gifts of tithes to the abbey of Chaalis to the north from lands at Corbeil in the south.[286] In his charters he entitled himself as both *miles* and bailli of the king. Another name appearing in the *Nomina* survey for the castellany of Corbeil is **Baudouin de Corbeil**,* who also happens to have produced the charter declaring Guillaume Pastez's gift of tithes to Chaalis.[287] Baudouin was the son of **Jean** de Corbeil, married to Carcassonne. Jean, who was related to the vicomtes of Corbeil, owed castle-guard at Montlhèry and was prominent in the area.[288] The seals of Jean, Carcassonne, and Baudouin contained only their names.[289]

Farther to the south on the Seine, the castellany of Melun contained one particular family of note, the **Andresels**,* represented in the *Nomina* survey by two brothers, **Aubert** and **Jean**.[290] They were the sons of Aubert d'Andresel and his wife Agnès de Garlande, daughter of Anseau-Rance de Garlande, the lord of Tournan-en-Brie. Agnès later married Simon de Poissy, who is also named in the *Nomina* survey,[291] but Agnès still retained her connections at Andresel as mother of Aubert and Jean. This relationship is clearly revealed in 1222 in a well-documented dispute between the sons Jean and Aubert and the canons of Saint-Martin de Champeaux over justice and other revenues at Champeaux. In the final settlement, Jean and Aubert recognized owing liege homage to the king for the revenues, but the settlement was achieved with the consent of their mother, Agnès, and her husband Simon de Poissy.[292] The family's many donations went primarily to the southern abbeys of Saint-Maur-des-Fossés, Saint-Martin de Champeaux, and Barbeau, whose cartulary contains Jean's testament of 1226.[293] Amaury de Montfort's survey of fiefs names Aubert as lord of *Baconcellis* with eleven vassals.[294]

Finally, four families escaped notice in the hierarchic lists and the *Nomina* survey but deserve attention both for their service in the royal court and for their activities around Paris. Contemporary to the earlier generation of Gautier the Chamberlain (the Father), **Philippe de Lévis** (Lévis-Saint-Nom) issued from a family that was closely allied with the Montlhéry-Chevreuse castellans south of Paris.[295] He accompanied the king on the Third Crusade; on his return he was an *assessor* at Étampes and was responsible for redrawing the boundaries between the castellanies of Montlhéry and Paris. He was one of the king's closest and most trusted agents early in the reign.[296] For example, with the elder Gautier the Chamberlain he was charged with the delicate commission to punish the *prévôt* of Paris for his maltreatment of the scholars at Paris in 1200.[297] At his death about 1203 his lands around Paris were divided among five sons, of whom **Milon** and **Guy** were most noteworthy.[298] Milon continued royal service as bailli of the Cotentin in Normandy, but Guy made his fortune in the Albigensian Crusade as marshal of the army and close counselor to Simon de Montfort.[299] From 1209 to 1216 he participated in the major operations of the war, including the battle of Muret, and was rewarded with the lordship of Mirepoix near Pamiers. To the west of Paris, they were instrumental in founding Notre-Dame de la Roche and converting it to a family necropolis.

A second family is represented by **Barthélemy de Roye**, who was undoubtedly the most successful of all the knights in Philip Augustus's court.[300] Appearing in the first document to be retained in the royal archives in 1194, he was soon known as "royal pantler" and was appointed to the post of grand chamberlain in 1208 at the death of Mathieu, count of Beaumont.[301] No layman was more assiduous in the king's business. He was present at all important occasions, performed missions, conducted inquests, and judged cases, eventually replacing Gautier the Young as chief judge at the exchequer of Rouen. With Gautier the Young and Brother Guérin he formed the inner council of the king's advisers. As a knight he had accompanied the count of Blois on the Third Crusade, but from 1202 he directed the military preparations for the conquest of Normandy, was present at the capitulation of Rouen, and participated in the campaigns leading to Bouvines. At Bouvines, he fought next to the king at the center of the battlefield, for which he received the custody of the count of Flanders. In addition to his family lands at Roye and Montdidier the king rewarded him handsomely with houses, clothing, jewels, and lands at Paris and important fiefs at Mantes and Montchauvet and at Acquigny in Normandy.[302] He was equally rewarded with family alliances. Although the younger son of a minor lord of Roye in Vermandois, he married, with royal consent, Pétronille, the daughter of Simon IV de Montfort, the baron. The king gave Barthélemy's daughters to the sons of highborn families—the counts of Alençon, the lords of Nesle, and the Créspins in Normandy. Among his numerous gifts to churches he contributed substantially to the rebuilding of Ourscamp and founded the Premonstratensian abbey at Joyenval near Poissy, which became the family necropolis.[303] The chapter of Chartres sang masses for his soul during his lifetime and thereafter in perpetuity.[304] His generosity was recognized in the obituaries of the major abbeys around Paris and the cathedrals of Paris, Chartres, Laon, and Amiens. The obituary of Morienval eulogized him effusively as "the venerable and illustrious lord Barthélemy de Roye, knight, chamberlain of France, brilliant in honor, feeder of the poor, a most faithful comforter, true restorer, embellisher and attentive lover of churches, not only of the church of Joyenval where his body rests in Christ but of all churches."[305] Before his elevation to a position at court he placed only his name on his seal, but after becoming chamberlain the title was included as well.[306]

A third family that escaped notice in the hierarchic lists and the *Nomina* survey was that of the brothers **Pierre** and **Renaud de Béthisy**, two royal baillis who worked together as a team in Vermandois and Artois.[307] Pierre, married to Luciane, directed most of his activities farther to the north around Amiens, where he was *prévôt*, but Renaud, married to Emmeline, was well established around Paris, where he made donations to Saint-Corneille de Compiègne, Chaalis, Ourscamp, and Noyon.[308] In his charters Renaud calls himself *miles* and occasionally *prévôt* or bailli of the king; his seal contains only his name.[309]

Another bailli, and perhaps the most important of the baillis in this biographical dictionary, was **Pierre du Thillay**, from the Croult valley to the north of Paris, near Gonesse.[310] First appearing in 1200 as *prévôt* of Paris with Robert de Meulan, he reappeared at Orléans in 1202 collaborating with the bailli Guillaume de la Chapelle.[311] He received a permanent appointment as bailli of Caen in 1205, a year after the conquest of Normandy, a position that he held for the next two decades. Although primarily known for his Norman activities, he styled himself in his private charters "lord and knight," and his obituary used the same titles. In 1208 he donated one hundred arpents of land from his ancestral estates to found the Hôtel-Dieu at Gonesse; later, he made donations from his Norman estates to found the collegiate church of canons at Notre-Dame de Fribois in the Pays d'Auge. His chief holdings to the north of Paris lay at Gonesse, Tessonville, and Sarcelles, but he held the church and tithes at Le Thillay and the manor and land at Dugny from another lord, Mathieu le Bel, who, in turn, held them from the abbot of Saint-Denis.[312] From the vicomte of Corbeil he held Bonneuil-en-France.[313] Pierre married Aveline, daughter of Eudes de Saint-Cyr, and gave his daughter Héloïse to Eudes de Tremblay, a royal bailli and neighbor to the east of Le Thillay. At the end of his life he may have converted to the Order of Knights Templars, joining the Temple established outside of Paris.[314] Apparently around 1219 he felt the need to put his affairs in order. In that year he requested the king to confirm his ecclesiastical foundations at Gonesse and Fribois,[315] but, most important, he commissioned a landbook of his holdings, not only of his extensive estates in Normandy, undoubtedly accumulated during his long service to the king, but also of his three family estates to the north of Paris.[316] In his landbook he bequeathed to his family a record of the extent of his holdings and the revenues they produced. Although such accounting had been previously performed by churches in Normandy and the Paris region, this is the first landbook produced by a lay lord in northern France. It therefore offers a minute but detailed account of the landed riches of a minor aristocrat from the Paris region.

My biographical dictionary (see Table 1), therefore, contains seventy-two names (not counting spouses and many other family members mentioned above) drawn from thirty-three aristocratic families surrounding Paris. Of the thirty-three families all but seven can also be found on the banneret list (1204–8) attesting to their military service to Philip Augustus.[317] We shall see that an equal number of these families were enregistered in the feudal surveys taken by the king,[318] and of greatest importance to their suzerain, half of the families appeared on the field of Bouvines to ensure his victory. Few of these families were missing from the lists that mattered most to Philip. It is also noteworthy that most of these families are not found on another list. Only a quarter of the thirty-three families received *fief-rentes* directly from the king.[319] The *fief-rente* was a fixed sum of money paid annually to a knight in exchange for liege homage. It functioned less as remuneration (it was often only a minor amount) than as a means for establishing lordship over a *réseau* of vassals. In the Paris region, it was distributed evenly over the hierarchic spectrum. For example, at the summit, two *fief-rentes* were bestowed on the countess of Vermandois (100 and 128 *livres*), and among the knights below, two were bestowed on the family of Mauvoisin (5 and 12 *livres*). Both the distribution and small number of these *fief-rentes* suggest an absence of royal policy to provide direct subsidies to the aristocracy around Paris, unlike the king's pronounced interest in the Flemish region, where he deployed them abundantly to compete with the English in recruiting knights in preparation for his military offensive in 1214.[320]

Supplied by the inventories of the royal registers, my biographical dictionary therefore embodies the king's interest in the top level of aristocracy surrounding his capital of Paris. As the most powerful seigneur of the region, Philip Augustus would allow few aristocrats of importance to escape notice.

Prosopography

Seventy-two individuals are, of course, a minute sample of the thousands of aristocrats living around Paris. In contrast, the royal inventories and the monastic charters provide an abundance of names for a prosopography of the region.[321] The *Scripta* and *Nomina* inventories together cover eighteen castellanies around Paris and provide the names of 351 direct vassals. The principal persons involved in the transactions of the 1,729 ecclesiastical charters drawn from thirty-two cartularies of the region add another 951 names to the list of 351 direct vassals, for a total of 1,302 individual names, all of which I have been able to alphabetize to minimize duplicates. In addition to this relatively firm figure are the subvassals in the eighteen castellanies (659), plus those subvassals of major lords (Beaumont, Nesle, and Gisors) who have been listed in separate sections of the *Scripta* survey (264), plus those vassals in the *Nomina* survey who did not hold from the king (128), amounting to another 1,051 names, which because of their number and complexity have not been alphabetized in order to eliminate duplicates. Beyond the royal and cartulary sources, other major lords of the region like Mathieu le Bel, Gautier the Chamberlain, the abbot of Saint-Germain-des-Prés, the bishop of Paris, and Amaury de Montfort inventoried their fief-holders, producing another 498 names. Finally, in the 1,729 ecclesiastical charters, another 378 feudal lords are mentioned, not as principal actors but as approving the business transacted, for a grand total of 3,229 names. Of this last figure at least two-thirds have not been checked for duplicates.

The deficiency of such numbers, however, can be demonstrated by comparing the figure of 1,302 alphabetized names with the tenants given in Pierre du Thillay's landbook for Gonesse, Tessonville, and Sarcelles. Of the twenty-eight tenants who were identified as "lords or knights" owing Pierre *cens*, two can be found in the *Nomina* survey (Baudouin d'Andilly and Amaury *de Vilers*) and two in church cartularies (Guillaume Pastez and Raoul de Gonesse).[322] Twenty-four out of twenty-eight local aristocrats in this minor region therefore have escaped the royal surveys and monastic cartularies. At this rate of underreporting we can deduce that even the expanded figure of 3,229 names derived from other surveys does not approximate prosopographical reality. The documentary record merely skims the surface of aristocrats residing in the Paris region.

Those that have been captured from the documents can be alphabetized and incorporated in the format of a telephone book. Whatever its merits, such prosopography is not demography. Each of the names conceals other members of the family including wives, daughters, and underage sons. Nor does such a list include the clergy of both sexes or the infinitely more numerous free and unfree peasants who constituted the vast majority of medieval population. As for the last group, Pierre du Thillay's landbook lists some eighty tenants who were not identified as lords or knights. Most of these people were most likely peasants, but they too represented only a fraction of the total because they were certainly the most prosperous, being able to afford the *cens* that they paid to their lord. Once again it becomes apparent that it is impossible to plumb the demographic depths of the Paris region.

Dealing with a confined space and employing tax records, demographers have estimated at 200,000 the population of the city of Paris itself at the end of the thirteenth century, composed of bourgeoisie and clergy. By extrapolation they have deduced that about 50,000 lived within the walls of Philip Augustus in 1200 (again, a purely speculative figure). It appears that with all its deficiencies the estimation of the sum total of the surrounding aristocracy cannot attain even that level of precision, but few other means are available to make plausible comparisons.

Self-Representation

Questions of self-identification and self-representation are of equal interest: By what titles did the aristocracy around Paris introduce themselves in their charters and on their seals attached to their charters? In the numerous letters to his vassals drafted and preserved by the royal chancery Philip Augustus employed the conventional formula "our knight" (*miles noster*) and "our friend and faithful person" (*amicus et fidelis noster*). In the feudal surveys the chancery clerics concentrated on the name and paid little attention to titles. The monastic cartularies, however, contained thousands of charters that were purportedly composed by the aristocracy themselves in which they identified themselves by their names and titles. We remember that these charters were actually written by churchmen themselves and could have been reexpressed or even recopied carelessly, but the existing evidence is so massive and its conclusions so clear that it would be fastidious to count the usages of titles. Among the counts, to cite three examples, those of Dreux and Beaumont-sur-Oise invariably entitled themselves *comes*, while Aliénor de Vermandois adopted the titles of her many husbands. When she became free, she chose "countess of Saint-Quentin" and "lady of Valois." The vicomtes of Corbeil and of Melun always identified themselves as such. Others used the particular honors to which they were entitled: Gautier the Chamberlain and his sons identified themselves as "chamberlains of the lord king," Barthélemy de Roye as "chamberlain of France," and the butlers of Senlis as "butlers of Senlis" or "butlers of the king." (Only at the end of the period did the descendants of Gautier call themselves lords of Nemours or Méréville.) The vast majority, however, chose between lord (*dominus*) and knight (*miles*), or they omitted the title altogether. For the period before 1180 historians have often interpreted the two terms *dominus* and *miles* as signifying seigneurial authority and chivalry (that is, the culture of the knight) respectively, but they have not been able to come to firm conclusions.[323] In our period there were also no firm rules, but certain tendencies nonetheless appear. Those classified as barons on the hierarchic list normally identified themselves as lord—Montfort, Montmorency, Livry (Garlande), and Nesle. (Although the Montforts did not neglect the titles inherited from their Anglo-Norman ancestors or those acquired in their southern conquests, at home they preferred "lord of Montfort.") Those identified as castellans also preferred the title of lord—Marly, Meulan, Neauphle, Chevreuse, Île-Adam, Chaumont, Gisors, and Mello. But *dominus* could also be adopted by important noncastellan families such as the Andresels, Nanteuils, and Garlandes at Tournan. In fact, lordship could be claimed by any family when it served to express authority over a place. The title of knight, however, was the most persistent category. Certain families like the Barres, Mauvoisins, the Poissys, and Pomponnes appear to have been satisfied with it, as were the royal agents—members of the Béthisy, Pastez, and Lévis families—but the Garlandes at Livry likewise used it frequently as did the Chevreuses. The interchange between lord and knight therefore was frequent. The omission of a title, of course, could be due to scribal negligence, but certain families, such as the Livry Garlandes, the Île-Adams, and especially the Montforts appear to have practiced the habit.

Beneath the knight a new figure began to make its appearance in the church charters, a young member of a family of knights who was not yet formally knighted. After 1200 the titles of *domicellus* and *armiger* were attached to males who were not *milites*.[324] Rare among the charters were recognitions of dubbing or the creation of new knights.[325] About the same time, the king's registers began to compile the names of valets (*valeti*) along with knights and widows from the southern bailliages, but not around Paris. In the bailliage of Orléans, for example, the bailli counted sixty-six knights and twenty-five valets (or 38 percent the number of knights).[326]

The monk and cleric wrote the charter in the name of an aristocrat, but the aristocrat added his contribution by attaching to the charter a seal by means of cord or strips of parchment. In our period the sealed charter had become ubiquitous.[327] So mandatory was the seal that it was announced invariably in the charter with the phrase "so that this remains firm and established, I have strengthened the present charter with my seal." This phrase was retained even in the copy that was made for the cartulary where the seal could not be seen.[328] Composed of fragile wax, most seals have disintegrated and disappeared from the original charters, but their presence was constantly recalled. Extant survivals show that the usage of seals exploded at the turn of the century, passing from dozens to thousands of cases.[329] Seals had first been employed by the king, then were adopted by bishops, but by the end of the twelfth century every knight and many ladies who had transactions with the church that required charters now possessed his or her own seal. At the end of his life Guillaume le Maréchal sealed his testament with a private seal.[330] This represented a substantial economic outlay. Much like the artisans who worked for mints that coined money, a seal engraver created a matrix, usually of bronze or iron. Intricate and doubtless expensive skill was required to form the image on the matrix that would be impressed on wax to create the seal. Of the thirty-three families in my biographical dictionary, twenty-eight have charters preserved in the Archives nationales with their seals intact or sufficiently readable.

These seals served a double purpose: they authenticated documents and they represented the owner. As authentication, the seal performed the constraining function of "auto-coercion." With his seal the owner guaranteed that he would perform the obligations detailed in the charter. By means of the seal, therefore, churchmen enforced compliance with the terms in the charter. The seal itself became the sign of the aristocrat's compliance.[331] Beyond constraint, however, it also provided a mode of self-representation.[332] The face of the seal generally contained the legend encircling its perimeter and a figurative image represent-ing the seal. In our period the legend was always written in Latin, the language of the charter, and it always contained the baptismal name and place-name of the sealer, for example, "the seal of Guillaume de Garlande" (*Sigillum Villermi de Garlande*).[333] The aristocratic owner provided identification, even if it was in the language of the ecclesiastics. Normally the seal did not provide the title of the sealer except in cases of high status. As in the charter, counts and count-esses acknowledged their title as the count of Dreux, of Beaumont-sur-Oise, or the countess of Saint-Quentin and lady of Valois.[334] The vicomtes of Corbeil and Melun and the butlers of Senlis likewise insisted on their titles.[335] The family of Gautier the Chamberlain identified themselves simply as "chamberlains," and Mathieu de Montmorency proudly bore the title of constable of the royal court (*constabularius domini regis Francie*).[336] What is more significant is that only a few families availed themselves of the title of lord (*dominus*) despite its more fre-quent use in the charters. The influential baron Jean de Nesle understandably used it in 1232, and the lesser knights Florence de Hangest (but not Aubert) and Anseau de Garlande, lord of Tournan, expressed their authority over their lands in this manner,[337] but many other barons, such as the Montforts, the Garlandes (the branch of Guillaume-Alix at Livry) and the Montmorencys (before receiv-ing the office of constable), as well as almost all of the castellans, omitted titles, styling themselves simply by their names. For example, Simon de Montfort was without title on his seal (Plate 5B); Amaury called himself "count of Montfort" only in 1230 after Montfort was made a county (Plate 6B).[338] More significant, from my sample of seals (seventy-six different seals from charters of aristocratic families in the Paris region in our period) never was the title of knight (*miles*) engraved on a seal, despite its ubiquity in the charters.[339] If the lords and knights were discreet about their titles, neither did the size of the seal indicate their rank. Most seals varied between fifty and seventy millimeters. Only great lords like the Montforts, Montmorencys, and the Nesles occasionally produced seals reaching eighty millimeters, but the rest paid little attention to the size.

Equally important to the personal identification in the legend of the seal, the imagery of the seal also offered the aristocrat the opportunity of self-representation. In our period the sealer was offered two choices: either an image of a knight on horseback or a representation of heraldry that identified either him personally or his family. The equestrian image, if used, was always placed on the face of the seal; the heraldry could be depicted on the shield of the knight or on the reverse of the seal, thereby producing a counterseal. We shall explore the equestrian choice in this chapter and reserve the heraldic option to the following chapter on the aristocratic family. In my sample of seventy-six seals, one-half (38/76) took the equestrian option, which had long been the traditional image of the aristocratic seal. Raoul, count of Vermandois, Aliénor's father, was one of the first to adopt the equestrian image in 1135, when he pictured himself as a banneret on horseback carrying a lance to which a banner was attached. This image was appropriate for a great lord. A later example, from 1161, is the seal of Robert de Vitry (Plate 15).[340] By the beginning of our period, however, the banner had disappeared to be replaced with a sword, and the gait of the horse increased from a gentle amble to a forceful gallop. Thereafter, with only one exception, all the equestrian seals from our sample, no matter the rank, carry the image of the armed knight bearing a sword with the right arm raised above his head, and holding a shield with his left in a manner to display the heraldry, if heraldry was included (Plate 6B, for example). Protected by trappings, the horse advances usually to the right at full gallop. The exception to this battle posture was adopted by Simon de Montfort, who pictured himself more peaceably on horseback, garbed for hunting and blowing a horn. At his feet are his dog and a small tree (Plate 5B).[341] Naturally individual engravers could impose variations on these images, though the details are difficult to detect at times because of the diminutive size and the wear of time. Eventually the armor appears more distinctly as chain mail, and the knight's tunic and the horse's trappings become more decorated. The most evident change, however, is the eventual replacement of the conical helmet with nasal piece by the all-encompassing cylindrical helmet.[342]

Military imagery was, of course, inappropriate for women's seals. As with her father's seal, the pattern chosen by Aliénor de Vermandois was followed by others in our sample. As countess of Beaumont in 1177 she is pictured standing, robed in a long gown with full sleeves and holding a budding scepter in her right hand and a falcon in her left. To accommodate this figure the seal is shaped as a mandorla. A second seal made for her as countess of Saint-Quentin around 1212 simplified the form and placed her left hand on her hip. This standing posture was adopted by Alix de Garlande (wife of Guillaume, d. 1216), Agnès de Gisors (widow of Hugues, d. 1223), and Jeanne de Garlande (wife of Jean, count of Beaumont) with slight variations. Alix and Agnès hold birds in their hands while Jeanne has a fleur-de-lis.[343] In a different mode, Carcassonne, widow of Jean de Corbeil, placed on her seal two birds, back to back, separated by a bush.[344]

In contrast to the elegant lady with her attributes of love and pleasure, the aristocratic man chose to present himself with the forceful image of a knight charging into battle, no matter how high his social rank and despite the fact that the term *miles* never appears in the legend. This valorization of the military function of warrior is perhaps the closest we shall come to the heart of his self-representation. The equestrian image moreover underscores the solidarity of the aristocratic class. It was employed not only by the simple knight but throughout the aristocratic ranks by castellans, barons, and counts as well. Only the king and ecclesiastics refrained from the image. The lay aristocracy thereby stood united within the chivalric image.

Did the equestrian image also express a concept of nobility? Since nobility includes heritability, we shall return to the question in the next chapter when we consider family and heraldry. We can nonetheless conclude here by noting one salient factor: in the thousands of charters issued by counts, lords, and knights and collected in the ecclesiastical cartularies, the Latin term *nobilis* rarely appears, nor is it ever found in the legends of their seals.[345] This does not mean, however, that the term is unknown. While *nobilis* rarely appears in the charters issued by the counts, lords, and knights, *vir nobilis* and *mulier nobilis* (typically without further definition) were used frequently by abbots, bishops, and even popes to address aristocrats.[346] Whatever it might mean to churchmen, the designation "nobility" was a term reserved for ecclesiastical usage; it was totally absent from the aristocrat's Latin vocabulary in his charters at the turn of the century. Nor did the term "noble," meaning a status defined legally and inherited by blood, surface in the vernacular documents from our period. (Vernacular French did not enter the charters or the seals of our aristocracy around Paris until well into the thirteenth century.) Although equivalent notions were suggested, the actual term was nearly absent from the *Histoire de Guillaume le Maréchal*, the poems of Gace Brulé, and the romance of Gerbert de Montreuil.[347] A hereditary nobility was not yet enunciated in the Paris region. The heroes of romance were *preu* not *noble*.[348] *Nobilitas* remained a term that was employed only by the ecclesiastical authorities and clerical authors of Latin works.[349]

Chapter 3

Family

The Nuclear Family

The names we considered in Chapter 2 establish the individual identity of the aristocrat, but of equal importance was membership in a family that endowed position in society. Throughout the twentieth century the nature and evolution of the aristocratic family have absorbed the attention of medieval historians under the influence of anthropologists. In general, they have viewed the aristocratic family as the interaction between the extended-horizontal family (*Sippe*) of brothers, sisters, uncles, and aunts and the vertical-linear structure (*Geschlecht*) of grandparents, husband, wife, and children. Certain historians have discovered a radical shift from the first model to the second around the year 1000; others have found continuity in the vertical-linear (nuclear) family before and after, but in most cases historians have agreed on the eventual process of "progressive nuclearization" by which the family shrank to the nuclear unit of father, mother, children, and their immediate relatives.[1] In the period between 1180 and 1220 the most abundant documentation for the aristocratic family in the Paris region comes from the ecclesiastical charters. In the initial sample of 1,729 charters, over half (983, or 57 percent) contain the specific provision known as the *laudatio parentum* by which at least one member of the family gave his or her consent to the transaction proposed in the charter by the donor or seller (see Table 2). This resulted from the necessity to name the members of the family who consented to the transaction. Naturally these lists depended on the available biological stock, but the great majority of the consenters were drawn from the conjugal/nuclear family of the donor or seller: in 66 percent of the 983 charters containing a *laudatio parentum* provision, a husband or wife gave consent, and in 39 percent a son or daughter gave consent. Brothers or sisters (37 percent) and mothers or fathers (7 percent) consented usually in the absence of children. The husband and wife acted alone in 34 percent of the 983 transactions; the husband, wife, and their children acted alone, without other relatives, in 24 percent of the 983 transactions (see Table 3). Uncles, aunts, and cousins and spouses of children also appear occasionally, but their numbers are less significant. The picture that these charters present of two to three generations shows that the conjugal/nuclear family was clearly predominant in aristocrat-church transactions in the Paris region in the decades surrounding 1200.

What was the churchmen's rationale for this undoubted interest in the conjugal/nuclear family in the charters? I shall return to this question more fully in Chapter 7, but here it is essential to remember that these transactions involved the conveyance of property and revenue to churches. Such transactions were addressed in several ways by canon law current at the time. As seen in the treatise of Bernard of Pavia, the canon law adopted Roman law and envisaged that the normal means for conveying property to the church was the testament executed at the death of the conveyor (*donationes causa mortis*). Most of the transactions in the charters, however, did not involve testaments but were considered "gifts among the living" (*donationes inter vivos*) since they were enacted before death. Bernard treated donations *inter vivos* and donations *causa mortis* successively.[2] Furthermore, we shall see that the rights of the wife to her dowry (gifts from her family at marriage) and to her dower (gifts to her from her husband at marriage) were likewise protected in canon law and thereby demanded her consent when alienated.[3] This helps to explain the prominence of the wives in transactions involving a dowry or dower. Roman law further required that the husband, as *paterfamilias*, should, of course, be party to all transactions. At the time, canon law also adopted the Roman-law principle of *legitim*, which declared that children had an inherent right to succeed to the property of their parents and provided specific proportions for the inheritance of the property. Even in cases of intestacy (which applied when a testament was lacking) spouses and children nonetheless possessed a claim to their parents' property.[4] The conclusion is therefore evident that the principal rationale for churchmen to include the *laudatio parentum* in their charters was to protect these conveyances against future contests in law by the nuclear families of the donors and sellers.

My findings for the Paris region do not differ significantly from those discovered by historians for other regions where the consent of family has been studied intensively.[5] The clear predominance of the husband, wife, and children is confirmed, although it has been difficult to come to firm conclusions about the role of other members of the family. At times, however, historians have been tempted to use the evidence from the *laudatio parentum* to argue for the nuclear/conjugal model as inhering to the aristocratic family. While other evidence exists, the ecclesiastical evidence in itself is not determinative. The consent of father, mother, and children was an ecclesiastical principle that the churchmen imposed upon the aristocracy by means of the sealed charter. The family may have in fact been nuclear, and negotiations doubtlessly preceded the final terms, but it was the conjugal family's consent to the transaction that the clergy nonetheless needed. Whatever the ways in which charters reflected social reality, the *laudatio parentum* was demanded on ecclesiastical principle. For that reason, the charters are virtually devoid of evidence of marital aberrations such as divorce, bastards, and other irregularities reported by the chroniclers, particularly those of the early twelfth century. Philip Augustus's transgressions over his marriage to Ingeborg of Denmark, for which the pope placed the diocese under interdict for nine months in 1200, were the subject of many documents, but we know that Guillaume le Maréchal's father dismissed his first wife only from the testimony of Guillaume's biographer.[6] Divorces among the high aristocracy of the Paris region, such as that of Mathieu, count of Beaumont, and Aliénor de Vermandois, are detected mainly in their genealogies, not through statements in the ecclesiastical charters.

Lineage

The *laudatio parentum* of the monastic charters presents only a lateral picture of the members of an aristocratic family. Since the charters in our study are limited to two generations or three at most, they are less apt to portray the longitudinal dimension across generations. The longitudinal picture is supplied by the better-known aristocrats of our sample of thirty-three families whose genealogies have been constructed by historians.[7] With little doubt the general practice was agnatic or patrilineal, transmitting the family's name, major resources, and power through the male line. In other words, to survive as an identifiable entity, the family sought to produce a male in each generation. The most successful of these families was the Capetians, the royal dynasty itself. Philip Augustus, the reigning king, was the seventh male descendant in unbroken succession from Hugh Capet, elected in 987. Also successful were the butlers of Senlis with their chosen name of Guy and the Île-Adams with their alternation between Adam and Anseau. We have also noted that other families split into major branches and continued through our period with a succession of males as, for example, the Garlandes (Guy at Tournan, Guillaume at Livry), the Mauvoisins (Guillaume, Robert), and, at later points, the Montmorency and Montfort families.

Patrilineal succession was therefore apparent in practice but received virtually no written formulation in the Paris region at the beginning of the reign, nor was the crucial problem of the absence of males, which could produce crises in the family's continuity, expressly addressed. Normally, regulations governing the succession of families were expressed as customs (*consuetudines*). In our period, however, references to such customs in the Paris region are extremely rare in the ecclesiastical charters.[8] In 1213, however, Simon de Montfort, after winning the battle of Muret, sought to establish regulations under which his followers would live in the southern territories that they had recently occupied by publishing a series of *generales consuetudines* at Pamiers. Since most of his followers were from around Paris, he included a selection of customs from their region. Among the most important were those that governed the succession of heirs and inheritances and the marriage portions of women "according to the customs and usage of France around Paris."[9] The text, nonetheless, did not specify the details of such customs; it was assumed that they were already known through practice.

The lack of explicit rules governing the absence of male heirs, however, could not be ignored for long. As early as 1185, Geoffroy, the Anglo-Norman duke of Brittany, had issued an assize that sought to regulate the succession of baronies and knights' fiefs in order to prevent fragmentation. Among the conditions anticipated, for which the assize formulated specific rules, was the eventuality of daughters as the sole successors to inheritances.[10] In Champagne, Countess Blanche de Navarre likewise laid down regulations for such eventualities in her ordinance of 1212. Like the duke of Brittany, she sought to maintain the integrity of fiefdoms, particularly those that contained fortifications. She decreed that in fiefs succeeding to daughters the eldest should be given the most important of the family's castles and fortified houses, while other fortifications should be assigned to the remaining daughters according to age. The remaining properties and resources should be assessed and divided equally among all the daughters.[11] King Philip was presented with a similar situation when Guillaume-Alix de Garlande died in 1216, predeceased by his son Thibaut, thus leaving three daughters as heiresses married to Jean, count of Beaumont, Henri, count of Grandpré, and Guy, butler of Senlis, respectively. The royal court rendered a decision that the lands and movables both in fief and domain that Guillaume bestowed on his three daughters as dowry (*in maritagio*) would be divided into three equal parts. The distribution of houses, however, would follow a principle that had been enunciated in 1200 in a dispute on dowers, as we shall see:[12] the count of Beaumont, as husband of the eldest daughter, received the best residence (*herbergagium*) with its fortifications, whether located in France or in Normandy, while the count of Grandpré received the second best, and so on. What remained was returned to the common fund and divided equally among the three.[13]

At Pont-de-l'Arche in 1219 the king issued a statute that governed the case of a wife who died without direct heirs. The wife's family would not inherit lands and movables that the wife and husband had acquired during their life together, but all would remain uncontested with the husband except for the reasonable legacies made by the wife. The wife's family would retain only that which she had received from them (presumably her dowry), minus her legacies.[14] Once again the male patrimony was sheltered from claims of the female line.

If Count Jean of Beaumont benefited from the decision of 1217, his own inheritance also came before the royal court in 1223, when he, like his brother Mathieu, died without children. Unlike the Garlande inheritance, this was a case of an escheat of a county without direct heirs, but like the Garlande case, it raised the question of patrilineal succession. The closest successor in the male line was Thibaut d'Ully, son of Yves d'Ully, who was a cousin of Jean. Thibaut's claim was contested by the sons of two sisters of Yves, who argued that the inheritance should be divided equally among the three because their parents were siblings of the same degree. Thibaut countered that if his father and aunts were still alive the succession would devolve to his father alone because the customs of France (*usus et consuetudines Francie*) followed patrilineal succession, privileging male heirs. At Vernon the barons of the king's court agreed with Thibaut that the county of Beaumont should succeed to him intact as the next male heir according to the customs of France, but as the king had done with Aliénor de Vermandois, Philip exacted a price for this decision. After the other claimants renounced their rights, Philip and Thibaut divided the inheritance between themselves, with the king taking the county and the major fiefs, leaving Thibaut what remained and a compensation of seven thousand *livres*.[15] As with Vermandois and Valois, Beaumont was considered an escheat devolving to the king, but for the first time the principle of patrilineal succession was enunciated as the custom of France.

Family Alliances

The historians' genealogies also indicate the intricate skein of marriages that knitted together our sample of thirty-three prominent families around Paris. (These connections are often hidden in the charters, which reveal only the first names of women.) The Garlandes were undoubtedly the most successful in placing their daughters into prominent families. For example, Guillaume-Alix's sister was married to the Marlys and his three daughters to the Beaumonts, Grandprés, and butlers of Senlis, as we have just seen. Anseau de Garlande's daughters were given to the Andresels, Poissys, and Île-Adams. When Simon V de Montfort married Alix de Montmorency, he united the two most important baronies of the south and north. His sister married Barthélemy de Roye, the most influential knight of the royal court. Guillaume des Barres married the elderly wife of Simon IV de Montfort after the latter's death. To the north, the Île-Adams married

daughters of the Beaumonts, Pomponnes, and Corbeils, as well as the Garlandes. To the south, the Andresels made alliances with the Garlandes and the
Poissys, and the Chevreuses with the Corbeils and the Mauvoisins. Barthélemy
de Roye not only married the daughter of the Montforts but he gave his own
daughters to two Norman lords, as well as to the brother of Jean, lord of Nesle.
Doubtlessly, other alliances can be detected through careful scrutiny of the
genealogies.

This maze of alliances is reflected in the foundation of abbeys and churches.
Guillaume de Garlande's endowments to the house of regular canons at Livry
(the present Livry-Gargan) after the death of his son Thibaut in 1197 offer an
illuminating example, particularly because the king also participated, made
contributions on his own, and preserved the relevant charters in his registers.
In addition to major legacies from Guillaume and the king were contributions
from Dreux de Mello (d. 1218), Mathieu de Marly, Robert Mauvoisin (d. 1217),
Jean de Pomponne, and Jean de Gisors. All can be connected by marriage to
the Garlandes.[16] Similarly, Barthélemy de Roye's foundation of the Premonstratensian abbey of Joyenval in 1224 enlisted the contributions from the Montforts of his wife's family, from the Montmorency-Marlys related to his wife's
family, and from the Norman Créspins who married Barthélemy's daughter. The
Poissys also contributed through their connections with the Montmorencys,
even though they were also instrumental in founding the Premonstratensian
abbey of Abbecourt.[17] To the north the Cistercians at Val-Notre-Dame were
sponsored by the neighboring Beaumonts and Île-Adams. The Poissy and Chaumont families, likewise connected by marriage, also both gave to Val-Notre-
Dame. The Cistercians at Vaux-de-Cernay to the south were patronized not only
by the Montforts, Marlys, and Neauphles, but also by the Chevreuses, Mauvoisins, and Corbeils. The female house of Porrois received support from the Montforts and Marlys, as well as from the Chevreuses and Mauvoisins, while the nuns
at Yerres received support from both the Chevreuse and Corbeil families.[18]

Names

The first and primary marker of identity in the Middle Ages was the first name
(*nomen*) bestowed on an individual at baptism. Not surprisingly each age had
its preferences for naming. In the eleventh and twelfth centuries, before our period, Nicolas Civel discerned in the two sources he investigated a preference for
the masculine names of Hugues, Guillaume, Robert, and Pierre, though his two
samples showed little agreement beyond these names.[19] Taking a broader sample of 1,729 ecclesiastical charters from the Paris region between 1180 and 1220
I have been able to assemble a total stock of 138 masculine names and coinci-

dentally an equal number of female names (139) available to individuals.[20] In practice one-half (52 percent) of the males and one-half (48 percent) of the females were bestowed names from the twelve most popular names available. Among the males, Jean (8.8 percent) was clearly the most popular, followed by Guillaume (7.5 percent) and Pierre (7.1 percent). Then followed Guy (4.8 percent), Hugues (4.8 percent), and Robert (3.7 percent). Simon (3.3 percent), Renaud (3.2 percent), Gautier (2.5 percent), Eudes (2.4 percent), Thibaut (2.0 percent), and Philippe (2.0 percent) completed the last half. Among the females, Civel found a preference for Pétronille, Alix, Agnès, and Adèle in the earlier period. In my sample, Agnès (8.6 percent) was clearly the most popular, followed by Alix (7.2 percent), Elisabeth (5.8 percent), and Marie (5.0 percent), and then by Mathilde (3.8 percent), Emmeline (3.1 percent), Isabelle (3.0 percent), Béatrice (2.8 percent), Helvide (2.7 percent), and Margarita (2.7 percent), and ending with Pétronille (1.8 percent) and Jeanne (1.6 percent). In the male pool, Christian saints' names accounted for four of the twelve most popular names. Jean and Pierre took precedence; two other apostolic names, Simon and Philippe, were less popular. The second place of Guillaume and the majority of names that followed (Guy, Hugues, Robert, Renaud, Gautier, and Thibaut, and perhaps Eudes) indicate the popularity of Germanic nomenclature among the male aristocracy around Paris.[21] For females, undoubted Christian inspiration was found in the Saints Elisabeth and certainly Marie, the mothers of John the Baptist and Jesus, but Marie, to whom most cathedrals and many of the monasteries were dedicated, takes a less prestigious fourth place behind Elisabeth's third place. Agnès and Alix, the two most popular names, were Greek in origin and transmitted to the Latin West through early Christian saints. The same is true of the less popular Isabelle (often confused with Elisabeth) and Margarita. Pétronille and Jeanne are simply diminutives of the masculine Pierre and Jean that were popular among the men. The remaining are distinctly Germanic names: Mathilde, Emmeline, Béatrice, and Helvide. Many more Germanic names appear, although not as frequently. Of equal interest is what was missing from the baptismal names in the Paris region. Most of the local saints—Denis, Martin, Germain, and Geneviève, for example—were noticeably absent. The attraction to the royal names Philippe (2 percent) and Louis (absent) was also resisted. (The name Philippe was introduced from Macedonian stock by Anne of Kiev, wife of King Henry I; Louis was of Carolingian origin.) A contrast between males and females is revealed in the stock of names available. Although the stocks of names were of identical size, the index of condensation, that is, the average stock of names available in a sample of one hundred individuals, was three times greater for females than for males (twenty-two for females versus seven for males) because the number of females using 139 names was one-third the number of males using 138 names.

Therefore, the parents of girls had a much richer variety of choices. Germanic names provided some of the variety. Both Christian and Germanic-pagan names jockeyed for selection from aristocratic parents in the region around Paris.

As for a choice of a family name, nearly all of the males selected a toponymic to identify themselves. Thus the particle *de* was the universal custom for designating aristocrats in our period and suggests that knights as well as lords considered themselves as lords over the place from which they originated. Since most of the names of females are supplied from the lists of the wives, daughters, sisters, and mothers in the *laudationes parentum*, the *de* is concealed, but when they do act as principals in transaction, they too identify themselves with place-names. In the Paris region few lords and knights, therefore, made use of cognomens to individualize their identities. At times cognomens were merely descriptive: *dictus Flamens, cognomento li Bruns,* and *Ruffus.* Occasionally they were denigrating: *li bougre, Villanus, lupus, li begues, sotum, monachus, malus clericus.* But most often cognomens were simply inherited surnames: *Bonemin, Malet, Prunelez, Balerie, Musavena. Joanne Carcasona cognomina* and *Sibille, priorisse cognomina,* are two of the scarce feminine examples of cognomens. The most distinguished of those using a cognomen were the Mauvoisins, whom we have already met, but the negative connotations of their name had evidently disappeared.[22]

There is little doubt that the place-name became the hereditary marker of aristocratic families of the Paris region, but the two to three generations represented in the *laudationes parentum* are not sufficient to determine whether the cognomens became hereditary as well. (The Mauvoisins, whose name was indeed inherited, are the exception here.) Nonetheless, we have already seen that within our "who's who" dictionary certain families showed a preference for a single baptismal name or an alternating succession of names. The pattern was established, of course, by the Capetians, who had alternated between Philippe and Louis since the eleventh century. The Montforts switched between Amaury and Simon, the Montmorencys and Marlys between Bouchard and Mathieu, and the Île-Adams between Adam and Anseau. The butlers of Senlis limited themselves to Guy; the Garlandes and Barres exhibited a penchant for Guillaume. Doubtlessly this repetition of baptismal names conveyed a sense of lineage, if not nobility, to these families.

Heraldry

The knight needed more than a name to identify himself on the battlefield.[23] Mounted on his charger, protected by chain mail, his head encased in a metal

helmet, he was barely distinguishable to his friends or foes. By the beginning of
the twelfth century it became imperative that he adopt a sign or symbol to establish his identity in battle or on the tournament field. Thus a heraldic sign or
blazon was affixed to the knight's banner, his shield, and eventually to the *surcot* covering his armor and to the trappings of his horse. The cloth and wood
has since disappeared, but the knight also commissioned an engraver to inscribe
heraldry on the shield in his seal. At least twenty-one of these blazons on equestrian seals have survived from thirty-three families in our biographical dictionary of the Paris region. The first to produce heraldic images on their shields
in their seals were Raoul, count of Vermandois, the father of Countess Aliénor,
and Galeran, count of Meulan, the father of Count Robert of Meulan and Roger
de Meulan. The diffusion of heraldry engraved on the face of seals exploded in
the region around Paris. A map of France shows a mere sprinkling of occurrences before 1180 and contrasts with a second map before 1200 that depicts a
spectacular concentration in northeastern France between the Loire and Meuse
rivers.[24] This period of acceleration between 1180 and 1200 coincided with the
development of armor that introduced the cylindrical helmet that completely
hid the knight's face, and also with the increased popularity of tournaments,
which like warfare absorbed the knights' energies.

The period between 1180 and 1220 also witnessed a significant transformation of the knight's seal from the use of equestrian images to heraldic images
(*armoiries*). On the equestrian seal, the knight, galloping normally to the right,
held his shield on his left arm, but it was positioned in such a manner to be fully
visible on the right. The shield on which the heraldry was displayed, however,
was necessarily tiny and easily defaced on the fragile wax. (Heraldry appears in
small format on the knight's shield in twenty-one of the thirty-eight equestrian
seals. See Plate 11B, for example.) A counterseal was therefore placed on the reverse of the seal displaying the heraldry in a larger format. Eventually the heraldic image replaced the equestrian image. Our sample of seventy-six different
seals of aristocrats in the Paris region includes fifty-one such heraldic seals,
whether displaying the large-format heraldry on the face (Plate 12B, for example) or on the counterseal. (Some seals contain both an equestrian image with
heraldry on the face and the large-format heraldry in a counterseal on the reverse.) This shift suggests that the knight was willing to replace his identity as
a warrior with that of an individual who identified with his family by means
of a distinguishing sign.

The heraldic sign was composed of fixed elements of animal, vegetable, and
geometric shapes, and distinct colors such as gold, silver, red, blue, black, green,
and purple, as well as furs such as ermine and squirrel. A specific vocabulary was
devised in French to identify these elements. Although colors did not appear

on seals, they were nonetheless used on shields and armor and acquired specialized names. Red, for example, was *gueules*; blue, *azure*; black, *sable*; and green,
sinople. From this vocabulary a particular language was created in contemporary
French literature to read (*blazoner*) the heraldic signs. Around 1200, to cite
one example, the author Jean Renart described the heraldry of Richard, count
of Normandy: "Ses escus ert d'azur et d'or / Bendé[s] a flors de l'un a l'autre" (translated "Son écu fut bandé d'azur et d'or, semé de fleurs-de-lis de l'un en l'autre").[25]
Already at the tournaments depicted in the *Histoire de Guillaume le Maréchal*,
heralds of arms, who announced the identities of knights, make their appearance, though the heraldic blazons themselves remain absent in the *Histoire*.[26] In
the course of the later thirteenth century, however, heralds of arms began to acquire an expertise in identifying these signs, thus transforming the heraldic language into a science with rules for interpreting their use. Toward the end of the
century the heralds produced rolls of arms (armorials) that depicted the heraldry
in color and facilitated the identification of individuals and their families. During our period, however, for depictions of heraldry we depend solely on wax seals,
which were colorless. The first contemporary use of color comes in the clerestory
windows of the choir of Chartres cathedral installed around 1218.[27] With the
absence of color, therefore, there is little evidence of heraldic codes and regulations in the Paris region of our period.

Diversity and disorder characterize the seals from the sample of thirty-three
elite families in the Paris region during the reign of Philip Augustus.[28] One of
the earliest emblems was the four eagles separated by a cross that was placed
on the equestrian seal of the Montmorencys and was shared with their relatives
the Marlys.[29] Another early example was the three sheaves of wheat found on the
counterseal of the butlers of Senlis.[30] The most popular figure was the rampant
lion with a forked tail depicted on the shield of Simon de Montfort,[31] which was
adopted by families close to him—the Garlandes,[32] the Meulans,[33] the Lévis,[34]
and the Neauphles.[35] Blackbirds were adopted by the Île-Adams,[36] the Mellos,[37]
the Neauphles,[38] and Poissys.[39] Philip Augustus was the first Capetian to use the
fleur-de-lis as royal heraldry, but it did not appear on a royal seal until that of
Prince Louis in 1214, both on the shield of his equestrian figure and on the counterseal (Plate 2B).[40] Those close to the king also adopted the fleur-de-lis: the
Béthisys,[41] the Garlandes,[42] the Nanteuils,[43] and the Montforts,[44] for example.
Numerous families did not restrict themselves to one heraldic device. The Montforts and the Garlandes, for example, employed both the lion and fleur-de-lis.
The Barres made use of a castle and an anchored cross.[45] The prolific Poissys
adopted not only the blackbird, but also bezants, a flowering cross, diamonds,
and rings.[46]

Because of the limitation to two or three generations it is difficult to detect dynastic continuity among the aristocratic seals in our sample, but Amaury de Montfort, the eldest son, did adopt the rampant lion with a forked tail of his father Simon (Plates 5B and 6B).[47] The continuity of the four eagles of the Montmorency-Marly clan provides another example (Plate 12B). Equally important in expressing a sense of family continuity was the custom of "breaking" (*briser*) the father's seal. While the oldest son retained an exact replica of his father's seal, younger sons modified their father's seals to retain their identity as members of the family.[48] This was accomplished normally by placing a diagonal stripe or a lambel (a kind of comb) across the father's heraldry. Thus the heraldry of Guy de Montfort, a younger brother of Simon V, was broken with a lambel as was that of Robert de Poissy.[49] A number of *brisures* are found in the heraldry of younger sons depicted in the stained glass of Chartres (Plates 7, 11, 13, and 14).[50] In the absence of direct testimony it is difficult to assess how aristocrats viewed heraldry, but assumptions can be deduced from practice. When they replaced their belligerent equestrian image with their heraldic device, they were evidently shifting their identity from a class to a family. When they extended their personal emblems to their eldest son and provided modifications for younger sons, they were surely developing a consciousness of agnatic lineage. Later in the thirteenth century heraldry became closely associated with nobility, but to what extent this result was obtained before 1220 is not clear, particularly since the aristocracy never employed the term for themselves in their charters or seals.

Women: Dowry and Dowers

The female is the indispensable constituent of the biological family, as is attested by the navel implanted in the midriff of every human being. Although the navel is ever present, it is also little noticed, especially by males. In an analogous way women are not nearly as visible as men in the extant documentation of the Middle Ages. Because the king was preoccupied with military service secured by patrilineal succession, women figure less in the royal inventories and charters except when they held fiefs in the absence of husbands or sons. In the *Nomina* survey, 2 percent of the tenants were women; in the *Scripta* surveys for the region around Paris, 3 percent were women. When the royal baillis surveyed areas south of Paris (but not around Paris) they recorded the names not only of knights but also of widows and valets. In their report on the bailliage of Orléans, 14 percent were widows, identified most likely because they were fiefholders.[51] Within the sample of 1,729 monastic charters, however, the presence of women is more pronounced. Not only did they consent to transactions with churches as wives, daughters, sisters, and mothers in the *laudatio parentum*, but in at least 10 percent of these transactions they acted alone as principals. Equally important, they intervened in another 5 percent of the cases when their dowries and dowers were concerned.[52]

Dowry (*maritagium, hereditas*) was wealth, generally found in property, that the father bestowed on his daughter at the time of the wedding.[53] (Since the Latin vocabulary is not without ambiguity, at times the terms can be understood only from the context.) Designed to support her children, the dowry was inherited by her children after the death of the mother. It supplies only a small number of the cases in the 1,729 ecclesiastical charters (twenty-three cases, or 1 percent). Among these, for example, is Dreux, lord of Cressonessart, who in 1202 gave his daughter Heresendis certain lands *in maritagio* as his portion of her *hereditatis*. When Heresendis gave this *hereditatem* to her son, it appears to be her dowry, but not all cases *de jure hereditario* are as clear.[54] For example, Agnès d'Andresel gave a rent *in maritagio suo* to endow her daughter as a nun at Yerres in 1213, and in 1196 Alix de Montcheval with the assent of her heirs gave to the Hôtel-Dieu of Paris from her *matrimonium* for the soul of her husband, but since we are not told the origin of the gifts, we can only assume from the terminology that they are dowries and not dowers.[55] In all of the extant examples dowry is alienated with the wife's consent. When the husband alienates dowry in favor of a church, he promises to reimburse his spouse for the dowry. For example, in 1198 when Gautier de Neuilly (Neuilly-sous-Clermont) gave land to Ourscamp from the *hereditas* of his wife Margareta with her consent, she received other property in exchange.[56] Or in 1202 Jean d'Apilly and his wife Pétronille gave arable land to the abbey of Longpont in return for a *beneficium* of fifty-three *livres*. Because the land belonged to Pétronille *jure hereditario*, Jean recompensed her with other lands.[57]

With the more frequent case of dowers (seventy-six cases, or 4 percent), that is, the gift of the husband at marriage, the ambiguity decreases. Time and again when the wife gives her consent to her husband's donations of property *ratione dotalicii*,[58] or when she exempts her holdings from her husband's benevolences *salvo ejus dotalicio*,[59] we can be sure that dower (*dos*) is involved. In practice the dower belonged to the wife for her lifetime; at her death it reverted to the husband. In a third of the cases (twenty-six of seventy-six) the husband compensates his spouse for alienating the dowers that he or they had bestowed on churches. For example, in 1201 Jean, lord of Montescort, bestowed land on the local priest with accompanying revenues. His wife Aude resigned her dower but received from her husband revenues on another territory.[60] Other examples suggest another important characteristic of the dower: the husband was accustomed to designate one-half of his property as dower. When Hermilphus de Magny sold a rent to a canon of Noyon in 1212, he specified that his wife had one-half of all his goods *ex jure dotalicii*.[61] The proportion of goods, however, is rarely specified in the ecclesiastical charters. Moreover, while the charters allude to numerous dowries and dowers that are alienated to churches, rarely do they report their constitution. An early example of a specified dower occurred in 1124: "I Geoffroy accept Jacqueline, daughter of *Dodonis Villani*, as wife and give her *in dotem* a fief that I hold from the *domina Hydeburgi* .... Furthermore, I give her *in dotem* the fief which Emelina, the daughter of Chevalier, holds from me and whatever I have at Tremblay."[62]

Royal documentation supplements these mentions of dowry and dower in the ecclesiastical charters. The king took notice of dowries and dowers among the aristocracy around Paris when successions were disputed or when he favored the knights of his court with marriages to heiresses. Around 1200 a dispute arose among the children of the two wives of Adam de Montfermeil over their inheritances and in particular what they received from their mothers' dowers. The question was put to the barons assembled in the royal court, who began by considering both the dowers of the two wives and the inheritance that remained outside the dowers. They assigned to the first unnamed wife's dower one-half of all of Adam's lands and, following the same principle as we have seen applied to the succession of the Garlandes in 1217, the best of the residences (*herbagagiis*). They assigned one-half of the remaining half and the second-best residence to the dower of the second wife, Mathilde. The remaining quarter of all of Adam's lands that were not assigned to either dower were to be divided such that the children of the first wife received one half (one-eighth of the total) and the children of the second wife received the other half (likewise one-eighth of the total).[63] We know from the local charters that Adam de Montfermeil had a son Guillaume who was the oldest (*primogenitus*) from the first unnamed wife, but thereafter Adam married Mathilde who bore him four sons—two laymen, Jean and Henri, and two canons, Raoul and Eudes.[64] In effect, then, Guillaume received from his mother's dower one-half of all Adam's lands and the best residence as his mother's dower, plus one-eighth of Adam's remaining lands. Mathilde's four sons, however, received only one-quarter of Adam's lands and the second-best residence as their mother's dower; in addition, they also divided among themselves one-eighth of Adam's remaining lands. Guillaume as the sole son of the first wife was therefore better-endowed by comparison to the others. It is not surprising that he appears in the inventory of knights in the castellany of Paris who possessed an income of at least sixty *livres*. We shall see that the Montfermeils were established both at Montfermeil and at Roissy-en-France.[65]

The Garlande dossier in Register C likewise included cases of dowry and dower. The dossier included four charters devoted to Alix de Châtillon, whom the king gave in marriage to Guillaume de Garlande in 1193. Since Alix's father was dead (d. ca. 1170), her brother Gaucher was responsible for her dowry in 1193. In an exchange with the king, Gaucher gave the king Pierrefonds and the king gave Gaucher a rent of eighty *livres*, drawn on Clichy outside of Paris, to fund Alix's dowry (*maritagium*). Philip also gave Montreuil to Guillaume and Alix as reward for Guillaume's services.[66] (The sum of eighty *livres* proposed by the Châtillons to the Garlandes was relatively modest on the contemporary scale, but doubtlessly befitted knightly standards.) A second charter confirmed Guillaume's dower (*dotalitium*) to Alix. Elaborating the principle that the monastic charters only suggested, Guillaume bestowed on his bride a house at his chief fief of Livry, one-half of his inherited lands, one-half of his acquired lands, and one-half of what he might acquire in the future. However, because the house at Livry was in the dower of his mother and was not available until her death, he substituted a house at Croissy not thus encumbered.[67] In a third charter of 1195, the king confirmed that Alix's brother increased her dowry with possessions at Viarmes. This dowry would be Alix's and Guillaume's in perpetuity.[68] Finally in 1215 shortly before his death Guillaume bequeathed to Alix an unspecified gift in dower that was confirmed by the counts of Beaumont and Grandpré who we remember were Guillaume's sons-in-law and potential heirs in the absence of a son.[69]

Thus by 1217, when the matter of the inheritances of the three daughters of Guillaume de Garlande was settled after Guillaume's death, the royal court had confirmed the assignment of one-half the husband's patrimony along with the principal residence as the customary dower for the Paris region. We have seen that this proportion also appeared occasionally in the monastic charters.[70] Later in the century, Philippe de Beaumanoir declared that the custom of one-half dower had been established throughout the realm in 1214, thus superseding the proportion of one-third in Normandy, which followed the customs of Anjou and England.[71] In addition, the judgment of the barons in 1200 regarding the children of Adam de Montfermeil demonstrated that the dower should be kept separate and inviolate as long as the dowager was alive, and this practice was observed also by the women of the Garlande family. The economic substance of both dowries and dowers consisted of all forms of landed wealth. Although real property was probably preferred, revenues and even tithes were also frequent.

Both the royal documents and the ecclesiastical charters illustrate how the dowry and dower created means for supporting women in their marital functions, particularly in raising children. Reporting decisions of the king's court, the royal charters privileged the proportion of one-half of the husband's estate to be assigned to the wife's dower. The church charters emphasized the obligation to obtain the wife's consent to all alienations of the dower and dowry and to compensate for any such loss. The canon lawyers who set the rules for the procedure of church courts likewise discussed the issue of dowry. As in the question of succession, canon lawyers such as Bernard of Pavia had no unique doctrine of their own on dowry, but discussed the institution (which they confusingly called *dos*) by following the precepts of Roman law.[72] Dowry was governed by Roman law and appropriately enforced in civil courts, but because it was connected to marriage it was also considered to be a spiritual matter and therefore under the jurisdiction of the church court. Essential to dowry was the Roman law principle that insisted on the wife's consent to any alienation. As for the gift of the husband (in practice the dower), it was not called a *dos* but a *donatio ante nuptias* (a gift before nuptials) that followed rules analogous to dowry and therefore required the wife's consent as well. Although considered to be of Germanic origin, dower, as we have seen, appeared more frequently than dowry in the ecclesiastical charters. That ecclesiastical practice invariably required the wife's consent to any alienation of a dower suggests that churchmen were protecting themselves against appeals to the alienation of the wife's dower before an ecclesiastical judge. Consent, after all, was the hallmark of the canonists' doctrine in the formation of marriage. When canon law taught that a wife must consent to any transaction involving her marriage, it is no coincidence that the same practice is abundant in the monastic charters.

Chapter 4

Aristocratic Castles and Residences

Military Castles

In an often-quoted passage the ecclesiastical chronicler Raoul Glaber noted that around the year 1000 the French countryside had donned a new white mantle of churches.[1] More precisely, he referred to the extensive use of stone for the building of churches and monasteries. It is likely, however, that he preferred not to notice that the countryside was equally covered with a brown mantle of earthen castles that housed rapacious lords who menaced the surrounding churches. In the eleventh and twelfth centuries France had become "incastel-lated," that is, virtually carpeted with castles. At first they emerged as simple mounds of earth surrounded by an encircling ditch or moat, the interiors of which formed summits that were crowned with wooden stockades. It was not until later in the twelfth century that certain of these structures were converted into stone, which then competed with the previous mantle of white churches. Because of the combination of earth and wood the earlier structures have been called "motte and bailey" castles to distinguish them from the later stone keeps. Designed primarily for military purposes, they provided defensive shelter for small garrisons to enable them to sortie beyond the stockade and coerce the surrounding countryside into submission. For that reason, they were ideally spaced within such a distance to allow their occupants time to exit and to return on horseback by nightfall before neighbors could organize reprisals. Often they were situated on hills and promontories or near populous centers for both defensive and prestigious reasons. Punctuating the horizon, their prominent silhouettes endowed their lords with a distinctive symbol of power that proclaimed not only a threat to neighboring churchmen but also resistance to overlords, be they counts or king.

Around 1100 the abbot Suger of Saint-Denis noticed that the region around Paris was dotted with such castles. From his opening pages he pictured King Louis VI occupied in attacking the castles of the rebellious aristocracy whom he was intent to submit to his authority. Thus we see him laying siege to Montmorency against its lord Bouchard, taking the castle of Luzarches from the count of Beaumont, besieging Montlhéry, which had caused his father so much grief, and attacking the Garlandes at Livry, as well as engaging in the more extensive campaigns against Le Puiset to the south and the castles of Thomas de Marles at Crécy, Nouvion, and Coucy in the Laonnois.[2] By the reign of Philip Augustus, as we have seen, rebellious families like the Garlandes and the Montmorencys had submitted to royal authority, but the king had acquired numerous important castles in the region like Meulan, Poissy, and Corbeil, had modernized others like Gisors and Montlhéry, and had constructed new ones like the Louvre in Paris and, to the south, Dourdan and Yèvre-le-Châtel. This prompted his chancery to draw up a list of all the royal castles in the realm and to reorganize the region around Paris according to castellanies in which the king demanded from his vassals quotas of castle-guard and military service.[3] We shall return to the royal castles of the region in the next chapter when we examine fiefs, castles, and castle-guard.

Beyond these bastions of royal authority, the Paris region remained nonetheless heavily "incastellated" by the aristocracy. Because of intense urbanization, however, all that remains of hundreds of castles are sites bearing their names. A sample of ruins and vestiges that have survived, however, focusing principally on the castles held by the counts, barons, vicomtes, and castellans introduced in Chapter 2, will suggest the extent and prestige of their former holders.[4] At Beaumont on the banks of the Oise, for example, the massive fortifications announced the power of the counts of Beaumont, accompanied by their smaller castles nearby at Luzarches and at Conflans on the Seine (see Map 2). The restored vestiges at Brie-Comte-Robert, Fère-en-Tardenois, and Nesles-en-Tardenois demonstrate the pretensions of the counts of Dreux. The castles of the barons of Montfort survive impressively as ruins not only at Montfort-l'Amaury, but also at Houdan, Rochefort-en-Yvelines, and Beynes. The topography of the town of Montmorency still reveals the dimensions of the baron's castle there. From the ranks of castellans, the fortifications of the Chevreuse family remain clearly prominent, and the vicomtes of Melun are impressively remembered at Blandy-les-Tours. Among those families close to the king, the celebrated lords of Barres built a castle at Diant, the Cléments at Mez-le-Maréchal,[5] and the descendants of Gautier the Chamberlain at Nemours. All three of these survive impressively. This entire sample of fifteen castles exists, of course, as stone structures, which accounts for their survival. Roughly half (seven) originated before 1150. Three have been dated to the second half of the twelfth century while the remaining five were constructed after 1200.[6]

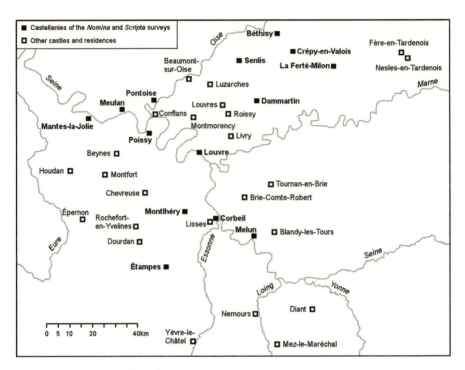

Oise

Béthisy ■

Fère-en-Tardenois
□
□
Nesles-en-Tardenois

■ Crépy-en-Valois

Beaumont-
sur-Oise
□

■ Senlis

La Ferté-Milon ■

Marne

Seine

□ Luzarches

Pontoise
■

Meulan
■

Louvres □

■ Dammartin

□ Conflans
□

□ Roissy

Mantes-la-Jolie
■

Montmorency

Poissy
■

□ Livry

Beynes □

■ Louvre

Houdan □

□ Montfort

Chevreuse □

□ Tournan-en-Brie

□ Brie-Comte-Robert

Épernon
□

Rochefort-
en-Yvelines □

Montlhéry ■

Lisses □

■ Corbeil

Melun
■

□ Blandy-les-Tours

Dourdan □

Essonne

Seine

Étampes ■

Eure

Loing

Yonne

0 5 10   20   40km

Nemours □

Diant □

Yèvre-le-
Châtel □

□ Mez-le-Maréchal

Map 2. Castles and residences

Two aristocratic castles in particular in the above sample, both of which have received extensive attention from archaeologists, illuminate the functions of castles both as military structures and as residences. Chevreuse, dating to the second half of the twelfth century, conformed to an older style in which the main structure was the heavily fortified donjon. Brie-Comte-Robert, likewise dating to the second half of the twelfth century, was constructed in a new style. Lacking a donjon, its outstanding feature was a strong, square perimeter of courtines, which were flanked with circular towers. In the past castellographers and archaeologists have concentrated their attention principally on the military features of castles. Before examining these two castles as residences I shall briefly look at their military function, which provided, of course, the initial motive for their construction.[7]

Chevreuse

The site of Chevreuse had long been in the hands of the castellans who took their name from it. Since there are indications of fortifications there since the eleventh century, its archaic features have prompted archaeologists to date the existing structure to the second half of the eleventh century. More recent excavations, however, have moved the date forward to the second half of the twelfth century, which would assign the construction to the castellans Simon de Chevreuse (d. before 1191) and his two successors, Guy (d. 1209) married to Aveline, and Guy (d. 1263) married to Helisende. One of these Guys acknowledged liege homage to Eudes, bishop of Paris (1197–1208), for the *castrum et castellaniam de Caprosia*, owing service of twenty-five *sous* of wax due to the bishop, and received in turn a gold ring from the bishop to confirm the investiture.[8] Perched on a hill above the town of Chevreuse on the banks of the Yvette River, the present donjon conforms to the classic Romanesque style of the eleventh century. Rectangular in shape (26.5 × 12 m), it encompassed 318 square meters on the ground. Its walls are 1.2 and 1.8 meters thick supported by external buttresses at all corners and in between. The present structure stands at an imposing height of 19 meters. Its interior contains four wooden floors, and the walls are pierced by few apertures. Common to such fortresses, the single doorway does not lead to the ground floor but to the second floor, thus requiring entry by ladder. An old-fashioned structure, its chief features were the thick stone walls and inaccessibility that relegated its defenders to the rooftop, where they were doubtlessly protected by crenellations. At the beginning of the thirteenth century it was modernized by a surrounding courtine encompassing an *haute cour* of 3,000 square meters, with a gate defended by towers. Higher on the hill above the courtine was a moat filled with water from a nearby reservoir.[9]

Numerous ruins resembling the older rectangular style of the donjon at Chevreuse are still extant in the Paris region. The counts of Beaumont-sur-Oise, for example, constructed there a larger donjon (a footprint of 508 square meters) as well as smaller examples at nearby Luzarches (Saint-Cosme, 271 square meters) and Conflans-Sainte-Honorine on the Seine (194 square meters).[10] Conflans, like Chevreuse, was held in liege homage from Eudes, bishop of Paris. The counts received two gold rings from the bishop confirming the investiture of the fiefs.[11] The lords of Montfort also built a small version of the rectangular donjon at Rochefort-en-Yvelines (224 square meters).[12]

Despite the massive walls and the imposing silhouette, the rectangular donjon presented two major disadvantages: it offered flat walls that were vulnerable to the projectiles of siege engines and sharp angles that protected attackers from the arrows of the defenders. The obvious solution to these weaknesses was the round tower, which had been employed since the time of the ancient Romans. The curved surface deflected projectiles and afforded the attackers no corners behind which to hide. The Capetians erected a round tower at the royal palace on the Île-de-la-Cité at Paris as early as the reign of Louis VI, and Philip Augustus retrofitted the round tower that he inherited from the Normans at Gisors in the Vexin. The family of Montforts also produced a simplified version at Montfort-l'Amaury and a more elaborated round tower at Beynes.[13] Furthermore, Philip Augustus made extensive use of the round tower by erecting at least twenty such structures throughout the royal domain, which he produced with assembly-line rapidity.[14] The largest and most celebrated example was the round tower of the Louvre at Paris, which he began in 1200. It measured 15.6 meters in diameter and an estimated 32 meters in height with walls 4.2 meters thick. It was encircled with a dry moat 7.5 meters wide. By 1209, however, he added a new feature by surrounding the tower with a substantial square courtine fitted with flanking towers at the four corners, between the corners, and also at each side of two gates. Enclosing a courtyard of 5,700 square meters, the ensemble has become known as the Philippine model.[15]

Brie-Comte-Robert

Since the time of Robert (d. 1188), son of Louis VI, the counts of Dreux had been fortifying their lands at Dreux, but their first significant construction was on their lands at Braye (now Brie-Comte-Robert).[16] So closely did it resemble the Philippine model that castellographers have assumed that it was constructed by Count Robert II (d. 1218) and was transmitted to his second son, Pierre Mauclerc, duke of Brittany (d. 1250), although the latter spent little time there. More recent excavations have set the date of construction back to the second half of the twelfth century, however, thus making Brie-Comte-Robert contemporary with Chevreuse and questioning the Philippine model as a source of inspiration. However that problem is resolved, Brie-Comte-Robert, although smaller than the Louvre enclosure, presents an imposing example of an aristocratic castle. Formed exactly in a square, its courtines measure 58 meters on each side (thus encompassing 3,360 square meters) and were fitted with round towers at each corner measuring 7.6 to 8.6 meters in diameter. Two sides contain similar flanking towers at midpoint; the other two on opposite sides contain fortified gates, surmounted by rectangular towers that defended the entries with portcullises, *assommoirs*, and wooden swinging doors that were barred from within. The tower gate facing the town of Brie was probably not as high as the opposite one (now known as the tower of Saint-Jean), which as the tallest tower of the ensemble proclaimed the power of the counts of Dreux. The corner and flanking towers are of equal dimensions, but, unlike the Louvre, there is no dominating central tower or donjon. The emplacement, unlike Chevreuse, is located below the town of Brie, but it is encircled with a moat fed by the steams that flow through this lower region.[17]

According to castellographers, the principal advantage of these courtines flanked by corner and midpoint towers was that it permitted the defenders to avoid blind corners and cover the extensive walls through openings in the round towers called *archères* through which archers and crossbowmen could fire their missiles. Triangular in shape with an angle of around ten degrees at their opening on the exterior, they presented only a narrow slit on the exterior but permitted greater room to the archer or crossbowman on the interior. Thus they offered maximum strength for the walls and greater flexibility for the defenders. Castellographers have taken particular interest in these apertures, attributing their emergence to the innovations of the Philippine castle. Following the example of the Louvre, they were placed systematically to cover the entire space of the walls. (Since the normal range of a bow and crossbow was 100 meters, with greatest accuracy under 30 meters, the flanking towers typically were spaced around 25 meters apart.)[18] At Brie the towers are placed 23 meters apart so that the walls are amply protected from towers on either side. Castellographers have further postulated that the disposition of the Philippine model with courtines and flanking round towers made the *archères* an essential feature. Surprisingly, however, at Brie-Comte-Robert there are not sufficient *archères* or other apertures to ensure this function of the towers, thus relegating the defense of the walls to the summit of the courtines and the flanking towers. (Castellographers, however, have further noted that existing examples of these openings attain a lateral range of coverage of 180 degrees only with difficulty, and experimental archaeologists using bows and crossbows have discovered that the confined shape of *archères* is minimally conducive to their deployment.) Whatever the problems posed by *archères* and the defensive deficiencies of Brie-Comte-Robert, the latter's grandeur and symmetry nonetheless proclaimed the pride and authority of the counts of Dreux.

With differing dimensions, the Philippine model, moreover, was employed extensively by both the king and the aristocracy close to him. In the Orléannais, for example, Philip Augustus erected Yèvre-le-Châtel with four towers and courtines encompassing 374 square meters but no donjon.[19] At the end of his reign he produced the most refined example of the Philippine model at Dourdan, which measured 4,800 square meters and replaced one of the corner towers with a larger master tower serving as the donjon.[20] The family of Dreux built a smaller replica at Nesles-en-Tardenois measuring 3,500 square meters.[21] The family of royal marshals, the Cléments, also built a version (3,170 square meters) at Mez-le-Maréchal, and the Barres family, descendants of Guillaume, the celebrated knight, erected a castle of the same model at Diant (3,600 square meters).[22]

Aristocratic Residences

If the castle's initial function was military, it also provided residential space. The royal circular castles housed garrisons who manned the *archères* and dominated the countryside, but the towers provided minimal space for inhabitants. The largest of them, the central tower of the Louvre, for example, had walls so thick (4.2 meters) that the interior space was limited to about 7 meters in diameter, or 41 square meters on each floor. The aristocrats who inhabited castles, however, required space to accommodate the private needs of their families for sleeping, eating, praying, and the holding of public meetings for their vassals and peasants. An important indicator of the aristocrat's status, therefore, was the amount of interior space that was allotted to these private and public functions.[23] The most recent archaeologists have therefore turned their investigations to castles as aristocratic residences as well. Not many have yet been examined in this light, but the two restored examples at Chevreuse and Brie-Comte-Robert serve as important exceptions, which I shall use to investigate how their respective families, the castellans of Chevreuse and the counts of Dreux, inhabited these fortifications.

Since Chevreuse has been the most recently and extensively excavated, it best illustrates the residential functions of the archaic rectangular donjon. The donjon contained four floors made from wooden planks, with each floor measuring around 197 square meters. We have seen that the ground level was not accessible from the outside and therefore served as a storage room, as with many such older castles. The second floor was the *étage noble* that doubtlessly housed the Chevreuse family. The third most likely served a similar purpose but could have included the garrison as well. The purpose of the remaining upper floor cannot yet be determined. The chief amenities for residential space consisted of windows for light, fireplaces for warmth, and nearby latrines for convenience. Although windows were placed on the second and third floors, the massive defensive walls of the donjon limited their number and effectiveness. Both the second and third floors were fitted with shallow fireplaces for efficient heating and both contained latrines in the walls. On the second floor the latrine was warmed by its proximity to the fireplace. The residential floors were connected by staircases within the walls—spiral steps to provide access to all the floors for the servants and a straight staircase to link the two residential floors. The donjon of Chevreuse therefore provided a potential of 788 square meters of livable space for its aristocratic lords. By the second half of the twelfth century about

3,000 meters were enclosed by courtines of the upper court that doubtlessly contained service buildings such as the kitchen but also a structure known as the "hall" (*aula*), which provided further space for public functions. A chapel dedicated to the Madeleine was placed in the lower court, from which the castle later derived its name.[24]

Although much less remains and although it has been less thoroughly excavated, the donjon at Beaumont-sur-Oise doubtlessly provided the counts there with similar conditions but on a grander scale. The number of floors cannot be determined, but each measured 270 square meters, thus allowing the aristocratic family at least 810 square meters of living space. *Archères* pierced the walls between the buttresses, permitting a minimum of light, and the walls contain at least one spiral staircase. On the northeast end of the donjon was attached a chapel in stone, shaped as an apse, which offered religious space for the family within the walls. By the turn of the twelfth and thirteenth centuries the donjon was surrounded by a courtine that enclosed a space of about 7,000 square meters and was fortified with a moat and at least eight defensive towers. It also contained the Cluniac priory of Saint-Léonor served by six monks who provided religious services for the counts. The smaller castle at Conflans afforded the Beaumont family 111 square meters of space on the ground floor, thus permitting a comfortable room on the second floor fitted with a fireplace and twin windows. The three floors of the castle afforded 333 square meters of residential space in total. Luzarches provided 117 square meters on the ground for a total of 234 square meters of residential space.[25]

We have seen that the counts of Meulan close by to the west of Paris had disappeared after the conquest of Normandy, but they were survived by a residential castle located at Vatteville-la-Rue west of Rouen. Reconstructed in the first half of the twelfth century, this stone residence offered at least 400 square meters on two floors. The ground floor was separated into two rooms by a masonry wall that provided a fireplace for cooking on one side and an oven on the other, thus creating the unusual situation of incorporating the kitchen directly into the stone structure. Including at least one latrine, the residence was distinguished by the unusual dimensions of the windows that offered more light. Wooden annexes in the adjacent courtyard completed the residential services, but no chapel has yet been located.[26]

The least damaged of the Montfort castles survives at Houdan. Dating from the twelfth century, it consists of a central cylindrical donjon flanked by four demi-cylindrical towers. It stands 25 meters high and contains at least two floors made of wooden planks in addition to the ground floor. The ground floor contains small windows and a spiral staircase in the wall. The second floor provides a chapel in one of the flanking towers and a latrine in another, but there is no evidence of a fireplace. A ladder led to the third floor furnished with small rect-angular windows and a possible fireplace. Since the three residential floors in the central donjon measure about 75 square meters each, offering only 225 square meters between them, it is probable that the Montfort family did not depend on this castle for residence.[27] They were not better served by another castle at Beynes whose original donjon provided 40 square meters on the ground floor for a to-tal of 120 square meters of residential space. However, their chief castle at nearby Montfort-l'Amaury, now in ruins, provided at least 570 square meters on three floors, thereby more than doubling the residential capacity of Houdan.[28]

At Blandy-les-Tours the vicomtes of Melun constructed extensive fortifica-tions, which by 1217 (that is, before the vicomte Adam departed on Prince Lou-is's English expedition) included a large rectangular stone donjon. Since only a basement survives, it is not yet possible to determine the extent available for the family.[29] At Nemours the loyal family of Gautier the Chamberlain also raised a rectangular donjon occupying 209 square meters on the ground and presently flanked with round towers at the four corners. It was surrounded with a quad-rangular wall with a high square tower. The ground floor contained a stone col-umn supporting two or three wooden floors above that accommodated a *grande salle* of 109 square meters and a chapel in one of the corner towers.[30] At least 436 square meters of potential residential space was provided. As often oc-curs in these residential castles, remodeling in the late Middle Ages makes it difficult to recover the earlier structures.

Since the massive walls of the rectangular or cylindrical donjons of the twelfth century severely limited living space to 800 or 900 square meters at most, it is not surprising that aristocratic families as well as the royalty sought new formulas for increasing the residential space in their castles. Perhaps the earli-est and certainly the best explored and restored was the Philippine model that the counts of Dreux created at Brie-Comte-Robert. Within the fortress complex encompassing 3,360 square meters Count Robert I not only constructed a de-fensive wall of courtines, flanking towers, and fortified gates, as has been seen, but he also integrated into the enclosed courtyard a series of buildings that served the residential and domestic needs of his family. Anchored to the courtines stretching between the two gates on the right side when entering from the town, he constructed a series of six rooms with masonry walls sufficient to add a floor above and an attic. The rooms measured around 7 to 8 meters in width and var-ied between 5 and 21 meters in length, each containing one to two stone col-umns to support the structure above on wooden beams, thus creating living space of 563 square meters on the ground floor that was duplicated on the sec-ond floor for an impressive total of 1,126 square meters. The two most easterly rooms on the ground floor (comprising 142 square meters) may have been devoted originally to the kitchen. Even if this space was set aside for the kitchen, just under one-half of the courtine walls supported aristocratic living space. On the second floor, above the largest space on the ground floor (167 square meters), was the *grande salle*, which served as the most prestigious room. One straight staircase and other spiral cases were incorporated into the dividing walls, but most access to the second floor was provided by wooden steps, the most important of which were situated in the courtyard. All of the rooms on both floors, save for two, were finished with fireplaces whose chimneys were incorporated into the courtine walls. The provision of windows is difficult to ascertain since only the courtine walls survive, which as defensive structures were not pierced with openings. Two towers provided latrines for three of the rooms that were accessed by passageways through the walls. The latrines were furnished with sophisticated water systems fed from the outside or supplied from interior reservoirs of captured rainfall. Both latrine towers were evacuated into the moat outside the walls. Hard dirt provided flooring for all of the rooms on both the ground and second floors. Tile flooring is found in only one of the storage towers, but all of the chimneys and the central columns on the ground floor were artistically sculpted in limestone.

A chapel from the original building has not been found, but it is likely that one existed in the largest of the gate towers, which was replaced by another chapel in the fourteenth century (the chapel of Saint Jean, situated in the courtyard). Only one well can be found in the courtyard, but entrapments for rainwater are more common. Two service rooms erected with solid masonry continued the buildings along the courtines across the gate from the kitchen, and less solid structures, doubtlessly also of a domestic nature, occupied the left courtines facing the residential rooms on the right. The three towers on the left side provided more permanent storage space; the one whose floor was tiled could be entered only through an aperture from the second floor to maintain a constant temperature and to discourage rodents. The deployment of corner and flanking towers as latrines and storage areas helps to explain the lack of *archères*; what few can be detected were so positioned as to be of little use for defense.[31]

Greatly expanding living and domestic space, the castle at Brie-Comte-Robert, while retaining essential defensive functions, nonetheless clearly increased the residential component by multiplying living space as well as space for domestic support and accompanying amenities. Of the Philippine imitations only the royal castle at Dourdan (4,800 square meters) has been subjected to study and restoration comparable to that of Brie. (The Louvre of Philip Augustus, which had a footprint of 5,700 square meters, remains inaccessible for further study beneath the Cour Carrée of the present palace.) Nonetheless, the Philippine model had a future if mainly on a lesser scale. The king built a smaller example at Yèvre-le-Châtel (374 square meters) and the counts of Dreux at Nesles-en-Tardenois (3,500 square meters). The royal marshals of the Clément family continued the series at Mez-le-Maréchal (3,170 square meters). Doubtlessly the goal remained to create more amenable living space for aristocratic families.

Despite the impressive archaeological progress that has been made in exploring these residential castles, there is one absence that should not be forgotten: horses. No evidence of stables has been detected in the courtyards or the surroundings of the castles, remarkable because the phosphoric acid of horse urine and the chemistry of manure leave permanent traces in the soil. The explanation may lie in the restriction of space investigated. In the densely urbanized areas around Paris the excavation of aristocratic sites is rare, and those investigated do not range far beyond the immediate fortifications. At Chevreuse, inhabited houses crowd around the archaeological site; at Brie-Comte-Robert the royal occupant Jeanne d'Évreux had the castle cleaned out in the fourteenth century. It is possible that archaeologists have not been looking in the right places. The missing horse nonetheless remains a mystery to archaeologists.[32]

Houses

Only kings, counts, barons, and castellans could afford the expensive stone structures that constitute the surviving castles. In the thousands of transactions between churches and the aristocracy we catch only momentary glimpses of castles, as for example, an unidentified castle belonging to Aliénor, countess of Vermandois, or that of Ermenonville belonging to Guy IV, butler of Senlis.[33] The near totality of knights inhabited dwellings identified in written documentation as houses (*domus*) or manses (*mansus, herbergagia*), which were certainly more modest. While there is no doubt that every knight possessed a roof over his head, the term "house" or its equivalent nonetheless appeared rarely in the written documentation. In a refined sample of property transactions between the principal aristocrats of the Paris region and churches, the conveyance of houses to churches accounted for only 4 percent of the transactions.[34] (On rare occasions aristocrats received a house in an exchange.)[35] When the king inventoried his vassals of the region in the *Scripta de feodis*, houses occur slightly more frequently: 9 percent of aristocrats reported houses among their possessions; in addition, another 2 percent reported *maisons fortes* (*domus fortes*) or fortresses (*firmitates*).[36] Although the actual numbers probably represent low reporting, it is clear that in both the cartularies and the feudal surveys most houses belonging to knights were not considered worthy of notice. Moreover, it appears that monasteries preferred to receive property other than houses from the aristocracy.

Only the agents who surveyed the vassals of the Montfort lordship in the 1220s obtained results that approach plausibility. In addition to liege homage, castle-guard, subvassals, and revenues, the possessions of each vassal were noted. Of the six castellanies surveyed, two paid no attention to houses and two smaller inventories reported houses for a third of the vassals, but in the two major castellanies, Épernon and Montfort, 92 percent of vassals and 80 percent of vassals, respectively, declared houses.[37] In both surveys, vassals occasionally acknowledged holding two to four houses, but for the most part, vassals were content to report single houses. In the castellany of Montfort itself, vassals from major families like Guy Mauvoisin, Gace de Poissy, Pierre de Richebourg, and Aubert d'Andresel made no mention of houses, which suggests that they were most likely located elsewhere. The neighboring castellan, Guy-Helisende de Chevreuse, declared a fortress (*fortericiam*) at La Ferté, otherwise unidentified. I have made few attempts to locate the houses, but many can be deduced from the names of their holders. Most were situated in hamlets, villages, and *bourgs*, that is, within clusters of the local peasant population. They average a little more than one per square kilometer.[38]

Roissy-en-France

Despite their undoubted ubiquity, houses remain scarce as well in the archaeological evidence surviving from the Paris region. Two explanations account for this scarcity: the heavy urbanization around the capital that obliterated minor structures and the low attraction to archaeologists who prefer to concentrate time and resources to uncovering the early Middle Ages when written documentation was scarce. Unexpected surprises, however, cannot be excluded. When a chain of hotels chose to build at Roissy-en-France, next to the Charles de Gaulle Airport, the archaeologists from INRAP were called to survey the site to determine the remains from the past beneath the surface. They discovered none other than aristocratic habitations from the twelfth and thirteenth centuries that have opened a window of opportunity on these rare survivals. Working under the constraints of time from 1999 to 2002, the archaeologists in fact uncovered the fragments of three successive buildings at Roissy.[39] Situated in the valley of the river Croult to the north of Paris, the excavation site lies close by the east of the village. At the first level of occupation from the first half of the twelfth century, the archaeologists found twenty-four postholes (averaging 98 centimeters in diameter) which outlined a rectangular structure measuring 12.5 by 17 meters, or just over 210 square meters in total. A surrounding ditch and seven silos (underground depositories) located both within and without the structure preserve remnants left by the first inhabitants of this dwelling. Two large silos were designed to store agricultural produce. Since only wood and soil remain at this level, the building was constructed entirely of wood. The absence of tiles and plaster indicates that the roof was of vegetable matter. It was undoubtedly a primitive structure consisting of three naves, but important remnants of wheat and pork in the silos suggest that the occupants enjoyed the amenities of well-off peasants if not yet claiming lordly status.[40]

A second and more abundant phase dates to the second half of the twelfth century and the beginning of the thirteenth when the first structure was replaced by another of smaller proportions outlined by some forty-five postholes (averaging 57 centimeters in diameter) but constructed from more solid materials. The structure consisted of a house (17.5 m × 8.6 m = 150 square meters) to which was attached on the south side a shed (17.5 m × 3.4 m = 60 square meters). The posts of the house were anchored in foundation trenches composed of plaster and limestone. The walls consisted of a wooden framework between the posts, which was covered with wattle, interwoven with twigs and finished with plaster. Interior postholes suggest that the main house was divided into rooms with two central passageways that intersected. One can hypothesize that the western side of the house was devoted to two separate storage rooms for provisions; the central part was the great hall containing the hearth for the fire and the table for dining; and the eastern side was the sleeping chamber. Both the interior and exterior posts were positioned close enough to support a second floor or attic, which probably extended over only part of the ground floor. The roof was supported by a wooden framework and was doubtlessly composed of straw or similar materials since no tiles or slates have been found. Large silos were located both within and without the building. In the interior three were in the western storage rooms and a fourth in the sleeping chamber. Their contents indicated they served the domestic needs of the inhabitants and were not used to store animal fodder. The floors of the house were doubtlessly covered with straw or other leafy plants. The shed that was attached to the south served to protect animals whose presence is fully confirmed by the impregnation of the soil with phosphates and by a canal for the evacuation of urine. The best hypothesis is a pigsty that could accommodate about twenty animals. A fragment of a ditch suggests that the entire complex was surrounded by a shallow moat and a wall, but there is no clear indication of attempts to fortify the site. Outside the walls to the north and northwest of the central house further silos and postholes suggest additional habitation and activity toward the end of the twelfth century.[41]

In the first quarter of the thirteenth century the wooden buildings were replaced by a rectangular stone structure erected on an earthen platform comprising 800 square meters and surrounded by two moats, an inner dry moat 5 to 6 meters wide and an outer moat 2.5 meters wide. On the mound created from the moats was raised a rectangular stone edifice that measured 14 by 9.3 meters on the exterior (covering 130 square meters). The walls were 1.4 meters thick yielding about 73 square meters of interior ground space. Since the walls that were excavated contained flat external buttresses at the corner, there were probably ten buttresses in all. Their presence allows the hypothesis that at least two floors above the ground were topped by a tile roof for which the evidence is abundant. This would allow a minimum of 146 square meters of residential space. The ground floor may also have contained a previously existing cellar for storage. No amenities such as latrines or fireplaces have survived. A pair of large postholes bordering the large moat suggests a foundation for a wooden bridge that gave access to the mound and stone house. The discovery of decorated floor tiles and a fragment of stone sculpture indicate a residence for an aristocratic lord. Although each successive building was reduced in size (from a footprint of 210 to 150 to 130 square meters), the rapid destruction of the wooden houses to be replaced finally in stone nonetheless indicates unbroken continuity of the inhabitants at Roissy. What was lost in space was undoubtedly gained in prestige.[42]

As yet no other site has been excavated in the Paris region that can be profitably compared to Roissy,[43] but the fragments at Roissy nonetheless fit the larger evolution of rural housing that took place in northern Europe from the early Middle Ages to the thirteenth century.[44] During the twelfth and thirteenth centuries appeared a new form of habitation occupied by peasants who were well off. These were veritable farms composed of a central house of large proportions and multiple annexes laid out in a quadrangle. The house itself was of mixed usage, serving as residence, as storage for agricultural products, and as shelter for animals. Because of the abundance of forests in northern Europe, the construction was almost entirely of wood, as contrasted with the predominance of stone buildings in the Mediterranean region. Such houses could be constructed quickly: modern efforts to reproduce them estimate that ten men could erect one in a month.[45] But they were "sub-buildings," not designed to last. It is likely that most of the local aristocracy who acknowledged a *domus* in the written documentation were not housed much differently than these well-off peasants.

Around 1200 the historian Lambert d'Ardres wrote a description of a more ambitious but nonetheless comparable house made for Arnoul, lord of Ardres, in Picardy to the north of Paris. Designed by a local carpenter, it was constructed entirely from wood and consisted of three floors. The ground floor provided space for storing food, supplies, and implements in chests, kegs, and vats. The second was divided between the sleeping chambers for the lord and his family, the domestic rooms for the bakers and butlers, and the kitchen, which had access to the ground floor where the pigs and fowl were kept. The third floor or attic housed the lord's older sons and daughters, servants, and also a chapel at the summit. All of these spaces were intricately connected with corridors, passages, and stairs. Although the chronicler may have been tempted to embellish when he compared it to the complexity of Daedalus's labyrinth, it nonetheless outlines the contours of a wooden aristocratic residence.[46]

At Roissy the archaeological evidence suggests that the lords there followed the general evolution of aristocratic housing. The earliest remains in the first half of the twelfth century fit the early pattern. Although the width of their wooden house spanned 12 meters and offered an impressive 210 square meters of floor space, the supporting posts were planted directly in the soil and the building was in fact replaced within decades. The structure of the second phase reveals a continual perfecting of techniques for building wooden houses. The posts were anchored in stone foundation trenches, the walls were roughly plastered, and a second floor was added that nearly doubled the interior space, but the building nonetheless retained the mixed character of a peasant house with a straw roof, close proximity to animals, and frequent use of silos to store grain. By the end of the twelfth century the lords at Roissy housed themselves in a manner comparable to their prosperous peasant neighbors.

At the beginning of the thirteenth century, however, they took steps to distinguish themselves by introducing the stone structure, capped with a tile roof and presumably equipped with amenities. The 73 square meters of interior ground space in the residence was greatly inferior to the 197 square meters of the castellans of Chevreuse and the 270 square meters of the counts of Beaumont; its closest contemporary was the 80 square meters for the lords of Rochefort-en-Yvelines. Comparison of total residential space, however, is more difficult to assess because in many cases like Roissy we can only estimate the number of floors available to the family. If we liberally assign them three floors, their 219 square meters puts them in the same league as the barons of Montfort at Beynes (120 square meters) or Houdan (225 square meters) but certainly not with the counts at Beaumont (810 square meters), the castellans of Chevreuse (788 square meters), or the lords of Montfort at Montfort (573 square meters), and especially the counts of Dreux at Brie-Comte-Robert (1,126 square meters). The defensive value of this small stone tower, whatever its height and the encircling moats, was minor in contrast to the great rectangular stone fortresses like Beaumont and Chevreuse or the Philippine fortresses like Brie-Comte-Robert; it nonetheless fitted into the dominant pattern of "residential castles or fortified houses" that began to appear elsewhere in France throughout the thirteenth century.[47] Their chief value was symbolic and proclaimed the prestige of whoever was lord at Roissy.

The Families of Roissy and Montfermeil

If the archaeologists have demonstrated the continuous occupation of Roissy since the early twelfth century, the documentary evidence has not kept pace in providing the name of the family to match.[48] Chiefly two families appear in the charters from the period who had sustained property rights at Roissy, those who took the name of Roissy and, secondly, the Montfermeils, whom we have already met in a dispute over inheritance. One might assume that those who took Roissy as their family name were in fact the lords of Roissy. A scattering of personal names bearing the place-name does appear in the charters. For example, in 1174 a Mathieu de Roissy and his sister Richilde sold woods at Roissy to the abbey of Saint-Victor.[49] There were other families, though, who also had significant holdings at Roissy,[50] and the charters do not show a continuous succession of persons with the Roissy name at Roissy until the second decade of the thirteenth century. It is possible that the property of the family of Mathieu and Richilde was passed through the female line. Richilde married Guy de Groslay and perhaps transmitted her possessions at Roissy through their daughters Agnès and Richilde.[51] Whatever the case may be, a male Roissy does not reappear until a certain Reric de Roissy and his son Philippe. In 1225, Philippe de Roissy is identified as son of Reric de Roissy and "knight and lord of Roissy" (*miles et dominus de Rossiaco*).[52] By 1238 Philippe's brother Guillaume was called the "first lord" (*primus dominus, feodo primo*) of Roissy as was Philippe later in 1253.[53] This first appearance of Philippe de Roissy and his descendants in the male line coincides with the completion of the stone house on the site. If they belonged to the family that occupied the previous wooden structures illuminated by the archaeological evidence, their ancestors were hidden in the documentary evidence, perhaps explained by their female connections descending from Richilde de Roissy in the twelfth century.

The most prominent family who had rights at Roissy were the lords of Montfermeil nearby to the south. We have already met Adam de Montfermeil, whose descendants disputed the division of dowers between his two wives in a case that was brought to judgment before the king's barons around 1200.[54] Adam's first-born (*primogenitus*) from a first wife, who is unnamed, was Guillaume. Guillaume received the greatest share of his father's inheritance and headed the dominant branch of the family as far as the charters show. Philip Augustus's survey of the castellany of Paris listed him among the knights whose revenues were more than sixty *livres* but who did not hold their fiefs from the king.[55] He married Agnès de Clacy[56] from another prominent local family, possessed a grange at Roissy as early as 1205, held minor tithes at Roissy in 1209, 1211, and 1218 and major tithes there in 1228.[57] By 1254 his daughter Alypidis possessed a house at Roissy as well as land.[58] Three years later when Alypidis de Montfermeil sold the house to Sainte-Geneviève de Paris, Marie *de Oisseriaco*, widow of Guillaume de Roissy, approved the sale as lady of the "first fief" (*primi feodi*).[59] We remember that Guillaume de Roissy was the first to claim the title of "first lord of Roissy." As far as can be ascertained by the charters, the Montfermeils never asserted the title of Roissy. Instead, Adam de Montfermeil, father of Guillaume de Montfermeil, was identified as "lord of the town called Montfermeil,"[60] and Guillaume de Montfermeil himself claimed other ancestral lands at Montfermeil and Paris.[61] If we knew the family of Guillaume's unnamed mother, we might have an explanation for the Montfermeil family's Roissy holdings, as was the case of the Groslay family's property at Roissy. Whatever the earlier claims of the Montfermeils at Roissy, however, the Montfermeils eventually acknowledged the lordship of the family of Roissy by midcentury.

Houses at Paris

During the reign of Philip Augustus the aristocrats surrounding Paris resided on lands that were located deep in the countryside. Never did a lord identify himself as a *burgensis*, that is, a citizen of a town. They were all nonetheless neighbors to the king's capital which was newly surrounded with walls and constituted the largest, most populated urban conglomeration north of the Alps. When the king surveyed those knights who were worth more than sixty *livres* of revenues from the castellany of Paris, not one was located in the city. Since the *censives* of landholders in the city did not appear until a later date, the only documentation available is contained in ecclesiastical charters that recorded the houses that the aristocrats gave to or occasionally exchanged with churches. From the principal lords of the region I have found seventeen who held at least thirty-two properties at Paris, evenly distributed between the Right (nine) and Left Banks (ten), with a slightly higher concentration on the Île-de-la-Cité (twelve). Those knights in the king's direct service naturally possessed most of these residences. For example, Barthélemy de Roye, the king's most trusted knight and later royal chamberlain, claimed seven properties, distributed evenly throughout the city. One was located outside the walls of the Left Bank between the Seine and Bièvre rivers.[62] Gautier the Father, the royal chamberlain, held five, all located on the Right Bank. Pierre du Thillay, formerly *prévôt* of Paris and later bailli of Caen, possessed multiple houses on the Right Bank near Saint-Magloire and near Les Halles on the rue des Prêcheurs, doubtlessly to accommodate him when he reported on business at the capital.[63] Guillaume de Garlande had a house on the rue Neuve that led into Notre-Dame.[64] Simon de Poissy, who was formerly responsible for the town criers of Paris, held properties on the Left Bank, principally at the Thermes and in the *censive* of Saint-Étienne-des-Grès.[65] In a house next to Saint-Denis-de-la-Chartre on the Cité, Mathieu, count of Beaumont, installed a chapel dedicated to Saint Catherine.[66] Pierre de Petit-Pont provided an unusual example of a knight who adopted a Parisian site as his family name.[67] The values of these properties varied greatly. Barthélemy de Roye paid 450 *livres* for a house on the rue Saint-Germain-l'Auxerrois on the Right Bank;[68] Hugues de Chaumont sold four houses near the Petit-Pont for fifty-three *livres*;[69] Guillaume de Milly sold half a house behind Saint-Denis on the Cité for two *livres*.[70] The relentless modernization of Paris, however, has eradicated all traces of private dwellings from the reign of Philip Augustus. Roofed with straw, some houses were very narrow and could have attained three to four stories, but like the sale prices, they undoubtedly varied greatly in size and amenities.

Embellishments and Movable Objects

In the castles and residences that have been excavated archaeologists have not only been able to discern the architecture, but they have also obtained glimpses into how the owners embellished and furnished them with objects that sought to improve the quality of life. At Brie-Comte-Robert, for example, numerous fireplaces have survived because they were incorporated into the outer walls of the courtines. The family of Dreux may not have tiled the floors of their spacious residence, but they did decorate their fireplaces. Characteristically, the Dreux family framed the fireplaces with elegant stone columns mounted on circular bases and crowned with capitals composed of four leaves that were popular in the second half of the twelfth century.[71] Although the lords at Roissy-en-France were of considerably less wealth, they nonetheless placed decorated tiles on the floors of their stone building of the thirteenth century and surprisingly invested in an artistically sculpted figure (a caryatid or atlas) in the same style that can be found in the *voussures* of the central portal at Notre-Dame in Paris. (At Roissy it survived because it was reused in the wall of the seventeenth-century château.)[72] When Queen Jeanne d'Évreux inhabited Brie-Comte-Robert in the fourteenth century, she had the site cleaned of its previous movables, thus eliminating traces of the preceding Dreux family. The sole exception is a small leaded glass window bearing the heraldry of Aliénor de Saint-Valéry, the wife of Count Robert III. This precious survival was probably installed in a chapel window and was later incorporated into windows of subsequent chapels.[73]

Most evidence of the ceramics and glass that were in use at the various sites is found in the abundant remnants discarded in the moats and ditches by the inhabitants. Chevreuse, for example, yields examples of ceramic pitchers and cooking vessels from the second half of the twelfth century that resemble those that were current at the royal castle of Dourdan.[74] Once again, more surprising are the remnants surviving at Roissy from a continuous occupation of the site from the twelfth to the eighteenth century. The entire twelfth century is represented by a variety of pitchers with beaks, lamps, and cooking vessels (*oules*) made from semi-granular (*sableuse*) clay colored in beige-rose. These were essentially vessels for cooking and drinking that were traditional to rural villages, thus underscoring the characteristics of early aristocratic habitations that were common to peasants.[75] In the thirteenth century these traditional pitchers, cooking vessels, cups, lamps, and lids to saucepans were continued but with greater variety. Two kinds of clay were used, glazing was more common (in particular green glaze) along with decorations with motifs that were similar to those produced in contemporary Paris. Although still rare, glass also makes its appearance.[76] Evidently, with their increasing wealth, the lords of Roissy began to import from the capital furnishings to improve their style of life.

Food

In the earliest house at Roissy at the beginning of the twelfth century cooking was most likely performed over the hearth in the middle of the great hall with provisions supplied from the storerooms to the west. With the second house at the end of the twelfth century it probably took place in one of the outbuildings in the courtyard, as it most certainly did with the stone house of the thirteenth century. This was also true for the lords of Chevreuse. At Brie-Comte-Robert the Dreux family constructed service buildings on the northwest side of the courtyard, which contained their kitchens. It is more difficult to describe what these kitchens served.

The most vivid accounts of what aristocrats ate from their tables come from the vernacular romances written for their entertainment. It was Chrétien de Troyes who established the romance tradition of glorifying the aristocratic meal in the great festivities portrayed in his Arthurian tales. For example, in *Erec et Enide* at Erec's Pentecost feast, King Arthur was not stingy but ordered his bakers, cooks, and butlers to provide bread, wine, and venison in such abundance that all could satisfy their desires (vv. 2006–14).[77] As a good storyteller, however, Chrétien would not waste words on details because he has more important things to say (vv. 6872–78). His successor Jean Renart, however, was not so inhibited and took evident delight in providing those details in his *Roman de la*

Rose. At Lïenor's banquet at Mainz, for example, he expatiates on the diversity of the courses: boar, bear, deer, crane, geese, roast peacock, lamb ragout (it was in May), fat beef, and fattened gosling served with white and red wine (vv. 5449–58).[78] The romance menu was so well established by Gerbert de Montreuil's time that he felt justified to abbreviate it in his *Roman de la Violette.* Eurïaut served her guest meat (*viande*) in great profusion, roasted fowl (*oisiaus en ross*) and venison (*venison*), and fresh fish (*poisson fres*), followed by plentiful dishes (*mes*) (vv. 485–95).[79] These romance descriptions represent the most voluminous evidence available to us of what aristocrats might have wanted to eat in our period. It is nevertheless clear that the romance authors were serving their audiences menus of culinary fantasy. The young knight Guillaume le Maréchal was too busy winning his tournaments for his biographer to pay much attention to his diet, but at the end of each contest the hero circulated through the hostels talking and feasting on dishes that were left undescribed. At the tournament of Pleurs, however, a magnificent pike two and a half feet long was awarded to him as the prize for being best knight of the day.[80] Presumably he was hungry enough to have eaten it or shared it with his companions. Clerics writing in Latin were naturally reluctant to celebrate a gourmandise that could hardly be judged virtuous by their standards. This excess clearly signaled that the dishes were no ordinary fare for the aristocratic table, but rather romance embellishment to nourish the gastronomic fantasies of the aristocracy, the ultimate audience of the romance.

To compensate for the meager evidence that has survived from kitchens archaeologists have enlisted their colleagues—carpologists and archaeozoologists—to examine the eating habits of the aristocracy. They adopt a radically different approach and their conclusions are not as colorful as the romances. They examine not what entered the mouth, but what exited into the latrine, was discarded in the moat, or was stored underground. The foodstuffs that they examine can be summarily divided between plants (the domain of carpology) and animals (the domain of archaeozoology). The picture provided by the carpologists is mixed. At the château d'Orville at Louvres north of Paris, which had been inhabited for centuries, rye (*secale*) was preferred over wheat (*bladum, frumentum*)—63 percent (rye) to 29 percent (wheat)—during the Merovingian period. By the eleventh century the proportions were reversed (wheat, 62 percent, to rye, 28 percent), which remained steady thereafter, indicating that wheat had become the preferred grain of an emerging elite.[81] In contrast, an extensive study at Chevreuse has found that 98 percent of the surviving seeds came from cultivated plants, but over half (54 percent) consisted of grape seeds with only slight traces of wheat.[82] It is possible that cultivation for wine was significant for the area, but the findings do not account for the importance of grain.

While Brie-Comte-Robert is completely devoid of evidence of food production, Roissy-en-France has produced the most interesting results for both cereal and meat over the three phases of its occupation from the early twelfth into the thirteenth century.[83] Confirming the trend established at Louvres, the presence of rye was low throughout the period, never attaining more than 5 percent. At the beginning of the twelfth century barley (*hordeum vulgare*) was high (80 percent) but then dropped to 40 percent and to 60 percent throughout the century and declined sharply to 20 percent by the beginning of the thirteenth. Wheat (*triticum aestivum*), on the other hand, entered the twelfth century low (5 percent), rose to about 40 percent throughout the century and then precipitously to 60 percent by the beginning of the thirteenth and continued its climb to dominate the grains thereafter. These comparisons are based on findings from the silos, which were designed for storage. The wheat, of course, was stored uniquely for human usage. Barley, moreover, although potentially animal fodder, was nonetheless shelled of its chaff, which rendered it fit for human consumption as well. This meant that most of the grain stocks were for humans either to be consumed at Roissy or to be sold on the market. The principal use of the grains was for bread or related products such as porridge, items that the vernacular authors of romance (except for Chrétien) accorded little notice. White bread baked from wheat rather than dark bread from rye or barley was nonetheless an indication of high status and confirmed the social pretensions of the lords of Roissy as they invested in their stone building. The storage silos of grain from the end of the twelfth century undoubtedly supplied the emerging cereal market. At that time the "plaine de France" where Roissy was located had become the wheat granary that furnished the bakers of the city of Paris. The absence of oats, moreover, is also noteworthy since it was the chief grain that could be shared with animals, especially horses.

What attracted the admiration of the romance writers was, of course, the great variety of meats that ladened the aristocratic table, not what accompanied them. The one archaeological sample that approaches the preferences of the romance table comes from Chevreuse, which established the following order of meats: pork (54 percent), fowl (17 percent), beef (11 percent), mutton goat (*capriné*; 11 percent), and venison (3 percent).[84] The menu that was unearthed by the archaeozoologists from the moats and ditches at Roissy, however, was simpler. Although there was variation depending on the location of the findings, the staples were undoubtedly pork, beef, and mutton goat. As at Chevreuse, pork dominated at the end of the twelfth (40 percent) and into the thirteenth century (31 percent). The establishment of a pigsty during the second phase of construction emphasized that the Roissy family not only consumed pigs but also produced them for the market. This is further confirmed by the discovery of at least three piglets in the first phase of habitation. No traces of animals of the age of reproduction, however, have been found. Mutton goat placed second at the end of the twelfth century (12 percent) and rivaled the position of pork into the thirteenth (31 percent). Beef ran third at the two intervals (7 and 25 percent). An anomaly was the occasional appearance of horses (6, 9, 3 percent). Their appearance may be due to other uses of horse skin and hair, besides their potential use as a comestible. Whatever the relative position of the three staples, they were undoubtedly meats of prestige. Lamb ragout and fat beef were worthy of praise from Jean Renart, but pork was omitted from the romance accounts; it was however the staple of the elite in Roman antiquity. Lower on the scale were chicken (9, 11, 2 percent), and goose (8 percent). Chevreuse recorded fowl (17 percent), but prestigious fowl like peacocks and goslings were missing from both Chevreuse and Roissy. Most surprising is the total absence of game meat and fish at Roissy, where there was no evidence of the boar, bear, and deer that headed Jean Renart's menu, while Chevreuse recorded 3 percent venison. The absence of fish may be due simply to the current agenda of archaeologists who have not yet programmed it for study. If not attaining the delights of the fantasies of Jean Renart or Gerbert de Montreuil, the trinity of pork, mutton goat, and beef nonetheless was not peasant fare and demonstrated the social aspirations of lessor lords like those of Roissy. The higher pretensions of the castellans of Chevreuse may have been reflected in archaeological remains that better approximated the fantasies of the vernacular writers. The lords of Roissy, nonetheless, were sufficiently modest at their table because it did not contain the delicacies of the hunt even though Guillaume de Montfermeil possessed a hunting park near the abbey of Livry.[85]

It must be remembered, however, that while aristocrats were landholders who as agricultural producers supplied the needs of the commercial market, they also provided for their own tables. It is likely therefore that the storage silos at Roissy contributed to the immediate demands of their owners. In the royal survey of fiefs for the eleven castellanies of the Paris region, revenues in kind accounted for only 4 percent of the items held by the aristocrats.[86] We notice occasional details of loaves of bread, poultry, eggs, wheat, oats, and barley in the *Scripta* survey. In the ecclesiastical charters, however, 13 percent of the transactions involved revenues in kind.[87] In other words, aristocrats of the Paris region were relatively quick to give away their agricultural produce.[88]

These aggregate statistics, however, are less helpful than the precocious landbook of Pierre, lord of Le Thillay, which provides a closer look into a neighbor of Roissy, close by to the west. When Pierre founded the Hôtel-Dieu at Gonesse in 1208 he gave the hospital important revenues of wheat (sixty *setiers*), as well as some oats (three *setiers*) and barley (three *setiers*). The wheat was certainly more than he would have consumed in a year at home. His landbook, however, shows that he kept for himself annual revenues of twenty-one capons and twenty geese from his lands at Tessonville and an additional twenty-five capons, as well as fifteen loaves of bread, a half *setier* of wheat, and twelve *setiers* of oats from his properties at Sarcelles. He also possessed twenty-two arpents of vineyards at Gonesse.[89] His landbook further reveals that he possessed more important revenues in kind from Normandy where he was stationed at Caen as royal bailli. Although he might have marketed the commodities raised around Le Thillay, they nonetheless supplied his yearly needs for poultry, bread, and wine. (The oats may even have fed his horses.) We can suppose that the lords of Roissy exploited their own lands for similar domestic consumption.

Chapter 5

Fiefs and Homage: The *Nomina militum* and *Scripta de feodis*

Warfare was, without question, the official function of the aristocrat. No matter his rank, he was a *miles,* a soldier equipped for combat. His seal, certainly the most explicit image of his identity, pictured him armed and wearing a helmet, charging on a horse at full gallop—whether he was a count or a simple knight. His normal support came from a fief (*feodum*), which fundamentally furnished a revenue derived from land. Most often he held this fief from another lord on the condition that he do homage and swear fealty (faith) to the lord. It was, of course, important to the great lords—kings, dukes, and counts—to keep track of these fiefs and the military services that they provided, but in France few such efforts appeared before the last quarter of the twelfth century. The first to do so were not kings but counts and dukes. In 1172 Henri the Liberal, count of Troyes, surveyed 1,900 lords and knights in Champagne grouped in twenty-six castellanies. He noted those who owed him liege homage and their length of duty as castle guards.[1] In the same year, Henry II, duke of Normandy, just as he had done in 1166 as king of England, counted the knights who were enfeoffed in the duchy: 1,500 knights held fiefs from him and 580 owed him military service. His survey was organized hierarchically starting with barons and proceeding to knights who were grouped together by bailliage.[2]

In 1204 when Philip Augustus captured the Norman capital of Caen and the ducal archives, his chancery copied Henry's Norman survey of 1172 into Register A, but since three decades had elapsed the scribes began immediately to correct the text and add information that brought it up to date.[3] It was superseded by a new survey in 1207, which asked the same questions as the 1172 survey, but rearranged the entries, grouping all vassals and fiefs by barony and bailliage.[4] In 1212, when the Capetian chancery initiated a second register, called Register C, it introduced new surveys for Normandy that expanded both the scope and questions of the previous ones. Finally, in 1220 a third register, Register E, combined all of these scattered surveys to provide a comprehensive inventory of the fiefs of the duchy distributed according to bailliages. For seven of the eight major bailliages of the duchy, the survey was based, as before, on the two traditional Norman questions—the number of knights enfeoffed and the service owed.[5] Within this comprehensive survey the Norman bailli Guillaume de Ville-Thierri proposed an entirely new format for the other bailliage—the Vexin castellanies to the northwest of Paris, both on the Norman and the Capetian side of the border. Modifying the previous inventories, he now asked four questions: (1) Who held from the king? (2) What fiefs did he hold? (3) What were the fiefs of his vassals? (4) What was his military service?[6] This revised format was adopted by the baillis for the newly acquired region of Vermandois and then applied also to castellanies south of Paris in the old domain where the inventory breaks off and is incomplete.[7] Following Léopold Delisle, I refer to these surveys as the *Scripta de feodis*. As I have explained in Chapter 1, to define the Paris region I have selected eleven of the castellanies surveyed in the *Scripta de feodis*—five of the closest castellanies in the Vexin (Gisors, Chaumont, Pontoise, Meulan, Mantes-la-Jolie) and two from the southern domain (Montlhéry, Melun), to which I have added four of the nearest castellanies from Vermandois (Montdidier, Chauny, Crépy-en-Valois, La Ferté-Milon).

Between 1212 and 1220 while Register C was still active, another survey was undertaken entitled *Nomina militum LX libratas redditus habentium* (Names of knights having an income of 60 *livres*). It posed two other questions, both important, but involving less detail: (1) Who held fiefs yielding sixty *livres* or more of annual income? (2) Who among these fief-holders held their fiefs from the king and who did not?[8] From twenty-one castellanies in this survey located haphazardly in the old Capetian domain I have selected ten that were closest to Paris (see Tables 5 and 6). In these two surveys, only three castellanies overlap—Mantes, Melun, and Montlhéry. Thus, toward the end of his reign, Philip Augustus's chancery had supplied two inventories of fiefs that systematically counted his military resources in eighteen castellanies in the Paris region. The dominant pattern for organizing these two surveys, the castellany, followed the pattern of neighboring Champagne rather than that of recently conquered Normandy and its baronies. Despite their deficiencies the surveys offered a store of information.

The king was not alone in inventorying his military resources from the Paris region. At the opening of the reign, the abbot of Saint-Germain-des-Prés, outside of the Paris walls, listed by diocese those lords who held fiefs from the abbey, forty-six of which were within the diocese of Paris.[9] Similarly the cartulary of Notre-Dame de Paris contains a list of forty-five fief-holders who held from the bishop at the time of Eudes de Sully (1197–1208), identifying their homage, their holdings, and the service owed.[10] Returned from the Albigensian Crusade after 1218, Amaury, lord of Montfort, moreover, undertook an inventory of 255 men who held from him, divided into six castellanies. Like the king, he inquired into their homage, military service, landed holdings, and those who held from them.[11]

What we can learn about the knights' military duties is, of course, limited by the questions formulated by the surveys. Both the *Scripta de feodis* and the *Nomina militum* were based on the regime of fiefs, that is, the land and its revenues that supported military service. We shall postpone to the following chapter the material nature of these landed fiefs. In this chapter we shall devote our attention to the following questions, which were proposed primarily in the *Scripta de feodis* and were addressed partially in the *Nomina* survey: (1) Who held fiefs directly from the king? That is, who were royal vassals? (2) Who held fiefs from those who held from the king (making them the king's subvassals) and who held fiefs from other lords? (3) Who owed homage or liege homage? (4) Finally, what military service was owed? That is, who owed castle-guard and who owed host and *chevauchée*? With these questions we shall be concerned not with the nature of fiefs themselves, but with the personal services, such as homage and military duty, that were gained from the fiefs.

To illustrate the nature of the two royal inventories from the Paris region I shall take the example of Pierre de Richebourg. He appeared twice in the *Nomina* survey that recorded the names of those who enjoyed revenues of sixty *livres* or more. He appeared first in the castellany of Mantes where he was the king's direct vassal and again at Paris where he did not hold from the king.[12] He also appeared twice in the *Scripta* surveys, first at Mantes and second at Nogent-le-Roi. These entries encapsulate the kind of information supplied by the *Scripta* inventory:

Pierre de Richebourg holds (*tenet*) from the lord king all that he has at Mantes, except the mill beneath the tower, and all that he has at Guerville except the street in which the *prévôt* of Guerville lives, from which he owes host and *chevauchée* (*exercitum et equitatum*) at his own expense; moreover he holds from the king 27 knights' fiefs (*feoda militum*) on this and the other side of the Seine.[13]

Lord Pierre de Richebourg holds (*tenet*) 100 *sous* of revenue from the *prévôté* of Nogent on the feast day of Saint John Baptist for which he was the vassal (*homo*) of the deceased count [of Blois]; and he holds the fief of *Chenoie* that lord Guillaume de Nesle, a knight, holds from him and the fief of *Levainfontainne* that Henri *de Poncellis*, a knight, holds from him, and one other fief at *Levainfontainne* that Amaury *de Probato Monte* holds from him, from which he owes host and *chevauchée*; and also the fief that Simon *de Merroles*, a knight, holds at *Merroles*.

In Register C this last text is preceded by the rubric: "These are the knights from the castellany of Nogent who hold in chief in the name of the king" (*Isti sunt milites de castellania Nogenti qui tenet capitaliter de domino rege*).[14]

Who Held Fiefs from the King?

The operative term is "to hold" (*tenere*), that is, to receive one's fief directly from a lord. In this case, it is held from the king. The fief, then, may also be called "tenure." Holding therefore involves the personal relationship of doing homage for the fief, that is, submitting to the authority of the lord and swearing fidelity to him, thus rendering the holder the "tenant" or vassal of the lord. The *Nomina* survey uncovered some 138 knights in the ten castellanies around Paris holding directly from the king fiefs that were worth sixty *livres* or more of annual income. From the eleven castellanies of the *Scripta* survey the king claimed 247 direct tenants. In sum, when duplicate names in the two surveys are accounted for, Philip Augustus could count on at least 351 knights in the Paris region who held their fiefs directly from him and were thereby his vassals.[15] Of all our statistical speculations this number is the most secure estimation that we possess. The total encompasses the spectrum of lords and vassals, including those at the highest level such as the counts of Beaumont and Dreux, the barons of Montmorency and Nesle, the castellans of Chevreuse, Marly, Gisors, and Hangest, as well as knights throughout the region such as the Poissys, Barres, Pomponnes, Mauvoisins, and Andresels. The sum of 351 vassals represents about 11 percent of the 3,229 names I have been able to assemble from the Paris region, but, as we have seen, the latter figure only scratches the surface of the potential aristocratic population, which remains impossible to fathom. The figure of 351 direct vassals was also greatly inferior to the 1,900 vassals of the count of Champagne and the 1,500 vassals of the duke of Normandy.

Who Held Fiefs from Other Lords?

Beside the royal vassals coexisted a much more numerous stratum of other knights. The *Scripta* inventory of the eleven castellanies named 659 subvassals of the king's tenants. In addition, the inventory listed scores of subvassals in individual surveys of the tenants of the count of Beaumont (90 subvassals), Jean de Nesle (149 subvassals), and Jean de Gisors (25 subvassals). Adding these together, the survey accounted for 923 vassals of the king's direct vassals.[16] Based on the available documentation, the 351 direct vassals of the two feudal surveys together with the 923 subvassals of the *Scripta* survey, while not representing the full extent of Philip's feudal resources in the Paris region, certainly constituted the core.

As we have seen in Chapter 2, the names of around two thousand other aristocrats can be gathered from various sources. However, the number of these who owed homage or military service is more difficult to determine. In the *Nomina* inventory, in addition to those who held directly from the king, were another 128 who held from other lords.[17] (Amaury de Poissy, for instance, was recorded in the *Nomina* survey as a knight not holding from the king in two different locations, yet he owed a quota of three knights.)[18] In our sample of 1,729 ecclesiastical charters from the Paris region, another 951 aristocrats, who were not among the king's direct vassals in the *Scripta* and *Nomina* surveys, are named as the principal actors.[19] Further, when churchmen acquired fiefs from the aristocracy through gifts, sales, and other conveyances, they demanded that the transfer be approved not only by the principal and his or her family but also by the lord of the fief in a clause known as the *laudatio domini*. At least 22 percent of the charters (or 378 charters) contained the phrase, suggesting an equal number of vassals named in the ecclesiastical charters.[20] Finally, alongside the royal surveys, major lords of the region including Mathieu le Bel, Gautier the Chamberlain, the abbot of Saint-Germain-des-Prés, the bishop of Paris, and Amaury de Montfort inventoried their fief-holders. Another 498 names can be gathered from these inventories, in addition to the names of the royal surveys and church charters.[21] Thus we can assemble a group of another 1,955 vassals in addition to the 351 direct vassals of the king and their 923 subvassals. Again, however, we recognize that these figures are certainly infinitesimal relative to the potential number of those who existed.

The Feudal Hierarchy

The *Scripta* survey inquired specifically about homage of the king's direct vassals and about the subvassals of the direct vassals. The church charters likewise were explicitly aware of the regime of fiefs, echoing the characteristic terminology of fiefs and homage.[22] The term "allod," which designated land that was not held as a fief, is virtually absent.[23] The monks of Saint-Denis were so sensitive to the regime of fiefs in the Paris region that their cartulary contained a special chapter, "De feodis," devoted to them.[24] Apparently the organization of fiefs in the lands around Saint-Denis was precocious. Abbot Suger of Saint-Denis was among the first to articulate the hierocratic relationship among lords and vassals. He noted, for example, that the count of Auvergne owed homage to the duke of Aquitaine, who, in turn, owed homage to the king.[25] The principle of hierarchy was also articulated in a contemporary charter in which a local lord, Mathieu le Bel, declared that he owed direct homage to the abbey and then named those subvassals who did homage for their fiefs.[26] The date of this charter has caused some confusion. When the monks of Saint-Denis copied the charter into their cartulary, they dated it to 1125.[27] They had good reason to assign this date. Not only can the date on the charter easily be read as 1125, the charter declares that Abbot Suger (1122–51) had initiated the inventory. Nonetheless, they appear to have been mistaken. The seal of the charter itself is that of Abbot Hugues Foucaut (1186–97), the names of several individuals in the charter match names in the *Nomina* survey for the castellany of Paris (ca. 1217) and in the landbook of Pierre du Thillay (1219–20), and a close look at the date on the charter itself reveals that it could easily be read as either 1125 or 1195. It appears therefore that in 1195 a revision was made of an original charter dating to Abbot Suger's time (the charter of Suger is lost) and that the revision was made for the descendant of Mathieu le Bel, who was likewise named Mathieu. In the revised version of 1195, the vassals' names were updated while Abbot Suger's name was retained. The charter thus incidentally illustrates the continuity of fiefs and vassals throughout the twelfth century. It also exhibits the underlying structure of fiefs in the Paris region. In 1195, Mathieu le Bel, a direct descendant of the former Mathieu, was a vassal of the abbot of Saint-Denis, and he himself claimed thirty-eight direct vassals who in turn claimed no less than forty-three subvassals. At the lower level, for example, Raoul, the younger brother of Mathieu, acknowledged sixteen subvassals; Jean de Pomponne, ten; Raoul *de Carni*, six; Raoul *de Grassi*, five; and so on. If in the first zone the hierarchy was decidedly flat (1 < 38), in the second zone it was much steeper (1 < 16 to 1 < 5). It therefore resembles a structure with a slightly sloping roof (one vassal extending over thirty-eight subvassals) and nearly vertical walls (one vassal extending over a handful of subvassals). The same characteristic was exhibited in the *Scripta* survey with vassals like Pierre de Richebourg reporting twenty-seven subvassals; the vicomte of Melun, sixty-eight, and Philippe de Nanteuil, thirty-two.[28] This flatness becomes exaggerated with the barons like the count of Beaumont (1 < 90), the lord of Nesle (1 < 149), not to speak of the lord of Montfort (1 < 255) in his own private inventory.[29] When Philip Augustus acknowledged 351 direct vassals, therefore, he was merely following the contemporary practice of the Paris region. None of these surveys exceeded three zones of subtenants.

The flattening of these hierarchies was encouraged by the king. With the agreement of six barons, Philip Augustus published in 1209 a new custom on the division of fiefs through inheritance or other means. When inheritances were divided, all vassals should hold their fiefs from the original lord and not through any intermediary such as an elder brother. The royal decree thus opposed the custom of *parage* practiced in Champagne and Normandy whereby fiefs distributed in a succession could be held from an intermediary, thus introducing a new lord who tended to sharpen the hierarchy.[30] Philip's policy of "immediatization" of fiefs was probably limited to the region of Paris where it had been practiced since Suger's time. It is not surprising that Philip's surveys as well as other local surveys proceeded no further than the two zones of vassals and subvassals, thus producing the large numbers of subvassals as we have seen. The policy of immediatization was also reflected in the *laudationes domini* of the monastic charters, where the agreement of the immediate lord was required to guarantee the vassal's transaction. Among hundreds of examples, the vast majority required only the consent of the immediate lord; only a handful (ten) mention an additional superior lord, as well.[31]

Liege Homage

With so many vassals offering homage to lords, confusion was frequent when a vassal did homage to several lords for different fiefs, and particularly when the lords opposed each other. The practice of liege homage, which favored one lord over the others, was devised as the solution to the problem. Among the local abbots, those of Saint-Denis were insistent that their vassals owed them liege homage for their fiefs, according to the custom of the Vexin (*ad usus et consuetudines Vulcassini*).[32] Among the laity, Anseau d'Île-Adam made a treaty in 1205 with his neighbor Mathieu, the count of Beaumont, in which he acknowledged that he was a liege vassal for designated fiefs, whereas the count held another fief from Anseau without homage or designation of military of service.[33] Hugues de Pomponne recognized liege homage not only to the abbot of Saint-Denis in 1224 but also to the king, Amaury of Meulan, and the count of Dammartin and Clermont.[34] It therefore became a major concern of the inventories of fiefs to distinguish the types of homage received from vassals. Eudes, bishop of Paris, counted 40 percent of his vassals as owing liege homage and 40 percent as owing simple homage.[35] In 1198, in the testament of Gautier the Chamberlain in which he assigned fifty-four fiefs to his four heirs, 35 percent (nineteen of fifty-four) were counted as owing liege homage.[36] The lord of Montfort was the most exigent: of 185 knights from four castellanies where homage was recorded,

42 percent were recorded as owing liege homage, 22 percent owed simple homage, and 26 percent gave guarantees with a simple oath (*assecuravit*).[37]

As supreme lord, the king was naturally in a position to demand liege homage throughout his kingdom. Along with his father, Louis VII, Philip demanded homage from the Angevin kings of England and most of the major barons of the realm as the occasion permitted.[38] Similarly, whenever the king granted a fief to a favorite, it was standard procedure to specify that the vassal owed liege homage to the king.[39] Anseau d'Île-Adam and Hugues de Pomponne, for example, included the king among their multiple lords to whom they swore liege homage,[40] and liege homage was frequently cited in monastic charters.[41] In the *Scripta* inventory of fiefs, distinguishing liege homage was a major task. In the castellanies surveyed, the percentage of vassals owing liege homage peaked at 54 percent in the castellany of Crépy-en-Valois (see Table 6). Overall, in the *Scripta* survey, 39 percent of those who held something from the king were recorded as owing liege homage and 34 percent as owing simple homage.[42] If it is assumed that the direct vassals of the king registered in the *Nomina* survey owed liege homage, a slightly higher percentage of the wealthiest vassals owed liege homage (42 percent) than did the vassals of the *Scripta* survey, who represented a broader spectrum of wealth.[43] Oscillating around 40 percent, the frequency of liege homage among the king's vassals did not differ markedly from the surveys of other lords. Surveys for the lord of Montfort reported 42 percent of vassals owed liege homage and 22 percent simple homage. In 1172, Count Henri of Troyes in Champagne counted 49 percent of his vassals as owing liege homage and 47 percent simple homage. Henri's report of 47 percent owing simple homage was doubtlessly due to better reporting of the alternatives to liege homage.[44] The general conclusion is nonetheless clear. The king and the major lords considered a little under half of their direct vassals as liegemen. What this meant in practice is more difficult to ascertain. We can easily imagine great confusion among the numerous vassals who owed liege homage to multiple lords when these lords came into conflict, but the advantage to the king is apparent. As the most powerful lord of the region, he experienced the least constraint in imposing his will and enforcing allegiance.

Being the supreme lord of the realm did, however, pose a particular problem for the king: could he, in turn, be the vassal of another lord? Louis VI, Philip's grandfather, faced this dilemma in 1124 when he discovered that as count of Vexin he was thereby vassal to the abbot of Saint-Denis. Philip Augustus dealt with the problem as it arose by making deals with the lords whose land he had acquired until finally in 1213, on the acquisition of the remaining portions of Vermandois and Valois from Countess Aliénor, he declared a general custom of the French kingdom that "none of our predecessors have ever done homage."[45]

During the last decade of his reign he was occupied with redeeming the homages that he had acquired when he annexed the county of Beaumont.[46]

Castles and the Service of Castle-Guard

By the reign of Philip Augustus, as we have seen, local lords around Paris such as the Garlandes and the Montmorencys had submitted to royal authority, thus enabling the king to put his hand on important castles. Between 1206 and 1210, shortly after the conquest of Normandy, the chancery clerics took the opportunity to compile in Register A a list of 110 castles that belonged to the king, distributed throughout the kingdom.[47] These royal castles provide a template for the king's domination of the Paris region. We shall see that they were staffed with garrisons of vassals who owed castle-guard and therefore no longer functioned as residences for the local aristocracy.

For the castles of Normandy, royal documentation reveals two practices that, though they had long been in effect, were used more frequently after the new territorial conquest. The king confided newly acquired castles to favorites and, once assigned, he imposed the obligation of "rendability."[48] That is, the recipient swore to return the castle at the king's demand, an oath that was reinforced by pledges who confirmed the agreement in writing. After the conquest of Normandy, numerous such charters were collected in the royal archives.[49] Such transfers occurred only rarely in the Paris region since the king had long dominated this area. Nonetheless, the king took an active role in the distribution of castles close to Paris, as is shown by the fact that miscellaneous concerns of local lords regarding castles and fortified houses surfaced in royal documentation. For example, the king declared that Guy de Garlande (d. after 1186) held his castle of Tournan-en-Brie in liege homage from the bishop of Paris. (The castle remained on Bishop Eudes's list in 1197–1206).[50] When Anseau de Garlande granted liberties to the bourgeoisie of Tournan in 1193, he demanded a *corvée* for work on the fortifications of the castle of Tournan.[51] The king intervened directly when fortifications became an issue between the abbot of Saint-Denis and his neighbors. In 1199 Mathieu, count of Beaumont, objected to Abbot Henri's fortification of a house at Lamorlaye and obtained the king's support in forcing the abbot to render the small fortress at the count's request.[52] On the other hand, in 1219 Mathieu de Montmorency promised the king that he would not fortify the island located in the Seine at Saint-Denis, which he held from the king.[53] At the same time, the king gave orders to demolish the fortified house of one of Mathieu's sergeants, but allowed another sergeant to build an unfortified house on the island of Châtellier as long as it did not exceed the height of other houses there.[54]

The royal interest in the castles of the Paris region is best seen, however, in the royal *Scripta de feodis* in which Philip's baillis listed fief-holders along with various other pieces of information, depending on the castellany. As landed wealth, the fief served many roles, but the king's immediate objective in requiring homage from a fief-holder was to obtain twofold military service—castle-guard (*custodia, excubia*) and host and *chevauchée* (*exercitum et equitatio*). In each of the castellanies surveyed in the Paris region, save Melun, the baillis recorded military services owed the king, whether castle-guard or host and *chevauchée*. For the service of castle-guard in the castellanies of Mantes, Meulan, Pontoise, Chaumont, Gisors, Montlhéry, La Ferté-Milon, Crépy-en-Valois, Chauny, and Montdidier, the baillis reported that out of 235 direct vassals in total, 115 owed castle-guard of various durations.[55]

Several of these castles were located in towns that contained communes that had long shared responsibility for maintaining the fortifications and supplying castle-guard. Two model charters in particular bear on the castles of the Paris region surveyed in the *Scripta de feodis*. The charter for the commune of Mantes (1150), originating in the previous reign, contained a clause that became the model for the others. It declared that common necessities such as castle-guard (*excubiae*), chains, moats, and fortifications were the commune's responsibility, a clause that was adopted by the Vexin communes of Chaumont (1182), Pontoise (1188), Poissy (1188), and Meulan (1188–90) during the opening decade of Philip Augustus's reign.[56] Second, in 1195 the king issued a new charter to Saint-Quentin based on customs from the time of Count Raoul of Vermandois, Aliénor's father, containing a clause that permitted the mayor and *échevins* to fortify the town. This clause was incorporated into the charters of Chauny (1213) and Crépy (1215) as well.[57] The precise contributions of these communes to their fortifications were not specified, but the king also garrisoned the nine castles of the *Scripta* survey reporting castle-guard with knights who recognized their obligation to perform castle-guard, calculated in months per year.

The findings of the royal inventory can best be seen in tabular form (see Table 6).[58] Of the nine castellanies surveyed, Montlhéry stood above the others: 63 out of 71 knights surveyed owed a total of 130 months of service, or an average of 10.8 knights owing castle-guard each month. The service was levied generally at the rate of two months per year, with only two knights owing four months each. Meulan in the Vexin was next where 10 out of 20 knights surveyed owed 47 months of service, or an average of 3.9 knights per month. Here the rate of service was more variable, ranging from one month to twelve months from each knight. At Chauny, 8 of 40 knights owed forty-four months of castle-guard, or 3.7 knights per month. (Of those owing castle-guard at Montlhéry, almost three-quarters held their fiefs either by liege homage or simple homage; at Meulan, half of those owing castle-guard held their fiefs by liege or simple homage.) Castle-guard in the remaining castellanies was perfunctory, ranging from 2.9 knights per month (La Ferté-Milon) to 0.33 (Chaumont). The results from Meulan (3.9 knights per month) and Chauny (3.7 knights per month) were each boosted by three knights who served the full twelve months. Of the 27 knights enregistered at Montdidier only one provided guard duty of two months, while five others acknowledged owing the service but did not know how much. At the end of Philip's reign, Amaury, lord of Montfort, surveyed castle-guard in four of his castellanies and obtained results comparable to the king's. Of 185 knights, 87 contributed 120 months, or 4.5 knights per month at Montfort castle, 3 at Rochefort, and 2.8 at Épernon.[59]

These results may be compared with those obtained by the vidames of Picquigny, which were exceptional. From the last decade of the twelfth century, a roll compiled for the vidame recorded the names of the vidame's vassals and the services they owed. In total, 61 knights owed 452.5 months of castle-guard at Picquigny, or an average of almost 38 knights per month. Thirty of the knights served the entire year.[60] The vidames of Picquigny had thus succeeded in establishing a permanent garrison in their castle. The closest that Philip Augustus came to this regime was at Montlhéry, which he had surveyed at least three times and which became a symbol of peace and stability in his kingdom. Perched on a hill commanding the road from Paris to Orléans, it had been held at the opening of the twelfth century by hostile castellans who disrupted communications between the two cities. When Philip's great-grandfather finally acquired it in 1105, he confessed that it had made him old before his time. A century and a half later, Philip's grandson Louis IX referred to the castle as "in the heart of France and a land of peace." Efficient garrisoning doubtlessly helped to contribute to its success.[61]

Although it is clear that the regime of fiefs was marshaled to support castle-guard, the implementation behind these inventories is not evident. How did the enfeoffed knights interact with the guards provided by the communes? Did the knights serve personally or could they commute their service for money? Most likely the number of guards did not remain constant but fluctuated seasonally. Except for Montlhéry, the number of guards appearing monthly appears derisory by comparison to Picquigny. Half of the castellanies reported virtually no service or no service at all. Most likely we can consider the service of castle-guard in the Paris region as an institution in decline that was increasingly transformed into court service.[62] The little interest that ecclesiastics took in such garrisoning was limited to parish jurisdiction. For example, in 1212 a dispute arose between the church of Saint-Vaast and the chapel of Saint Vulgis of the castle of La Ferté-Milon over the right to perform baptisms and burials of the knights on duty. Countess Aliénor of Saint-Quentin had adjudicated a similar dispute at the royal castle of Ribemont in 1200.[63]

The Service of Host and *Chevauchée*

If the regime of fiefs recorded in the *Scripta de feodis* produced perfunctory results in castle-guard, the obligation of host and *chevauchée* was taken more seriously. The formula *exercitum et equitatum* designated the service of an armed warrior on horseback who joined the king's army in warfare (host, *exercitum*) or on more sporadic raiding parties (*chevauchée, equitatum*). The men of the communes who owed repair and castle-guard were also obliged to perform this service, although they were not knights. The obligation was included in the charters granted to Mantes, Chaumont, Pontoise, and Meulan in the Vexin.[64] When the commune of Étampes was dissolved for disorderly conduct, the obligation of host and *chevauchée* was retained for the townsmen.[65] Saint-Quentin's charter, which became the model for Chauny and Crépy in Vermandois, also contained the duty, as did Roye adjacent to Montdidier.[66] The men of Mantes, Chaumont, and Pontoise, however, sought to limit the duty within the boundaries of the Seine and Oise rivers. Meulan specified that toward the Vexin, Seine, and Yvelines the service was confined to the distance in which one could return within a day. At Brie-Comte-Robert the men of the town and the *hôtes* of the chapter of Notre-Dame de Paris were required to arm themselves and to accompany their lord, the count of Dreux, or his *sergents* on *chevauchée*, provided that they could return to their homes that evening.[67] In other words, the service of *chevauchée* was integrated into the functions of the castle that protected a small garrison. The service allowed the garrison to sortie into the neighborhood as far as it could while returning to safety within the same day.

The baillis of the *Scripta* survey reported ten castellanies where the knights holding directly from the king owed him host and *chevauchée* (Table 6). The results were insignificant at Gisors and Montlhéry; at the latter military service was restricted mainly to castle-guard. The nonroyal survey at Montfort likewise produced negligible results (2 to 4 percent in different castellanies). If we eliminate Gisors and Montlhéry from the royal survey, however, the contribution of host and *chevauchée* was very high: from 100 percent (Pontoise, La Ferté-Milon) to 74 percent (Montdidier). All told, 142 knights from the ten castellanies owed the king this service. The castellanies from the Vexin declared that each knight served at his own expense (*ad costum suum*). The Vermandois castles were silent on this requirement except for Montdidier, where it was stated that knights served according to the custom of Vermandois (*ad usum Viromandesii*). Apparently there was no direct correlation between homage and castle-guard, nor was there an evident alternation between castle-guard and host and *chevauchée*—most of the knights recorded in the *Scripta* inventory were obligated to serve. The practical modalities of their service, however, remain open to question. Did their duty require that they serve personally, or could they supply a substitute? What was the length of service? Could they commute their service for money? The commutation of the service was, in fact, an important motivation behind the Anglo-Norman surveys.

When we return to the ecclesiastical charters, we remember that 22 percent of the transactions required the consent of the feudal lord (Table 2). Many fiefs involved in these transactions were encumbered with military obligations that needed to be addressed. For example, the church of Saint-Fursy de Péronne ceded land to its vassal Julien d'Allaines and his son, Étienne, adding to the fief Julien already held, in exchange for a rent from Julien or his son. But the church stipulated that the service attached to this land, which was owed to the chapter of Noyon, remained in effect. Étienne owed the chapter of Noyon each year service with a horse wherever in the diocese the chapter wished.[68] Or in 1202 a certain Pierre, son of *Girardi sicarii,* gave the church of Saint-Léger de Soissons twenty *sous* from land held in fief from the count of Soissons, but the donation did not release him from his *feodi servicium.*[69] Other mentions of feudal service did not involve knights directly, but involved men of the village who, like the communes of castles, owed host and *chevauchée,* or at least were alleged to owe such services. In 1183, the abbot of Saint-Denis and the count of Clermont agreed that the men of a village between Liancourt and Verderonne owed host and *chevauchée* but were not obligated to go to the lord's tournaments. In 1211, the monks of Saint-Denis complained that men of another village were wrongfully harassed by a certain knight, Renaudus, who claimed the men of the village owed him host and *chevauchée* and were obligated to accompany him to tournaments. In this case, all such claims by the lord were repudiated. In 1215, the monks of Compiègne agreed with a certain knight, Jean de Coudun, that the men of the village of Marest, north of Compiègne, were obligated to accompany Jean to tournaments and owed him *chevauchée.*[70]

Since the clerics of the royal chancery certainly had access to an abacus, they could have added up the findings of the surveys in the *Nomina militum* and the *Scripta de feodis* as I have done. In eighteen castellanies around Paris the king could count 351 knights who held from him directly (Table 5). In eight castellanies of the *Scripta* survey, with 216 reporting, 39 percent owed him liege homage and 34 percent simple homage (Table 6). As for castle-guard, in eight circumscriptions he could have received 321 months from 115 knights for an average of 3.3 knights per month per castellany. In ten castellanies, 142 knights, or 60 percent, owed him host and *chevauchée,* presumably at their own expense.

We have no direct evidence, however, that the clerics ever performed these exercises of arithmetic, nor do we know how exactly they put these inventories to use. At the Temple outside of Paris, the king's clerics drew up accounts when the *prévôts* and baillis reported on their revenues and expenditure three times a year. These accounts were tallied on the abacus to produce totals, but they were actually designed to supervise the activities of the royal agents who reported.[71] It is most likely that the *Scripta* were employed not to add up feudal resources but to keep track of the vassals' obligations. This limited use, however, should not inhibit historians from profiting from this data for their own purposes.

The Vexin castellanies declared that the knight performed his military service at his own expense. No inventory or charter, however, specified his equipment, assuming, of course, that it was generally understood. Even vernacular literature such as the romances of Gerbert de Montreuil referred to knights' garb and equipment only when pertinent to the narrative. His knights bore a hauberk and helmet, carried a sword, lance, and shield, and rode a destrier.[72] The vernacular author of the *Histoire de Guillaume le Maréchal*, however, provides a rare account that specified the equipment required by a knight. (For so much of our knowledge of chivalric life, the *Histoire* is an unparalleled source.) At the tournament between Saint-Jamme and Valennes the author expatiated in detail on how knights prepared themselves on the eve of the forthcoming contest. They had their hauberks (*haubers*) and leg armor (*chauces*) polished; they tried their helmets (*hieaumes*) on for size; they adjusted their coifs (*coiphes*) and ventails (*vintailles*) to fit the links of mail (*mailles*); they called for their shields (*escu*), making sure that the neck straps (*guige*) and arm thongs (*enarmeüre*) were strong; their sturdy mounts were fitted with collars (*colieres*), blankets (*covertures*), saddles (*seles*), bridles (*freins*), breast harnesses (*peitrals*), and straps (*cengles*).[73] Here the author furnishes us with the precise vernacular terms for the equipment, except for the weapons, that a knight was expected to provide.

The Cash Nexus

The castle-guard, host, and *chevauchée* that were recorded in the royal registers were secured by oaths of homage and funded by landed fiefs. Very little cash was involved. Yet Philip Augustus, like the Anglo-Norman and Angevin kings, employed mercenary armies consisting of both foot soldiers and mounted knights whom he paid wages in cash. Our most revealing source for this military service is provided by the fiscal accounts of 1202–3, the only fiscal records to survive intact from Philip's reign.[74] The accounts illuminate Philip's opening campaign against Normandy down the Seine valley, which eventually resulted in the fall of Rouen and the conquest of the duchy. In these fiscal accounts we can learn how he amassed an army of some 2,250 men consisting of around 250 mounted knights, 240 mounted *sergents*, 70 mounted crossbowmen, 100 crossbowmen on foot, 1,600 *sergents* on foot, and various others. We can follow the details of where he moved them, from castle to castle, and the wages he paid to each category.[75] We can also see how he raised the money for their wages through a war tax originally called the *prisée des sergents*.[76] Based upon the numbers of *sergents* and wagons that the towns and abbeys of the royal domain formerly had owed as military service, eventually the service was commuted to cash that could be adjusted to the needs of each campaign.[77] Despite these details on this mercenary army, we do not know who these mounted knights were or the source of their recruitment. Although it is possible that some were also the king's vassals, it is clear that they were not remunerated with fiefs but with cash.

Despite this disjunction between the paid army and the military service supplied by fiefs, the latter vassals were not entirely free from the cash nexus. Beginning with Louis VII, following the example of the Angevin kings of England, the Capetians began to make cash payments called *fief-rentes* to their most valued vassals in return for homage, fealty, and occasional service.[78] Although resembling wages, the main goal appears to have been the establishment of a feudal relationship based on money. Like the conventional fief derived from land, it created a personal relation of homage and fealty between a lord and a vassal and often reinforced a landed bond. Not long after 1204, the chancery clerics drew up a list of *fief-rentes* that was organized by the *prévôté* on which they were paid. In Register A, 93 *fief-rentes* were paid out annually, disbursing 3,173 *livres*. By the completion of Register C in 1220 they had increased to 126, paying out 5,187 *livres*.[79] The recipients ranged widely from *sergents*, chamberlains, even foreigners, to knights and high lords, including the royal family. The sums paid likewise ranged from a few *livres* to hundreds. Out of roughly a hundred names, about two dozen can be identified from the aristocracy around Paris. As the following list of those best known to us demonstrates, they ranged from the royal cousins of the Dreux and Vermandois families to the lowly knight and trouvère Gace Brulé. Their emoluments were equally varied:

Count Robert de Dreux, 100 *livres* from Mantes, 500 *livres tournois* from Caen
Countess of Crépy, 100 *livres* from Bapaume; Countess of Saint-Quentin, 128 *livres* from Roye and Montdidier
Butler of Senlis, 30 *livres* from Paris
Gautier the Father (the chamberlain), 20 *livres* from Paris

Roger de Meulan, 100 *livres* from Évreux

Renaud de Pomponne, 7 *livres* from Pierrefonds; his son, 20 *livres* from
    Pierrefonds

Robert de Poissy, junior, 16 *livres angevin* from Vernon

Pierre Mauvoisin, 5 *livres* from Pacy; 12 *livres* from Mantes

Lord of Hangest, 40 *livres* from Roye and Montdidier

Gace Brulé, 24 *livres* from Mantes

With the exception of the count of Dreux, Philip's expenses on *fief-rentes*
were hardly exceptional, particularly if they are compared with those in the
Anglo-Norman realm. The biographer of Guillaume le Maréchal reported that at
the tournament at Ressons-Gournay Guillaume made such an impression that he
was offered 500 *livres de rente* by the count of Flanders, which was matched by
an equal offer from the lord of Béthune; Jacques d'Avesne could only propose
300 *livres* but included the lordship over his lands; later the lord of Béthune returned to the bidding with an extraordinary offer of 1,000 *livres* and his daughter
in marriage as well. Doubtlessly reflecting the hyperbole of his biographer, Guillaume was reported to have turned them all down, averring that he was not yet
ready for marriage.[80]

Attached to the *prévôté* of Mantes at the end of the inventory in the registers, however, was a long list of barons and knights from the Flemish region.
This was the result of Philip's policy to win over the Flemish nobility after the
death of Count Philippe at Acre in 1191, a policy that was countered by the English kings Richard and John, who also proposed *fief-rentes*. By 1212, however,
the scribes had crossed out most of the names indicating that Philip Augustus had
lost the bidding war against John over the loyalty of Count Ferrand and his followers. Despite this failure, the political function of the *fief-rente* in Flanders
was evident; its purpose for the Paris region is less clear except to bind local favorites to the king with additional ties of homage and cash. Little evidence has
surfaced that the *fief-rente* served any significant military purpose.

Winning a War: La Roche-aux-Moines and Bouvines

The final criterion for judging military effectiveness is, of course, victory in
battle. Philip Augustus went on the offensive against King Richard, attacking
him in 1193 while Richard was still absent from his lands. Despite some initial
successes Philip's military fortunes, however, were not brilliant. After Richard's
return from the crusade in 1194, most of the victories were won by the English
king. For this warfare we have only the French and English chroniclers who shed
little light on the logistics of the conflicting armies, but Richard's spectacular

victory at Courcelles-lès-Gisors in September 1198 offers an exception. The contemporary chroniclers differed on details, as was their custom, but all were agreed on Richard's stunning victory in which at least one hundred of Philip's knights were captured in the engagement. Fortunately for our purposes, the English chronicler Roger of Howden named forty-three of those captured. The families of at least five of the individuals on Roger's list can be found in the Vexin section of the banneret inventory (see below on this inventory, compiled between 1204 and 1208). The families of nineteen individuals, or nearly half of Roger's list, can be matched with names in the *Nomina* and *Scripta* surveys (1218–20).[81] While names are deformed and others difficult to locate, it is nonetheless clear that Philip drew a substantial part of his army from his vassals in the Paris region. On other occasions when Philip summoned the royal host, he relied on the military obligations of the prelates and barons. In the the campaign of 1202–3, as we have seen, he maintained a mercenary army of around 2,250 men, which included around 250 mounted knights. At Courcelles-lès-Gisors, however, Philip's army was a domanial affair.[82]

Shortly after Richard's victory at Courcelles-lès-Gisors, Richard's sudden and unexpected death in 1199 dramatically shifted the military balance. Richard's brother John lacked his sibling's military skills and Philip was able to apply good luck, superior finances, and shorter supply lines to conquer Normandy by 1204 and drive the English out of the Loire valley by 1206. The final denouement, as is well known, took place on the fields of La Roche-aux-Moines and Bouvines in 1214, which resulted in total victory for Prince Louis and Philip Augustus. The campaign had been long prepared by King John to recover his Norman and Loire fiefs. With ample subsidies the English king recruited his nephew, Emperor Otto of Brunswick, as well as the counts of Flanders and Boulogne and other dissident barons, to attack Paris from the north while he assembled his vassals in Poitou to approach Paris from the south. At this crucial moment Philip was forced to divide his forces, sending Prince Louis to meet John in the south while he proceeded to confront the allies in the north. At La Roche-aux-Moines outside of Angers John strangely refused combat with Louis, but he had succeeded in splitting the Capetian army. Philip met the allies at Bouvines outside Lille with half of his effectives but won a stunning victory. These battles were not a simple *guerre*, a seasonal conflict, but a true *bellum* that summoned the full resources of the kingdom and inflicted decisive defeat.

Preceding these victories, the Capetian chancery had drawn up new inventories. We have noted that between 1204 and 1208 the chancery clerics compiled in Register A an extensive list of some 566 "knights carrying banners" drawn from the kingdom north of the Loire.[83] As field commanders, these men hoisted their banners to lead squadrons of mounted knights, the basic units of cavalry warfare, into battle or tournaments. In the register they were grouped by region. The Vexin and Vermandois regions correspond roughly to the territory I have delineated around Paris for this study. In these two regions, the role of the vassals of his domain is immediately apparent, as it was at Courcelles-lès-Gisors. In the list for the Vexin, fifty-six bannerets are identified, drawn from forty-five families. Thirty-three of these forty-five Vexin families, or almost three-quarters of the families, also appear in the *Nomina* and *Scripta* surveys.[84] The figures are comparable for Vermandois: fourteen out of twenty banneret families, or 70 percent, can be found in the feudal inventories. This high correlation shows convincingly that the king relied heavily on his vassals from the Paris region for field commanders.

After 1212 when the chancery clerics initiated Register C, they drew up a new but unnamed inventory, which I shall call "knights' quotas." Placed on a separate page of Register C, it can be presumed to have been drafted after the documents that precede it, that is, after June of 1213.[85] The inventory contains the names of eight towns of the royal domain and fifty-one individuals, likewise drawn from the royal domain. To each town and to thirty-nine of the individuals the clerics assigned a quota of three or five or ten or more knights. In effect, the inventory is a muster list for the battle of Bouvines, devoted to recording the levies from the royal domain. In total, it accounted for the provision of 763 knights who were placed under the leadership of the inventory's bannerets. When this list is compared with the chroniclers' reports of the battle at Bouvines, it is found to be incomplete at the upper echelons of counts and barons, but these lacunae can be filled in with chroniclers' estimates of the contingents of the counts and barons. Altogether, with the 763 knights of the royal domain and around 560 knights supplied by the barons and counts of the realm, modern historians estimate that Philip fought at Bouvines with around 1,300 knights.[86]

The "knights' quotas" inventory is not organized geographically, but using the inventory of "knights carrying banners" as a framework, I have sorted the names into six regions of which the Vexin and Vermandois correspond roughly to the Paris region as I have defined it, and the results can be represented in tabular form (Table 7).[87] Almost half of the total number of knights tallied in the quota list, 338 knights out of 763, came from the Vexin and Vermandois. From the Vexin fourteen bannerets brought 118 knights on the field joined by 60 knights supplied by Dammartin and Pierrefonds and the Vexin generally, for a total of 178 knights. From Vermandois twelve bannerets produced 60 knights to which the castellanies of Chauny, Valois, Senlis, and Montdidier contributed another 100 for a total of 160.

Despite their fragmentary and incomplete character, the *Nomina* and *Scripta* inventories help to assess the feudal resources of the regions that supplied the above totals. Most obviously, they allow us to tally the resources of several of the bannerets who appeared in the "knights' quotas" inventory. Of the fourteen bannerets from the Vexin, ten appear in the *Nomina* survey, with nine holding their fiefs directly from the king. Of the twelve bannerets from Vermandois, seven appear in the *Scripta* inventory, with three owing the king liege homage and the other four simple homage. A mere six vassals in the quota list appearing in the *Scripta* survey enfeoffed 334 vassals of their own. For example, in the *Scripta de feodis* it is reported that Jean de Nesle had 149 vassals, Jean de Beaumont had 90, and Pierre de Richebourg had 27.[88] Such numbers were more than ample to fill their respective quotas of forty knights, twenty knights, and five knights. Equally apparent, the value of the fiefs of the castellan of Neauphle (estimated at 240 *livres parisis*), of Robert de Poissy (2,000 *livres*), and of Amaury de Poissy (300 *livres*) easily could have covered their quotas of five, five, and three knights.[89]

A general comparison of quota tallies with resource tallies for each region leads to the same conclusion. In organizing the "knights' quotas" names, I have defined the Vexin region broadly to encompass not only the castellanies of the Vexin proper but also the castellanies south of Paris (Étampes, Corbeil, Melun, and Montlhéry), Paris itself, and those nearby Paris to the north (Senlis, Dammartin, and Béthisy). As we have seen, Philip counted on a quota of 178 knights from this region. His feudal resources in these fourteen castellanies as reported in the *Nomina* and *Scripta* surveys included 250 direct vassals who reported 391 of their own vassals.[90] Unfortunately, the baillis inquired of military service in only five of these fourteen castellanies. For these five castellanies, 54 of 134 direct vassals reported owing host and *chevauchée*. From the Vermandois, Philip counted on a quota of 160 knights. His feudal resources in these four castellanies included 101 direct vassals who reported 268 of their own vassals. Of the direct vassals, nearly half (46) owed liege allegiance and 88 acknowledged owing host and *chevauchée*. Adding these together, as set out in Table 5, Philip drew from a military pool of 351 direct vassals and 659 subvassals inventoried in the eleven *Scripta* castellanies, to which can be added another 264 subvassals of three lords (Jean, count of Beaumont, Jean de Nesle, and Jean de Gisors) inventoried separately in the *Scripta* survey—a total of 1,274 knights to supply a quota of 338 knights! Characteristic of military statistics, potential effectives usually outweigh those who appear for action. Even so, from these tallies I conclude that Philip Augustus's feudal resources amply covered the requirements of the quota list.

By opening with three bannerets—Mathieu de Montmorency, the count of Beaumont, and Guillaume de Garlande, all from the Paris region and each accompanied by twenty knights—the quota list of Register C acknowledged their leadership on the field, which the royal chronicler Guillaume le Breton also recorded.[91] The striking contribution of the aristocracy around Paris to Philip's great victory is fully confirmed. We must also remember that before Bouvines, Philip divided his forces with Prince Louis, whom he dispatched to the west to confront John. The pool from which Philip and Louis drew for this second army is unknown, but according to Guillaume le Breton, it was composed of 800 knights.[92] The dense regime of fiefs around Paris easily supplied a quarter of the contingent of knights that historians believe Philip Augustus fielded at Bouvines. A pool of 1,274 knights could have supported Louis's army as well.

The battle of Bouvines was fought on 27 July 1214 and thereby raises a chronological problem for my calculations based on the two feudal surveys, which, although contemporary, cannot be dated precisely. The "list of bannerets" transcribed in Register A can be situated in the years 1204–8. The "knights' quotas" inventory in Register C can be dated very close to the battle of Bouvines. The *Nomina* survey is likewise found in Register C but cannot be dated with more precision than between 1212 and 1220.[93] The *Scripta* surveys of Register E are found in the hand of Étienne de Garlandon, the first scribe of the register, who began compiling it in 1220.[94] Parts of the *Scripta* survey of Register E were preceded by earlier drafts in Register C. Surveys concerning Jean de Gisors, Robert de Poissy, and the castellany of Montlhéry all appeared in the earlier register.[95] On the other hand, it is certain that the survey of the castellany of Crépy was conducted after July of 1218, as it contains mention of the king's gift of Bonneuil-en-Valois to Robert de Tournelle, which can be dated to that month.[96] All of the surveys took time to complete and were probably conducted years before their final inscription. There is no clear evidence that Philip Augustus commanded the surveys of fiefs to prepare for the battle, but whatever the king's intentions, the surveys nonetheless offer estimates of his feudal resources contemporary to the battle and show that he had ample resources to defend himself against King John at La Roche-aux-Moines and the allies at Bouvines.

The military campaigns of 1214 were not phases of endemic warfare between competing lords but extraordinary challenges that demanded commensurate efforts. A standing army of 250 knights paid by royal revenues such as were levied in 1202–3 was not sufficient to meet the challenge. As in 1124 when Louis VI, Philip's grandfather, prepared to meet an invasion from the German emperor, Philip met this new invasion from the east with extraordinary measures. He drew upon his rights as supreme lord to recruit vassals from northern France who owed him liege homage. At the fore of these recruits were his vassals from the Paris region. It was as feudal lord that Philip Augustus survived the challenge of 1214.

Historians have recently and frequently maintained that the medieval phenomenon of "feudalism" is actually a modern construct devised in the early modern period by antiquarian scholars beginning with Henry Spelman in England and Montesquieu in France.[97] If, however, we understand the word to mean the encompassing regime of fiefs, feudalism in the Paris region at the turn of the twelfth and thirteenth centuries was more properly a construct of the Capetian kings of France. Like the dukes of Normandy and the counts of Champagne, the French king, as supreme lord of the lands around Paris, sought to organize the fiefs of the region and to control those fiefs through liege homage, thereby supplying himself with the necessary military services of castle-guard and host and *chevauchée* to meet his political goals. Like the counts of Champagne, he assembled these fiefs into castellanies, each centered on a strategic castle. Most important, he ordered extensive inventories of fiefs, homages, and military service to be recorded in his registers. Although unfinished, these written surveys fashioned a "feudal system" for his Parisian lands just as those of the dukes of Normandy and the counts of Champagne had done for their dominions. Historians may continue to argue about the origins of the fief, but around Paris Philip Augustus created feudalism.

Chapter 6

The Landed Wealth of Lay Aristocrats

As far as broad generalizations are valid, it can be asserted that the medieval economy around 1200 was primarily based on land. Agriculture, therefore, not industry, commerce, or finance remained the underlying source of wealth for aristocrats. For them the exchange of wealth was accomplished more through land than money. We have seen that at the end of the twelfth century it was still more common to exchange the fief (land) for military service than it was to buy this service with money, despite the existence of mercenary armies. Land, therefore, not money was the blood circulating through the arteries of the aristocrats' economy. This condition remains true for the region around Paris during Philip Augustus's reign despite the size and dynamism of the capital city itself. Although the urban conglomeration probably approached 50,000 inhabitants, making Paris the largest city of northern Europe, and its industrial and commercial activities as well as its political functions were growing vigorously, its urban money economy nonetheless had less effect on the landed economy of the surrounding aristocracy. We shall see, for example, that 52–66 percent of aristocratic wealth was in land as opposed to 1–10 percent in rents paid in cash (*cens*).

Since land involves agriculture, its economic value was realized by the peasants who worked it and harvested its fruits. Most peasants were unfree in some sense, that is, they were burdened with servitudes that inhibited their movement, marriage, and possession of property. Equally significant was the peasant's subjection to a lord. Just as a vassal who performed homage was subject to his lord in the regime of fiefs, so a peasant owed obedience to the authority of the vassal in whose fief the peasant's lands were situated. The lord-peasant relationship has often been labeled "seigneurialism," which French historians have been inclined to treat together with the regime of fiefs because of similar functions. Anglophone historians have tended to separate the two regimes because of the gulf between free and unfree status. In my study I have decided to eliminate consideration of peasants for practical reasons. Not that they are unimportant, but their treatment involves an intense and subtle reading of the documents that exceeds the practical boundaries of this study. In dealing with land, therefore, I shall attempt to treat not how wealth was created but, once created, how it was distributed among local lay and ecclesiastical lords themselves. Admittedly I am dealing only with the surface of the economy.

Aristocratic Land: Royal Surveys

Both king and churchmen took interest in the landed wealth of the aristocracy of the Paris region but for different reasons. We shall see in the next chapter that clerics and monks endeavored to investigate the land that they received from the aristocracy by gift, sale, and other means in order to acquaint themselves with what they had received. Philip Augustus sought to uncover the wealth that sustained the vassals who owed him homage and supplied his castles and feudal host. The previous inventories of the counts of Champagne had counted only homage and castle-guard, and the inventories that Philip inherited from Normandy posed only the two traditional questions of the number of knights enfeoffed and the services owed. Guillaume de Ville-Thierri's survey of the Vexin, however, proposed a new format. Not only did he inquire about these issues but, equally important, he asked what kind of landed wealth each royal vassal possessed. In the Paris region, for the *Scripta* surveys, these questions were applied to the eleven castellanies that we examined in Chapter 5. (The central castellanies found in the *Nomina* survey were not involved.)

Amassing a great amount detail, the investigators fortunately followed a standard format that allows us to codify the landed resources into three major categories as follows:

1. Landed property (p)
   - (pt) *terrae*, agricultural fields, meadows, vineyards identified by place-names
   - (pd) *domus*, houses
   - (pc) *castella, firmitates*, fortified houses
   - (pn) *nemora*, woods
   - (pm) *molendina*, mills
   - (pp) *pressoria*, presses
   - (pf) *furni*, ovens
2. Landed revenues (r)
   - (rc) *cens*, regular payments in money
   - (rk) produce, regular payments in kind
   - (ru) forest usage, forest customs
   - (rt) tithes

(rf) *fief-rentes*
(rm) money, cash sums
3. Jurisdiction (j)
   (jj) justice
   (jh) *hospites, hôtes*, serfs
   (jp) *pedagia*, tolls
   (jd) dowry or dower

The *Scripta* survey makes little effort to indicate the quantity of the items or to assess their value in money or in other fungibles. Only on occasion will the baillis note, for example, thirty arpents of arable land, fifty *sous* of *cens*, or rent, thirty *muids* of wheat, or twenty-seven capons. On one rare occasion Hugues de Gisors's fiefs were evaluated at sixty *livres*.[1] The chief concern was to identify individual items. These inventories are of little use in assessing the value of landed wealth in money, but they do portray the kinds of wealth on which an aristocrat relied to support his feudal obligations. In modern terms the inventories present not values in money but portfolios that distinguished categories of landed assets possessed by an aristocrat. By counting and reducing to percentages of individual items (totaling 652), I can present the following portfolio at the disposition of 272 aristocratic tenants in eleven castellanies.[2]

From Table 8, we see that agricultural lands (fields, pastures, and vineyards) were the aristocrat's greatest asset of wealth, representing 52 percent of the assets ascribed to him. Houses, both domestic and fortified (11 percent), woods (6 percent), and mills (4 percent) were the next most frequent properties. Among revenues, the *cens* in money (10 percent) and produce in kind (4 percent) were his most valuable sources. *Hôtes* (4 percent) and tolls (2 percent) were his most important jurisdictions. Equally noteworthy is the minimal importance of tithes (1 percent). Moreover, if we compare twenty-five tenants from the *Nomina* survey whose wealth was also recorded in the *Scripta* inventory, we find no striking differences (Table 8, row B). The knight of the *Nomina* survey enjoying sixty *livres* of income or more differed from his peers only by slight increases in his agricultural property (66 percent) and houses (13 percent), as might be expected. The comparison of aggregates (Table 8, row A totals) sums up the situation: to perform his services for the king, the knight relied on a portfolio that was overwhelmingly based on landed property (74 percent), relatively little on revenues (17 percent), and minimally on jurisdictions (8 percent).

Although the bailli Guillaume de Ville-Thierri and his imitators in Vermandois and the south offered few monetary evaluations of landed wealth, his colleagues Thibaut le Maigre, bailli of the Vexin, and Bernard de Poissy did provide monetary assessments of aristocratic wealth. In 1217, about the time that the

Scripta was compiled, they recorded an assessment of the fiefs of twenty-nine knights from the castellany of Poissy, which was copied into Register E.[3] Consisting of rounded figures, the assessments ranged from Robert de Poissy's 2,000 *livres* to Roger Revel's 15 *livres* and totaled 5,510 *livres* for the twenty-nine knights. Fortunately Robert's fiefs at Poissy were also described in greater detail in Register C and then in Register E in a format congruent with the *Scripta*.[4] They included unspecified properties at Poissy, land and a house at Béthemont "in fief and domain," woods at Marly (*Cruie*) with usage of live and dead wood, tolls at Maisons-Alfort for boats ascending and descending the Seine, his brother Amaury's holdings at Les Alluets-le-Roi (*Alues*), and three other subfiefs. Like his father Gace, Robert was a forester at Marly with rights of justice and hunting.[5] Little from this description, however, would account for the high assessment except the tolls at Maisons, which were located advantageously on the Seine and most likely were extremely lucrative. In this sense the Poissys were exceptional in benefiting more from the commerce on the Seine than from their landed assets. Nevertheless, Robert had already gained a reputation for his wealth. In the quota list for the battle of Bouvines he was called "rich" (*Robertus de Pissiaco Dives*), and he appeared at the battle with a squadron of five knights.[6] In fact all of the Poissys were well off. Robert's brother Amaury was assessed at 300 *livres* and their cousin Simon de Poissy at 800 *livres*, the second highest sum on the list. Since there was great disparity between the highest and lowest, the most representative figure would be the median value of 80 *livres*, which was a little more than the 60 *livres parisis* set as the standard in the *Nomina* survey. In fact, eleven of the twenty-nine knights of the castellany of Poissy appear in the *Nomina* survey as well, ranging from Robert de Poissy down to Hugues de Poissy (60 *livres*). The fact that all eleven of these knights in the *Nomina* list earned 60 *livres* or more according to the assessments of the fiefs of the castellany of Poissy offers confirmation that the knights of *Nomina militum* indeed possessed revenues of 60 *livres* or more, just as the list claimed.

Aristocratic Land: Ecclesiastical Charters

Churchmen were likewise motivated to record an aristocrat's wealth because the aristocrat was their principal benefactor. I shall examine aristocratic donations in greater detail when I turn to aristocrats' dealings with the church in the next chapter, but the monastic charters nonetheless present a reckoning of landed wealth fully congruent with the format of the royal surveys. The archives and cartularies of churches have long been the most abundant source for modern historical studies of aristocratic lands, but at the outset it is essential to recall that they record not what the aristocracy held at the time, as was recorded in the royal surveys, but what was alienated. It is therefore of interest to compare the ecclesiastical statistics (a portfolio of properties alienated to the church) with the findings of the king's agents (a portfolio of properties retained, most of which were held in fief). When the aggregate results of the 1,729 charters assembled for this study are juxtaposed, important differences emerge. As noted above, the aggregated portfolio of aristocrats was based mainly on property (74 percent of the inventoried items), with much smaller contributions from revenues (17 percent) and jurisdictions (8 percent). In contrast, 45 percent of the charters pertained to landed property, 55 percent pertained to landed revenues, and 10 percent pertained to jurisdictions (Table 8, rows A and C). Because the data of the charters and the royal survey are commensurate, I have constructed a second and more refined portfolio of aristocratic wealth drawn from 610 of the 1,729 monastic charters. The 610 charters are from aristocrats located closest to the eleven castellanies involved in the royal inventory and contain 832 transactions. (The following percentages are percentages of the total number of items instead of percentages of charters.) The resulting portfolio of wealth the aristocracy disbursed to the church differs even more from the portfolio of the properties the aristocracy retained. Landed property accounted for only 40 percent of the portfolio of alienated property, contrasting starkly with the 74 percent of the king's findings (Table 8, rows A and D). Revenues accounted for 46 percent of the portfolio of alienated wealth, and jurisdictions for 14 percent, compared with 17 percent and 8 percent in the portfolio of retained wealth. It is evident that the elements of the two portfolios differ in their proportions. The aristocrat was relatively slow to part with his agricultural lands, given that they constituted 52 percent of the portfolio of retained properties but only 27 percent of the portfolio of alienated properties. He was relatively quick to part with both his *cens* (10 percent of the retained portfolio versus 18 percent of the alienated portfolio) and his produce in kind (4 percent versus 13 percent). Jurisdictional rights, especially tolls and dowries and dowers, also constituted a larger share in his donations than in the properties he retained. Equally noticeable is that 9 percent of his donations came from tithes, which were a miniscule percentage of his holdings, a point that will be discussed in the next chapter. As for the transactions in landed property (40 percent of alienations), we should keep in mind that not all were donations. As is reported in Table 2, roughly 35 percent of all alienations were sales, gift-countergifts, or exchanges, which will be discussed later. They are included here because they represent property transferred to the church even though the aristocracy received remuneration. In comparing these two portfolios of retained and alienated properties the important conclusion nonetheless remains: the aristocrat of the Paris region was relatively reluctant to alienate his landed property but was relatively generous with his revenues.

These comparisons raise an ultimate question: Are the landed resources identified in the feudal surveys the same as those destined for churches? Throughout both sets of records we find property held "in fief and in domain."[7] The customary distinction posits domain as supporting the lord and his family and fiefs supporting his vassals, but it remains unclear how this distinction bears on the properties, revenues, and jurisdictions that were alienated to the churches. To approach this question, I have considered a sample of properties. While the compiling of the feudal inventories appears to be systematic, and the coverage of properties in monastic charters is fortuitous, overlap between the properties mentioned in the two sources does occur. In the eleven castellanies around Paris surveyed in the *Scripta de feodis*, 247 persons belonging to 216 families held fiefs directly from the king. Of these 216 families, at least 77 families, or 36 percent, may also be identified in contemporary monastic charters.[8] In the feudal surveys of these 77 families, thirteen properties are named that are also named in transactions with the churches. The fact that only thirteen properties of these 77 families are named in both sources shows at first glance that there is little overlap between the portfolio of the feudal surveys and the portfolio of alienated properties. Nonetheless, this small sample of thirteen properties does offer a close-up of the transfer of aristocratic wealth to the churches. In one instance, an entire property was bestowed on an abbey.[9] In three other cases only parts of the property (fields, meadows, *champarts*) were sold to the monasteries before the properties themselves were declared in the survey.[10] On the other hand, revenues from nine properties, including *cens*, produce, and tithes, were offered to churches either before or after the survey.[11] It is significant that six of these revenues were tithes. The alienation of nine revenues compared to four properties in the sample confirms the same propensity of aristocrats that we found in the larger portfolio—that they were more willing to part with revenues than with landed property.

Pierre du Thillay, a Local Landlord

A micro-study of the landed wealth of Pierre du Thillay serves as a conclusion to this investigation of aggregate statistics. We have seen that Pierre was *prévôt* of Paris in 1200, then royal bailli at Orléans around 1202, before Philip Augustus transferred him to Caen in Normandy, where he served as bailli until 1224. Before his entry into royal service, Pierre was a knight at Le Thillay outside of Gonesse to the north of Paris, direct vassal of Mathieu le Bel, and subvassal of the abbot of Saint-Denis. In 1208 he made major donations to endow the Hôtel-Dieu of Gonesse. What is of interest about Pierre is that he not only provided two charters (dated 1208 and 1215) of the lands and revenues he bestowed on the Hôtel-Dieu, but he also drew up a landbook accounting for the land and revenues he retained for himself at Gonesse, Tessonville, and Sarcelles. Pierre's detailed accounting confirms my conclusions from the aggregate statistics of the Paris region. He kept for himself nearly three times the land that he gave to the Hôtel-Dieu (148.3 hectares versus 52 hectares) but dispensed nearly three times as many revenues as he reserved for himself (31 *livres*, 14 *sous* versus 10 *livres*, 19 *sous*, 7.5 *deniers*).[12]

The Landed Economy

Our two portfolios of aristocratic wealth from the *Scripta* survey and the charters, of course, do not uncover the agricultural products that produced that wealth. Certain aspects of the portfolios are clear enough. Agricultural land and vineyards, for example, produced crops and wine that could be marketed. Regular payments in money (*cens*) furnished cash that was immediately expendable. However, the classifications of property (fields, vineyards, mills . . .), revenues (payments in money and kind, tithes . . .), and jurisdictions (justice, tolls . . .) do not reveal exactly what generated wealth. The closest insight into specific crops and products is furnished by the category of payments in kind, even though the category constituted only a fraction of the two portfolios—only 4 percent of the wealth retained in the *Scripta* survey and 13 percent of the wealth donated in the charters (see Table 8). Despite the small contribution of revenues in kind to the two portfolios, a closer analysis of the category yields results on the main features of aristocratic landed wealth (see Table 10).[13] While the contours of this wealth do differ according to what was retained and what was given away, the two portfolios can be combined to show what was finally at the aristocrat's disposal. The conclusion is striking: aristocrats were first and foremost involved in growing wheat. Of the revenues in kind that were retained, 32 percent were in wheat, and of the revenues alienated, 66 percent were in wheat, for an average of 59 percent (83 of 141 total revenues in kind). By comparison, oats, which were shared with horses, constituted only 9 percent of the production, as did wine (9 percent). Although not dominating, these two commodities nonetheless clearly were present. The remaining items—bread, capons, cocks, eggs, pork, herring, even salt and chestnuts—are mostly haphazard and only of anecdotal interest. These conglomerate statistics can be confirmed from the concrete example found in the charters and landbook of Pierre du Thillay. That his major crop on his lands around Gonesse, Tessonville, and Sarcelles was wheat is indicated by his donation of sixty *setiers* to the Hôtel-Dieu of Gonesse, as contrasted with donations of three *setiers* of oats and three *setiers* of barley. He also possessed vineyards at Deuil-la-Barre (2 arpents) and at Gonesse (23.75 arpents), as well as ample supplies of bread (fifteen loaves each year), capons (forty-six), and geese (twenty), which were barely discernible in the aggregate statistics.[14] These last items were much more plentiful at his Norman estates where they were known by the customary term of *regarda*.

The overall picture provided by the *Scripta* survey and the charters, and confirmed by Pierre du Thillay's records, does not, of course respond to questions normally posed by historians who study the medieval economy.[15] The limitations imposed by my personal choice preclude important issues both in time and space. By confining the focus to fifty years, or three generations at most, my exploration cannot detect secular change in cycles of production or secular increases and decreases in prices, not to speak of permanent shifts in the nature of the economy. Although brief, even my selected period was not stable within itself. For example, in 1194 Rigord, the royal chronicler, reported unprecedented rain and hail that destroyed fruit trees, vines, and harvests. The next year, the dearth drove prices of a *setier* of wheat to sixteen *sous* in Paris, and a *setier* of barley to ten *sous*. A *setier* of *méteil* went for thirteen *sous* and a *setier* of salt for forty *sous*. The floods continued into 1196 when the Seine broke down the bridges at Paris. In 1198 the chronicler remarked that harvests had not been sufficient for three years. By 1202–3, however, the price of wheat had descended to a range between five *sous* and six *sous*, eight *deniers*.[16]

By limiting my research to the Paris region, moreover, I have not been able to detect differences from other regions or interactions with other regions. Nonetheless, since the time of the Roman conquest, the Paris region was reputed for the quality of its wines, and because of its fertility the *plaine de France* to the north of the city became known as the breadbasket of Paris. At the center of the *plaine* in Gonesse, Pierre du Thillay competed with the Cistercians of Chaalis in growing wheat. By the 1220s the monks had constructed at Vaulerent an immense stone barn (still standing) that measured 1,650 square meters on the ground, one-third the floor plan of Notre-Dame at Paris. Ten kilometers to the north of Gonesse, this imposing structure was filled with harvests reaped from 1,000 arpents of arable land that more than doubled the size of Pierre's 400 arpents.[17] Further south was Paris, which sheltered 50,000 inhabitants. The largest city north of the Alps, it was the veritable motor of the regional economy, like Toulouse to the south. Our sources are limited as to the many ways the capital doubtlessly dominated and transformed the economy of the region,[18] but it would be safe to speculate that many aristocrats of the region like Pierre du Thillay competed with the neighboring monks to supply the millers, bakers, vintners, and tavern keepers with the bread and wine to feed the capital.

Chapter 7

The Landed Wealth of Churches
and Monasteries

Lay Donations to Churches

Land undergirded the economies of the king and aristocracy by means of fiefs. It also supported the church for the construction of edifices and the maintenance of religious communities. Before the eleventh century, however, one of the leading processes for distributing land was through despoiling and plundering. Enjoying the advantages of castles and military force, aristocratic lords frequently usurped the lands of their weaker neighbors, most notably the properties and revenues of churches. (The despoiling of churchmen is better known to us than the despoiling of their lay neighbors because churchmen possessed the written means to advertise their losses through chronicles and charters.) During the eleventh century through the peace and truce of God movements, churchmen began to persuade rapacious lords through peaceful means to return these lands. Land now circulated more often as gifts and less by plunder. The principal inducements to the transfer of land were spiritual benefits that earned salvation in the world to come or threats of eternal punishment, means we shall explore more fully in the following chapter. Concurrent with this peaceful transfer of property, churchmen also persuaded the aristocracy to perform these acts through written charters, which, when sealed, were increasingly accepted as authoritative instruments of transfer. By the beginning of the twelfth century, the written charter had become the chief vehicle for land circulation.[1]

Since the act of writing was performed exclusively in Latin, its exercise fell to the clergy who enjoyed the clear monopoly over literacy. Now considering land more as an economic than a religious resource, the clergy began to take advantage of their literacy to administer their lands by means of written records. They began to document their lands in charters and papal confirmations and draw up accounts of their resources, which they persuaded the laity to accept as authoritative records. Of equal importance, by the beginning of the twelfth century they had begun to collect these charters and documents in books called cartularies. At that time Abbot Suger of Saint-Denis was one of the principal innovators who took advantage of written records to administer the resources of his abbey, although the monks of Saint-Denis did not actually produce a full cartulary (the *Cartulaire Blanc*) until the second half of the thirteenth century. By our period, that is the turn of the twelfth and thirteenth centuries, scores of ecclesiastical cartularies had appeared in the Paris region.[2] From these I have selected thirty-two of the most prominent and accessible, and from them I have collected 1,729 charters that recorded land transactions between the regional aristocracy and the churches and monasteries.

In this period, moreover, the aristocracy constituted the primary source from which the churches and monasteries increased their lands. The charters that record these acquisitions therefore remain both unsurpassed in documenting the growing landed wealth of the churches and monasteries in the Paris region and in providing a brilliant spotlight on the aristocracy's contribution to this wealth. The extraordinary munificence of the aristocracy combined with the church's claim to be an immortal corporation (it rarely alienated its wealth) rendered the church the richest landholder by the end of the Middle Ages. The church's wealth, however, is not my concern here; rather, I want to explore the behavior of the aristocrats who were the principal contributors to that wealth.[3] My first goal then is to record the transfer of this wealth and to reserve for the next chapter the spiritual benefits that were realized from this transmission, recognizing always that these benefits were never absent from consideration.

Commercialization

Because of this abundance of documentation historians have long been preoccupied with this transfer of wealth. Availing themselves of anthropological insights, they have privileged the role of gift exchange and the reciprocal bonds that it created.[4] The church received material wealth for which it conveyed corresponding spiritual benefits to the donors as well as equally important associative benefits. In becoming the friends of the neighboring monks and their saints, the aristocrats enjoyed their protection. In recent years, however, historians have noticed a basic shift in this paradigm of gift exchange that began about 1150 and continued for the two centuries that followed. The shift has been illustrated with precision by Richard Keyser in an analysis of the charters of the Champenois abbey of Montier-la-Celle.[5] He has shown that while the transfer of wealth in land persisted, the exchange took on a commercial character that minimized the emphasis on piety of the earlier period and its accompanying reciprocity. The transactions were increasingly expressed in the form of contracts or binding agreements that were precise and systematic. Pure gifts were replaced by sales and exchanges that were expressed in monetary terms.[6] Furthermore, the predominance of the king and the high nobility of the earlier period was replaced by simple knights as the principal donors. This was accompanied by a decrease in the size of the land parcels that were conveyed. Testaments effective after death began to replace charters of conveyance between parties still living. And the accompanying spiritual benefits were expressed increasingly in standardized formulas and contractual obligations. Montier-la-Celle was situated on the outskirts of the city of Troyes, the site of one of the principal fairs of Champagne that supplied the commercial nexus for northern France. Perhaps for this reason the charters of Montier-la-Celle were precocious in reflecting the shift to commercialization. Likewise, the burgeoning commerce of Paris doubtlessly hastened the commercialization of the Parisian countryside. In this shift of paradigms, our chosen period of 1180 to 1220 lies at the beginning and thus displays the attributes of a transitional epoch.

A significant marker of this seismic shift between pious reciprocity and commercialization is the appearance of a new kind of charter transferring wealth between the aristocracy and the churches and monasteries. Previously the charter was issued by a prelate (a bishop or abbot), a great lord, or the king. To establish its authenticity, not only was the charter sealed by the prelate or secular lord, it also recorded numerous witnesses at the end. The actual transfer in the charter was preceded by an elaborate preamble that expressed the donor's remorse for injuries to churches, regrets for past sins, fears of illness and impending death, and finally and most important, the need for the church's intercession. Take, for example, a charter from 1138 issued by the chapter of Chartres in a dispute with a certain Ours de Meslay:

> Whatever regards the honor and common utility and peace of the poor of the church is a necessary thing which ought to be attended to with utmost care by those who seek this with right intention, lest they lose their work and effort in silence, and lest what they have labored for mightily, for the sake of the peace and harmony both of those present and those to come, become a nursery of discord and contention through negligence and forgetfulness. On this account all of us brothers of the chapter of Chartres wish to make it known to the present and the future that the lord Ours de Meslay unjustly was receiving tolls in a certain part of the land of Notre-Dame at *Belsia*. Summoned by the canons, he was unwilling to come to justice and finally was excommunicated. However, by the mercy and inspiration of God, having a change of heart, he came to the chapter and there acknowledged his guilt and placed a pledge of satisfac-

tion into the hands of the dean and afterward, with many witnessing it, both clergy and laity, humbly placed his pledge on the altar of Notre-Dame.[7]

Now compare the following charter from our period, drawn from thousands of others like it, which illustrates how much has changed:

> I, Ferry de Gentilly, knight, make known to all the faithful of Christ to whom the present letter has come that I have given in perpetual alms (*elemosinam*) to the church of Saint-Martin-des-Champs all the tithes in grain and in wine and in other things that I had at Gentilly and whatever rights of justice I held in the territory of *Tour*, and the winepress, and the rent which Gautier *Cent Mars* and his brother Revenuz de Louveciennes and Petronille la Bigote de Vitry owe me each year at the feast of Saint Remy. And so that it remains firm and established I have strengthened the present charter with my seal. Done this year of grace 1217, the month of October.[8]

We notice immediately that the charter is abbreviated, an explanatory preface is lacking, and its terms are expressed precisely in a stereotyped formula and standardized vocabulary, all suggesting a commercial transaction. The religious motivation is either omitted or shortened to "in perpetual alms." The witnesses have disappeared and the seal has become the sole authentication of the charter. The concluding formula, "so that this remains firm and established I have strengthened the present charter with my seal," or other phrases to the same effect, was never omitted, even in the copies that survived only in the cartularies where the seal could no longer be present. Bishops and abbots continued to issue such charters, although at times the bishop was replaced by his *officialis*. Great lords became less numerous, but most significant was the appearance of the knight who took their place and issued the charter in his own name and sealed it with his own seal.

Compensation to Aristocrats

The quasi-totality of the transactions contained in the 1,729 charters consisted of the conveyance of property and landed revenues from the aristocrats to churches and monasteries. For that reason the ecclesiastics naturally included these charters in their cartularies. From this massive transfer of property, however, not all was lost to the aristocracy. As shown in Table 2, more than one-third of the transactions were accompanied by compensation for the aristocrat through sale (22 percent), countergift (8 percent), exchange (3 percent), or pledge (2 percent). When dealing with sale (*venditio, emptio*), the canon lawyers of the church largely had adopted the principles of Roman law in which sale was simply defined as the exchange of a thing (*res*) for a sum of money, with the stipulation that the price be declared. Bernard of Pavia, who summed up the current canon law in his *Summa decretalium*, quoted Justinian's *Institutes* by stating succinctly, "Buying and selling is contracted after a price has been agreed upon. . . . The buyer is held to pay the price and the seller to hand over the thing."[9] Without a price, then, there was no sale. Evidently this requirement was familiar to the clerical scribes, because, with few exceptions, they name the price in the transaction. The monks of Saint-Denis, for example, paid as much as 300 *livres* for a meadow and 60 *livres* for vineyards, and the chapter of Notre-Dame de Paris 250 *livres* for land at Orly.[10] Most prices for arable land, meadows, and vineyards ranged from 5 *livres* to 200 *livres*. Occasionally prices were accompanied with the number of arpents, which permits calculation of the price per arpent. Saint-Victor paid Guillaume de Poissy 5 *livres* per arpent for fourteen arpents of arable land at Lay (L'Haÿ-les-Roses) and 10 *livres* for another arpent in the same locale.[11] Houses sold for as much as 50 *livres*.[12] Other figures that stand out include 431 *livres* for part of a grange bought by Saint-Germain-des-Prés, and 400 *livres* for a mill bought by Saint-Denis.[13] Remembering that 60 *livres* was a standard annual revenue for a knight, these maximum prices suggest how much churches were willing to pay for real estate. More impressive were the prices churches offered to redeem tithes. The 1,000 *livres* that the chapter of Notre-Dame paid for both the grange and tithes of Soignolles-en-Brie is difficult to interpret because the property is conflated with the tithe,[14] but the regularity with which churches paid sums ranging from 200 to 400 *livres* for tithes is noteworthy.[15] A sum of 80 *livres* was offered for a *cens* that produced an annual rent of 5 *livres*,[16] and 90 *livres* for an annual rent of three *muids* of grain.[17] Purchases of jurisdictions ranged from 120 to 200 *livres*.

Closely related to sale was the practice of combining a gift with a countergift, which accounted for 8 percent of the transactions. For example, Gobert de Thourotte donated to the abbey of Ourscamp his mill for which the monks gave him 200 *livres de beneficio*, and Ansel de Brunoy gave a *cens* on land to Saint-Lazare in return for 2 *livres de caritate*.[18] The presence of the phrases announcing *beneficium* and *caritas* suggests that the monks sought to distinguish these contracts from the legal requirements of sale despite the economic similarities. At times the countergift combined money with property, which would apparently compromise the transaction as a sale,[19] but in the majority of the gift-countergift transactions the counterpart was in money, which rendered them an economic substitute for sale. In any event, this type of transaction was more modest than sale because rarely did the countergift exceed 100 *livres*. Another recourse that compensated for loss of property was exchange, which performed the same economic functions as gift-countergift. In Roman law *permutatio* was the exchange of one item for another. Following the Roman lawyers once again, Bernard of Pavia explained that exchange (*permutatio*) was governed by the same conditions as sale, differing only in that in a sale a sum of money is given for a thing received, whereas in an exchange something is given for some other thing received.[20] In the charters the equivalent term was *commutatio* and usually involved comparable entities (land for land, tithes for tithes), but money supplemented the transaction as well.[21] Exchange is at times apparent only from the nature of the transaction, thus introducing uncertainty into its identification. It accounted for only 3 percent of the transactions between churches and aristocrats.

A final technique for converting land or revenue into sums of money was the pledge or gage (*vadimonium*) by which the aristocrat temporarily bestowed property or revenue upon a church in exchange for a loan of money. When the time expired, the money was returned to the church and the pledged item to the aristocrat. This contract constituted 2 percent of all transactions. Again following Roman law, Bernard of Pavia called the pledge a *pignus*, which placed a thing in obligation for a debt, providing greater security to the creditor because it was easier to recover a thing than to act against a person. The creditor was held to return the pledge when the debt had been paid in full.[22] In practice the pledge consisted not only of property but also of jurisdiction or revenues from *cens* and produce, but usually it was based on tithes.[23] The sums of money obtained ranged from 5 to 420 *livres* with 20 to 199 *livres* most frequent.[24] On occasion the length of time was stipulated at three years, on others at five or six years,[25] but most transactions mentioned no time span. In this context, the pledge functioned economically as a loan without time limits with the tithe serving as collateral or security. It provided aristocrats opportunity to raise money temporarily. Along with sale and gift-countergift it converted landed assets into cash.

The sample of 1,729 charters demonstrated that the aristocrats received compensation in 35 percent of their transactions with churches and monasteries (Table 2). A classification of transaction types does not, however, capture the types of wealth transmitted by the aristocrats. For that reason it became necessary to conduct a second and more refined survey of aristocratic wealth, for which I selected 610 ecclesiastical charters containing 832 transactions. For this survey, the format adopted was the same as that used for the survey of aristocratic lands drawn from the *Scripta de feodis* (described in Chapter 6 and summarized in Table 8, row A). From the thirty-two cartularies, it focused on those originating nearest the eleven castellanies of the *Scripta* survey. (As with the *Scripta* survey results, percentages are of total transactions.) We can now determine with better detail what kind of wealth the aristocrats alienated by sale, gift-countergift, or exchange with churches, as is seen in Table 8, row Db. Property (14 percent of all transactions), with agricultural property clearly at the head (10 percent), was preferred; revenues (7 percent of all transactions) were divided fairly evenly between money rents (*cens*, 2 percent), tithes (2 percent), and payments in produce (3 percent).[26] All jurisdictions combined accounted for a minimal 3 percent of transactions.

The 22 percent in sales combined with 8 percent in gift-countergifts (Table 2) did not attain the level of 60 percent in sales found in the charters of Montier-la-Celle at the end of the thirteenth century,[27] but the figures show that the Paris region was headed in that direction. More significant, the ubiquity of monetary evaluations, not only in sales (dictated, of course, by the Roman-law definition of sale) but in the other contracts as well, is another sign of the commercialization doubtlessly prompted by the influence of Paris as a commercial center. Except for the money of Provins to the east and the Norman money to the west, the overwhelming currency quoted for the region was the *livre* of Paris, divided into *sous* and *deniers*. That the prices frequently reached the hundreds of *livres* is also noteworthy. Around 1209 the knight Jean de Montmirail, future candidate for sainthood, contemplated departing on the Albigensian Crusade. To finance his venture, he arranged the sale of a portion of woods in the Cambrésis for 7,000 *livres*, but his wife would not consent to the sale.[28] The potential buyer, be he an ecclesiastic or a layman, is not mentioned, but the price is astronomical when compared to those of the contemporary charters. It may simply be, therefore, the exaggeration of his hagiographer writing after 1217, but the fact that the figure was even proposed suggests that it was not beyond the realm of credibility. It also suggests that the commercialization of the countryside was well under way. Although the full story is not revealed, the influence of Paris is nonetheless strongly suggested.

Pure Donations to Churches

In contrast to sales, gift-countergifts, and exchanges, donations or pure gifts offered aristocrats only nonmaterial benefits in return. From the sample of 1,729 ecclesiastical charters transferring wealth, 65 percent recorded donations (Table 2). In my second and refined survey of 610 charters involving 832 transactions, this figure rises to 74 percent (Table 8, row Da). This high percentage of gifts corresponds with the findings at Montier-la-Celle where gifts in the decades up to 1220 typically represented 70 percent or more of the monks' acquisitions, thereafter declining relative to purchases and exchanges.[29] The refined survey also allows us to see more detail both in what type of wealth the aristocrats conveyed and in how they conveyed that wealth. While in the aggregate study of

1,729 charters, 45 percent of aristocrats' charters concerned property, in the second and refined survey, property constituted 40 percent of all transfers to the church, and property conveyed specifically as a gift constituted 26 percent of all transfers to the church. The basic component of landed donations was agricultural land (18 percent of all transactions), followed by forests (4 percent), houses (2 percent), and mills and presses (1 percent each). When aristocrats conveyed property, in roughly two of every three instances they conveyed the property as a pure donation (26 percent gift versus 14 percent sale, gift-countergift, or exchange). Revenues accounted for 46 percent of aristocrats' transactions, while revenues conveyed specifically as gifts accounted for 37 percent of all transactions. These gifts consisted of *cens* (16 percent of all transactions), produce (10 percent), tithes (7 percent), and forest use (3 percent). When they conveyed revenues, in roughly four of every five instances they conveyed the revenue as a gift (37 percent gift versus 9 percent sale, gift-countergift, or exchange).

A not-uncommon practice was to combine donations with sales. For example, in 1210 Geoffroy d'Orgenoy gave three-fifths of certain designated lands to Saint-Victor but sold the rest for 90 *livres*. Raoul de Cornillon sold eight arpents of land to Chaalis for 45 *livres* and donated the *cens* on the land. Eudes de Touquin gave one-third of the revenues of Rozay-en-Brie to Notre-Dame de Paris, but sold the remainder for 300 *livres*.[30] In this hybrid form of gift giving the seller acquired both the proceeds of the sale as well as the spiritual benefits of the donation.

Testaments

Donations, then, were by far the most common means for transferring this massive wealth from the aristocracy to the church. The vast majority of these gifts were considered by the canon lawyers to be donations between living persons (*donationes inter vivos*). Following Roman law, Bernard of Pavia defined a donation in general as "a gift motivated by generosity" (*liberalitas*), and he divided such donations into two kinds. The first kind is between living persons, "when the thing that I give I wish another to have rather than myself." The second kind arises *causa mortis* (because of death), "when I wish to have the thing rather than another, but I prefer someone other than my heir."[31] (In other words, a donation because of death is a gift of a thing I would like for myself but prefer to give it to another rather than to my heir, who would normally inherit it.) Thus, after treating donations *inter vivos*, he turned to donations *causa mortis* and testaments. "A gift because of death is customarily executed by testament."[32] Most charters of donation, making no mention of death, clearly were understood as donations *inter vivos*. About 20 percent of donation charters, as we shall see, did mention a religious motive of penance, which was an implicit consideration of the eventuality of death. Even these charters, however, were not *causa mortis* unless they were included in a formal testament. It appears, therefore, that nearly all of the donations to churches mentioned in the ecclesiastical charters were considered to be gifts between living persons because they were not formally part of a testament. Before turning to the evidence of testaments proper, one special case treated by Bernard of Pavia in his section on donations *inter vivos* should be noted. Bernard concludes the section remarking that "those things that are given to a cleric in consideration of a church are acquired by that church, and those things which are given to a cleric in consideration of his person are counted among the goods of the cleric himself."[33] This meant that all donations of the former type were eventually absorbed by the churches of these clerics because the cleric was not permitted to keep the gift in his own right.

In Roman law the testament was the normal means for providing for the succession of heirs and for the distribution of property after death. During the reign of Philip Augustus most of the surviving examples, called *testamenta*, come from either the monarchy or from those at the highest level of society. Before departing on the Third Crusade in 1190, the king himself drew up his *testamentum*, which was, for the most part, an ordinance (*ordinatio*) regarding the administration of the realm during his absence. Approaching death in 1222, he drew up a second testament in which he distributed his property and alms.[34] In 1225 Louis VIII used his testament to provide for the succession of his sons.[35] When the young king Henry of England fell sick in 1183, he employed his last will to engage Guillaume le Maréchal to fulfill the king's crusading vow. In 1219 at the point of death, Guillaume himself, now a great baron of the realm, drew up his testament, which he authenticated with his private seal. His biographer detailed provisions to his children, gifts to churches, alms for the poor of London, and distribution of robes for newly dubbed knights at Pentecost.[36] Those close to the Capetian court, such as the families of Gautier the Chamberlain and Barthélemy de Roye, likewise availed themselves of such instruments.[37] Aveline, lady of Chevreuse, petitioned the king and his baillis to execute the last will of her husband Guy de Chevreuse.[38]

Scattered throughout our sample of charters are occasional references to the existence of *testamenta* now lost. At the highest level of aristocratic society, Jean, count of Beaumont, as he "labored in grave illness," drew up his testament and assigned the archbishop of Reims, who was a relation through his wife, and the prior of Saint-Léonor and four knights to be its executors, "just as it was drawn up in a charter," but the charter (the testament itself) has not survived.[39] Similar references are found for Pierre, count of Auxerre,[40] and Guy, the firstborn son of Jean, castellan of Noyon,[41] as well as for lesser figures such as Pierre the

Marshal and Adam de Clacy in the cartulary of the Hôtel-Dieu of Paris,[42] and Adam de Châteaufort[43] and Hugues *de Robore*.[44] When Guillaume de Poissy, son of Gace de Poissy (d. 1189), donated alms amounting to forty *sous* from the *cens* of his lands at Lay to Saint-Victor of Paris, the canons copied the details into their cartulary. Guillaume accounted for forty-one tenants who paid him a *cens* of twenty-five *sous* on fifteen lands and twenty-seven vineyards. In addition, another six tenants owed fifteen *sous* for the *cens* on his press. Thus a virtual *censier* was transformed into a testament confirmed by Guillaume, bishop of Paris (1220–23), and by Guillaume de Poissy's feudal lord, Mathieu de Marly.[45] A more common format was the legacy (testament *de legato*) of the deceased knight Jean de Andresel, son of Aubert, transcribed by the monks of Barbeau in 1226. Rather than the sources of his alms, he listed the legatees. By his reckoning he distributed twenty-five *livres* among forty-four recipients, eight of whom received twenty *sous* or more and thirty-six of whom received five *sous* each. The abbey of Barbeau was favored with one hundred *sous*, which explains why Jean's testament is found in the abbey's cartulary. These sums were assigned on the *cens* of Andresel, and his wife Agnès gave her assent.[46] This testament was little more than a detailed account of one of the 132 donations of *cens* revenues that constituted 16 percent of all transactions in the sample of 610 charters.

Tithes and Jurisdictions

The mention of tithes above (9 percent of transactions in the 610 charters) calls for further comment. The tithe (*decima*, meaning literally one-tenth, but often variable in practice) was an ecclesiastical tax imposed on the revenue of parishioners for the benefit of the parish priest, his church, and the bishop. In the early Middle Ages these tithes were widely usurped by aristocratic laymen who acted as patrons of the individual churches, so that the tithe became part of the aristocrats' customary revenues. In the eleventh century, reforming churchmen opened a campaign to recover these tithes by excommunicating all laymen who held them. The procedure for absolving the excommunicated required the layman to hand the tithes over to the bishop who then returned them to the church, but most often not to the original parish church but to a neighboring monastery, who then assumed the place of the former lay patron.[47] This campaign, however, was only partially successful. Many aristocrats still enjoyed this income at the turn of the twelfth and thirteenth centuries. Although tithes were a negligible part of the aristocratic portfolio in the royal survey (six cases, or 1 percent, most likely an artificially low number due to a reluctance to report them), they were a significant part of the portfolio of wealth distributed to the church. They appeared in 17 percent of the 1,729 ecclesiastical charters (Table 2) and accounted for 9 percent of transactions in the refined sample of 610 charters (Table 8). Mostly tithes were donated, but churchmen also were willing to buy back tithes for high prices, as has been seen. Rarely do the ecclesiastical authors of charters restate the churchmen's reforming efforts. An exception was Maurice, bishop of Paris (1160–96), who declared that Guy d'Aunay had unjustly held the small tithes of Leudeville and Vert-le-Grand for a long time, for which he was excommunicated. Guy had turned them over to Maurice's predecessor as bishop, Thibaut (1143–57), and received absolution. Maurice eventually conferred them on Sainte-Geneviève.[48] (In the *Scripta* survey, a Guy d'Aunay, undoubtedly a descendant of the Guy who had held the tithes, reported on his holdings at Vert-le-Grand and made no mention of tithes.)[49] Similarly, in 1198 Robert de Chennevières resigned the tithes of Fontenay to Eudes, bishop of Paris, who then conferred them on Saint-Victor,[50] and in 1219 Jacques, bishop of Soissons, reported that when Emiardis and her husband Mathieu *de Doy* sold to Saint-Jean-des-Vignes the tithes of Verberie for 240 *livres*, they had first turned over the tithes to the bishop who in turn invested the abbey with them.[51] The majority of the gifts and sales of tithes, however, went directly to monasteries who duly noted them in their cartularies. The fact that fief-holders were reluctant to report their tithes in the *Scripta de feodis*, while tithes constituted a not insignificant part of wealth given or sold to churches in the ecclesiastical charters, suggests that aristocrats may have considered them as toxic assets to be abandoned.

Tithes were not only unlawful for laymen. They could also be awkward for churchmen. Churchmen could possess them legally, but when they served as pledges, questions were raised. Since we have seen that these pledges were de facto loans, the holding of tithes by the party lending money, in this case a monastery, could be considered unlawfully usurious. Pledges remunerated the holders of the loan without diminishing the principal, which was one of the classic definitions of usury. In 1163 Pope Alexander III declared them *mortgages* (dead pledges) and usurious because they did not, in fact, reduce the principal. The theologians at Paris, however, considered pledges based on tithes to be an exception to the rule on *mortgages*. Because the laymen's retention of tithes was unlawful, churches could accept them, even temporarily, as pledges, with the justification that stolen goods were being recovered, and thus churches were not thereby obligated to deduct the gain from a pledged tithe from the principal that had been loaned.[52] For that reason the monastic charters openly reported the pledges based on tithes but were more reticent about pledged property, *cens*, and produce, which did not qualify for the exception.[53]

After considering the transfer of aristocratic wealth to churches through property and revenue, it remains to consider the last category, jurisdiction. Of the 1,729 charters, 10 percent concern the transfer of jurisdictions, while in the refined sample of 610 charters, the transfer of jurisdictions accounts for 14 percent of the transactions. Of this 14 percent, most transactions were donations (11 percent donations versus 3 percent sales, countergifts, and exchanges). Of these donations of jurisdictions, the largest part came from great lords like the counts of Beaumont and the lords of Poissy who granted monks exemptions from their tolls on the Oise, the Seine, and elsewhere.[54] The small number of donations of jurisdiction over *hôtes* (2 percent of transactions), of course, does not represent the large role played by the peasants in the landed economy of the aristocracy.

Cash

One of the most obvious signs of commercialization is, of course, the flow of cash. That 22 percent of charters recording transactions between churches and aristocrats consisted of sales meant that the churches were willing to pay considerable amounts of cash for property and revenues. The gift-countergift transaction likewise included money on occasion and increased the cash that churches paid out. Rarely do the charters express the motives for selling property, but in 1209 Arnulf, knight of Magny, admitted that he was "burdened with debts and compelled by necessity" to sell a revenue of wheat from his tithe barn to a certain canon of Noyon. (The price however, is not mentioned.)[55] Similarly, Rericus and Simon d'Ozouer (Ozouer-le-Voulgis) sold tithes and arable land to Saint-Victor for 140 *livres* to pay their debt to the Jews.[56] We can imagine, however, that such motivation was, in fact, frequent.

If there was a growing stream of cash flowing from the churches to aristocrats, the reverse is less evident. Overall, donations of cash to churches (distinct from donations of revenues) accounted for only 2 percent of transactions in the refined sample of 610 charters.[57] In two rare charters, the monks of Saint-Denis sold properties for substantial prices. A charter of 1201 records their sale of forests to Milon de Lévis, Guy de Lévis, and Renaud de Cornillon for the sum of 800 *livres*. In 1207, they sold sixty arpents of woods to Anseau de Garlande, lord of Tournan, for 70 *livres*.[58] And in an unusual glimpse into the commercial scene, in 1220 *Ansellinus Silvaticus*, knight of *Cremonsis*, gave in alms to Sainte-Geneviève a revenue of 16 *livres* in the money of Provins. The 16 *livres* was derived from a revenue of 80 *livres* drawn from the carriage of wine at Provins and the fairs there. The fief of the carriage of wine had been granted to him by Countess Blanche of Troyes and her son, Count Thibaud.[59]

Since the majority of transactions recorded in the ecclesiastical cartularies consist of gifts from the aristocracy to the church, another rare charter from the cartulary of Notre-Dame de Paris stands out because at first glance it appears to declare a gift from a church to an aristocrat. In 1219 Étienne, dean of the chapter of Paris, gave to Étienne de Hautvillers (*Alto Villari*, near Chevreuse) one hundred arpents of woods at Vernou (Vernou-la-Celle-sur-Seine).[60] The reason for this unaccustomed liberality becomes clear by the stipulation that the aristocrat engaged himself to make the land arable and return an annual *cens* of four *deniers* per arpent in the money of Provins. Apparently the transaction was actually an exchange of land for its cultivation that allowed the church to exploit the land by collecting a rent. In effect the church was monetizing its landed resources.

Women

In addition to approving transactions by their husbands, fathers, sons, and brothers, adult women also joined these men as the principal actors and donors in transferring landed wealth to the church. In the sample of 1,729 charters women participated in 15 percent of all the transactions (Table 2), but this figure includes their special intervention in consenting to the disposal of their dowries and dowers as well as their own initiatives. In the refined survey of 610 charters, female initiatives in sales, gift-countergifts, and exchanges were negligible, but women were responsible for 15 percent of the gifts (or 11 percent of the total 832 transactions).[61] In Table 9, I have compared the 612 gifts of men and women in the 610 charters. As Table 9 shows, their profile of giving varied little from that of men, though it had a slightly heavier emphasis on revenues over property and jurisdictions. The chief difference was that men were twice as prone to include tithes among their donations.

Guarantees

After the aristocrat and the individual church agreed on the terms of the transfer of wealth by sale, exchange, or gift, the next concern was to assure that the contract be respected in the future. Because the church was an immortal corporation and intended to keep its assets in perpetuity, this assurance was vital for both the immediate and distant future. In practice, three sets of parties could be called upon to assure future compliance: guarantors, family, and feudal lords. Guarantors (*fidejussores* and *plegii*) were employed in other regions to enforce the contract but were rare in the Paris region,[62] but the other two groups were regular features around Paris. As has been noted, over half of the 1,729 transactions in the monastic charters (57 percent) included consent of the family (*laudatio parentum*) to the transaction (Table 2). By this means churchmen sought to forestall future noncompliance or objections from the immediate heirs.[63] Who

precisely was available for consent, of course, depended on the existing composition of the biological family. We remember from Table 3 that the most frequent
were the living spouses of the seller or donor (66 percent), followed by the
children (39 percent) and siblings (37 percent). These groups appear in all possible combinations, but the most frequent was husband and wife alone (34 percent)
and husband, wife, and children (24 percent). Uncles, aunts, cousins, and spouses
of the children, particularly of daughters, were also employed, but in config-
urations too complex to measure. Mothers and fathers were present in only
7 percent of charters, mainly to support sellers and donors without progeny.
The wife's consent was privileged by canon law if the transaction involved her
dowry or dower. The complexity of combinations has puzzled historians who
have studied them,[64] but what is clear is that churchmen demanded explicit
consent from the conjugal or nuclear family to protect their future interests. In
all likelihood those consenting to the transaction were already agreed upon before the charter was drafted, because there are few records of dissent. For example, in 1193 when Dreux Buffe gave to Val-Notre-Dame his woods *de
Guarreria*, his brother Gautier refused consent, but later relented.[65] Likewise
Gilduin de Chantereine resisted a gift of tithes to the abbey of Josaphat by his
father Robert, a knight, but had come to terms with the gift by 1217.[66] Apparently, the future saint Jean de Montmirail also had difficulty obtaining the agreement of his family to his charitable ventures. When he proposed to sell his
woods in the Cambrai region for 7,000 *livres* to finance his participation in the
Albigensian Crusade, his wife objected. Later, his eldest son refused consent to
Jean's gift of a house at Gandelu to the abbey of Longpont and dispatched his
sergeants to prevent the abbey from collecting the small tithes there.[67] By emphasizing the nuclear family, however, churchmen protected themselves only
for the next generation. It would be more difficult to assure the distant future.
After the family, further consent was required from the feudal lord if the property or revenue was enfeoffed. This *laudatio domini* is found in 22 percent of all
charters (Table 2). The guarantees of family and lords were applied to all transfers of wealth without distinction but with special emphasis on gifts and sales.

Litigation

Despite these precautions disputes nonetheless arose that required resolution
through litigation. Reports of such settlement appear in 14 percent of the 1,729
charters (Table 2). The subjects of dispute were varied and often multiple, but
they chiefly concerned lands, particularly woods, and tithes, and there is a discernible concentration on customs, tolls, and rights of justice. The judges in such
cases were recruited from prominent leaders both clerical and lay—bishops, their

officiales, abbots, feudal lords, and the king—but traveling papal judge-delegates and royal baillis were notably active because as local agents they were expressly assigned to deal with local issues. With so many cases to choose from we can offer only a few examples to illustrate the variety of issues involved. For example, in a case of 1206 between the abbey of Saint-Jean-en-Vallée and Geoffroy de Lèves over a mill and woods, the latter refused to show for the trial and lost the decision, being judged *in contumacia*.[68] Or in 1219 the abbey of Saint-Nicolas de Ribemont brought suit against Jean de Dercy, a knight, to recover arable land. The damages awarded the abbey included sums not only for losses suffered but also for the legal expenses of bringing suit.[69] The resolution of the disputes was largely subjected to arbitration (*compromissum*) entrusted to judges or to designated panels of clerics and knights, with the royal baillis being particularly busy. The judgment was frequently preceded by a formal inquest (*inquisitio*) to determine the facts of the case, and the final decision was expressed in summary terms.[70]

Only occasionally do the customary proofs of ordeal by battle or water appear in the decisions. In 1192, the abbot of Morigny contested the knight Arnulf d'Auvers over the mills *de Vaus* in the presence of four royal baillis, including Philippe de Lévis. When the witnesses could not agree, a judicial duel was proposed, but both parties declined, doubting the outcome of the ordeal, and agreed on a peaceful solution: the abbot offered Arnulf forty *livres* for renouncing his rights over the mills.[71] Similarly, in 1214 the brothers of Ourscamp abbey brought to the king a complaint against the men of Tracy, saying that they had burned properties of Ourscamp, killed animals, and broken game enclosures. Three baillis appointed by the king to conduct an inquest brought together eight men of Tracy whom public opinion most suspected of the injuries and many *persone nobiles* of the regions, including Jean, lord of Nesle, Raoul his brother, Aubert de Hangest, and the three castellans of Noyon, Nesle, and Coucy. The eight men of Tracy swore they had nothing to do with the injuries, but "when it became clear to the eight men that their promises did not suffice," the men of Tracy added that, if the brothers suffered injury in the future and if they or their sons or other relations were held suspect by the king or by his baillis, they would voluntarily prove their innocence before the bishop of Noyon by undergoing judgment by the water ordeal.[72]

Even when more details are offered, it is difficult to assess what was gained or lost by each party without a thorough knowledge of the context. For example, among the unusual number of litigations found in the cartulary of Saint-Denis are several involving the lords of Montmorency. But only a thorough study of them would reveal how these lay barons were able, in fact, to encroach on the lands and rights of the abbey.[73] Since virtually all of the available cases of litigation are preserved in ecclesiastical archives (even those presided over by the king),[74] we may be permitted to assume that those decisions favorable to the church have survived, or at least those which contained significant elements favorable to the church involved. A great number of the decisions were expressed simply as "amicable" resolutions (*pacem amicabiliter fecerunt*), and doubtlessly they were favorable to the church that recorded them. This conclusion is reinforced by the frequent acquittals of property and revenues that the laity accorded to the church at the end of the charter. For example, in 1194 Mathieu, lord of Marly, and his wife Mathilde mediated a controversy between the abbey of Sainte-Geneviève and Garnier de Rocquencourt over the tithes of *Malo Nido*. A *forma pacis* was obtained in which Garnier acquitted to the abbey his rights over the tithes in return for eight *livres*.[75]

One particular case illustrates the essential features of this litigation. In 1201 Geoffroi, bishop of Senlis, Geoffroi, prior of Saint-Arnould de Crépy, and Hervé, prior of Sainte-Marguerite d'Elincourt, arbitrated between the priory of Saint-Leu d'Esserent and Enguerran de Boves in a dispute over the tithes that Simon, lord of Clermont, gave to the church. After a diligent inquest the judges came to an agreement (*compositio*) whereby Enguerran resigned the tithes to the church. For Enguerran's benefit, however, the monks made him a countergift *de caritate* of thirty *livres* for the crusade for which he was preparing. He did, in fact, take part in the Fourth Crusade, but like Simon de Montfort returned home after the decision to attack Constantinople.[76]

Chapter 8

The Kingdom of Heaven

Penance and Purgatory

To compensate for the vast transfer of wealth from the aristocracy to the church, churchmen may have proposed financial remuneration or the benefits of association, but they always offered an ultimate recompense: entrance to the kingdom of heaven.[1] Without doubt the most fundamental doctrine with which churchmen inculcated the laity was that of salvation. After death all souls were destined to one of two fates, either eternal bliss in heaven or eternal punishment in hell. The prospect of the last judgment in which Christ would return to earth to separate the blessed from the damned and assign them to their final fate was the most publicized drama of the Christian religion, portrayed vividly on the portals of the cathedrals at Paris and Chartres. The scenario would take place at the end of time at the sound of the trumpet. All of the dead would arise from their tombs to receive their just judgment and be assigned their destiny. But what is the fate of these souls before the last judgment? To answer this question churchmen began to consider an intermediate state between heaven and hell eventually called purgatory, where those who were not incurably damned would purge their sins before becoming fit to enter heaven. The elaboration of the scenario of purgatory was the work of the theologians at Paris in the second half of the twelfth century. All Christians were required to cleanse themselves through penance of the sins they had committed on earth. Penance consisted essentially of contrition, confession, and satisfaction or good works. Contrition involved sorrow for past sins; confession, the oral acknowledgment of them to priests; satisfaction through good works included not only righteous behavior but also giving to the poor and especially to churchmen whose prayers for the eventual salvation of those in purgatory would thereby be elicited. What sins had not been cleansed in one's lifetime would be purged after death in purgatory. It was this final aspect that played the primordial role in the relations between churchmen and the laity. If the laity would give to the clergy, the latter would pray for them, to hasten their passage through purgatory. In the theologians' hands the relationship acquired the commercial aspects of a contract: gifts to the church were converted directly into prayers for the departed in purgatory. By the close of the twelfth century the theologians at Paris had clarified the procedure of purgatory by which the donations of the faithful generated calculable merit that could be tallied up to reduce the donor's time in purgatory and hasten his or her entry into heaven.[2] Giving to the church became an efficacious means for obtaining eternal salvation.

In Chapter 7 we examined an eleventh-century charter from Chartres in which churchmen had prefaced a layman's donation with an elaborate preamble that expressed the donor's remorse for injuries to the church at Chartres.[3] Another elaborate charter from early in our period (from 1181) described the agreements between Henri *de Hunvilla* and his family and the abbey of Saint-Jean-en-Vallée, also at Chartres. Henri had given the monks half of his mill for the salvation of his soul and of his ancestors, for which the monks had given him the sum of forty-three *livres* of Chartres in gratitude (*tanti beneficii gratia*). A few days later Henri fell from his horse and broke his leg. Fearful of dying, he was brought by his wife and two daughters accompanied by their husbands to the monastery where he was received into the monastic community. After Henri's death, his wife and sons-in-law reconfirmed the original gift with an additional gift of eleven *livres*.[4]

We have also noted how radically these charters had changed at the turn of the twelfth and thirteenth centuries.[5] Not only do the clerical scribes abbreviate the charters and cast them in businesslike terms with stereotyped terminology and formula, but to express religious motivation for the donations, they employ terse phrases like "for the salvation of my soul and my ancestors" (*pro salute anime mee et antecessorum meorum*) or "burdened [by sins] at the point of death" (*laborans in extremis*). Occasionally the clause could be linked specifically to sickness or bodily injury (as was the case with Henri *de Hunvilla*), or to childbirth, to youthful sins or to making amends for injuries against the church.[6] Rare was the positive avowal of Ida, widow of Jobert de Ribemont, who declared that she was "in the prime of life, with a sane mind" and was moved not by fear or remorse but "by divine goodness, for the remedy and salvation of my soul and of my ancestors."[7] Others proposed burial at the beneficiary church[8] or the establishment of chaplains or canons to sing masses for the departed, for which the phrase "to perform my anniversary" (*anniversaria*) became a frequent clause.[9] More substantial was the foundation of chapels,[10] often in castles, of which Guillaume de Garlande at Livry and Guy de Chevreuse are notable examples,[11] and, of course, the endowment of entire churches or monasteries.[12] One noticeable attractor of gifts from the Poissy, Mauvoisin, and Île-Adam families

was the devotion to Saint Thomas Becket, the recent and popular saint now en-
shrined in Canterbury in England.[13] A final example is the charter of Ferry de
Gentilly of 1219, which I have cited in the preceding chapter to illustrate the businesslike brevity adopted by churchmen. Ferry's sole enunciation of religious
motivation for his gift is the use of the term *elemosina* (alms), that is, gifts specifically designated for the church.[14] This was the most frequent religious marker
in the charters of our period. What I have not previously noted regarding these
succinct and stereotyped expressions is that they preface no more than 20 percent of
the refined sample of 610 charters collected from the churches and aristocrats
of the Paris region.[15] Most of the transfers of landed wealth were therefore recorded without mention of religious motivation. This omission does not imply
absence; it merely indicates that in the short and businesslike charters the salutary
motivation was assumed by the clerical scribes. Salvation doubtlessly remained
the chief motor for the massive transfer of wealth. Even if prayers, masses, or
churches were not mentioned, the spiritual credit that accrued to the benefactor
was understood.

Obituaries

If the clergy sought guarantees through guarantors and the consent of family
and of feudal lords, the laity likewise needed reassurance that the clergy's prayers
and intercessions would continue into the future. One solution was to inscribe
the name of the benefactor on a calendar at the date of his or her death to re-
mind the clergy to offer prayers or masses for the donors. Designated *anniversaria*, these inscriptions were frequently mentioned in the charters. By the end
of the twelfth century and culminating later in the thirteenth, contemporane-
ous with the appearance of the cartularies, these calendars with their lists of
names were copied into codices called obituaries or necrologies. Throughout
their development the obituaries were overwhelmingly populated by the names
of the clergy, but gradually they began to introduce the lay members of their
own families and finally other laymen who were not relatives but who had benefited the church. Early inclusions consisted naturally of the powerful in
society—kings and their families and the high aristocracy, in addition to bishops and abbots—but eventually lesser lords and knights were enrolled in notices, together with descriptions of their material donations. Through these
obituaries the laity were assured that they were not forgotten after death. Seven
of these obituaries survive from the Paris region.[16] Their fortuitous emplacement
and uneven coverage exclude the compilation of aggregate statistics, but they
are sufficient to illustrate the obituaries' function in serving the religious needs

of the aristocracy. Fortunately, all but one of these churches (Saint-Léonor) also produced a surviving cartulary, which permits comparison of their contents.[17]

The chapters of Notre-Dame de Paris and of Saint-Victor, just outside the walls of Paris, produced the most developed obituaries of the region that included not only the date and name of the laity but also a description of his or her legacy. It is clear that Notre-Dame favored castellan families who had members already established in the chapter. For example, Hervé de Marly (dean ca. 1184–92) recruited his brother Mathieu for donations, and Geoffroi de Chevreuse (canon) relied upon his relative Guy de Chevreuse to fund his own anniversary.[18] Hugues Clément (dean 1195–1216) and his brother Eudes (archdeacon) were instrumental in providing anniversaries for their brothers Aubry, Henri, and Robert (Aubry and Henri were royal marshals), as well as for their parents, Robert (a tutor of the young Philip Augustus) and Hersende.[19] Other royal knights and familiars of Philip Augustus's court included Gautier the Chamberlain, Barthélemy de Roye, Guillaume de Garlande, and Guillaume des Barres.[20] Of some thirty lesser knights who gave or sold property to Notre-Dame, however, only Adam de Montfermeil and Pierre du Thillay, the royal bailli, were recognized in the obituary.[21] (None of Adam's donations precisely detailed in the obituary can be found in the cartulary, and the obituary listed no donations of Pierre du Thillay.)[22] Saint-Victor's obituary was later and followed Notre-Dame's in format and in contents. The favored families of the Marlys, the Chamberlains, the Royes, Garlandes, Barres, and Chevreuses, already in the obituary of Notre-Dame, reappeared in Saint-Victor's. They were joined by the barons of Montfort and the butlers of Senlis, as well as the Montmorencys, the cousins of the Marlys.[23] From the lower strata more knights like Mathieu le Bel, Frédéric de Palaiseau, and Ferry de Massy and his wife can be detected.[24] What distinguishes the obituary of Saint-Victor is a close connection between the obituary and the cartulary. Over half of the donations described in the obituary can be found in the cartulary.

Outside Paris the monasteries employed a simpler format but enlarged the lists to include more knights. The rich Cluniac house of Saint-Martin-des-Champs kept a massive obituary that was simply a list of names arranged according to date of death. Alongside the powerful and favored families, which now became common,[25] they added the counts of Beaumont and the castellans of Île-Adam.[26] The knights included Guillaume de Nanterre, Guillaume d'Aulnay, Guillaume *de Cornellon*, Baudouin d'Andilly, Ferry de Gentilly, and Robert de Chennevières; over half of their donations can be found in the abbey's cartulary.[27] The Cistercian houses likewise adopted the abbreviated format. To the north of Paris the monks of Val-Notre-Dame were mindful of their powerful neighbors, the Beaumonts, Montmorencys, and Île-Adams, as well as the Montforts and Garlandes,[28] but they also reached down to Guy de Thourotte, Robert *de Fresnes*, Enguerran de Trie, Jean *de Montecaprino*, Dreux de Pierrefonds, Agnès de Franconville, and Gérard de Vallangoujard.[29] Despite the fragmentary nature of their cartulary, there was a high correspondence with the obituary. To the south of Paris the Cistercian women of Porrois (Port-Royal) also favored their powerful neighbors, the Montforts, Chevreuses, Marlys, and Lévis.[30]

The Cistercians of Val-Notre-Dame and Porrois relied heavily on neighbors for their patrimony, but other monasteries were, in fact, foundations of single families. The Premonstratensian canons of Joyenval, for example, owed their creation to the royal chamberlain and favorite Barthélemy de Roye. Their obituary illustrates this dependence by the massive representation of the Roye family coupled with their marriage alliances to the Montforts, Nesles, and Créspins. Understandably, the important neighbors—the Marlys, Poissys, and castellans of Neauphle—were also included.[31] Similarly the Cluniac priory of Saint-Léonor was founded by the counts of Beaumont to serve as their necropolis, and its obituary faithfully reflects this dependence. Count Mathieu was responsible for the principal buildings and his wife Aliénor and brother Jean made important donations as well.[32] Cartularies and obituaries, therefore, form a working partnership in documenting the great legacies of the aristocrats as they increased the patrimony of the neighboring churches and monasteries around Paris.

Mortuary Rolls: Guillaume des Barres

The obituaries supplied prayers for the deceased from a single community on their anniversary date. Since the ninth century, however, monks had employed a system whereby this service could be shared with other houses by circulating mortuary rolls. The names of the departed brothers and sisters were inscribed on a roll of parchment that was carried to other establishments that acknowledged receipt of the names and engaged the community to pray for the souls of the deceased, thereby multiplying the prayers for the dead. Guillaume des Barres, arguably the most celebrated knight of his day, was one of the first laymen to benefit from this system when the Fontevraudist nuns at the priory of Fontaines-les-Nonnes near Meaux created a mortuary roll on his behalf. During his lifetime Guillaume had made donations to other monasteries in the Paris region such as Saint-Maur-des-Fossés, Val-Notre-Dame, Chaalis, Saint-Victor, Yerres, and Saint-Martin-des-Champs.[33] He had also founded an anniversary of his death with a gift of fifty *livres* for the construction of Notre-Dame at Paris, where he was remembered as a "vir nobilis, miles strenuissimus."[34] In 1182, however, he had made gifts to Fontaines-les-Nonnes for the soul of his father, and his gifts continued through 1194 and 1214.[35] Perhaps it was the fact that he had placed his daughter Amée as a nun at Fontaines that persuaded him finally to choose the house for his own burial. When he died there on 23 March 1233 he had put on the monks' habit as a "brother for aid" (*frater ad succurrendum*). Although this house was apparently female, his acceptance may be explained by the origins of Fontevraudists who began as a mixed order of men and women.

Throughout the month of April the nuns worked to prepare an elaborate mortuary roll, which they had richly embellished with illuminations, doubtlessly executed by the flourishing artistic ateliers at Paris.[36] Under a protective cover, the first parchment of the roll pictures Guillaume on his deathbed garbed in a Fontevraudist habit, flanked on one side by two clerics and three nuns and the bishop of Meaux, who absolves him, and on the other side by two weeping nuns, perhaps relatives of the deceased because above them is the Barres heraldry. Over the scene Christ sits in majesty surrounded by two angels, one of whom presents Guillaume's soul to the Savior. The four evangelists conventionally frame the entire picture.[37] The second leaf of parchment transcribes a formal encyclical letter addressed to all future recipients that opens with a theological discussion of redemption and continues with a eulogy of Guillaume's chivalric and Christian virtues. It announces his date of death and requests prayers for the salvation of his soul. Further, if the recipients also desire prayers for their recent dead, the nuns of Fontaines were prepared to reciprocate. The letter concludes by commissioning a certain Roger, whom Guillaume had raised from childhood, to act as the roll's courier on its intended journey. Those who receive Roger during passage are requested to provide his necessities.[38] To these initial parchments (measuring eighteen centimeters in width) are sewn one to another fifteen additional parchments of various lengths, which add up to a total of ten colossal meters. Undoubtedly attached one by one as needed, these blank sheets provided space for the recipients to record the house, the date, and acknowledgment of prayers as the roll traveled from church to church.

On 3 May 1233 the roll departed from the cathedral of Meaux on a journey that covered much of northern France, with travels extending as far north as Boulogne-sur-Mer on the Channel, and east to Laon and Troyes, south to the Auxerrois and Loire, and west to Chartres and Rouen.[39] At the center it crisscrossed back and forth in a maze of directions passing through Paris at least three times, but rarely stopping at the same church. It covered all of the establishments at the same location with amazing rapidity (five foundations at Meaux, ten at Sens, twelve at Paris) and then moved quickly on. With the exception of Chaalis, all of the churches that Guillaume had formerly favored were likewise visited. Although the courier Roger did not keep the sheets in chronological order, he nonetheless recorded that on his return on 27 August 1233, that is, in four short months, he had visited 220 churches and monasteries. Each community dutifully reported its name and the date and acknowledged that it would pray "for his soul and for the souls of all future deceased so that they might rest in peace through the mercy of God." At times they specified which office would be devoted to the anniversary and requested reciprocal prayers for their own deceased whom they named. The indefatigable travels of Guillaume des Barres's servant had succeeded in multiplying massively the intercessions for his master's soul. Undoubtedly Guillaume's long service as a seasoned warrior had generated the need for such intercession.

Not all of the roll was devoted to piety, however; the nuns of Fontaines had permitted the Barres family to display its heraldry and had depicted the deceased knight in full armor. Within the encyclical letter, Guillaume is eulogized as a "sweet and noble lord" as well as a counselor and defender of the kingdom of France who opposed its enemies with his own body. He was above all princes and barons in fidelity, distinguished in blood, of handsome face, tall, with strong, well-formed members, but also humble, eschewing pride, wise. He was a just man who nourished the poor. Unbelting the sword of knighthood, he donned the habit of the nuns' order with humility and renunciation of wealth.[40] Always addressing Guillaume as "nobleman" (*nobilis vir*), the recipients occasionally echo similar epithets: "leader and defender of the French" (*Francorum dux ac defensor*) or the "flower of knighthood" (*flos milicie*). The sisters of Fontaines-les-Nonnes thus found little problem in accommodating the worldly pomp of a celebrated knight within the humble walls of their cloister.

Monastic Conversion

Guillaume des Barres's deathbed conversion to the monastic life designates another portal into eternal life in addition to the giving of alms. Since the unfree (meaning mostly the peasants) were excluded from the clergy by ecclesiastical law, it is obvious that the aristocracy was the major source of clerical and monastic recruitment. (The townsmen were only beginning to enter.) Most of the hundreds of monks and nuns enrolled in the obituaries, therefore, belonged to aristocratic families. We have already noticed that families like the Marly-Montmorencys, the Chevreuses, the Garlandes, and the butlers of Senlis, whose genealogies are among the better known, populated the secular clergy of Notre-Dame. My survey of 1,729 transactions from thirty-two cartularies of the Paris region, nearly all of which were monastic, nonetheless contains only forty cases of conversion to the monastic life. This touches barely 2 percent of the hundreds of aristocrats whose transactions are recorded in the sample. The forty conversions detected in this survey clearly do not account for the hundreds if not thousands of clerics, monks, and nuns in the churches and monasteries of the Paris region. Obviously the ecclesiastical charters were underreporting.

The forty conversions divide equally between monks and nuns, even though houses with female religious produced only four of the thirty-two cartularies in my sample.[41] Although Guillaume des Barres's deathbed conversion was spectacular, he was followed in this sample by five others. The brothers Pierre *li Vermaus* and Renaud de Coucy were assigned a place of burial at Ourscamp. The conversion of Manasses, "miles de Escencuz," was recorded in the cartulary of Saint-Jean-des-Vignes. Robert, knight of Mézières, and his wife, with their end drawing near, were received by the monks of Saint-Nicolas de Ribemont *ad surrurendum.*[42] Only three examples surface of oblates, that is, children under age, offered by their families to be reared by monks, thus suggesting that regulations against the practice were beginning to take effect. One of the rare cases, for example, involved Pétronille de Montfort, whose mother Alix funded her upbringing at Saint-Antoine until the age of twelve.[43] At that age, if Pétronille decided to become a nun, the foundation would be doubled. Most transactions, however, involved the endowment of adult men and women. At times the candidates made provisions for themselves, like Bouchard de Montmorency at Val-Notre-Dame and Mathilde de Chaumont at the Hôtel-Dieu de Paris.[44] Most often it was the family that provided for their children or siblings. Many examples survive of fathers and mothers endowing daughters, at times with the mother's dowry or dower.[45] Eudes de Tiverval and his wife gave to Porrois on the condition that the nuns accept one of their several daughters.[46] The kind of wealth that was offered did not differ from the donations in general. Landed property was preferred, but rents in produce followed closely. As a way of divesting toxic wealth, tithes were frequently employed. Since the overt sale of entry into a monastery was judged to be a crime of simony according to canon law, the terms of the transactions avoided the language of quid pro quo, adopting instead the concise and businesslike language of the various types of donations.[47] The articulation of penitence is virtually absent.

In the sample of forty converts, many of the prestigious families appear. Besides those mentioned already at Notre-Dame de Paris were the Montmorencys, the Île-Adams, and the Meulans. The prominent female houses of Yerres and Porrois to the south attracted recruits from the nearby Montfort, Andresel, and Chevreuse families. Well over three-quarters of the recruits, however, came from the lower ranks of the aristocracy, whose names were recognized only locally. In saintly reputation, none of the knights of the Paris region were as celebrated as Jean de Montmirail who came from the neighboring Champenois region, enlisted with the Cistercians of Longpont in the Soissonais, and, as we shall see, nearly achieved the crown of full sainthood.

Crusaders

One particular means for performing satisfaction for one's sins was to make a pilgrimage, that is, to take a journey to the tomb of a saint to venerate his or her relics. Popular pilgrimage sites for France were Saint-Jacques in Spain and Saint-Gilles in Languedoc, but the aristocracy around Paris left little evidence in their charters of undertaking such voyages. A rare exception occurred in 1198, for example, when Dreux, lord of Cressonessart (Cressonsacq, dép. Oise), gave woodland to Ourscamp before he departed for Saint-Jacques. If, perchance, he died on the trip, he promised to double the gift.[48] The most prestigious pilgrimage destination was, of course, the tomb of Christ, but since 1187 it was no longer accessible because of the Muslim capture of Jerusalem.

When an aristocrat entered a monastery, he renounced both the world and his warrior profession, but churchmen offered an alternative that allowed him to retain his profession, shed blood, and still be admitted to the kingdom of heaven. This was the crusade, which for over a century had dispatched military expeditions to the Near East to liberate the holy places from the hands of the infidel. The crusader was an armed pilgrim who enjoyed both temporal and spiritual privileges but, most of all, an indulgence. Although the exact meaning of the indulgence was ambiguous, it promised release from penance if not remission from all sins, as many crusaders believed.[49] Three major crusades materialized during Philip Augustus's reign: the Third Crusade (1189–91) which was led by King Philip, King Richard of England, and Emperor Frederick; the Fourth Crusade (1202–4) of Pope Innocent III that was intended for the Holy Land but ended at Constantinople; and the Albigensian Crusade, which Innocent preached against the Cathar heretics in the south of France (1209–18).

Recruitment for these three expeditions from the Paris regions can be perceived in the sample of 1,729 charters, of which 107 contain explicit mentions of crusaders. This figure represents about 6 percent of the charters, which is better reporting than the 2 percent alluding to entry into monasteries. Although the notices are explicit only about pilgrimages to Jerusalem or against the Albigensians, in most cases the dates of the charters indicate which crusade they joined.[50] Half of the crusaders (forty-eight) accompanied Philip Augustus to the Holy Land in 1189–91 and included prominent lords such as Raoul, count of Soissons, Guy, castellan of Coucy, Guillaume de Garlande, Adam, castellan of Île-Adam, Guy de Chevreuse, and Philippe de Lévis. Ten names may be linked with families appearing in the feudal surveys (the *Nomina* and *Scripta* surveys), but the remainder were from the lower echelons of the aristocracy. Unfortunately, we have little corroboration of these figures from independent sources because Philip Augustus's expedition, unlike Richard's, did not attract the attention of major chroniclers. What is best known is that the king brought with him on the Third Crusade the chief barons of his father's generation, such as the counts of Flanders, Blois, and Clermont, and left them buried in the Palestinian sands at the siege of Acre in 1191.

Recruitment for the Fourth Crusade was opened on 28 November 1199 with the charismatic preaching of the priest Foulques de Neuilly to the knights assembled for a tournament at Écry in Champagne (the present Asfeld, dép. Ardennes) where hundreds received the cross.[51] The sample of 1,729 charters captures 31 from the Paris region (or one-third of the 107) including the well-known figures Simon, lord of Montfort, Mathieu, count of Beaumont, Guy, castellan of Coucy (once again), Mathieu de Marly, Robert de Mauvoisin, and Enguerran de Boves.[52] From this group the chronicler Geoffroi de Villehardouin identified all but two (Beaumont and Marly) as having taken the cross at Écry, mentioning as well the lesser knights Ferry and Jean d'Yerres, who are likewise found in the charters.[53] He noted that that they came "from France," but there were many others in the charters who were not included in his narrative. Of the remaining twenty-two names from the charters, only two appear in the *Nomina* survey.[54]

To promote the campaign against the Albigensians Pope Innocent extended the scope of the crusading indulgence to include all the benefits of a pilgrimage to the Holy Land for those who spent only forty days fighting the heretics no farther away than southern France.[55] Despite this incentive, only thirteen crusaders can be found in the sample of 1,729 charters. They naturally included Simon de Montfort, the renowned military leader, and his brother-in-law Mathieu de Montmorency.[56] Of the remaining eleven, only Simon de Chavigny and Robert de Poissy may be found in the *Scripta* survey.[57] The Montfort-Montmorency allies receive the attention of Pierre, the chief chronicler of the crusade from the nearby abbey of Vaux-de-Cernay,[58] but even the rich cartulary of that monastery, patronized by the Montforts, identified no crusaders from the local area.[59] This low representation from the Albigensian Crusade is all the more surprising since, unlike the Third Crusade, it occurred during a peak period of charter production.

Whatever the deficiencies of the documentation, the steady and clearly delineated decline of crusaders in the sample (forty-eight crusaders to thirty-one to thirteen) suggests a waning interest among the aristocracy in the Paris region, despite the greater coverage accorded by the chroniclers Geoffroi de

Villehardouin and Pierre des Vaux-de-Cernay. The monastic charters nonetheless uncover a sector of the crusading armies hitherto hidden to historians. The royal inventories and chroniclers reveal great lords and bannerets who contributed to the Capetian victory at Bouvines, and the chroniclers likewise noticed these men on crusade, but the charters provide the names of around seventy lesser knights from the region of Paris who soldiered off to fight the infidel and heretic.

Since the 1,729 charters were drafted with the purpose not of identifying crusaders but of recording the transfer of wealth, they are more useful in uncovering the financing of the crusades. Moreover, since the monks were less interested in the money that they gave away than the wealth they gained, they record very few cases of direct subventions. On the eve of the Fourth Crusade in 1202, not on the eve of the Albigensian Crusade, Simon de Montfort acknowledged the receipt of forty *livres* "freely and charitably" offered by the prior of Saint-Thomas d'Épernon and certified that it was voluntary, not of necessity.[60] Similarly in 1193 Mathieu de Montmorency declared that when Raoul *Pilatus* bestowed vineyards on Val-Notre-Dame, it was with the condition that if he wished to go to Jerusalem, he could seek both permission (*licentiam*) and aid (*auxilium*) from the church.[61] Direct loans to crusaders and pledges were also rare.[62] For example, Payen *de Soisy*, about to depart to Jerusalem in 1192, gave his tithes at Soisy-sur-Seine to Saint-Spire de Corbeil as pledge for eighty *livres*. This arrangement acted as a loan because presumably he would repay the sum on his return.[63] Most transfers, however, follow the customary schema of transactions as seen in Table 11 (gifts, sales, gifts-counter-gifts). Of immediate benefit to the departing crusader was the sale of assets for cash, which accounted for 9 percent of the transactions. The aristocrat thereby pocketed sums ranging from forty to one hundred *livres* for the sale of property and revenues.[64] Closely comparable were gifts and countergifts, which account for another 13 percent of the cases. For example, Guillaume de Garlande gave to Saint-Martin-des-Champs his woods at Noisy in exchange for one hundred *livres* (*de caritate*).[65] Well over half of these exchanges were for money, ranging from seven to one hundred *livres*, rather than for property or revenues in kind, which would be of little use on the expedition. The overwhelming remainder of cases (70 percent) consisted of pure gifts to the church with no material compensation. When Gace de Poissy (d. before 1193), for example, was on his deathbed in the Holy Land at an undisclosed date, he was unusual in giving to Abbecourt forty *sous* in cash.[66] As would be expected, the kind of wealth that crusaders bestowed on the church did not differ from what they were accustomed to give in alms, but the proportions of their giving had changed. They gave less property (31 percent of the crusaders' transactions as shown in Table 11 versus 45 percent of all transactions as shown in Table 2) and about the same in revenues (51 percent versus 55 percent) and more in jurisdiction (17 percent versus 10 percent). Of particular interest was their reluctance to dispose of their toxic assets of tithes (5 percent versus 17 percent). A good number of the donations were delayed until after the death of the crusader.[67] Before departing on crusade Mathieu de Marly confessed that he was unable to assign a gift of fifteen *livres* of revenue from Meulan since he was impeded by important affairs.[68] The most significant aspect of these gift charters, however, is the striking absence of compunction. The few exceptions stand out. When the knight *H. Baloeir* gave his tithes to Saint-Corneille de Compiègne in 1189, for which he received a countergift of fifty *livres*, he confessed that he had held them unjustly.[69] Before departing against the Albigensians in 1216 Guy de Pierrelaye resigned to Saint-Denis the woods of *Hosseel*, which he and his father had held unjustly.[70] And Jean de Trie and Nicolas de Bazoches in 1189 and Count Mathieu de Beaumont in 1206 made formulaic requests for their souls and placed their gifts on the altar.[71] The overwhelming majority of donations were made in the contractual language of business transactions with not a word of contrition. As departing crusaders, nonetheless, these warriors were undoubtedly aware that they were pilgrims whose souls benefited from the penitential indulgence. In the end, the church's immeasurable recompense for their sacrifice was, as always, speedy salvation.

Templars and Hospitalers

Conversion to the monastic life provided the knight with one set of advantages; recruitment to the crusade, another. It was probably predictable that the two institutions would eventually be joined, thus producing the crusading orders, the Knights Hospitalers and the Knights Templars. As monks they took the vows of obedience, chastity, and poverty, subjected themselves to monastic rules, and were organized into communities that resembled monasteries, but they were also knights fully equipped and trained to wage war. Their mission was to protect pilgrims to the Holy Land and when necessary to defend the holy places against the infidel. The earliest were the knights of the Hospital of Saint-Jean de Jerusalem whose order was founded during the First Crusade at the end of the eleventh century at the hospital in the holy city, but they were never as numerous as the knights of the Temple at Jerusalem. Around 1120 a group of knights from Champagne led by Hugues de Payns and residing in Jerusalem decided to associate themselves with the regular canons who served the church of the Holy Sepulchre. When the great Cistercian abbot Bernard of Clairvaux composed the treatise *In Praise of the New Knighthood* (*De laudibus novae militiae*) for their guidance, he became their special patron. He promoted the ideal of "Christ's knight" (*miles Christi*), which, in turn, valorized the mission of the monk-crusader. Although their reputation as knights was redoubtable, they suffered heavy losses against Saladin in the battle of Hattin (1187) but later contributed to the taking of Acre in 1191. From the 1120s the Templars recruited widely in France but with particular success in Champagne (through the influence of Hugues de Payns and Bernard of Clairvaux), Burgundy, and Languedoc, areas where the Cistercians were strongest. Thanks to their close association with the Cistercians, the Knights Templars founded numerous houses in the first half of the twelfth century.[72] They attracted support from many aristocratic families and established hundreds of commanderies before the order was dissolved by King Philip the Fair at the beginning of the fourteenth century.

At Paris they caught the attention mainly of the monarchy. They established a Temple there by the reign of Louis VII (around 1140), who endowed them with numerous revenues, especially from contributions exacted from the money changers in the capital.[73] At Acre in 1191 Philip Augustus exempted them from paying fees to the royal chancery for the royal charters that confirmed their transactions.[74] At Paris, the Temple became Philip's treasury for which the Templar Brother Haimard served as chief treasurer. (Brother Guérin, a Hospitaler, became Philip's chief cleric in charge of the chancery.) Well established at their house in Paris, the documentation created there, however, has virtually disappeared, leaving few traces, doubtlessly connected with the dissolution of the order by King Philip the Fair.[75] The most that is known about the Temple at Paris are the names of the masters or procurators of the house, who survive with their first names or last names unrecognizable among the local aristocracy.[76] The few charters that the historians of the Hospitalers have recovered reveal patronage from the high aristocracy not unlike the other monasteries we have seen. For example, we find donations from Guy, butler of Senlis, Robert, count of Dreux, Aliénor, countess of Beaumont, Amicia, lady of Montfort, as well as from the royal family, such as Adèle, the queen mother.[77]

The modern editor of the cartulary of the Paris Temple declared that they had many possessions in the Île-de-France, even if few notices have survived.[78] Scarce charters, however, do afford a glimpse of Templars in 1217 in a dispute regarding their possessions at La Ferté-Gaucher (dép. Seine-et-Marne, on the borders of Champagne) with Mathieu de Montmirail, of the family of Jean de Montmirail.[79] In April 1192, a year after the capture of Acre, where the Templars subsequently had transferred their headquarters, a knight Raoul gave to the house twenty *aissinos* of his land at Ressons-le-Long (dép. Aisne). Doubtlessly arriving in the Holy Land as a crusader with Philip Augustus, he specified that he had abandoned the secular world to take on the garb of the Temple. His donation was confirmed and sealed by Raoul, count of Soissons, and witnessed by

Plate 1. A. Chartres Cathedral
(Notre-Dame de Chartres), window
no. 100, the Virgin Mary. Photo by
Céline Gumiel, Centre André Chastel.
B. Seal of the chapter of Notre-Dame
de Chartres. Douët d'Arcq II, no. 7150
(1207). Photo by Clément Blanc-Riehl,
Archives nationales.

Plate 2. Prince Louis.
A. Chartres Cathedral window no. 107 rose, Prince Louis. Photo by Céline Gumiel, Centre André Chastel.
B. Seal of Prince Louis. Douët d'Arcq I, no. 186 (1214). Photo by Clément Blanc-Riehl, Archives nationales.

Plate 3. Thibaut VI, count of Blois.
A. Chartres Cathedral window no. 109 rose, Thibaut VI, count of Blois. Photo by Céline Gumiel, Centre André Chastel.
B. Seal of Thibaut VI, count of Blois. Douët d'Arcq I, no. 958 (1213). Photo by Clément Blanc-Riehl, Archives nationales.

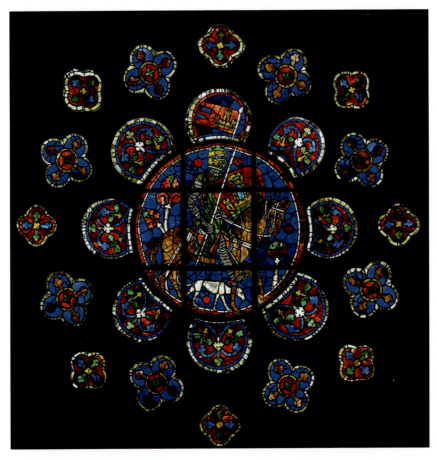

Plate 4. Alfonso VIII, king of Castile.
Chartres Cathedral window no. 111 rose, Alfonso VIII, king of Castile. Photo by Céline Gumiel, Centre André Chastel.

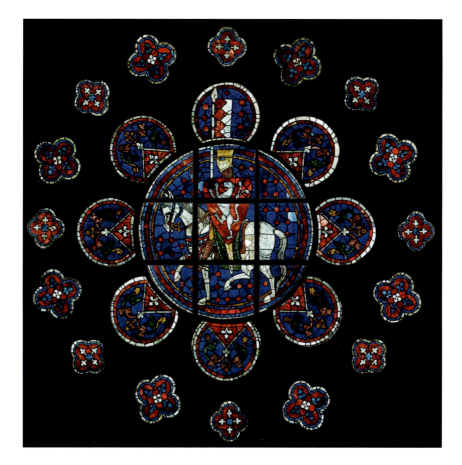

Plate 5. Simon de Montfort.
A. Chartres Cathedral window no. 108 rose, Simon de Montfort. Photo by
Céline Gumiel, Centre André Chastel.
B. Seal of Simon de Montfort. Douët d'Arcq I, no. 708 (1211). Photo by
Clément Blanc-Riehl, Archives nationales.

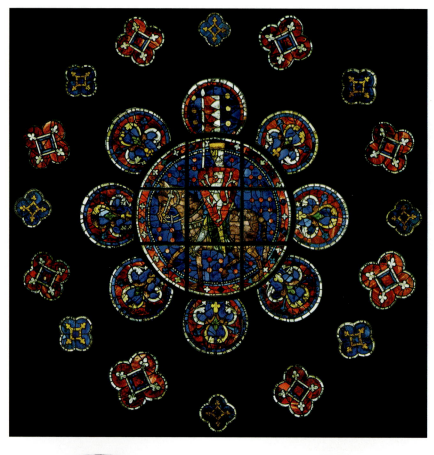

Plate 6. Amaury de Montfort.
A. Chartres Cathedral, window no. 110 rose, Amaury de Montfort. Photo by
Céline Gumiel, Centre André Chastel.
B. Seal of Amaury de Montfort. Douët d'Arcq I, no. 710 (1230). Photo by
Clément Blanc-Riehl, Archives nationales.

Plate 7. Robert de Courtenay.
A. Chartres Cathedral window no. 112 rose, Robert de Courtenay. Photo by
Céline Gumiel, Centre André Chastel.
B. Seal of Robert de Courtenay. Douët d'Arcq I, no. 274 (1232). Photo by
Clément Blanc-Riehl, Archives nationales.

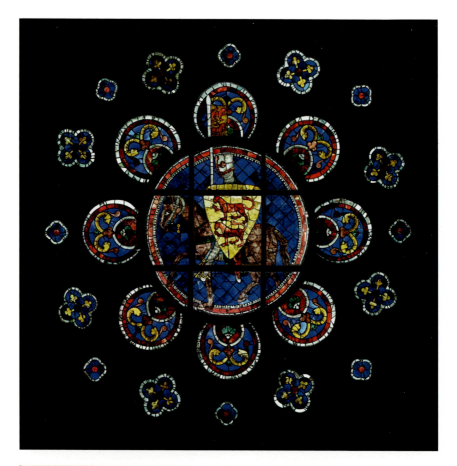

Plate 8. Robert de Beaumont.
A. Chartres Cathedral window no. 114 rose, Robert de Beaumont. Photo by
Céline Gumiel, Centre André Chastel.
B. Seal of Robert de Beaumont, Gaignières drawing. BnF Est., Rés. Pe 1p, fol.
70. Photo courtesy of the BnF.

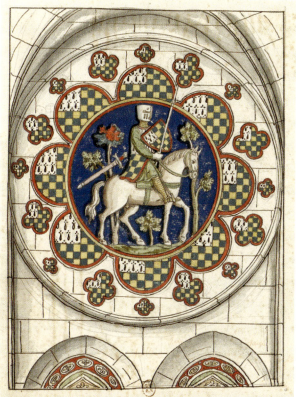

PIERRE de DREUX dit Mauclere Duc de Bretagne, Armé
+mort en 1250 en guerre, pris sur les vitres de l'Eglise de Notre Dame de Chartres.

Gaïg. 94

Plate 9. Pierre de Dreux, duke of Brittany.
A. Gaignières drawing of Chartres Cathedral window no. 124 rose, Pierre de Dreux. BnF Est., Rés. Oa 9, fol. 80 (Bouchot I, no. 94). Photo courtesy of the BnF.
B. Seal of Pierre de Dreux. Douët d'Arcq I, no. 534 (1220). Photo by Clément Blanc-Riehl, Archives nationales.

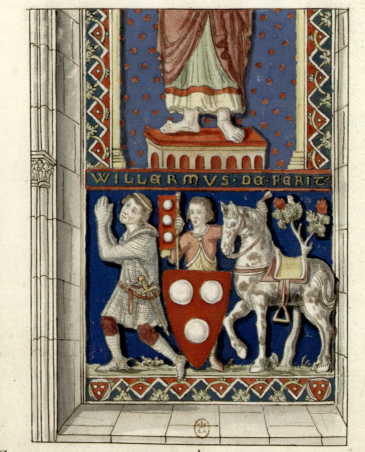

WILLARMVS · DE · FERIT ·

GUILLAUME de la FERTE-Hernaud au Perche, fait un concession
à l'Abbaye de S.ᵗ Pere de Chartres estant à la Ferté, par un titre du mois de May
1207. & par un autre de l'an 1221. il confirme une donation de dismes faite par
les Abbé & couuent de cette Abbaye à M.ᵉ Jean Lambert, l'un & l'autre Scellez comᵉ
il est marqué icy sont en original dans leur Chartrier⌡ pris sur les vitres de l'Eglise
de Notre D.ᵉ de Chartres.

Gaig. 65

Plate 10. Guillaume de La Ferté.
Gaignières drawing of Chartres Cathedral window no. 108 left lancet,
Guillaume de La Ferté, with Guillaume's seal. BnF Est., Rés. Oa 9, fol. 45
(Bouchot I, no. 65). Photo courtesy of the BnF.

Plate 11. Étienne de Sancerre.
A. Chartres Cathedral window no. 108 right lancet, Étienne de Sancerre, Gaignières drawing. BnF Est., Rés. Pc 18, fol. 28 (Bouchot I, no. 1746). Photo courtesy of the BnF.
B. Seal of Étienne de Sancerre. Douët d'Arcq II, no. 3574 (1281). Photo by Clément Blanc-Riehl, Archives nationales.

Plate 12. Bouchard de Marly.
A. Chartres Cathedral window no. 114 left lancet, Bouchard de Marly. Photo by Céline Gumiel, Centre André Chastel.
B. Seal of Bouchard de Marly. Douët d'Arcq I, no. 2714 (1224). Photo by Clément Blanc-Riehl, Archives nationales.

Plate 13. Jean de Beaumont-du-Gâtinais.
A. Chartres Cathedral window no. 115 left lancet, Jean de Beaumont-du-Gâtinais. Photo courtesy of the Centre André Chastel.
B. Seal of Jean de Beaumont-du-Gâtinais. Douët d'Arcq I, no. 1360 (1237). Photo by Clément Blanc-Riehl, Archives nationales.

SDIONISIVS

Plate 14. Jean Clément.
A. Chartres Cathedral window no. 116 right lancet, Jean Clément. Photo by Christian Lemzaouda, Centre André Chastel.
B. Seal of Jean Clément. AN Supp. seals, no. 7438 (1226). Photo by Clément Blanc-Riehl, Archives nationales.

Plate 15. Seal of Robert de Vitry. Douët d'Arcq II, no. 3928 (1161). Photo by Clément Blanc-Riehl, Archives nationales.

Plate 16. Louis IX depicted on a *clef de voûte* in the choir of Chartres Cathedral. Photo by Céline Gumiel, Centre André Chastel.

Jean de Nesle, brother of the count, and Guillaume, another Templar from Ressons.[80] Undoubtedly the order possessed other houses in the Paris region since the border with Champagne was crowded with Temples,[81] but the disappearance of their archives has obliterated further testimony to their presence around Paris. Our sample of thirty-two cartularies contains not one charter from the Templars. They are absent from our 1,729 transactions. The Templars in the Paris region are, therefore, another example of how dependent historians are on the survival of documentation.

Death: Thibaut de Marly and Hélinand de Froidmont

The churchmen's program for attaining the kingdom of heaven through contrition, confession, satisfaction, giving to churches, converting to the monastic life, and participating in crusades was oriented toward death, the definitive moment of human existence, after which the human soul passes into the hands of God to receive its due reward or just punishment for the life it has lived on earth. This program, which was championed by the theologians at Paris at the turn of the twelfth century, might best be called "contritionism," that is, being sorry for one's sins for which one does penance during this life.[82] Before the twelfth century, however, churchmen had introduced another approach that might be called "attritionism" through which the fear of death itself becomes the primary motivation for preparing for death during one's lifetime.[83] Attritionism, furthermore, was usually accompanied by a *contemptus mundi*, that is, a disdain for the present world. Attritionism was normally articulated in the clergy's liturgy and in sermons composed in Latin. While sermons may have been occasionally preached orally to the laity in the vernacular, they were almost always recorded in Latin. Earlier in the twelfth century Bernard, the influential abbot of Clairvaux and the guiding leader of the Cistercian movement, had directed his attention particularly to the aristocracy of which he himself was a member. His example doubtlessly encouraged the Cistercians of the Paris region to apply the "attritional" approach to the local aristocracy. At the end of the twelfth century two Cistercian writers appeared who subscribed to the program, but unlike Bernard they confronted the laity directly in their own vernacular tongue. From the half dozen Cistercian houses surrounding the capital, Val-Notre-Dame produced the writer Thibaut de Marly, and the more distant Froidmont in the diocese of Beauvais harbored the celebrated poet Hélinand.

Thibaut de Marly occasionally has been confused with a later homonym, Saint Thibaut of the Cistercian house of Vaux-de-Cernay, who, we shall see, was his great-nephew from the same distinguished family of Montmorency-Marly. The earlier Thibaut was the uncle of the celebrated Mathieu de Montmorency, who became royal constable in 1218, and the brother of Hervé, dean of Notre-Dame (1184–92) and later abbot of Saint-Martin de Montmorency. In the Montmorency-Marly succession, around 1160, Bouchard, the eldest brother, was given Montmorency and Thibaut received Marly, which he then passed to a younger brother Mathieu after his monastic conversion. As lord of Marly, Thibaut made a pilgrimage to Jerusalem in the years 1173–75, the terms of which were recorded in the cartulary of Notre-Dame de Paris. With the concurrence of his brother Bouchard, before departure he gave his holdings at Gonesse and Montmorency to his brother Hervé in "fraternal charity" for the sum of twenty *livres*. Hervé was permitted to give, sell, and pledge these properties as he wished. (Later, as dean, Hervé probably bequeathed them to Notre-Dame since the transaction was preserved in the church's cartulary.)[84] Thibaut was already involved in making donations to the Cistercians at Val-Notre-Dame before he entered the house as a monk between 1182 and 1185. Dying early in the 1190s, he had lived as an influential lord from the Paris region for at least two decades before his retirement from the world.[85] Between 1182 and 1189 he wrote a long poem of 850 lines, simply entitled *Les Vers*, devoted to the themes of the fear of death and the contempt of the world. Throughout this work he provided virtually no information about himself except for an initial confession that he "knew no letters" (*ne sai lettres*, v. 5), meaning doubtlessly that he was ignorant of Latin, having been raised as a layman. His work confirms this admission because he appears to ignore the Latin sources of his themes, including both the church fathers and the contemporary theologians, but in their place he inserts passages that resemble the long prayers found in contemporary *chansons de gestes*. His concluding verses appear to be derived from the *Quinze signes* of the end of the world that circulated both in Latin and vernacular versions.[86] Extant in only three manuscripts, the poem apparently had a limited circulation.

What makes Thibaut's *Vers* pertinent is the explicit awareness of the aristocratic world, as might be expected from one who had long exercised lordly authority. After a prefatory biblical history of the world, he opens with a jongleur's technique of name-dropping by asserting "I shall not mention Auchier or Landri" (vv. 196–97). This opening is taken directly from the *Roman d'Alexandre* and was specifically remembered in Paris by Pierre the Chanter and Gerald of Wales as referring to the habit of jongleurs to change their repertory when they saw that their initial offerings were not appreciated by their audience.[87] "I shall not mention Auchier or Landri, but rather Simon de Crépy," he continued (vv. 196–98). He had just named Guichard de Beaujeu (v. 193) and Milon de Lagny (v. 194 and later v. 223) and proceeded with Gérard de Montigny (v. 220). With the exception of Guichard de Beaujeu, who was Burgundian, these personalities most likely originated from the Paris region.[88] Simon, the heir to the important lordship of Crépy-en-Valois, became a monk at Saint-Oyand in the Jura in the eleventh century. He was widely celebrated in the early twelfth century as an example of an aristocratic knight who had become a saint of exemplary holiness.[89] Somewhat later, Guichard de Beaujeu was a powerful seigneur in Burgundy who also forsook his secular life to become a monk at Cluny and to whom was attributed a verse sermon in the vernacular.[90] Milon de Lagny and Gérard de Montigny have not yet been identified, but along with Simon and Guichard, Thibaut evoked their names as exemplars of knights who abandoned the world for a more holy monastic life. Another knight, Renaud de Pomponne, who came from the well-known family situated nearby Paris on the Marne, served Thibaut as an example (v. 320) that death strikes suddenly. Renaud's family were vassals of the abbey of Saint-Denis and his descendants still used the name Renaud at the turn of the century. In the *Nomina militum*, the family appeared in the castellany of Senlis.[91] Beyond these personages, Thibaut alluded vaguely throughout his verse to various knightly concerns that illustrated the vanities of aristocratic life, such as family inheritance (vv. 229–30, 645), seigneurial injustices, tournaments (vv. 503–9), and crusades (v. 825).

Thibaut de Marly's long poem, which begins with the creation of the world and concludes with the last days, covers a loose collection of themes discursively arranged around the contempt of the secular world and the imminence of death. He returns frequently to the scene of the last judgment as portrayed on the facade of Notre-Dame de Paris in which all classes of society are portrayed as arising from their graves. In his tableau, knights with their horses, bourgeois in their furs, ladies in their *bliauts*, tavern keepers with their false measures, money changers, and furriers are all judged equally and assigned their fate before the divine judge (vv. 578–90). If there is a principal leitmotif, however, it is that death strikes all without warning. The most notable example was taken directly from the saints' lives composed about Simon de Crépy. When Simon wished to move the grave of his father, Count Renaud, who had died in possession of many castles, he discovered that his father's cadaver was so horribly eaten by worms that he was shocked into abandoning his lordly life to become a charcoal burner and to beg for his livelihood (vv. 196–215). Similarly, Renaud de Pomponne was suddenly slain by a servant boy and did not benefit from his former reputation for prowess, handsomeness, riches, and castles (vv. 320–23). In a series of litanies Thibaut creates a procession of fortuitous deaths that encompassed all ages, from the womb of the mother to advanced age (vv. 607–10), and every kind of people grouped by antinomies (poor/rich, foolish/wise, small/great, and illiterate/literate, vv. 112–20), as well as famous figures of history—Charlemagne, Oliver, Roland, and King William "who conquered to the ports of Ireland" (vv. 326–30). Family patrimonies will not last: a father and mother raise a child only to bury him before he can inherit (vv. 229–31). "'This is my house,' claims an heir. 'My father claimed it while living. . . .' But he is dead under six and a half feet of soil, and the king is under just as much" (vv. 653–59). Occasionally Thibaut suggests that true contrition for one's sins may mitigate one's fate, but usually he relies on the fear of unforeseen death as the driving motive for repentance. When asked by his lord what to do, his considered advice is simply, "If one does not abandon the world, the world will not let go of him. . . . The more one takes delight in it, the more one is harmed." (*S'il ne guerpist le siecle, qu'il ne guerpisse lui. . . . Cil qui plus s'i delitent plus sont maleüré*, vv. 100, 103).[92] Thibaut concludes his *Vers* with a detailed critique of contemporary aristocratic behavior: God will not praise you if you fight in a foreign land against the Saracens or make a pilgrimage, but he will love those who feed, clothe, and provide shoes for the poor, lodge the homeless, and visit the poorhouses. For these small services God will make one richer than Lohier (Charlemagne's oldest son) and endow him in paradise with castles constructed without chalk or mortar and with riches that will never be diminished (vv. 825–33, 845–58).

Hélinand, monk at Froidmont in the diocese of Beauvais, was another Cistercian who addressed the aristocracy directly in their tongue. Originating from a noble Flemish family that had taken refuge in France after the murder of Count Charles of Flanders in 1129, Hélinand studied grammar with Master Raoul at Beauvais. He appeared in Paris in the 1180s where he was identified as a jongleur at the royal court and was acquainted with the circle of Pierre the Chanter, and was as well a collaborator with Brother Guérin, Philip Augustus's head of the chancery and chief ecclesiastical adviser. Around 1190 he entered the Cistercian house of Froidmont, where he remained until his death sometime between 1223 and 1237. His Latin writings consist of a chronicle, political and moral treatises, and numerous sermons, but his chief fame is based on a vernacular poem, *Les Vers de la mort*, that he composed between 1190 and 1197 after his monastic conversion. Drawing upon his past as a jongleur, he composed fifty stanzas that meditated on death and abandoning the world with such vivid imagery that they obtained wide circulation in at least twenty-four manuscripts.[93] Although his themes echoed those of Thibaut de Marly, his poetic talent far exceeded that of his predecessor.

Hélinand's *Vers de la mort* identifies his immediate audience by direct address. Those addressed include the two reigning kings, Philip Augustus and Richard (st. 20), a half dozen counts (st. 18), the papal court and cardinals of Rome (sts. 13–14), the hierarchy of bishops in France (Reims, Beauvais, Noyon, and Orléans, sts. 15–17), and also two personal but unidentified friends, whom he calls Bernard and Renaud (sts. 7, 8). These contemporary names serve as markers of his political universe and may express his displeasure with the king's current divorce proceedings against the queen, Ingeborg of Denmark. All of the identified bishops and at least two of the counts had participated in the council of Senlis in 1193 that had granted the separation that King Philip wanted, but Hélinand does not explicitly reproach them for the decision. Within this high level of society, he appears to be most concerned with the aristocracy and especially its youth. He reminds them of their wealth derived from revenues, jurisdictions, and markets (st. 3); he recalls the banners and catapults of siege warfare (st. 22), but most important, he contrasts the old men whose imminent death is on their faces with the elegant youth who are so absorbed with the pleasures of hunting with dogs and birds and with performing homage to tasty morsels that they ignore that they too will die at midday before night falls (st. 24).

Throughout the poem Hélinand, like Thibaut, recognizes the vanity of the world, but he develops his major theme on the suddenness of death more than Thibaut. The first twenty-five of his stanzas open by addressing Death directly:

Mort, you have placed me in a cage to shed, as sweating in a bath, the excesses that my body has committed in this world. (st. 1)

Mort, go sing to those who sing of love and boast of vain things. (st. 2)

Mort, you who collect your rents in every place, who take the sales in all the markets, who know how to despoil the rich. (st. 3)

As the stanzas progress, the rhythm of suddenness increases: it takes the son before the father; it gathers fruit before the flower; it comes as the thief in the night (st. 23); it takes those in full youth, at twenty-eight or thirty years, who imagine themselves to be at the peak of their years and who dress and make themselves beautiful (st. 25); it changes sunshine into rain, inundations into drought; it takes everything in an hour; it converts purple and miniver into sack and haircloth (sts. 28, 29). "By right death is called sudden (*sobite*)" (st. 27). After an entire poem devoted to the menace of death, Hélinand finally introduces the remedy of "contritionism": "Without distinction we all await first death and then judgment. To confront the two there is one remedy, to repent quickly and to purify ourselves completely of everything of which our conscience accuses us. He who does not act before dying will excuse himself too late and in vain when God exacts vengeance. Before he sets sail from the harbor he carefully caulks the boat so that he can voyage in complete safety" (st. 49). After combining "attritionism" with "contritionism," Hélinand makes his final adieu: "Away with debauchery, away with lust! I do not want costly meals; I prefer my peas and my soup" (st. 50).

We remember that the nuns of Fontaines-les-Nonnes prefaced their encyclical letter for Guillaume des Barres with a brief survey of the divine plan of redemption from Creation to the Incarnation, just as Thibaut de Marly had opened his *Vers*. Moreover, like Hélinand they addressed Death in the second person singular: "Hélas, many times hélas, O dreadful fate, O cruel death, sparing no one, dragging all, you have struck our flock miserably when you have carried away from us our sweet and noble lord Guillaume des Barres." The monks of Salmaise echoed in reply: "Unholy death cruelly seized the soul of this Guillaume whose life was blessed."[94]

By concentrating on "attritionism" both Thibaut and Hélinand seek to motivate their aristocratic audiences in their own tongue through the fear of an unforeseen demise. Sudden death in tournaments, warfare, and crusades was certainly the occupational hazard of the warrior class. It is worthy of note, however, that their final goal is personal conversion, not necessarily to the monastery, but at least to a more perfect Christian life. Moreover, never do Thibaut and Hélinand succumb to the temptation to use the imminence of death as an incentive to contribute to the monks for their prayers. Despite the steady transfer of wealth from the aristocracy to the church, these two are remarkably restrained for not dealing the economic motive as their final card.

Tombs

Once the point of no return had been reached, a final word was nonetheless granted to aristocrats on their tombs. This postmortem came, of course, not from beyond the grave; it was composed by the deceased while still living or by his family not long after, but it voiced future expectations. From the thousands who died at the turn of the twelfth and thirteenth centuries in the Paris region only a handful of tombs can be located today, their survival being due to their placement inside churches. Fortunately, however, at the end of the seventeenth century the antiquarian-genealogist Roger de Gaignières commissioned a team of collaborators to canvass the churches of the region in search of tombstones of the clergy and nobility, for which they made sketches.[95] Since many of the tombs and the churches are no longer extant, the Gaignières sketches are the only record.

Among these tombstones, the clergy, both men and women, naturally outnumbered the laity by far. This was particularly true of monasteries, which buried most members of the community in the church's cemetery or in the conventual buildings. Since monasteries recruited massively from aristocratic families, most of the tombs were aristocratic. Of the forty aristocratic conversions to the monastic life that have surfaced in the charters of the Paris region, we may assume that all, at whatever age they entered the monastic life, were buried in clois-ters. Certain ones—for example, Renaud de Coucy—indicated that they entered at the end of their life to die and be buried, presumably "for aid" (*ad succurren-dum*) as monks, as had Guillaume des Barres.[96] As monks and nuns, therefore, their tombs rarely revealed their class because their recorded names were those of religion and not of their families.

The vast majority of aristocrats, however, died as laymen and laywomen who had already made their donations to churches while they were alive or in testa-ments to be executed after their death. Occasionally the donation specified that the donor chose to be buried at the church receiving the gift.[97] For example, a Guillaume *de Horrevilla* requested burial with the Cistercians of Vaux-de-Cernay, and Pétronille, wife of the royal chamberlain Barthélemy de Roye, announced her intention to be buried at the Premonstratensian house of Joyen-val, which her husband had founded. Since both were acting at the end of their lives (*laborans in extremis*), it is not entirely clear whether this request implied deathbed conversion "for aid" (*ad succurrendum*) or, more likely, that they were simply buried as laity.[98]

Since burial in sacred ground contributed to the soul's salvation and since ecclesiastical authorities possessed a monopoly over cemeteries, all matters con-cerning burial fell under the church's jurisdiction. Bernard of Pavia's *Summa decretalium* offers a succinct statement of the canon law applicable at the time.[99] Because the dead must necessarily be buried, he begins, the church has the right of burial (*ius funerandi*), which encompasses a whole range of issues such as which churches have the right of burial, at which church one should be buried, who is prohibited from burial, who chooses when and where the burial takes place, and what share of the donations the church should have. This broad ju-risdiction encompassed all classes of society, but certain details applied specifi-cally to the aristocracy. Although as a general rule Christians should be buried in the cemeteries of their village or parish churches, private chapels were per-mitted to the great lords (*magnates*) in their courts or houses for the convenience of their families. In principle these private chapels did not have the right of burial, although families doubtlessly negotiated exceptions. If one chose to be buried outside the parish, the local church was compensated up to half the normal contribution. All excommunicates were forbidden burial in sacred ground, in-cluding notorious usurers and knights who had died in tournaments. Appar-ently aristocrats questioned this last restriction as too severe because the issue was raised at Paris in the school of Pierre the Chanter. After debating the pros and cons, Pierre decided that if a knight showed signs of remorse at the point of death—if, for example, he made the sign of the cross—this gesture would per-mit him to be interred in sacred ground. The best-known case was that of Count

Geoffroy of Brittany, the boon companion of Philip Augustus, who reportedly had been killed in a tournament in 1186 but whom the king had buried with full rites and honors in the choir of Notre-Dame.[100] As for the numerous other questions that arose over burials, Bernard concluded that many could be decided by local custom.

The tombs that have survived in the Gaignières collection, therefore, were the result of collaboration between the clergy who made the regulations and the aristocracy who paid the expenses. Within this framework, how did aristocrats seek to represent themselves on their tombstones? The Gaignières collection has preserved at least twelve tombs of males from the Paris region whose names can be recognized from the written documentation. This form of representation, however, poses overlapping problems for interpreting the images: since families were prone to use homonyms, the same name appears over generations; since it is difficult to determine whether the tombstones were commissioned by the deceased or later by family members, they can be difficult to date.

At the turn of the twelfth and thirteenth centuries the tombs normally consisted of a sarcophagus placed on the ground and covered with a stone slab on which a simple decoration was engraved. With time the decoration became increasingly ornate and the figure of the deceased developed from an engraved sketch to a three-dimensional effigy surmounting the cover. From the Gaignières sample, the simplest was the tomb of Guy de Garlande, "dit le Jeune," lord of Tournan, from the collateral line of the powerful Garlande family. Located at the abbey of Jouy-en-Brie, the rectangular slab was completely unadorned except for the Latin inscription around the perimeter that identified him as *Guido de Gallanda . . . Iuvenis*.[101] At the Cistercian abbey of Barbeau the brothers Jean and Aubert d'Andresel engraved on trapezoid slabs their swords in scabbards framed in an architectural arch to which their first names were added. Jean's sword is attached to a belt and is inscribed *dominus de Andesello*, while Aubert's lacks the belt and is engraved *frater eius*. Most likely these two are the Jean and Aubert who issued charters together in 1222.[102] Eudes, from the celebrated family des Barres, followed a similar pattern at the abbey of Preuilly except that he placed the sword in the upper right quadrant and identified himself with an inscription along the perimeter as *Odo de Barris, miles quondam dominus de Pleisseto de Buneis*.[103]

An important advance was taken when the simple engraved sword evolved into a three-dimensional effigy of a knight resting supine on the tomb. At the collegiate church of Notre-Dame de Poissy, Guillaume de Poissy was dressed in mail armor from head to toe (Figure 1).[104] Encased in an ornamented Gothic arch, his head rests on a pillow and his feet are warmed by a dog below. In his right hand he holds his sword upright and at his left side his shield displays his

2.pied.

Figure 1. Tomb of Guillaume de Poissy at Notre-Dame de Poissy, Gaignières drawing. BnF Est., Rés. Pe 11a, fol. 43. Photo courtesy of the BnF.

heraldry, "losangé d'or et de gueles," which matches the seal of Simon de Poissy.[105] This preoccupation with the knight's métier of arms and family heraldry culminates in the image of Thibaut de Vallangoujard whose tomb was located at the Cistercian abbey of Val-Notre-Dame (Figure 2).[106] Although the image is engraved, the iconography is identical except that the knight's head is bare and his hands are clasped in prayer. The framing is increasingly ornate and the inscription is in French, giving the date of death as 1243. The heraldry on the shield is a simple cross, whereas in 1214 Thibaut's seal bore "une croix cantonnée de quatre aigles." He was identified as a squire (*armigerus*) in a charter of the same year.[107]

The emergence of family heraldry is fully apparent in the effigy of Gaucher de Nanteuil at his family foundation of Nanteuil-le-Haudouin (Figure 3). Like Guillaume de Poissy, the figure is comfortably recumbent with his head on a pillow and feet on a dog, but he has discarded his armor for a lordly tunic (*bliaut*) over a chemise, and his shield is placed across his legs and prominently displays the family heraldry of the fleurs-de-lis, "broken" (*brisée*) in the right quadrant with a blank space. His scabbarded sword entwined with a belt lies to the side.[108] At a date difficult to determine, the tomb of Eudes des Barres at Preuilly was joined by another more elaborate tomb of a member the same family. Placed in the wall at Preuilly, it displayed the same imagery as Gaucher de Nanteuil's but was now sculpted in full relief (Figure 4). The shield bore heraldry (a single cross) that replicated the seal of Guillaume des Barres ("une croix ancrée, brisée d'un bâton").[109]

Another shift in imagery appears on the tomb of Barthélemy de Roye, royal chamberlain and the leading knight of Philip Augustus's court (Figure 5). On the tomb at his family foundation of the Premonstratensians at Joyenval, Barthélemy has discarded the markers of the military profession for a *bliaut* lined with squirrel (*vair*) over a chemise. A purse (*aumônière*) hangs at his belt. His hands are placed at his belt and neckline in a courtly pose. Instead of a helmet is a simple cap, encircled on either side by angels swinging censers. Enclosed in an elaborated Gothic arch is a Latin inscription that proclaims his founding of the abbey, his service to the king, and his other virtues. At this point the royal knight has been transformed into the distinguished counselor of the royal court. His family heraldry, now absent, has become irrelevant.[110] Adam the Chamberlain, lord of Villebéon, who was descended from the loyal family of Gautier the Chamberlain through Gautier the Young, likewise adopted this courtly pose (Figure 6). In a flat engraving at the abbey du Jard he is pictured similarly in his *bliaut*, but now, because he is further removed from the court, he restores a heraldic shield displaying the arms of his family, as displayed, for example, on

Figure 2. Tomb of Thibaut de Vallangoujard at Val-Notre-Dame, Gaignières drawing. BnF Est., Rés. Pe 1c, fol. 128. Photo courtesy of the BnF.

Figure 3. Tomb of Gaucher de Nanteuil at Nanteuil-le-Haudouin, Gaignières drawing. BnF Est., Rés. Pe 1b, fol. 35. Photo courtesy of the BnF.

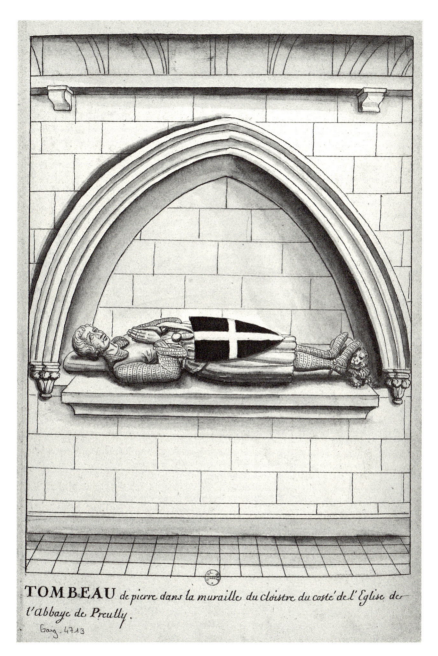

TOMBEAU de pierre dans la muraille du cloistre du costé de l'Eglise de l'abbaye de Preully.

Gay. 4713

Figure 4. Tomb of a member of the family des Barres at Preuilly, Gaignières drawing. BnF Est., Rés. Pe 11a, fol. 205. Photo courtesy of the BnF.

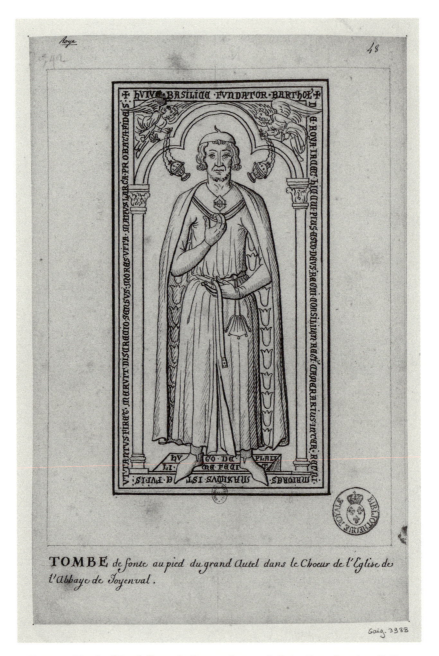

Figure 5. Tomb of Barthélemy de Roye at Joyenval, Gaignières drawing. BnF Est., Rés. Pe 5, fol. 27. Photo courtesy of the BnF.

Figure 6. Tomb of Adam de Villebéon at the abbey du Jard, Gaignières drawing. BnF Est., Rés. Pe 6, fol. 26. Photo courtesy of the BnF.

the seal of Ours (d. 1233). An inscription in French announces his death in 1264.[111]

Two counts from the royal cousins of Dreux complete the sample of tombstones preserved by Gaignières. Count Robert II, lord of the castle of Brie-Comte-Robert, had himself portrayed in the courtly tradition at Saint-Yved de Braine, one of the abbeys patronized by the family (Figure 7). Unarmed in his *bliaut* and chemise, he holds a fleur-de-lis in his right hand. In the upper corners is placed the heraldry of Dreux ("échiqueté d'or et d'azur"), surrounded by a lengthy inscription.[112] In the same church, however, his bellicose son Pierre (*dit* Mauclerc), to whom Philip Augustus gave the duchy of Brittany, adopted the knightly tradition (Figure 8). He lies clothed in full armor and a robe with his bare head on a pillow and his feet on a dog. His sword is covered by his shield bearing the exchequer heraldry of the Dreux family but *brisée* "au franc canton d'hermine," the heraldry of Brittany. His hands are clasped in prayer while angels hover in the upper corners.[113]

Within the precincts of churches and monasteries of the Paris region, the ecclesiastical authorities therefore permitted the aristocracy to display both the armor and swords of their knightly profession and the heraldic shields of their family heritage. Occasionally they are pictured in prayer with angels at their side. They repose in comfort with their heads on cushions and their feet warmed by dogs. Their faces are calm; Adam the Chamberlain's eyes are closed in sleep. What is remarkable about these aristocratic representations is the complete absence of fear of sudden death or eternal torment beyond the grave, which they heard about from the Cistercians Thibaut de Marly and Hélinand de Froidmont. Even the tombs surviving in Cistercian houses display only vague premonitions of anguish. On the contrary, the aristocratic knights remain confident in their belief that their donations to churches and monasteries and the intercessory prayers received in recompense will see them safely through the perils of the next life. "Whose soul by God's mercy may rest in peace" (*Cuius anima per misericordiam dei requiescat in pace*) is inscribed on Eudes des Barres's tomb. Equally remarkable is the repetition of the emblems that marked their high position in society within the precincts of the church. As on their seals during their lifetime, they continue to display their swords and heraldry on their tombs after death.

Their wives and daughters, however, were represented by fewer surviving tombs. The two legitimate queens of Philip Augustus's reign were provided with effigies appropriate to their rank. At Notre-Dame in Paris Isabelle de Hainaut (d. 1190) bore a crown on her head and carried a scepter in her right hand (Figure 9). Her left hand points to the neck of her chemise over which she wears a long *surcot* (overcoat). The crude Gaignières sketch suggests that her clothing

Figure 7. Tomb of Robert II, count of Dreux at Saint-Yved de Braine, Gaignières drawing. BnF Est., Rés. Pe 1, fol. 75. Photo courtesy of the BnF.

Figure 8. Tomb of Pierre Mauclerc at Saint-Yved de Braine, Gaignières drawing. BnF Est., Rés. Pe 1, fol. 98. Photo courtesy of the BnF.

was richly embellished.[114] In the church of the commandery of Saint-Jean-en-l'Île-lez-Corbeil, her misfortunate successor Ingeborg was accorded a more elaborate effigy, provided by the artisan Maître Hugues *de Placliago*, in the same style in which he depicted the royal knight Barthélemy de Roye at Joyenval (Figure 10). Like Isabelle, she is crowned and holds a scepter; her other hand is free to finger the neckline of her chemise. Her sleeveless overcoat (*surcot*), however, is elaborately lined with ermine, and she is framed in a Gothic arch accompanied by angels swinging censers.[115] A *surcot* over a chemise became the standard garb in the few surviving tombs of aristocratic ladies of our period. For example, a lady from Nanteuil, of the same family as Gaucher de Nanteuil, wears a simple chemise and *surcot* and a hood (*coiffe*) tied around her chin (Figure 11). Her hands are clasped before her chest in prayer since they are not encumbered with a royal scepter. Like Gaucher her head rests comfortably on a pillow and a purse (*aumônière*) hangs from her belt.[116] The tomb shared by Alix, wife of Pierre, duke of Brittany, and their daughter Yolande is more decorated according to their high station (Figure 12). Yolande adopts the same pose as the lady of Nanteuil, but her mother, Alix, more pretentiously holds a scepter in her right hand although she does not bear a crown but a *coiffe*.[117] In our period aristocratic women normally rested in tombs separate from their husbands, but at the abbey du Jard, Adam the Chamberlain, lord of Villebéon, father of the other Adam de Villebéon buried at the same abbey, shared his sarcophagus with his wife (Figure 13), a disposition that became increasingly common in the future. In this image Adam reposes in a simple *bliaut* with his hands clasped and his feet on a dog. His wife assumes the usual female pose but her garments are strikingly richer than her husband's. In particular, her *surcot* covers her head and is lined with ermine, and her purse (*aumônière*) hangs from a decorated belt.[118] As with the men, the women assume an attitude of calm repose. The inscription on this last tomb was almost entirely effaced when the Gaignières sketch was made but what still can be read—"at rest" (*an repos*)—matches the demeanor of the couple depicted. It was not until the Black Death a century later that effigies assumed the agony, macabre, and decay that has characterized medieval tomb sculpture.

Sainthood: Thibaut de Marly and Jean de Montmirail

The highest benefit that churchmen could confer on aristocrats was the posthumous fame of sainthood. Enrollment among the company of saints, the heroes of the church, guaranteed immediate entry into heaven and was, of course, extraordinarily rare, especially to those who had died as laity. Until the beginning of the thirteenth century virtually all of the newly canonized saints were chosen directly and exclusively from the ranks of the clergy, at times secular, but

TOMBE de marbre noir au milieu du Chœur de l'Eglise Cathedrale de Paris. Elle est d'Isabel de Hainault premiere femme de Philippes Auguste Roy de France, laquelle mourut en 1190 a l'aage de 20 ans.

(oxford collect.º Gaignières)   collationné conforme al l'original

Figure 9. Tomb of Isabelle de Hainaut at Notre-Dame de Paris, Gaignières drawing. BnF Est., Rés. Pe 1a, fol. 21. Photo courtesy of the BnF.

Figure 10. Tomb of Ingeborg of Denmark at the commandery of Saint-Jean-en-l'Île-lez-Corbeil, Gaignières drawing. BnF Est., Rés. Pe 1a, fol. 22. Photo courtesy of the BnF.

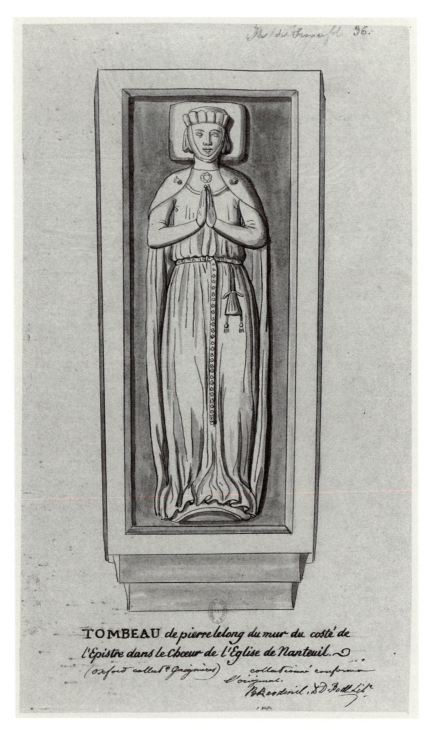

TOMBEAU *de pierre le long du mur du costé de l'Epistre dans le Chœur de l'Eglise de Nanteuil.*

(oxford collect.º gaignières)   collectionné conforme
                                   à l'original.
                                   B. Bandinil. SD Bodl. Lib.

Figure 11. Tomb of a lady of Nanteuil at Nanteuil-le-Haudouin, Gaignières drawing. BnF Est., Rés. Pe 1b, fol. 36. Photo courtesy of the BnF.

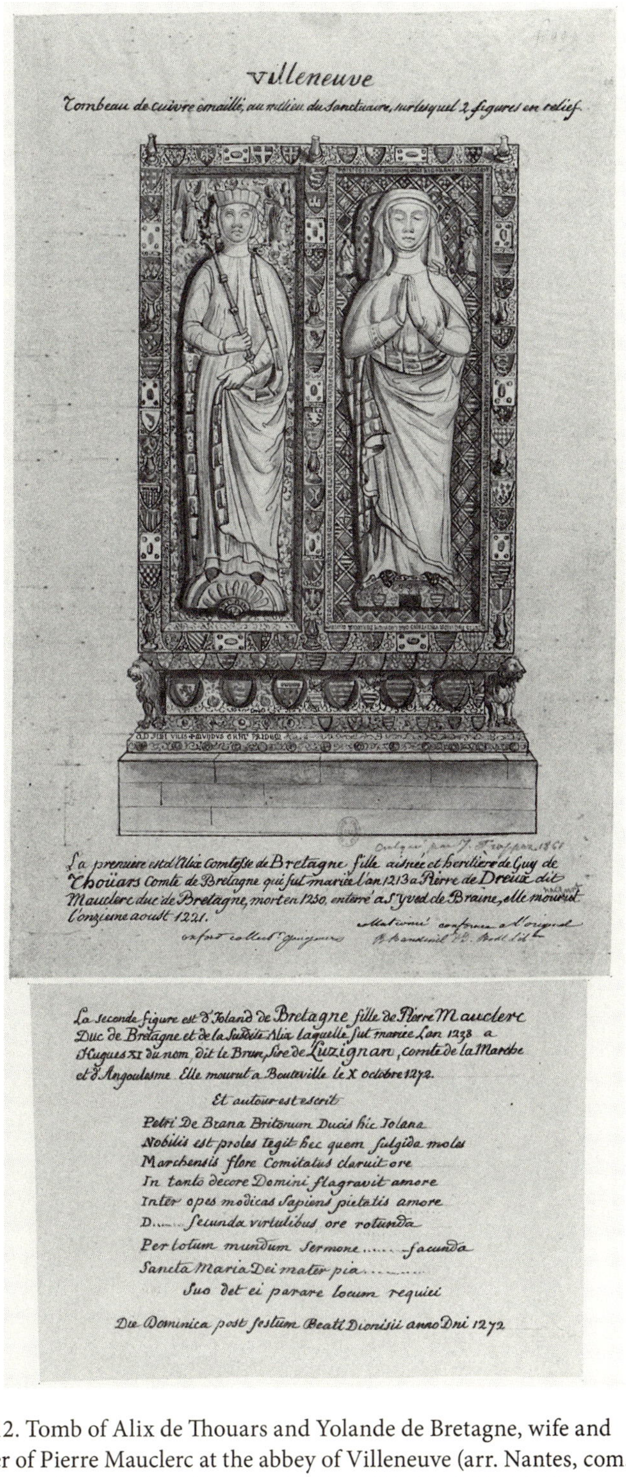

Figure 12. Tomb of Alix de Thouars and Yolande de Bretagne, wife and daughter of Pierre Mauclerc at the abbey of Villeneuve (arr. Nantes, com. Les Sorinières), Gaignières drawing. BnF Est., Rés. Pe 1, fol. 99. Photo courtesy of the BnF.

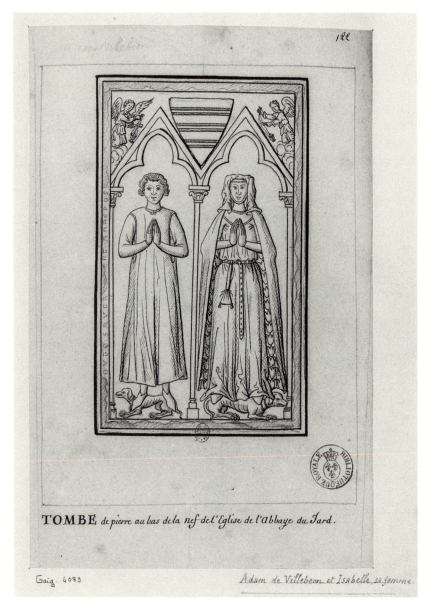

Figure 13. Tomb of Adam de Villebéon and his wife, Isabelle, at the abbey du Jard, Gaignières drawing. BnF Est., Rés. Pe 6, fol. 25. Photo courtesy of the BnF.

mainly monastic. Since virtually all the male and female clergy were recruited from aristocratic families, these men and women were clearly eligible, but their entrance into sainthood nonetheless passed through the door of clerical status. Occasionally their recruitment into the secular clergy or conversion to monasteries came late enough in their life to prompt their biographers to recognize their previous worldly existence in their accounts. From the eleventh century in the Paris region, for example, two local saints appeared. Bouchard de Vendôme, count of Corbeil, Melun, and Paris, was patronized by the monks of Saint-Maur-des-Fossés.[119] Simon de Crépy-en-Valois, a prominent lord in the Vermandois, was sponsored by the influential abbey of Cluny.[120]

Beginning with the pontificate of Alexander III in the second half of the twelfth century, the papacy began to intervene directly by taking charge of the canonization of modern saints. Archbishop Thomas Becket of Canterbury, martyred in 1170 and canonized in 1173, and Bernard of Clairvaux, who died in 1153 and was canonized in 1174, were the among the first to benefit from his intervention. Both of these saints gained immediate fame on the international stage. Although Thomas's relics remained at Canterbury where he was martyred, he became the favorite saint of the masters and students at Paris and attracted numerous gifts from the aristocracy of the Paris region, as we have seen.[121] On the other hand, the impact of Saint Bernard's canonization produced the result that in France most of the saints in the following century were drawn from the Cistercian order of which he was the leading abbot. An example from our region and period is Thibaut de Marly who entered the Cistercian abbey of Vaux-de-Cernay in 1222, became prior circa 1230, and was elected abbot in 1245 before he died in 1247. His pieties and austerities won him the reputation of sainthood, which was publicized locally by his abbey, but Thibaut did not gain papal recognition. As his biographer asserted, he was of noble birth (*nobili genere procreatus*) and the eldest son and direct heir to his father Bouchard de Marly, whom we have met as one of the leading lords to the west of Paris. His life before entry into Vaux-de-Cernay was summarized by the hagiographic cliché: "Among the great lords of those lands he became a great knight in the secular world, vigorous in warfare and tournaments" (*armis et torneamentis strenuus*).[122]

This backdrop serves to highlight the unique characteristics of the early career of Saint Jean de Montmirail. His birth, lands, and feudal allegiances rendered Jean a vassal of the counts of Champagne, but his early attachments to Philip Augustus at the royal court and his choice in entering the Cistercian abbey of Longpont in the Soissonnais bring him into the orbit of our region. Before entering Longpont, Jean was already well attested in the local charters and feudal rolls as an important lord. The only son of André de Montmirail and Hildiard d'Oisy, he inherited the lordships of Montmirail, Oisy, La Ferté-Gaucher, the viscounty of Meaux, and the castellanies of Château-Thierry and Cambrai. He married Helvide de Dampierre, the sister of the constable of Champagne, with whom he had at least seven, perhaps ten children. In the feudal rolls of Champagne he was listed in 1190 as owing castle-guard at Château-Thierry and in 1200–1201 as one of the "great barons" of the county.[123] In 1198 he was enrolled among the Champenois subscribers for the young count Thibaut when Thibaut pledged homage to Philip Augustus.[124] We shall see that his subsequent embrace of extreme religious practices alienated him from the affections of his wife and eldest son, but while he was still in the secular world he collaborated closely with Helvide in making gifts to the abbeys of Saint-Jean-des-Vignes in 1195 and Mont-Saint-Martin in 1206.[125] In 1208, however, they were found to be acting separately in disputes with monastaries.[126]

His *vita*, composed by a monk at Longpont after his death in 1217, naturally follows Cistercian conventions in recounting his life, but it also takes care to report unique aspects of his aristocratic career that were unusual for this genre of saints' lives.[127] In hagiographic fashion the account is divided into four sections: (1) a secular knight in a secular life, which is treated summarily; (2) a religious knight in a secular life; (3) a monk in a religious life; and (4) his miracles and influence after death. The author reassures his readers that while he will not neglect Jean's holy life and miracles, he will also bring to memory, with God's help, his secular knighthood with its manifold deeds and battles, but without detracting from his spiritual virtues.[128] (The plausible historicity of several of these accounts has warranted that I cite them at appropriate points in this study.) The *Vita* finds it worthy of note that Jean was beloved by King Philip Augustus who preferred to call him "Jean le preux" (*Johannes probitas*) rather than Jean de Montmirail. Not only did he wage war successfully against the enemies of the French, but in a particular Norman campaign against Richard, the French king found himself surrounded at Gisors with his army defeated and lacking reinforcements. Jean succeeded in rescuing the king from imminent death and summoned reinforcements.[129] For these exploits he was honored with rich clothing, but Jean preferred fighting with interior humility as a "knight of Christ" over receiving exterior royal decorations. We also know that after the death of his mother, and then of his father, his stepmother Alix de Courtenay, of royal lineage (she was the king's niece), placed the orphan in the royal court where he was received as a close friend of the king because they were both of the same age (born in 1165). On the Third Crusade in 1190, however, he accompanied Count Henri of Champagne to Acre and not the king.[130] Nonetheless, his associations with the royal court were doubtlessly responsible for the characterization of his family as royal (*regia generis nobilitate*).[131] Like contemporary knights Jean was also an enthusiast of tournaments in which he indulged with extravagant generosity that descended into prodigality, reminiscent of Guillaume le Maréchal and the romance heroes. He later remembered that he had spent 1,000 *livres* for just one tournament, which had dissipated his family's wealth and possibly that of his wife. This expense may explain his reconstitution of Helvide's dower in 1200 by replacing alienated property with new property.[132]

At an unspecified date, the *Vita* reports that Jean began to take frequent counsel from a religious-minded regular canon who did not flatter him for his military victories, but, like the biblical daughter of Jephtha who had advised her father on his return from battle, he questioned Jean on the ultimate value of these youthful tournaments and warlike activities. In their place the monk proposed a religious program that would encourage Jean to descend from the heights of secular power to cultivate the monastic values of humility and poverty. Jean adopted Abbot Bernard of Clairvaux's ideal of "the knight of Christ" (*Christi miles*), which opened the second phase in his *Vita*—a religious person living in the secular world (*in seculo non seculariter vivebat*), to which the author devoted two chapters.[133]

As a *miles Christi* Jean inaugurated his new vocation by following Philip Augustus's example. As a good farmer he not only planted virtue but also rooted out weeds and thorns sown by prosperous Jews. Like the king in the royal domain in 1180/81, Jean began confiscating synagogues in his lands, expelling the Jews, and canceling their debts, which had been lent in money compounded with usury. Unlike the king, however, who thereby enriched himself, Jean built and endowed a hospital at Montmirail at his own expense where the poor, strangers, pilgrims, and the sick were charitably received.[134] Jean's biographer then proceeded in hagiographic fashion to detail numerous accounts of his charity and humility that were totally beyond the pale of a secular lord. Oblivious to the stench, Jean took delight in personally burying the dead, kissing the putrified breast of a poor woman, and frequenting and kissing lepers. When out of cash, he shared his tunic with a poor leper in the tradition of Saint Martin, the ancient sainted knight. He gave a costly warhorse to another needy leper. Continuing in this hagiographic tradition for two chapters, his works of self-abnegation were located at specific places throughout his lands that could be identified— for example, at Cambrai, Montmirail, Oisy, Provins, Crèvecoeur, and Soissons. Throughout this catalog of piety, the author carefully noted that the *Christi miles* remained in the secular world and still attended to his seigneurial duties, if unconventionally. When making a routine visit to one of his domains, for example, he steadfastly refused to judge the complaints that came before the court because of his preoccupation with higher spiritual affairs. On another occasion, a blind man interrupted Jean's dinner to confess that he was a notorious sinner accused of robbery, witchcraft, adultery, sacrilege, and other crimes, whose eyes Jean had ordered put out as fit punishment for his misdeeds; this judgment had, however, brought about the criminal's reformation and saved his soul from eternal damnation. Declining gratitude from the repentant, Jean further rewarded him in his new life. As a powerful lord himself, he was irritated by the multitude of knights and horses that crowded his castles at Oisy and Crèvecoeur and preferred the company of the poor and needy. When his familiars and knights had gone to sleep, he invited the poor to share his bed while he slept on the floor. This may have suggested to cloistered readers that he and his wife had taken mutual vows of chastity, but the acknowledgment of seven children amends that hypothesis. In all events, while practicing vigils, prayers, and austerities during the hard winter months, Jean finally resolved to escape the tumult at Montmirail and to retreat to a forest cabin called eponymously "Le Bois," where he abandoned knightly glory and became a hermit, a true "knight of Christ."

The year must have been 1209 because it coincided with Pope Innocent III's preaching of the crusade against the Albigensian heretics in the South. Jean prepared to take the cross, now as a committed *Christi miles* in Bernard's original sense. Seeking sufficient money to give alms to the poor while en route, he attempted to sell his woods in the Cambrésis for 7,000 *livres*, as we have seen.[135] Once again, however, his temptation for chivalric glory was called back to order by a faithful servant who reminded him that the proposed pilgrimage would only divert him from his final purpose to escape the secular world as a hermit. Jean commissioned the servant to inquire from a celebrated anchorite in the diocese of Liège where he might best pursue this path, but the response came as a surprise. Jean's purpose would be best served not as a solitary hermit but as a monk in a monastery, preferably that of the Cistercian order.[136] Now it was Jean's turn to require a second opinion. Like other candidates for monastic orders he sought the advice (*responsum, consilium*) of the theologians teaching at the nascent university of Paris. Arriving with his lordly retinue, he was greeted by the congregation of theologians, probably at the cloister of Notre-Dame. After an honorarium of thirty *livres* was offered, the customary procedure for drawing up such a committee was proposed: ten of the most distinguished theologians were to hear the request and choose three members, who as the "sounder and better part" (*sanior* of the *maior pars*) would then make the decision and finally obtain confirmation from the seven others. The result was unanimous, but unsurprising—that he should join the Cistercian order. At the time the faculty of theology was still under the influence of the celebrated theologian Pierre the Chanter, who not long before had donned the monastic habit at the Cistercian abbey of Longpont in the diocese of Soissons, before his death in 1197.[137] The final question was, therefore, which house should he choose? At least seven Cistercian monasteries lay within his family lands, but the ever-original Jean sought to follow the Lord's command to Abraham: "Leave your native land, abandon your family and your father's house." Hoping to avoid all further seigneurial entanglements, Jean chose, again unsurprisingly, Longpont, beyond the western borders of his lands. Still pretending to depart for the crusade, Jean left his grieving household with a few companions and was received as a monk at Longpont on Ascension Day (27 May) 1210.[138] Besides the date of his death, this is the only date recorded in his *Vita*: it was a high point in the abbey's history.

Now cloistered at Longpont, Jean entered the third phase of his career—a monk living in a monastery—but this did not abate his passion for expressing humility in unconventional ways. On Ascension Day he prostrated himself before Abbot Gaucher, who later became abbot of Cîteaux, and submitted to the customs of the Cistercian order with its vigils, labors, and observances, as well as an austere dietary regime. It was the degree of abstinence that brought Jean into his first conflict with his superiors. While the monks were served one loaf of bread each day in the refectory, Jean preferred the rotten bread left for the dogs. This extremity unsettled the brothers' routine and provoked a dispute between Jean and the prior over his disobedience to constituted authority, which was nonetheless resolved in Jean's favor.[139] Jean continued in his eagerness to perform unpleasant tasks such as cleaning the vomit of a sick monk at night and disposing of it in the latrine.[140] Jean also created problems with his own familiars who had joined him at Longpont. A former servant named Amandus wished to continue his former task of cleaning his master's shoes at night, considered to be a degrading task. When discovered, Jean became overwrought at this affront to his own humility, but peace was finally achieved when the prior persuaded the lord to reciprocate the task with his former servant each evening so as to preserve the lord's humility with the servant's respect.[141] Following all this internal friction, it was not surprising that the prior was prompted to ask the knight whether he was satisfied with the Cistercian order. Jean affirmed that he preferred no other order. When the prior pursued as to what Jean now desired, he replied that if he were to enter again, he would come not as a monk but as a *ribaud* (*ribaldus*), that is, as a stable boy. Beyond their reputation for immorality, stable boys were assigned the cleaning of stables and the removing of dung, for which they ate their bread in the sweat of their face but were considered precious in God's sight.[142]

Jean's cloistering, however, apparently did not prevent him from exiting Longpont on external business, as further anecdotes reveal. Outside, he returned to his penchant for removing dead animals from the roads and kissing lepers wherever he found them; for such bizarre activities he was greeted with jeers from other workers. At his castle of Gandelu in Brie Jean donated a house in pure alms to his abbey against the opposition of his oldest son, also called Jean, who prohibited the monks from taking possession, but he did consent to the monks contributing minor repairs. The father immediately seized the opportunity to carry tiles to the roof on his own shoulders. Later he gave to his abbey the minor tithes at the same castle, but again the eldest son objected and prevented their collection. Jean's tenuous relations with his family became evident whenever he passed by Montmirail. On one occasion he and his prior received only perfunctory hospitality at the express command of his son; on another when he had business at his ancestral home, he asked to see his wife, but was informed that she was taking a bath and could not be disturbed. Jean received the refusal with good nature and proceeded to visit his stepmother at La Ferté-Gaucher where he was entertained with honor and pleasure. "At least you are not taking a bath," the humbled monk observed.[143] (After his father's death, however, the son Jean, his namesake and heir, began making donations from Montmirail and Crèvecoeur for the soul of his ancestor.)[144] While at La Ferté-Gaucher Jean continued to exercise his peculiar manner of administering justice. Sentenced by the countess, a certain person who was held in prison for robbery was about to have his members amputated or his eyes blinded. Jean pleaded with his stepmother to spare the culprit the corporal punishment in exchange for receiving the cross to depart overseas on a crusade. When the perplexed woman invited her stepson to take charge, he refused to serve as judge in the affair, but still recommended the proposed remedy. Upon his release from prison, the man prostrated himself to thank Jean, and Jean, in turn, reciprocated to guarantee his humility. To the evident question—how can a convicted criminal justly escape punishment, protected by the sign of the cross?—Jean's answer was that as a monk he had the right to liberate sinners through works of mercy.[145] The *Vita beati Joannis* is filled with many more such anecdotes of which this bare summary does slight justice. The author of the *Vita* also agreed that it would be difficult to detail the humilities, vigils, austerities, and tears of this athlete of Christ, but it was time to turn to the intercessions and cures after his death.

Jean de Montmirail expired on the vigils of Saint Michael's (28 September) in 1217, the other date noted in his *Vita*. The last two chapters of his *Vita* return to a more conventional narration of the saint's postmortem influence, freed now from the idiosyncrasies of his earthly existence. The night in which Jean died, the prior Hugues had a vision of the monks singing in procession with their candles, among which one burned brighter. A *conversus* experienced a similar vision except that he saw the visage of the saint descending in the form in which the Lord was depicted in stained-glass windows.[146] Numerous miracles of healing were performed at his tomb and at the invocation of his name. Among them were healings of serious illnesses such as the loss of speech, fevers, and multiple tumors, and of minor ailments such as arthritis, migraines, and diarrhea. A pious Norman woman reported a vision on the feast of the archangel Michael in which she saw the saint on his deathbed received by angels. Although he was still burdened with a few minor lapses (*leves negligentias*) for which he had not done penance, with God's help he spent only three days in purgatory before entering the glorious company of the saints.[147]

Jean was first buried outside of the church, but when it was decided to move him to another location, a stonecutter from Pacy conjectured that the coffin did not contain the saint's bones because the monks had thrown them to the dogs. For this blasphemy God punished the stonecutter with a hideous deformity of the mouth that could not be healed until the miscreant, who sought healing at other saints' tombs, returned repentant to Jean's grave. His tomb was transferred to the chapter house and inserted into the wall behind the monks' seats, where it again became the occasion for further miracles.[148] This may have occurred during the construction of the new Gothic edifice that was consecrated in 1227.[149] In 1236 the chapter of Longpont applied to Pope Gregory IX to canonize their saint, for which a papal commission was appointed, but without result. The reputation of the miracles nonetheless culminated in 1253 when the Cistercian order granted permission to Jean's daughter Marie, wife of the powerful Enguerrand III de Coucy, to transfer the body to the Gospel side of the main church of Longpont, where she constructed a grandiose Gothic tomb in two levels (Figure 14). The upper displayed the tonsured saint to full view in his Cistercian cowl. Beneath and partially obscured by architraves lay the effigy of the knight, clad in mail armor from his metal cap to his feet. The inscription read: "He who lies under this stone at Longpont wished to submit voluntarily to following Christ; he whose ashes are here was the heir of Montmirail; his name was rightly 'Grace of God,' Jean; thanks be to Christ who honors us in him." (Isidore of Seville had glossed the name Jean with "Grace of God.") In testimony of his Montmirail heritage two trilobes decorated the tomb with four figures in one and six in the other, representing his ten children—three more than genealogists have discovered. Only three had survived by the time the tomb was fashioned. Rarely had a knight-saint been represented in his duality more sumptuously, poignantly, and faithfully.[150]

In stark contrast to the conventional, stereotyped, and abbreviated life of Saint Thibaut de Marly, the lengthy *Vita* of Saint Jean de Montmirail is a fascinating, even historical document. Framed in the narrative structure of traditional hagiography, the actual deeds of humility and poverty that the featured saint performs surely surpass the contemporary conventions of sainthood both

Figure 14. Tomb of Jean de Montmirail at Longpont (dép. Aisne), Gaignières drawing. BnF Est., Rés. Pe 1e, fol. 92. Photo courtesy of the BnF.

in their originality and extremity. Lest we dismiss them as the fantasies of an overenthusiastic hagiographer, however, they are embedded in a historical narrative that not only enlivens the life of an eminent knight but also illuminates the conditions of aristocratic life at the turn of the twelfth and thirteenth centuries. We see a historical knight serving the king on *chevauchée* and amusing himself at tournaments, presiding over seigneurial justice and founding hospitals, despoiling Jews and departing on crusade, quarreling with his family and seeking advice from the schools at Paris—all of this activity being situated in localities precisely identified by recognizable place-names on the frontiers between the Paris region and Champagne. Even in his Cistercian cowl Jean de Montmirail becomes recognizable as an authentic aristocrat during the reign of Philip Augustus.

Chapter 9

The Voice of Vernacular French

The vast majority of records that pertain to the aristocracy around Paris were composed in Latin by clerics and monks, all men of the church, including the clerics in the service of the king. In principle, however, a knight (*miles*) was deemed to be illiterate (*illiteratus*), that is, he did not benefit from a Latin schooling. This condition did not, of course, exclude exceptions, nor did it prevent aristocrats from using clerics to read or write for them in Latin so that with the collaboration of clerics they became functionally literate. Nonetheless, as early as 1180 the vernacular author of *Ipomedon* averred that "if the laws and letters in Latin are not translated, they are scarcely understood."[1] The maternal language of the aristocracy was, of course, vernacular French, which they spoke and heard daily. During the second half of the twelfth century an occasional layman read and wrote French, thus producing the *chevalier lettré* (literate knight) as opposed to the *miles illiteratus* of Latin.[2] In one of the earliest survivals of written French, the *Vie de saint Eustache*, the author explained, "Both clerics and laymen are accustomed to use the vernacular; that is why I wish to speak in French."[3] (Normally, of course, saints' lives were composed in Latin.) By 1200 a considerable body of vernacular literature appeared that separated into two principal genres—the epic, or *chanson de geste*, epitomized by the classic *Chanson de Roland*, and the romance represented by the well-known Chrétien de Troyes, both of which were written for the listening and reading pleasure of aristocratic audiences. This vernacular literature spoke most directly to the lords, ladies, and knights themselves at the turn of the century, but it was composed almost entirely of fictional tales. Actual deeds and events were recounted for the most part in histories, which remained in Latin, the exclusive language of churchmen.

Many activities relevant to aristocrats were nonetheless recorded exclusively in the vernacular. The aristocratic world painted by these writers, of course, overlaps with that of the Latin histories and the ecclesiastical documentation, but it also expands the boundaries, introducing subjects that the Latin authors were reluctant to address. Thus we are introduced to women who do more than confirm their husbands' transactions, to romantic love between knights and ladies, to chivalric courtesy, prowess, and largesse, and to the pastimes of tournaments and hunting that were the passions of aristocratic society. While the forms of aristocratic society remain the same as in Latin, the colors of that society are brilliantly enhanced by the vernacular writers. Any account of the aristocracy omitting these perspectives would be seriously deficient.[4]

Vernacular History: The *Histoire de Guillaume le Maréchal*

One important exception to the domination of history written in Latin nonetheless appeared in the *Histoire de Guillaume le Maréchal*, which was commissioned in the 1220s by one of the leading baronial families of England in order to recount the biography of their scion, Guillaume le Maréchal, earl of Pembroke, who rose from being a simple knight to become a great baron and regent of the realm.[5] What was exceptional about the *Histoire* was that it was composed not in Latin but in vernacular French. That Guillaume was an English baron would certainly disqualify him for my purposes except that from boyhood he was raised in Normandy, and as a young man he participated in warfare and tournaments in the neighborhood of Paris from the 1180s until around 1200 when Philip Augustus finally expelled the English from northern France. His biography remains, therefore, perhaps the most detailed and accurate history of northern and western France at the end of the twelfth century. It would lead me far from my project to rewrite the biography of Guillaume le Maréchal, which has been done well and often,[6] but I cannot neglect a source that illuminates aristocratic society so vividly around the fringes of the territory and at the beginning of the period that concerns me. It was composed by a layman named Jean (*Johans*), otherwise unidentified, who originated from western France, perhaps from the Touraine or Anjou, and wrote in a standard literary French of the West, that is, in octosyllabic verse with rhymed couplets.[7] Not only did he profit from personal experience, good informants, and reliable documents to furnish an unusually accurate account, but as a lay vernacular author he was also acquainted with romance literary conventions and at times they color his work. Many modern accounts of medieval society have relied so heavily on his *Histoire* that French chivalry has often become little more than the *Histoire de Guillaume le Maréchal* writ large; nonetheless I cannot neglect his testimony that impinges on subjects of interest to me.[8]

Vernacular Romance

The royal court of Philip Augustus was particularly proud of the language it spoke. When a Picard trouvère, Conon de Béthune, appeared at the court, the king and queen mother, Adèle de Champagne, made fun of his French, reproaching him for not having been raised at Pontoise.[9] Despite this linguistic snobbery, historians of French literature have come to recognize that the region around Paris produced little vernacular writing during the reigns of Louis VII and Philip Augustus, perhaps due to the reputation of the Capetians who were openly hostile to the entertainment profession. The dominant area of literary production in this period was not Paris, Picardy, or Flanders but the county of Champagne where Chrétien de Troyes wrote five celebrated romances in the standard literary language of octosyllabic verse with rhymed couplets: *Erec et Enide*, *Cligès*, *Le Chevalier au lion* (*Yvain*), *Le Chevalier de la charrette* (*Lancelot*), and the *Conte du Graal* (*Perceval*). While in the past literary historians have associated this standard language with the region around Paris, more recently they have conceded that its center of production was in Champagne, the homeland of Count Thibaut, Countess Marie, and the queen mother Adèle. These romances, which took few pains to disguise their fictionality, retold the adventures of King Arthur and his knights and were accepted as classics. Without doubt the aristocrats of the Paris region were acquainted with these romantic and enthralling tales. In the first decade of the thirteenth century, however, a new genre of romance was announced in Champagne by the appearance of the *Escoufle* (ca. 1200) and the *Roman de la Rose* (ca. 1209) attributed to Jean Renart.[10] Posing under this pseudonym, Jean composed fictional stories in Chrétien's standard literary verse and style, to which, however, he added a striking innovation, the "reality effect" (*effet de réel*). This was the addition of details and episodes from actual life that enhanced the realism of his narrative. For example, rather than setting his stories in the never-never land of Chrétien's Arthurian mythology, Jean placed them in identifiable settings, in particular, in the territory stretching from the Liégois to Lorraine along the eastern borders of the kingdom of France with the German Empire. Although the principal actors of his stories are patently fictional, he populated his romances with secondary figures like King Richard the Lionheart, Michel de Harnes, and Guillaume des Barres, who were historical personages, easily recognizable to contemporary audiences. By such *effets de réel* Jean attempted to mediate between romance and history for the pleasure of his aristocratic audiences. When Jean dedicated the *Escoufle* to the contemporary Baudouin IX, count of Hainaut, and the *Roman de la Rose* to Milon, *prévôt* of the chapter of the cathedral of Reims, he declared his allegiance to Otto of Brunswick, the Welf contender to the German Empire, who became Philip Augustus's principal rival to the east. Jean confirmed this political posture by organizing a fictional tournament at the actual town of Saint-Trond near Liège in which a party of knights, all identifiable partisans of Otto, bested a party of French knights, all identified as loyal to the Capetian king. Obviously, Jean did not expect that his romances would be appreciated by the aristocracy around Paris who remained faithful to their overlord.

Gerbert de Montreuil: The *Roman de la Violette*

Yet Jean found a close imitator in Gerbert de Montreuil who composed a *Continuation* to Chrétien's *Conte du Graal* (1226–30) as well as the *Roman de la Violette* (1225–31).[11] As noted in Chapter 1, from Montreuil located on the northern coast of the county of Ponthieu, Gerbert dedicated his *Violette* to Marie, countess of Ponthieu (d. 1251), who was married to a rebellious baron of the Paris region, Simon de Dammartin. Much of the action of the *Violette*, as in Jean's *Rose*, takes place at Cologne and Metz in the middle space between France and the Empire. In the *Violette*, again like Jean in the *Rose*, Gerbert eschews Arthurian mythology. His story, he proclaims, "is not about the Round Table, nor of King Arthur and his men" (vv. 34–35). And like his mentor, he adopts the crucial technique of the *effet de réel*, expressed in an abundant use of precise geographic settings and identifiable historical personages. Gerbert nonetheless makes a decisive break with Jean's political context by shifting the stage from the Empire and the fictional Emperor Conrad to the Capetian heartland and King Louis VIII, Philip Augustus's son. Jean had opened the *Rose*, "In the Empire where the Germans have been for many days and years . . . once there was an emperor . . . Conrad" (vv. 31–35). Gerbert echoed, "Once there was a king in France, handsome, *preu*, and brave . . . Louis" (vv. 65–66). Gerbert's story begins with the Easter court of the king of France at Pont-de-l'Arche (v. 86) downstream from Paris and then continues upstream at Melun (v. 698), both favorite residences of Philip Augustus at the end of his reign.[12] At the end of the *Violette* Gerbert retains this Capetian setting by staging a tournament at Montargis on the southern border of the royal domain, south of Mez-le-Maréchal on the Loing River. As in Jean's *Rose*, the itineraries of the participants to this event are delineated with such precision that they can easily be traced on a map. Most important, like the *Rose*, Gerbert's *Violette* confirms his political allegiance by identifying the participants of the two contending parties at Montargis (vv. 5912–58). While the defeated party led by the villain Lisïart, count of Forez, consisted of turbulent barons recruited, as we shall see, from the Auvergne and Beaujolais, the victorious side was championed first by the historical Amaury (d. 1241), count of Montfort, and second by the fictional hero Gerart, count of Nevers, and was composed entirely of those who were faithful to the Capetians in the 1220s and 1230s. It included, for example, Philippe Hurepel, a royal son and count of Boulogne; the royal cousins Pierre and Robert de Dreux (d. 1234), counts of Brittany and Dreux; as well as two royal knights from the Paris region, the lords of the Garlande and Barres families. Later, Barthélemy de Roye, too old to participate in the contest, was brought on the scene. At least four of these figures had stood by the king on the field of Bouvines.[13] It is true that the dedicatee of Gerbert's *Violette* was Marie, countess of Ponthieu, who was wedded to the rebellious baron Simon de Dammartin. At Bouvines, Simon had joined his brother Renaud de Dammartin, count of Boulogne, against Philip Augustus and was captured and exiled.[14] (Marie's petitions with Louis VIII and then with the regent Blanche of Castile finally succeeded in obtaining permission that her husband Simon might return to his domain, albeit under strict conditions.) It must be remembered, however, that Marie was also of Capetian blood, the daughter of Guillaume, count of Ponthieu, and Alix de France, daughter of King Louis VII and Constance of Castile. Unlike her husband, her father Guillaume had remained faithful to the king and had fought with him at Bouvines. Marie was, therefore, Philip Augustus's niece and Louis VIII's cousin, thus accommodating her to Gerbert de Montreuil's Capetian orientation.

In imitation of Jean Renart's *Rose*, Gerbert's *Violette* adopts the plotline of the *cycle de la gageure*, that is, of the virtuous maiden who is calumniated. When Gerart, count of Nevers, brags about the virtue of his *amie* Eurïaut, the villainous Lisïart, count of Forez, challenges him with a wager that the girl can be seduced and proposes the county of Nevers as the prize. Although Lisïart is unsuccessful as a seducer, he nonetheless surreptitiously obtains compromising knowledge that Eurïaut has a birthmark on her breast in the shape of a violet (just as the heroine in Jean's romance had a rose on her thigh) and wins the wager. Gerart loses Nevers, and Eurïaut is dismissed in disgrace, but when Gerart learns the truth about the stratagem, he sets off in quest of his *amie*. His travels take him through the border space between France and the Empire where he proves his prowess in countless battles, often against overwhelming odds, but he nonetheless survives because of his love for his *amie*. In the end he rescues her from burning at the stake in the nick of time; with his Capetian allies he challenges Lisïart and his companions to a tournament of Montargis; he proves Eurïaut's innocence in a judicial combat against the villain; he regains his county and marries the heroine. If the reality effects of geography and historical personages were calculated to capture the attention of an aristocratic audience around Paris, Gerbert has nonetheless produced a work that continued to exploit the fictional characteristics of Chrétien's romances. In a territory that was impoverished for lack of vernacular writing I have therefore found the *Roman de la Violette* to be useful in sketching the ideals, dreams, and fantasies of the mental world of the aristocrats surrounding Paris.

Gerbert de Montreuil shared a final innovation with Jean Renart. As was noted in Chapter 1, both Jean and Gerbert proudly drew attention to the fact that they had included songs and melodies in their stories.[15] Thus in addition to telling charming stories, both romances were transformed into anthologies of lyrics popular at the time. As Jean promised, he inserted forty-eight lyrics into his narrative and thereby created a new literary genre of lyric anthology.[16] Gerbert's manuscripts include between forty and forty-four lyrics in his narrative, two of which are also found in Jean's.[17] Moreover both proclaim that the lyrics were to be both read and sung: "No one will ever be tired of hearing it because he can sing and read it, if he wants. It is made with such delight that all who will hear it sung and read will take such pleasure" (*Rose*, vv. 18–21). "The story is beautiful and noble which I wish to recite and recount to you, because one can both read and sing therein" (*Violette*, vv. 36–38). Just how these texts were meant to be read and sung at the same time is not made evident, but it appears nonetheless that both authors conceived of their romances as virtual musical comedies in which music was intermingled with narrative. The manuscripts of neither romance contain musical notation, which was only supplied in later manuscripts called *chansonniers*. Although Jean quotes a strophe or two and Gerbert is normally content with the initial line, it is nonetheless clear that both suggest the appropriate lyrics that the reader would recognize or that a performer would supply. As in popular concerts, "everyone knows the song." Thus the lyrical insertions also played the role of *effet de réel* by reminding the audience of the songs of their day.

Gace Brulé

The songs anthologized by the two romances covered the whole repertoire of lyrics available at the turn of the twelfth century. They include translations into *langue d'oeuil* of the famous Provençal poets Bernart de Ventadorn and Jaufre Rudel, as well as songs from contemporary northern trouvères like the Vidame de Chartres and the Châtelain de Coucy, but the most frequently cited (seven lyrics) was Gace Brulé, the most popular of all trouvères.[18] As a songwriter, Gace's output was prodigious. By the end of the thirteenth century the *chansonniers* had collected over eighty of his poems and supplied the music for more than sixty, a record that placed him above all contemporary trouvères. As a historical personage, however, his figure is shadowy, and the information that he revealed about himself is oblique. In one lyric composed in Brittany he expressed nostalgia for Champagne; in another he seemed to suggest that he resided at Nanteuil,[19] but the place-name is so common that it is difficult to locate. His language resonates with the vocabulary of lordship suggesting that he was of knightly origins. A later *chansonnier* depicts him on horseback with a shield bearing the heraldry of *burulé* (alternating red and silver stripes) certainly associated with his name.[20] He often mentioned his friendship with Geoffroy, duke of Brittany, with the count of Blois, and with the countess of Brie (read Champagne),[21] which may have implied their patronage, but, as mentioned in Chapter 1, we are now aware of two other patrons whom he does not mention. He received an annual *fief-rente* of twenty-four *livres* from the *prévôté* of Mantes, and the household accounts of Prince Louis from the year 1213 recorded that he received ten *livres* from revenues, likewise at Mantes.[22] Moreover, one charter surviving from 1212 states that he held land at Groslières not far from Dreux to the west of Paris.[23]

It is difficult to identify the dialect of a poet because the text of his poems is most often determined by the linguistic preferences of the scribes who copied the text. The editor of Gace's poems concluded that he wrote in Champenois, but a Champenois that did not greatly differ from the standard literary language of his time. Thus Gace can be included within the Champenois orbit of Chrétien de Troyes, while not ruling out patronage of him by the Capetian royalty.[24] What is distinctive about his language is its orality. If Jean Renart and Gerbert de Montreuil were unclear as to how their lyrics were to be read and sung, Gace's poetry clearly exhibits characteristics indicating that it was composed for oral performance. The rhymes are often chosen to facilitate recall for the performer. Certain rhyme words are likewise repeated frequently, and *chanter* and *dire* are the two terms most frequently associated.[25] All of this befits the most popular songwriter of his day.

If Gace is reticent about himself, he nonetheless seasons his poetry with abundant contextual markers, not the least of which are geographical and political references and mentions of fellow poets. Despite nostalgia for Champagne and his allusion to residing at Nanteuil, the realm of France remains his encompassing geographic reference. In romance tradition, a "sweet lady is the most beautiful in all of France"; similarly, the French king provides the standard of comparison for everything desirable.[26] Like Jean Renart, however, Gace remains aware of the competition between the German Empire and the French kingdom when he refers to "a hope of being emperor and crowned king of France."[27] If a recently discovered *jeu parti* is genuine, he even discusses the contemporary dispute between Philip Augustus and Otto of Brunswick.[28] His most frequent contextual device, however, was to delineate a broad circle of contemporary poets. His *envoies*, that is, the concluding verses that address fellow trouvères to whom he dispatches his poems, name at least twenty personages. However, unlike his mentions of highborn patrons who can be readily identified, Gace employs pseudonyms, even *senhals* (poetic fantasies), to mask his recipients, thus engaging modern scholars in literary guessing games.[29] *Noblet,* for example, could refer to the Guillaume de Garlande who was married to Alix de Châtillon, and another address to a *Gallandois* may refer to the same person.[30] *Le Barrois* may refer to the eastern count of Bar, but it could equally have been sent to the ubiquitous Guillaume des Barres.[31] More opaque, the often cited *Gui de Pontiaus* masks the contemporary Guy, châtelain de Coucy, who also appears as *Chastelain*.[32] *Bochart* could refer to one of the Marly family, and *Amauri* to one of the Montforts.[33] Other trouvères, such as Blondel de Nesle (Jean de Nesle?) and Gautier de Dargies likewise return the compliment, addressing *Gasse* in their *envoies*.[34] Thus these trouvères created an enclosed poetic universe; they conceal their addressees for their esoteric amusement, but if some of these modern identifications are accurate, we cannot help but notice how many belonged to the aristocracy around Paris during Philip Augustus's reign. In particular, Guy, the châtelain de Coucy, was among the prominent lords of the Paris region who accompanied Philip Augustus on the Third Crusade, and in 1199 Geoffroi de Villehardouin counted him among those "from France" who took the cross at Écry for the Fourth Crusade.[35]

Gace Brulé and his coterie of trouvères who wrote in the northern dialect of *langue d'oeuil* were the direct heirs of an earlier and similar poetic tradition created by the troubadours of Provence who composed in the dialect of *langue d'hoc*.[36] Gace and the anthologists Jean Renart and Gerbert de Montreuil knew and quoted Jaufre Rudel and Bernart de Ventadorn, the most popular of these southern poets, and were well aware of their prominent themes concerning women and love. Doubtlessly the northerners considered themselves to be the continuators of the same tradition as their southern predecessors. While the influence of the troubadours on the trouvères is important to literary historians, it is unlikely that the contemporary audiences of the trouvères were led to draw similar comparisons; rather, they likely accepted the trouvères on their own terms without inquiring into their southern origins. For my part, commenting on the troubadours' influence would lead me too far from my own goals.

Raoul de Hodenc: The *Roman des Eles*

A final but short text, the *Roman des Eles*, also drawn from the periphery of our region, was composed around 1210 in octosyllables with rhymed couplets for the instruction of the aristocracy.[37] Despite its title, it was not a *roman* in Chrétien's sense but a didactic poem teaching the virtues of knighthood. It was organized around the schematic figure of a bird called "prowess" (*proesce*) with two wings—on the right, "largesse" (*larguesce*), and on the left, "courtesy" (*cortoisie*)—each possessing seven feathers. "Largesse" is further defined by the feathers on the right, but on the left "courtesy" includes more variety, ranging from respect of the church, to suitable speech, genuine joy, and concluding with the definition of love. The author identifies himself as Raoul de Hodenc. If this is Hodenc-en-Bray in the Beauvaisis to the north of Paris, Raoul was a knight and a nephew of the cleric Pierre de Hodenc who gained fame as chanter of the chapter of Notre-Dame at Paris and as one of the leading theologians of his day. The uncle's influence would thereby help to explain the scholastic coloring of this treatise that sums up the essence of knighthood for lay audiences.[38]

Lacking vernacular texts composed directly in the Parisian region during Philip Augustus's reign, I am obliged to draw on others from the peripheries of our region. The *Histoire de Guillaume le Maréchal* will therefore provide testimony from the biography of a historical knight who was active in the region during the opening decades of the reign. Composed at the end of our period, the *Roman de la Violette* offers a romance, a literary genre that encapsulates what aristocratic audiences expected for entertainment, while the *Roman des Eles* attempts to schematize chivalric culture. Finally, the lyrics of Gace Brulé and the Châtelain de Coucy offer songs that were most popular with these audiences. Through the fictions of these vernacular texts that spoke directly to aristocratic men and women I shall attempt to enter the mental universe of the aristocratic audience and to capture the fantasies, dreams, and ideals that embellished the life that they desired. The historian cannot ignore this mental world revealed in the vernacular fictions because it is as historically real as the events and deeds recounted in histories both in Latin and in the vernacular.

The Vernacular Lady: Women and Love

In the Latin ecclesiastical charters the female presence is largely limited to wives who consent to their husbands' transactions, particularly if they concern dowries or dowers. In the vernacular writings, however, women appear overwhelmingly as objects of love. Without doubt, love (*fine amors*) was the dominating theme of this fictional vernacular literature, but it was almost never homosexual. Only momentarily is Gerart, the hero of Gerbert de Montreuil's *Violette*, accused of preferring men, when he withstands the seduction of a hostess (vv. 3521–23). Women—noble ladies and maidens—are therefore the exclusive love objects of aristocratic men in the fictional romances and lyrics. In the *Histoire de Guillaume le Maréchal*, historical women are kept to the background, though they are not entirely absent. They dance with the Marshal before the tournament at Joigny (vv. 3455–76); the Marshal rescues a woman whose house is on fire (vv. 8753–60); another smuggles bandages to the wounded Guillaume (vv. 1759–84); and a noble lady awards the prize pike to the hero after the tournament at Pleurs (vv. 3042–51). Never does a lady's beauty catch the eye of the narrator;

only Guillaume's physical appearance is admired: he had brown hair, the face of a Roman emperor, a perfect body, and a broad crotch (*forcheüre*), valuable for one who lives on horseback (vv. 728–35).

Women abound in Gerbert's *Violette*. The romance opens in Pont-de-l'Arche at the court of King Louis who "cherished ladies and maidens." After dinner was served, the king proposed a festive ball for which the ladies hastened to prepare themselves. The tables cleared, the music was provided by the singing of ladies from the noblest families of France—Besançon, Burgundy, Blois, Saint-Pol, Coucy, and Niort. When the châtelaine de Dijon requested a song from the hero Gerart, he complied with verses of Gace Brulé: "Since a dear lady and true love request it, I shall again compose an elegant and lovely song" (Gerbert vv. 191–92; Gace no. 1, p. 2). The heroine Eurïaut is first to be introduced to the court at Melun with a full description of her clothing in accordance with romance tradition. Like Chrétien's Enide, she wears an embroidered violet tunic, a silk belt, and a green mantle lined with ermine, but Gerbert lavishes most attention on the gold, precious stones, and tiny silver bells that adorn her rich garments (vv. 812–56). Resplendent as are her clothes, they are nothing compared to Eurïaut's own appearance. Ten literary beauties—Helen, Dido, and Iseut among them—are called as evidence. Then follows Gerbert's description of Eurïaut from head to waist, following a canonical convention in romances:

> Her head of curls was a resplendent gold, her forehead as white as polished glass . . . her eyebrows brown, her eyes clear and pure, her nose straight and delicate. . . . The summer rose that opens in the mornings was not as radiant as her mouth and complexion. . . . Her cheeks were whiter than silver or ivory enhanced against the red. But of one thing I marvel, that she had a neck and chest more white than the lily or the pine in flower. She had white hands and well-formed arms. . . . Although not more than fifteen years of age . . . her small breasts were raised high and newly pointed. (vv. 868–900)

At this point Gerbert breaks off—only what was visible through the clothes was permitted in the romance canon.

While Eurïaut's feminine beauty is conventional, Gerbert de Montreuil takes an unusual step in noticing the physical characteristics of his masculine hero as well. Gerart, count of Nevers, is introduced to the court at Pont-de-l'Arche by King Louis. "His face was so fine, his body, arms, and hands so well formed, but nothing in comparison to the complexion of his face which was as the rose in May. . . . A lady's blood quivered at the sight" (vv. 164–70). In contrast to the knightly attributes of the historical Guillaume le Maréchal, Gerart's beauty appears to reflect the feminine qualities that Gerbert found in his heroine Eurïaut.

After Eurïaut's betrayal is alleged, Gerart wanders through the forest thinking dark thoughts about his *amie*. The women who betrayed Solomon, Samson, and Absalom in the biblical narrative come to mind momentarily, but this misogyny dissipates after he learns of her innocence (vv. 1292–1304). He regrets his lapse of faith and remembers Gace's lyric: "I say that it is great folly to try to test your wife or your beloved as long as you want to love her" (Gerbert vv. 1311–18; Gace no. 45, p. 150). Gerart therefore pursues his quest for the heroine, encountering en route dozens of seductive damsels in distress whom he rescues at perilous danger but at no loss of his virtue. At the final denouement it becomes clear that unlike other romance heroines (Jean Renart's Lïenor, for example) Eurïaut remains a passive figure whose final redemption is due entirely to the exertions of her lover. Gerbert adapts Eurïaut's steadfast loyalty to Gerart to exemplify the same virtue of his patroness Marie, countess of Ponthieu, who patiently endured disinheritance by the king (v. 6647).

When one of Eurïaut's suitors, the duke of Metz, contemplates her beauty, he also is inspired by Gace Brulé's song, which contains the lines, "Ah! lady, white (*blanche*) and radiant (*clere*) and rosy cheeked (*vermoille*), all my desires stem from you" (Gerbert vv. 1266–76; Gace no. 76, p. 252)—the standard romance attributes of female beauty. While Gace's lyrics are chiefly devoted to the sentiment of love, he is not unmindful of his object's physical beauty, but his attention is centered on her face, mouth, and eyes (no. 9, p. 28; no. 11, p. 30; no. 37, p. 128). With more discretion than Gerbert de Montreuil, the furthest he will proceed along the body is "her tender face, white hands, long and well-shaped fingers . . . beautiful arms, elegant white neck, head with shining blond hair . . . and mouth that can smile so well," but his motivation remains sensual: "which makes love burn and glow" (no. 71, p. 234). Indeed, he will enjoy "her loving, pleasing body" (no. 32, p. 112) because "God has created her great beauty and lovely body" (no. 5, p. 16). Unlike romance writers, however, who name the heroines they celebrate, Gace's lyrics are addressed to countless women who remain unidentified. Gace the trouvère is the consummate but ever-discreet lover.

Fine Amors

The *Roman de la Violette* therefore recounts a love story between a knight, Gerart, count of Nevers, and Eurïaut, his *amie*, whom he loves and loses along with his heritage through treachery and finally regains after numerous trials, while she remains steadfast to the end. Although Gerbert de Montreuil does not employ the term, *fine amors* is the subject of his romance. *Fine amors* was not only the pervasive subject of vernacular literature in the adventures of romance; it was also treated endlessly and repetitively in the songs of Gace Brulé. It remained the supreme virtue, but was also the impossible to define virtue, despite Raoul de Hodenc's clumsy efforts to include it in his didactic *Roman des Eles* as the seventh feather on the wing of courtesy. Raoul's maladroitness notwithstanding, salient characteristics of *fine amors* emerge from the romance poets.

Following the convention of the southern Provençal troubadours, *amors* required an inevitable alternation between joy and suffering, but from the pens of the northern poets suffering predominates.[39] The first lyric in the *Violette* that was intoned by a noble lady in the court at Pont de l'Arche begins, "Go softly; I suffer of love" (v. 104), to which the succeeding travails of the lovers testified amply. To illustrate this concretely Gerbert raised specific examples of lovesickness (*mal d'amour* or *amor heroicus*), which since ancient time doctors had identified with the symptoms of paleness, insomnia, and mental distress. It was first employed fraudulently by the villain Lisïart to gain Eurïaut's attention (vv. 401–10), but the symptoms of Gerart were genuine when he fell desperately ill at Cologne over the loss of his *amie* (vv. 2346–80). Hardly a stanza of Gace's poetry failed to treat *fine amors* without echoing the vocabulary of pain. For example, the first of the songs that Gerbert borrowed from Gace, sung by the hero of Gerbert's story, opens with, "Since a dear lady and true love request it, I shall again compose an elegant and lovely song" (Gerbert vv. 191–92). But the song concludes with the *envoie*, "Lady, I shall thus suffer as long as I continue to live" (Gace no. 1, pp. 2, 4). Another verse about supreme love (*haute amor*) begins forcefully with "Pain of love, torment, and misfortune have so dealt with me that I no longer know what to think; grief has turned into such a habit" (Gace no. 41, p. 140).

Many are the causes for this somber outlook. Borrowing from the Provençal troubadours, for example, Gace assigned the blame to "treacherous flatterers out of envy" (*felon losengier d'envie*; no. 17, p. 56), "wicked people" (*males gens*; no. 42, p. 142), "slanderers" (*mesdixans*; no. 80, p. 268), and even "jongleurs" (*janglors*; no. 3, p. 10), just as Gerart had held the slanderous Lisïart responsible for his grief. More generally, however, the problem was attributed to the seasons, to which Gace was particularly sensitive. Rarely was he able to boast that "I hold my lady dear in all seasons—in winter and in summer my love for her is young and new" (no. 28, p. 98). And only on occasion does he feel his love rise with the coming of spring: "In the sweetness of the new season, when everything turns resplendently green, when meadows and orchards and thickets are beautiful and the birds sing among the flowers, then I rejoice, for everyone else abandons love . . . I alone wish to love" (no. 38, p. 131). Most often, however, spring brings sorrow: "When the snow and frost and cold come to an end with the harsh season, when leaf and flower and grass return with the beautiful weather, then I sing without mirth" (no. 14, p. 42). Or again: "When I see the mild season arrive, when snow and frost come to an end and I hear the little birds warble on the branches in the woods, then my lady makes me feel a pain from which I never wish to be cured" (no. 10, p. 28). Summer brings little relief: "Upon the return of summer warmth, when the fountain stream flows clear and the woods and orchards and the fields are green and the rosebush flowers red in May, then will I sing, for the pain and distress which grips my heart will have lasted too long" (no. 29, p. 100). Naturally winter is no better: "When leaf and flower fade away and I see the cold come in, then I sing as I would cry" (no. 44, p. 146). Fall is the same: "When I see the weather beautiful and bright before there is snow or frost, I sing to console myself, for too much have I forgotten joy . . . when the best-loved lady in the world always tries to make me suffer" (no. 9, p. 26). Gace is acutely attuned to the changes in the seasons of northern France, but springtime is no cause for joy—only grief provides the inconsolable melody to his songs throughout the year.

There were other reasons, of course, for the lover's distress. On the wing of courtesy Raoul de Hodenc in his *Roman des Eles* likened love to the sea, to wine, and to a rose. The sea is governed by the wind, which can be fickle and treacherous, blowing one ship off course, bringing another to a good port. Like merchants, some lovers can be ruined and others become inordinately rich (Raoul vv. 509–50). Echoing the Tristan legend, Gerbert also adopts the sea imagery in the *Violette*. Gerart declares that he is not at sea without a mast or sail or rudder, unlike some whose love is unrequited and who cannot therefore come to port (Gerbert vv. 215–24).[40] In Raoul's schema, however, love is not all pain and misfortune; like wine and the rose, it can be a positive force. If left in the keg, wine clarifies and purifies itself of dregs. If love is born of the heart, the lover will always improve his qualities. Love, moreover, is like the rose, the most excellent and courteous of all flowers. When a rose is placed in a *chapelet*, it illuminates and enhances the other flowers, so love enhances other qualities, such as courtesy, generosity, and beauty (Raoul vv. 551–631). We shall see below that love also enhances the most important virtue of prowess. Like Raoul's *Roman*, Gerbert's *Violette* also concludes on a positive note. If the first lyric quoted is "Go softly; I suffer of love" (Gerbert v. 104), the last concludes, "Who loves well should not torment himself . . . without love no one can know true joy" (vv. 6616–20). And to this anatomy of *fine amors* a final observation about the *Histoire de Guillaume le Maréchal* cannot be avoided: if women remain in the shadows throughout, *fine amors* is likewise notable by its near total absence. The Marshal's masculine world around Paris in the 1180s was scarcely touched by the sentiments of the romances and trouvères.

Fine Amors and Absence on Crusade:
The Châtelain de Coucy

Chief among the causes for suffering from *fine amors* was the absence between lovers. I have postponed discussion of it until now because of its special pertinence to the historical context at the turn of the twelfth century. In the *Violette* we remember that Gerart's loss of Euriaut produced severe *mal d'amour* and generated the remaining adventures. When Gace Brulé proclaimed that one should not test the love of one's beloved, he has his lady respond with a blunt question: "When will you go overseas?" (no. 45, p. 150). In the contemporary setting she was anticipating, in effect, that he would depart on a crusade, thus bringing about the dreaded separation between lovers. This extreme form of absence thus generated a whole corpus of verse named by scholars the *chansons de croisade*,[41] produced by trouvères including the Picard Conon de Béthune and, most prominently, the Châtelain de Coucy, who, unlike Gace Brulé, is well attested among the historical aristocracy of the Paris region. The Châtelain composed a corpus of at least fifteen songs that continued to display Gace's characteristic themes, such as the effects of the seasons on lovers, the canonical beauty of the female body, and the torments of *fine amors*, leading to absence, and its most severe testing on the crusade. In two *chansons de croisade* the Châtelain explored the conflict of allegiance between *fine amors* and God that produced a crisis of faith and ended in blasphemy that blamed God for betraying love.

In his first and most popular lyric (it was also quoted by Jean Renart in the *Rose*, vv. 923–30), the Châtelain begins:

> The new season, May, the violets, and the nightingale all summon me to sing, and my courteous heart makes love so sweet that I cannot refuse it. Would that God grant me such honor that I might hold her naked one time in my arms before I go overseas. From the beginning I find her so sweet that I do not believe that I can endure the suffering, but her sweet face, her small fresh mouth, her beautiful, brilliant eyes, laughing and clear, have captured me before I can give myself to her. . . . Among all joys is that which is crowned, which comes from *amours*. God, what am I to do?[42]

The second *chanson de croisade* accuses God directly before fellow lovers:

Lovers! It is before you above all that I display my grief, because I must depart straightway and separate myself from my loyal companion. Losing her, nothing is left of me. . . . Great Lord God . . . what shall I do? Is it necessary to take final leave from her? Yes, by God, it cannot be otherwise. I must go without her into a foreign land. . . . Great Lord God, how can I abandon the great joy, the solaces, the company, and the sweet words that she spoke to me, who was for me lady, companion, and lover? . . . *Merci, Amour*! If ever God did baseness, he acted as a villain when he broke the bonds of loyal love . . . and still I must abandon my lady. . . . Now they will rejoice, those false traitors (*losengeour*) who have the possessions that I once enjoyed. But I would never be so perfect a pilgrim that I would wish them well; because of that I may lose the benefits of my pilgrimage. . . . I am leaving, my lady! To God the Creator I commend your body wherever I should be. I do not know if ever you will see my return. It will be by chance that I shall ever see you again. . . . And I pray God that he accords me the honor that I remain for you a true lover.[43]

Clearly blasphemous, *fine amors* is prized higher than defending God's cause.

The Châtelain de Coucy, however, was not only a trouvère but also a historical crusader. He was Guy (d. 1202), married to Marguerite, and the contemporary châtelain of Coucy.[44] His existence is attested in charters of donations to churches, such as Ourscamp and Saint-Crépin-en-Chaye in the Noyonnais and Saint-Vincent in the Laonnois, which his wife approved and Philip Augustus confirmed.[45] In particular, these charters illustrate his preparations for two crusades, the Third Crusade in 1190 and the Fourth in 1201. He returned from the Third and left again on the Fourth. According to the historian Geoffroi de Villehardouin, he sided with the crusaders at Corfu who refused to proceed against Constantinople. When the decision went against his party, he continued with the expedition but died while crossing the Aegean, and his body was buried at sea.[46] The local charters show that he was not alone on the Fourth Crusade but was joined by a cousin, Renaud de Coucy, and Renaud de Magny, the husband of his aunt Mauduite.[47] His own charters had prepared for the eventuality that he might not return. In announcing his intention to travel to Jerusalem in 1190, he affirmed that should he die on the pilgrimage or in any other place, without heirs of his wife, his donations would nonetheless remain valid.[48] In 1201 he reconfirmed the 1190 grant but added land from the dower of his wife with her consent.[49] In the end the couple remained childless, and the castellany passed to a Renaud, his aunt's descendant.

When compared with the self-image of the trouvère, the surviving historical documentation on Guy, the châtelain, poses intriguing questions. How does the trouvère who passionately resists leaving his *amie* for the crusade square with the historical Guy who carefully prepared two crusades with the apparent co-operation of Marguerite, his wife? Evidently the *amie* whom he wants to hold naked in his arms is not the wife. Is it possible that the châtelain's entire scenario is patently fictional yet illustrates a pervasive hostility against the crusading movement among aristocrats? The situation, however, becomes more complex. At the end of the century a certain Jakemes composed a romance in which the Châtelain de Coucy, now named Renaud, falls in love with the lady of Fayel.[50] When the lady's husband discovers the incipient affair, he tricks the châtelain into departing on a crusade where the latter conducts himself bravely but dies on his return. The husband has the crusader's heart served to the lady for dinner, which produces her death from shock when the gruesome truth is revealed. The theme of the *coeur mangé* was known to other romances, but of concern to us is the reputation of Jakemes's châtelain-trouvère as a fictional crusader, which outweighed the memory of Guy the historical crusader.

Romance Courtesy

Courtesy constituted the left wing of Raoul de Hodenc's bird of prowess, and joy was the fourth feather that counseled knights to listen gladly to songs (*chançons*), melodies (*notes*), fiddles (*vïeles*), airs (*sons*), and the delights of minstrels. If a knight heard a lady slandered in song, moreover, he should move to have the song changed (vv. 322–25). In the masculine and warlike *Histoire de Guillaume le Maréchal* women appeared briefly at the tournament of Joigny and invited Guillaume and his fellow knights to dance with them while they waited for the contest to begin. Guillaume, who had a good voice, provided the music, later continued by a young minstrel (vv. 3471–82). Guillaume sang not only as a young knight but also on his deathbed as the elderly and esteemed baron. To assuage his pain and restore his appetite he satisfied his urge to sing by summoning two daughters, the younger of whom he taught to sing the refrain of a *rotrouenge*, a dancing song (vv. 18531–80), perhaps recalling the tournament at Joigny. These brief notes heard faintly in a historical context swell into a voluminous "sound of music" in Gerbert de Montreuil's fictional *Roman de la Violette*. Jean Renart had boasted that the insertion of songs and melodies (*chans et sons*) into his *Roman de la Rose* was an innovation that enhanced his narrative as scarlet dye enriches fine cloth (vv. 1–17). Gerbert simply announces that "you will hear many courtly songs before the end of the story" (vv. 44–47), but he nonetheless fits his songs and music more adroitly to his romance.[51]

We remember that Gerbert opened the *Violette* at the royal court at Pont-de-l'Arche with King Louis inviting the members to dance to *chansons à carole* supplied by the singing of noble ladies. Dance music furnished well over half of the lyric insertions in the *Violette*.[52] Although Chrétien had included dancing among the festivities in his romances, he never presented his major characters as singers. Jean and Gerbert, however, assign solos to the principal actors of their dramas, and their repertoire consists mainly of the *grand chant courtois* with Gace Brulé the principal songwriter. Their predominant theme remains that of the pain and pleasure of *fine amors*. In the *Violette*, Gerart opens with Gace's "Since a dear lady and true love request it, I shall compose an elegant and lovely song" as a response to the lady's invitation (Gerbert vv. 191–92; Gace no. 1, p. 2). The song ends by avowing suffering (Gace no. 1, p. 4), as seen above. Nonetheless, in conformance with Raoul de Hodenc's advice, Gerart defies slanderers who would betray love (Gerbert vv. 193–97; Gace no. 1, p. 2). When Eurïaut opens, she immediately reacts against this danger by intoning Bernart de Ventadorn's "There is no trouble, deception, treachery, so I think, unless someone makes himself clever at guessing the love of others" (vv. 324–31), which she sings in the Provençal original. To withstand Lisïart's advances, she adopts Moniot d'Arras's *chanson de mal-marié*: "Leave me alone, do not ask me again; know truly that it is wasted breath" (vv. 447–49). The duke of Metz voices his incipient love for Eurïaut with Gace's "He who, advising me of love, says that I should detach myself from it does not know what arouses me" (Gerbert vv. 1266–75; Gace no. 76, p. 252). A *chanson de toile* served to recall Eurïaut's name to Gerart and to break the spell of the love potion (vv. 2303–9). After dozens of major pieces from Gace Brulé, Bernart de Ventadorn, the Châtelain de Coucy, and others, Gerart addresses Eurïaut with another of Gace's songs, a fitting hymn for their approaching wedding day. "Fields and orchards, gardens and woods give me no occasion to sing, but if it pleases my lady to command me, I cannot have a more fitting reason. It is therefore right that I tell of her merit, her graciousness and her true beauty. . . . True lover, I always say and would say that no man is a lover who fights against love. . . . No man can contend against its power" (Gerbert vv. 5790–98; Gace no. 67, pp. 219, 223). The music for these songs was assembled almost a century after the lyrics were composed.[53] In addition to being read silently, it was surely recited orally as well, but whether the melodies were actually sung cannot be determined. With song and music Gerbert de Montreuil has nonetheless transformed his simple narrative of adventure, if not into a grand opera, at least into a musical comedy.

Aristocratic Amusements: Hunting

Except to examine the moral qualifications and earnings of the profession of jongleurs, the ecclesiastical writers in Latin paid little attention to the amusements of singing and dancing.[54] Nor were they interested in other entertainments by which aristocrats passed their leisure hours. These activities, however, caught the attention of vernacular writers, particularly when they recounted festivities on high holidays. Despite the preoccupation with fighting throughout the *Histoire de Guillaume le Maréchal*, the author offers momentary glimpses into playing chess (v. 100), throwing stones for distance (vv. 1800–1828), and, predictably, dicing for horses, this time in the company of Guillaume des Barres (vv. 4178–96). Chrétien de Troyes's scene of knights and ladies amusing themselves with games in a pleasant meadow sets the paradigm for romance writers.[55] The trilogy of chess, tables, and dice were the standard amusements in Jean Renart's *Rose* (vv. 498–503). Gerbert de Montreuil follows suit when his hero visits Cologne (*Violette*, vv. 3223–24). Chess was played on a lined board (*eschiquier*) akin to the modern version. Tables included a variety of games, also on a diagrammed board, resembling English backgammon or French trictrac. Dice, the game of chance, was played with multiple cubes.[56]

High among the aristocratic pastimes, however, was that of the hunt, or as Chrétien called it, "the pleasure of woods and streams" (*deduit de bois et de riviere*).[57] *Bois* of course designated the forest, while *riviere* stood for the streams, the habitat of fowls that could be hunted with birds of prey. Jean Renart devoted sustained passages to hunting in both of his romances. In the *Rose* (vv. 138–223) a spring hunt for deer opens the narrative; in the *Escoufle* the hero Guillaume is portrayed as an experienced falconer. In great detail Jean describes his capture of a buzzard (*escoufle*), an episode that serves as a turning point and lends its name to the narrative (vv. 6725–66). In conscious imitation of the episode, Gerbert describes a similar scene in the *Violette* (vv. 4144–229) where Gerart also hunts with a bird of prey, this time with a sparrow hawk (*esprevier*). He exits Cologne on his horse with his hawk on his wrist to ride downstream along the Rhine in search of larks (*aloe*), quail (*quaille*), magpies (*pie*), and teals (*cerciele*). When he hears the song of a lark while it is in flight and before it has come to rest, he spurs his horse and releases his hawk's jess. The hawk takes off from Gerart's wrist and catches its prey as it attempts to escape. Both buzzard and lark play key roles in the plots of the two romances, but both allow the authors to demonstrate their knowledge of falconry—another *effet de réel* for the pleasure of their aristocratic audiences.[58]

When Robert III de Dreux (d. 1234) served with Prince Louis in 1214 to confront King John's expedition toward Paris from the west, we remember that he was captured by the English in a rash sally across the bridge at Nantes. His imprisonment in England, however, befitted his aristocratic status, as he was allowed to pursue the pleasures of hunting in the forests and streams. It is significant that the fact was noted by the vernacular chronicler of Béthune.[59]

Hunting was also the one aristocratic pastime that was referred to in the ecclesiastical charters, particularly when the charters involved the transfer of woods and forests. The acquisition of woods by churches occupied only a small fraction of their transactions with the aristocracy (6 percent of 610 charters),[60] but occasionally the rights of hunting were included. For example, Jean de Corbeil and Jean, castellan of Noyon, handed over their hunting rights with their woods,[61] but Gautier the Young, royal chamberlain, and Guy IV, butler of Senlis, retained their right to hunt in their donations.[62] Gace de Poissy, the father of Robert de Poissy, served as royal forester in the forest of Cruye with rights over hunting as well as other jurisdictions.[63]

The Vernacular Knight: Prowess (*Proesce*)

Since the *Chanson de Roland* and the romances of Chrétien de Troyes, prowess (*proesce*; adj., *preus*) has reigned supreme among the virtues of knighthood, but it has proved difficult to encompass it with a simple definition. Emphasizing the ideal of excellence, it included all the qualities appropriate to knighthood. Raoul de Hodenc demonstrates the difficulty in formulating a definition when he asserts that no knight "can be esteemed for prowess unless that prowess has two wings . . . largesse and . . . courtesy" (vv. 140–45). In other words, prowess is equated with the total sum of the virtues of knighthood. Among its facets, however, may be listed bravery, strength, and endurance, which reinforced the military functions of knighthood. Yet, the historical Guillaume le Maréchal, whom his biographer calls "le meillor chevalier del monde" (v. 19072), was never designated as *preus*. From 1186 to 1204, as he passed through the formative years of early manhood absorbed in the fighting of northern France, his biographer affirms: "Subsequently he led such a very fine life that many were jealous of him. He spent his life in tournaments and at war and traveled through all the lands where a knight should think of winning renown. In France and the Low Countries, throughout Hainaut and Flanders, came his high reputation for great exploits" (vv. 1513–20).

The dominant image of chivalric prowess in the romances was the solitary knight who had set out on a quest for exploits in battle. Inspired by Chrétien, the image was slighted by Jean Renart in the *Rose*, but his follower Gerbert de Montreuil took up the romance tradition again. After his hero Gerart de Nevers had lost Euriaut but had learned of her innocence, he traveled widely in search of her on the French and German border through Cologne, the Ardennes, and Metz and thereby encountered numerous adventures involving castles under siege and ladies in distress for whom he was obliged to fight a series of formidable adversaries in titanic battles under adverse conditions, all to prove his prowess and his love for his *amie*. Gerbert devoted more than half of the *Violette* to recounting these exploits. Since romance audiences had long demanded such adventures, Gerbert stereotyped them according to a conventional formula. The first combat against Galerans, lord of Gorgerans, outside the walls of Cologne in behalf of Lady Aigline, illustrates the essential features. The two champions challenge each other on horses, charge, and meet with such force that their lances splinter, their shields split, and they both fall to the ground, stunned. Characteristically, then, their time on horseback is brief; most of the battle is waged on foot and with swords. When they revive, they attack each other with such ferocity that their faces are blinded with blood and sweat. Each refusing to surrender, they fall again in exhaustion. A second time they rebound to continue, only to fall once again, this time with the hero Gerart on top. It is only the memory of Eurïaut that enables the hero to summon the strength to cut the laces of his opponent's helmet and demand his surrender. When the latter refuses, Gerart severs his head (vv. 1879–2032). Despite the great injuries incurred, a succession of such battles is repeated against five named opponents and one giant, occasionally on horseback, but mainly on foot in single combat with swords. It is important to note, however, the contrast between this romance cliché and what is known about historical practice. In two decades of combat in northern France, Guillaume le Maréchal was always depicted as fighting on horseback. Never did his biographer portray him as brandishing his sword on foot. The single combats were a romance convention with which Chrétien and Gerbert regaled their aristocratic audience. Equally significant, the combats were most frequently fought not for their pleasure but for the love of a lady. Not only did Gerart battle to defend Eurïaut's honor, but *fine amors* for his *amie* enabled him to triumph under the most adverse conditions. Single combat was therefore closely linked to *fine amors* as a romance fiction to please an aristocratic audience.

Gerbert's two final combats, however, assume a different form. They are transformed from single combat into judicial duels or trials by combat. At the end of his journeys Gerart finally discovers Eurïaut at Metz, about to be burned at the stake for a murder of which she is unjustly accused. Gerart offers to prove his *amie*'s innocence in battle against her malicious accuser Melïator. The ensuing combat follows the romance stereotype with the champions entering on horseback and finishing on foot. After Melïator loses his arm, he surrenders and confesses to his false accusation (vv. 5518–634). Then comes the final wager, before King Louis's court, to prove Eurïaut's innocence by battle against Lisïart's calumny. As a climax to the romance, the ensuing combat exaggerates the tribulations of battle to the limits of belief. After being unhorsed, the opponents plunge into seven assaults on foot. When Eurïaut's virtue is once more impugned,

Gerart again finds the strength to bring the battle to an end. As a final twist to the inevitable denouement, Lisïart loses his helmet and feigns surrender, thereby allowing him to stab Gerart with a dagger as the latter unsuspectingly tries to help. This final treachery results in the villain's full confession and execution. In depicting the two judicial combats, Gerbert de Montreuil is careful to follow contemporary procedure. Accusations and denials are formulated in oaths that are sworn on relics; counsel is taken from other parties; wagers are received; pledges are furnished to guarantee appearance; and mass is attended before battle. The fact that Guillaume le Maréchal had also proposed such trials by combat to clear his own name (vv. 5744, 5759, 5770–80) suggests that they were still practiced at the end of the twelfth century. In the 1220s, Guillaume le Breton, moreover, suggested that Philip Augustus was tempted to settle his differences with the count of Flanders by single combat at Boves in 1185.[64] (Whether or not this was proposed only to highlight the king's bravery, it was nonetheless offered as a plausible procedure.) Like tournaments, however, judicial battle had been forbidden by the church council at Clermont in 1130 and was included with the prohibition of ordeals by fire and water by the Lateran Council of 1215. Little notice was paid to these prohibitions, however, until Louis IX promulgated anti-dueling ordinances later in the thirteenth century.

The Making of a New Knight

Early in the twelfth century when knights began to identify themselves on their seals, they depicted themselves as riding with their swords prominently raised above their heads. We remember that the sword was also the earliest emblem to be engraved on a knight's tomb. The sword thereby became the consummate symbol of knighthood, and knighthood itself thereby began with the receiving of the sword by dubbing or by belting. In our period "belting (*cingulare*) with a sword," became the expression of inception into knighthood. As we have seen, adult male aristocrats accepted the classification of knighthood (*miles*) and began to distinguish themselves from nonknights who were designated as squires (*armigeri, domicelli,* and *valeti*). In the eleventh and early twelfth centuries churchmen had composed treatises in Latin prescribing ecclesiastical rituals requisite for creating new knights, but no further examples appear by the end of the century.[65] Only brief notices of knighting have surfaced in the thousands of ecclesiastical charters from our period. Around 1180, for example, Maurice, bishop of Paris, declared that Guérin, son of Renaud *de Grangiis*, pledged to give land and justice in alms to the abbey of Vaux-de-Cernay, and that "in the year in which he becomes a knight" (*anno quo miles fiet*)—that is, when Guérin would be legally competent to make the donation—Guérin would concede this gift.[66]

In 1210 Adam *de Viliers* declared that he had received the wardship (*ballum*) of the fief that Guy *de Viliers*, deceased, had held from Saint-Denis in liege homage. Adam affirmed that when Pierre, the son of Guy *de Viliers*, came of age—when Pierre became a knight—his wardship would end and Pierre would hold the fief.[67]

The principal testimonies in our period to the inception of knighthood come from vernacular literature and from occasional glimpses into historical practice provided by chroniclers. The *chansons de geste* had previously used the term "dub" (*adouber*) to indicate the giving of arms before combat, but it was Chrétien de Troyes who created a vernacular literature around the making of new knights. In his Arthurian romances usually the old king dubbed the heroes. The classic example, however, was the *Conte du Graal*, which offers a parody of Perceval, the young naïf stumbling into knighthood despite his mother's opposition. When he is finally belted by the *preudome* Gornemans de Golant, the whole ceremony has assumed a religious character consistent with the solemn goal of pursuing the Holy Grail. The young boy is blessed with the sign of the cross and admonished to adhere to the order of chivalry without wickedness.[68] In the *Escoufle* Jean Renart recounts the sumptuous festivities surrounding the knighting of the young Guillaume de Montivilliers by the count of Saint-Giles, but without reference to religious observances. Gerbert de Montreuil has no need for such ceremonies in the *Violette* because his heroes are of adult age, but in his *Continuation* of Chrétien's *Graal*, Perceval once again encounters Gornemans who again belts him with his sword, this time admonishing the young knight to do justice and defend the holy church (*Continuation*, vv. 3992–97, 5018–21).

With one important exception all of the historical occurrences of knighting in our period omit reference to religious ceremony. They do note, however, the common practice that the event was celebrated on the ecclesiastical feast day of Pentecost. On that day in 1209 at Compiègne Philip Augustus girded his oldest son Louis with the belt of knighthood with great solemnity in the presence of many magnates. The royal cousins Robert and Pierre de Dreux were also knighted as well as a hundred other knights. The chronicler Guillaume le Breton noted that the festivities were accompanied by an abundance of food and gifts that was never seen before or after that day.[69] In fact, however, the king had performed this ceremony on Pentecost every year.[70] For that reason Chrétien had punned that the day was so named because it cost so much.[71] Philip Augustus had withheld the belting of Louis until 1209 when the prince was twenty-two. Doubtlessly he wanted to protect his sole heir from the dangers of knighthood and in particular from the dangers of tournaments. At Compiègne Louis promised his father that he would attend such contests not fully armed but only with a simple hauberk and an iron helmet. Philippe Hurepel, Louis's half brother, made a similar promise in 1222.[72]

By the second half of the twelfth century it was apparently customary for the king of France to knight the major barons of his realm. In 1173 King Henry II of England desired that his heir, the young King Henry, be knighted by Louis VII, but the young Henry preferred to accord the honor to his boon companion Guillaume le Maréchal, "the best knight who ever was," much to the envy of the distinguished barons of France, including Guillaume des Barres and Bouchard de Montmorency. Henry handed the sword to the Marshal who belted him straightaway and with a kiss asked that God grant him prowess (*Histoire*, vv. 2071–2150).[73] Guillaume himself had been knighted by his patron the Chamberlain of Tancarville at the age of twenty-one in 1167 at Drincourt in Normandy. The Chamberlain "girded him with a sword with which he was to deal many a blow" (vv. 815–22). At the end of his life the Marshal was again accorded the honor of belting another king, this time the nine-year-old Henry III, just before his coronation at Gloucester in 1216 (vv. 15306–21).

These accounts of making new knights found in the contemporary Latin and vernacular chroniclers are silent about the religious dimensions of the ceremony emphasized in the ecclesiastical liturgies and the vernacular romances. The principal exception and the most explicit account of this ceremony in our period is furnished by the monastic chronicler Pierre, abbot of Vaux-de-Cernay, who related the events of the Albigensian Crusade in southern France. In 1213 at Castelnaudary, Simon, lord of Montfort, with his fellow crusaders requested the bishop of Orléans to knight his eldest son Amaury. The bishop first resisted but was later persuaded to perform the task. On the feast day of the nativity of Saint John (24 June) while celebrating mass, the bishop took Amaury on his right and Amaury's mother on his left. Before the altar on bended knee, the bishops of Orléans and Auxerre girded the boy with his knightly belt ("cinxerunt puerum cingulo militari"), intoning the hymn "Veni Creator." Thus with great solemnity the boy was made a new knight.[74] Doubtlessly the framework of the crusade endowed the ceremony with a religious emphasis that was usually practiced exclusively in military terms.

Besides the sword and lance the young knight required a horse and armor. After his knighting, Guillaume le Maréchal found himself at the tournament between Sainte-Jamme and Valennes without a horse. While his patron Guillaume de Tancarville attended to supplying him one, the occasion offered the biographer opportunity to describe how the knights prepared themselves on the eve of the contest, thus resulting in a recitation of the full lexicon of their equipment. The equipment of their horses was enumerated in detail: horse collars (*colieres*), horse blankets (*covertures*), bridles (*freins*), breast harnesses (*peitrals*), straps (*cengles*), and girths (*contrecengles*). But of more interest to the debutant knight was, of course, the armor: hauberks (*haubers*), leg armor (*chauces*), saddles (*seles*), stirrups (*estriés*), helmets (*hieaumes*), shields (*escu*), neck straps for shields (*guige*), arm thongs (*enarmeüre*), coifs (*coiphus*), ventails (*ventailles*), and chain mail (*mailles*) (*Histoire*, vv. 1232–46). In the *Violette* Gerart's adventures placed the hero in the similar position of lacking equipment, which then provided the author the opportunity to embellish with superlatives the armor he borrowed from Aiglante in defense against Galerans (vv. 1735–71), for example, or from Duke Milon to battle the Saxons outside of Cologne (vv. 2576–94). In battle against Galerans, his helmet came from Charlemagne and his hauberk had belonged to King Alexander. Against the Saxons, his helmet was surmounted with a panache of peacock feathers and his hauberk was finely worked with chain mail. Beneath his hauberk, he wore a tunic (*auqueton*) embroidered with gold. Over the hauberk, he wore a breast plate (*cuirie*) that was surmounted by a coat (*cotte*) woven by a Scottish lady. His leg armor was of iron and bound with sturdy straps (*coroies*). His spurs were of gold. Against the Saxons, both he and his horse were garbed in vermilion and he carried a shield and a lance with a banner. Against Galerans, his sword carried the inscription of a fabulous tale, which Gerbert took time to recount (vv. 1772–1829). Such embellishments undoubtedly were intended for his audience's pleasure.

Tournaments

It is noteworthy not only that Philip Augustus restricted his two sons' attendance at tournaments but that, more significantly, no tournament has been reported in the Paris region during his reign. The closest a tournament came to Paris was at Lagny on the Marne on the borders of Champagne. Evidently this absence conformed to the ecclesiastical ban on these military exercises promulgated at the council of Clermont in 1130 and then renewed at every major church council through the great Lateran Council of 1215. Despite this virtual "blackout" in the Latin documentation,[75] the vernacular sources both historical and literary vigorously testify that the tournament remained the most popular pastime of aristocratic society. The historian must turn to the accounts in the *Histoire de Guillaume le Maréchal* and the contemporary romances to obtain light on this important aristocratic activity. Most historians have done that, rendering the *Histoire* the classic text on the tournament at the end of the twelfth century.[76]

"At that time," the Marshal's biographer continued, "there was no war, so the Marshal took [the young King Henry] through many a region, as a man who knew well how to steer him in the direction of places where tournaments were to be held" (vv. 1959–62). "France, the Low Countries, Hainaut, and Flanders" were his favorite sites (vv. 1518–19). The contemporary chronicler Gislebert de Mons confirmed that Count Baudouin V of Hainaut likewise found this territory fertile for tournaments.[77] Even Gerbert de Montreuil has the fictitious Gerart, count of Nevers, tourneying nearby in Germany and Hainaut while remaining under the spell of the potion that induced forgetfulness (*Violette*, v. 3825). The *Histoire* names eleven sites in northern France where Guillaume attended tournaments during the last decades of the twelfth century. (In some seasons they were held every fortnight.) Since they always took place in the countryside, they were normally identified between two place-names. In fact, all eleven sites skirted the royal lands.[78] We have seen that the closest to Paris was at Lagny directly to the east on the Marne, at the border of Champagne. There the biographer had access to a tournament roll from which he recited the names of participants grouped by province, claiming that three thousand participated, including nineteen counts (vv. 4778–84). Those identified as French included great barons like Robert, count of Dreux, the count of Soissons, and Amaury, from the family of vicomtes of Meulan. Others recognizable from lesser families around Paris included the two Guillaumes des Barres (father and son), Adam, vicomte of Melun, Simon de Rochefort, Eudes de Plessis, and Thibaut de Vallangoujard. A Simon, named as the brother of the younger Guillaume des Barres, was perhaps Simon de Montfort (vv. 4481–540).[79] Evidently the French enjoyed a certain prestige as tournament fighters. At one unidentified contest they entered the field "with such a show of joy, as if they had already captured their adversaries" (vv. 2582–83). At Pleurs a good number of prominent barons of the kingdom made their appearance, among them the duke of Burgundy, the counts of Flanders, Clermont, and Beaumont, as well as the ubiquitous Barres (vv. 2909–20). If the contest at Lagny was held in 1179, it may have coincided with the coronation of the young king at Reims, but it is highly unlikely that the king, age fourteen, participated. Given the French enthusiasm for the sport, the complete absence of tournaments close to Paris confirms the royal policy.

Tournaments were an essential feature in literature as well.[80] Chrétien de Troyes recounted in detail four fictional tournaments, one in each of four romances. Jean Renart continued the tradition with the tournament at Saint-Trond to which he devoted nearly half of the *Roman de la Rose*, and Gerbert de Montreuil created another fictional one in the *Violette*, which took place under the auspices of King Louis VIII at Montargis, on the southern borders of the royal domain (vv. 5852–6067). After Gerart had rescued Eurïaut from the stake at Metz, the next item of business was to clear her name from Lisïart's calumny and to restore his rightful possession of the county of Nevers. When Gerart hears news of an approaching tournament at Montargis that would be attended both by Lisïart, count of Forez, and the count of Montfort, who had volunteered to champion Euriaut's cause, he joyfully makes preparations to attend. Garbing himself in white in romance fashion, he and his fellow knights arrive incognito. The contest is divided between two parties: barons and knights who are loyal to the Capetians under the leadership of the count of Montfort, as we have seen, and those who follow the villainous Lisïart, count of Forez. Although the names of the counts of Nevers and Forez are patently fictitious, the followers of the count of Forez, like the followers of the count of Nevers, were all identifiable historical personages. Gerbert omits their first names, but their families were easily recognizable—the count of Auvergne, dauphin of Montferrand, and lord of Bourbon; the counts of Chalon and Auxonne; the count of Sancerre and châtelain of Issoudun. Originating mainly from the mountainous Massif-Central, many of the families were intricately interrelated and were often allying or feuding with each other.[81] In contrast to the loyal Capetians, therefore, the opposing party was composed of disruptive barons, appropriate companions to the treacherous Lisïart. Further, the county of Nevers itself, like the *Violette*'s county of Nevers, had experienced a turbulent past, having been usurped with a tactic not unlike that of Lisïart.[82] At the time of Gerbert's writing, the count of Forez was Guy IV who in 1226 suddenly married Mathilde, the heiress of Nevers. Although the historical circumstances were different, Gerbert's audience would have known that the counties of Nevers and Forez recently had been united by marriage. As for the tournament of Montargis, the villainous Lisïart escaped, despite the valor of the French party on the field, thus requiring the final judicial duel to prove his guilt. Because the tournament of Montargis was not necessary to the main story, Gerbert devoted to it a scant two hundred lines, but in romance tradition a tournament could not be omitted.

If the *Histoire* shows how tournaments in northern France appeared to a vernacular writer in the last decades of the twelfth century, the *Violette* reveals what an aristocratic audience around Paris expected to find in the opening decades of the thirteenth. It will be useful, therefore, to compare the salient features of these two genres of vernacular writing. Naturally the Marshal's biographer was interested in the tactics of his hero's success, whereas Gerbert de Montreuil was understandably susceptible to romance ideals, especially those of prowess and love, but the two approaches were not mutually exclusive. The Marshal was not entirely immune to romance, and Gerbert's concern for the *effets de réel* oriented his attention to the current practices. We should therefore find the interplay of tactics and ideals within the same author.

In the *Histoire*, the knight rode to a tournament on a strong warhorse, protected by helmet, hauberk, and leg armor, bearing a shield hung from his neck, a sword attached to his belt, and a lance in his hand. Upon arrival on the field he joined one of two groups, for example, the Norman-English on one side and the French on the other (vv. 2579–80). At Montargis, those led by Amaury de Montfort were on one side and those led by Lisïart of Forez on the other (vv. 5912, 5938). Did the tourneyer usually engage as part of a group or individually? In the *Histoire*, some 2,500 lines devoted to the Marshal's tourneying career make clear that most tournament action was devoted to fighting in groups called squadrons (*conrei*, v. 1307), battalions (*bataille*, v. 1420), and troops (*rote*, v. 3627). Each one was commanded by a banneret—for example, the Chamberlain who carried a banner at Valennes and rallied his followers with the battle cry "Tancarville" (v. 963). Those who were able to keep their ranks tight and in good order ("li conrei seréement et sanz desrei," vv. 1417–20) were most often victorious. Between Saint-Brice and Bouère, for example, Guillaume noticed the difference between knights who approached in a disorderly fashion and those who rode in closed ranks (vv. 1417–20). Despite the French knights' high reputation, they rode in such disorder at a tournament between Anet and Sorel that Guillaume and his companions were able to drive through their ranks and put them to flight (vv. 2801–16). He who broke formation first was the first to be captured (vv. 2734–36). Never was there a better tournament than at Ressons and Gournay, exulted the author of the *Histoire*. Squadrons and battalions clashed so savagely and the field was so littered with broken lances and shields that it was impossible to spur one's horse through the debris. The tournament consisted of mêlées that broke out everywhere. The sounds of lances and swords drowned out God's thunder, and one truly remarked that the "brave and valiant are to be found between the horses' hooves" (vv. 6058–92). Lances splintered like glass (vv. 4856–59), swords and maces battered heads and arms (vv. 2509–11). Only restraint from killing one's opponent distinguished these mêlées from actual warfare. Although Gerbert de Montreuil has other priorities, he was nonetheless careful to retain a minimum of mêlées in the background at Montargis. After the initial clash between Lisïart and Gerart, the knights reassemble in formations (*routes*) led by bannerets and the resulting mêlée litters the ground with fragments of lances and banners (vv. 6011–20). The count of Auvergne later resumes an attack against the French battalions and squadrons (*batailles, conrois*, v. 6046), but two valiant knights, Barres and Garlande, parry his efforts. Gerbert's summary treatment, however, barely mentions the tactics that preoccupied the historical Marshal.

Gerart, the victor of so many combats against formidable adversaries, giants, and dragons was, of course, eager to display his prowess in romance fashion. In the king's presence, Count Lisïart passes between the parties and shouts a challenge to anyone who would oppose him. Although the count of Montfort is the first to attack, Gerart quickly takes over, adjusting his shield and lance and spurring his horse. Exchanging heavy blows, Lisïart breaks his lance on Gerart's shield, but the hero unhorses the villain and, passing by, utters his battle cry. These single combats on horses with lances were generally known as jousts (*joustes*). Not respecting the discipline of tight lines and closed ranks, Gerart then joins the mêlée, charging in all directions and gaining such glory that the king inquires about this white knight who has merited the grand prize of the tournament. In effect Gerart is simply following the romance tradition of Chrétien who had introduced tournaments to provide the stage on which his Arthurian heroes could display prowess in single combats and gain the prize of the day.

Although the fields of the *Histoire* are scenes of confusion, the Marshal's biographer does not lose sight of his hero. Guillaume is seen defending his patron, the young King Henry, capturing prizes and defeating opponents. For example, one knight lost a horse twice to Guillaume on the same day at Eu in Normandy (vv. 3272–73). In all of his tourneys, however, only one adversary who is defeated in single combat in romance fashion is named. Guillaume spies a certain Philippe de Valognes among the opponents, breaks ranks, seizes Philippe's bridle, and leads him off the field (vv. 1324–38). It is no surprise that the *Histoire* never records a defeat for the Marshal. Like the romance hero, after each tournament he is awarded the prize of the day. At Pleurs, for example, the prize is a splendid pike presented by a noble lady who commissions other barons to find the worthy recipient. When Guillaume is finally located at the forge, he has his head on the anvil where the blacksmith tries to extract his battered helmet (vv. 3041–43). The temptation to embellish the Marshal's exploits in romance fashion is always present. Although single combats are not the center of the *Histoire*, one out of three tournaments is preceded by a preliminary exercise called the *jostes de pladeïces* (*Histoire*, v. 1310) or *premieres commencailles* (v. 3214) in which young knights practice their skills in jousting, that is, with lances in single combat. Gerbert likewise prefaced his tournament at Montargis with new knights engaged in *commencailles* (*Violette*, vv. 5969–70).

Why does the knight engage in these ferocious battles on the tournament field? If the *Histoire* is to be judged, his motive was to acquire as much booty as possible. Guillaume entered his career in France as a landless knight dependent on the patronage of the Chamberlain of Tancarville and later the young King Henry. His biographer therefore paid particular attention to the prisoners, ransoms, and especially the horses he captured. In one case at Saint-Pierre-sur-Dives, for example, his prize came by chance. While the Marshal was at lunch, the opposing party instigated the combat early. When the mêlée moved into the village, a knight injured himself in his fall from his horse, thus affording a ready capture for Guillaume and the means to pay the lunch bill (vv. 7201–26), but most prizes were won with effort. The technique was to seize the bridle of the adversary's horse (*al frein*) and lead him off the field, as Guillaume did at Eu. He gained twelve on that day (vv. 3272–73) and fifteen at Anet (vv. 4020–21). Becoming successful, he went into partnership with a Flemish knight. A scribe who kept accounts recorded that they captured over a hundred knights in one season, besides horses and equipment (vv. 3420–22). On his deathbed Guillaume surmised that he had won more than five hundred ransoms over his lifetime (v. 18483). To add verisimilitude to his narrative, even if exaggerated, Gerbert de Montreuil likewise calculated Gerart's gains at Montargis to be in the thousands of *livres tournois*, including horses and seven knights, although he had not been able to capture Lisïart (*Violette*, vv. 6055–65). It was not a career of tourneying, however, that provided Guillaume le Maréchal his greatest fortune; it was his fame as the *meillor chevalier del monde* and his loyalty to the English crown that made him eligible to receive the heiress Isabel de Clare as wife and become one of the richest barons of the realm. For Guillaume, like the romance heroes of Chrétien and Gerbert de Montreuil, the tournament with its prizes became the theater of chivalric glory in which to display prowess.

We have seen that in romance, prowess was associated with *fine amors*. Under the spell of Chrétien's romance, knights fought for their lady's love. Gerart not only endured prodigious combats for Eurïaut's love, but at Montargis he decorated his helmet with her wimple and wrapped her head ribbon around his shield (vv. 5894–98). Entering the lists, "Chevaliers, mon amie Eurïaut," was his battle cry (vv. 6009, 6030). Chrétien de Troyes had established the tradition that tribunes be constructed to allow the ladies to observe the exploits of their lovers. In the *Histoire*, however, tournaments were not spectators' sport. The action traversed the countryside through fields and vineyards and descended on village streets, which explains the absence of female onlookers except at the beginning and the end of the event. Since tournaments were not a spectator sport, heralds were assigned to relate the feats of arms and minstrels were out front to witness the fine blows (vv. 977–79). While women were scarce in the *Histoire*, as were the traces of love, one exception reveals the influence of romance. We remember that at Joigny, while Guillaume and his companions waited for the tournament to begin, they passed the time dancing with noble ladies to the Marshal's singing. This episode was not merely an idle distraction; it improved the bravery and the skill of the participants. As the knights saw their adversaries approach, "because of the ladies' presence, the least courageous among them was emboldened to be the victor at that day. . . . They rode along at a measured tread in close formation, not one of them advancing in front of another. . . . And those who had been at the dance with the ladies put their bodies, hearts, and minds into performing well. . . . Just as lightning strikes down and flattens anything in its path, leaving nothing untouched, so those who had been in the company of the ladies continually got the better of the other side" (vv. 3524–52). It would be difficult to find better testimony of the power of a lady's love to enable prowess.

For Gace Brulé, the trouvère of love, however, the torments of love make him a better lover, not a braver knight. In Gace's vast repertoire of love poetry not a word is found about *proesce* except in a dramatic dialogue that records his name as a participant, which is unique in his collection. Although the word *proesce* remains absent, the dialogue involves two ladies, a false lady (*la fause*) and a good one (*la bone*), who discuss the merits of two knights. One knight is bad (*mauvais*) and the other noble, refined, and well spoken (*frans et cortois* and *beau pallier*). The outcome of such a schematic dialogue is, of course, apparent from the start, but what is of interest is the contrast between the two knights. The wicked knight is a coward (*coart*) who loves his lady for money, while the other, when he returns to the tournaments in his land, is without pride and excess (*sanz orguil et sanz folie*). The false woman, however, protests that she does not "love a knight who frequents tournaments, who wanders about and borrows and squanders money, and in winter dies of cold when his credit fails." She declares, "I do not need a lover to smash a big lance for his *amie*. . . . You take the honor; I'll take the money" (no. 81, pp. 268–73). If the verses are truly Gace's, the poet for once approves of the effects of love on those who fight.

Ladies observing a tournament from the distance suggests romance convention, but when they take over the spectacle themselves we can be certain that we have parody. An early trouvère from the Artois region, Huon d'Oisi, composed before 1190 a poem entitled *Tournoiement des dames*.[83] One year, he begins, when knights were created but refused to bear arms, a tournament was organized at Lagny by two prominent ladies, *la contesse de Crespi* (Aliénor, countess of Vermandois and Crépy) and *ma dame de Couci* (Alix de Dreux, wife of Raoul I, lord of Coucy).[84] We have seen that early in the reign of Philip Augustus Lagny was the closest to Paris one dared to suggest such an event. The text's objective was to identify some thirty-four aristocratic ladies who participated in the contest by offering their first names or family names or battle cries. Among them were the queen herself, Isabelle de Hainaut (*la roine*), three countesses—Marie de France, countess of Champagne (*la contesse de Campaigne*), Adèle de Breteuil, countess of Clermont (*la contesse de Clermont*), and Ida de Boulogne (*Yde*, crying *Bouloigne, Dex aie*)—and several other figures who can be recognized in the charters of the Paris region from their family names: *Trie, Marli, Triecoc, Poissi, Garlandon*, and *Cressonessart*. Huon's parodic intent is transparent in a situation where highborn ladies take over the chief amusement of newly created knights who refuse prowess in a region bereft of such opportunity.

Contrary to this pleasant female conceit, the tournaments were nonetheless serious masculine affairs perfectly comparable to the business of warfare as found in the *Histoire de Guillaume le Maréchal*. The anonymous author of Béthune who wrote history in the vernacular for his fellow knights underscored the resemblance between the battle of Bouvines and tournaments: Bouvines "was such a fine mêlée that the *preudomes* who were there testified that they had never seen such a good tournament as that battle."[85] Among those from the Paris region who distinguished themselves on the field was Mathieu de Montmorency who appeared on a mighty horse brandishing a scimitar (*faussert*). He rode with such force and unhorsed so many knights in the mêlée that no better knight could be recalled. Eudes, the duke of Burgundy, was dressed in the same coat of mail and bore the same shield as the valiant Guillaume des Barres. His feats of arms were reported as far as Syria (*surie*), but unfortunately they were attributed to Guillaume. When Eudes approached the Flemish, the latter were advised to turn flank lest they suffer from his attack.[86]

Writers of romance at the turn of the century often lamented the decline of chivalry in their time. When treating the exploits of the young King Henry in the 1170s, the biographer of Guillaume le Maréchal repeated the cliché by claiming that the young king's *proesce* had brought about the revival of chivalry, which had almost fallen extinct in his time (vv. 2635–41). However, in the biographer's own day (that is the 1220s) great men were so afflicted with sloth and greed that they bound *chevalerie*, along with largesse, in chains. To prove his point, he continued, "errantry (*l'esrer*) and tourneying (*le torneir*) have given way to jousting (*plaidïer*)" (vv. 2686–92). The full-scale battle had been replaced with the simple joust practiced by neophyte knights before the contest.

Vernacular Largesse

At Joigny ladies and *fine amors* were the source not only of prowess but of largesse as well.[87] While Guillaume and the ladies were dancing, a young herald took over the singing and began a new song, each stanza of which concluded with the refrain, "Come on, Marshal, give me a good horse." Needing no further prodding, Guillaume mounted immediately, rode out to the first advancing knight, unhorsed him, presented the steed to the herald, and rejoined the ladies without their having noticed his absence (*Histoire*, vv. 3483–516). At the end of each tournament the participants circulated from hostel to hostel to eat, drink, discuss the deeds of the day, and settle accounts. Winners collected their prizes, losers offered pledges to redeem their ransoms, but Guillaume was frequently depicted as giving away his gains. Those captured at Joigny had not really lost because the Marshal had forgiven their ransoms and bestowed his prizes on defeated knights and crusaders (vv. 3553–62). At Anet fifteen French knights were released at one time (vv. 4063–67). At Pleurs, where Guillaume won the pike, his biographer claimed that he had not come for gain but to do well and win honor (vv. 3007–12).

In the *Roman des Eles* Raoul de Hodenc emphasized the importance of *larguesce* by devoting to it the whole right wing of *proesce,* his metaphorical two-winged bird (vv. 144–266). The first feather links the virtue of largesse directly with bravery (*hardis*); then the successive feathers are employed to enumerate its practical application: for example, do not inquire into the value of possessions, give both to the poor and rich, never promise what one does not intend, and so on. Only the last feature suggests concrete gifts such as repasts and cloaks and connects largesse directly with prowess. Despite its desiccated nature, Raoul's discussion follows directly from Chrétien de Troyes's tradition for whom "largesse is the lady and queen who illuminates all virtues. . . . Largesse alone makes one a *preudome*; high birth cannot do it, not courtesy, wisdom, nobility, wealth, strength, chivalry, prowess, lordship, beauty, or anything else."[88] The two authors differ only in degree. In Chrétien's scheme largesse supplants prowess; in Raoul's it is one of two wings.

If the *Histoire* employed the tournament to illustrate Guillaume's largesse, the author was merely following romance tradition. Chrétien's Erec, for example, displays his liberalities at Evroïc.[89] Jean Renart's hero Guillaume de Dole entertains lavishly after the tournament of Saint-Trond and, like the Marshal, releases prisoners, gives away horses, and leaves town poorer than when he arrived (*Rose*, vv. 2868–959). We have seen that Gerart de Nevers took prisoners and horses at Montargis, but when he arrived at his hostel that night to receive congratulations, he is preoccupied by his painful failure to capture Lisïart and forgets the romance obligation (*Violette*, vv. 6055–88). On the field, however, the counts of Boulogne and Ponthieu were noted for their generosity (vv. 5919, 5924). Largesse also exerted its influence on Jean de Montmirail, the Champenois knight who was preparing himself for the monastic life. He was so prodigious in his liberalities that he expended a thousand *livres* at one tournament alone. His monastic mentor chided him on the worthlessness of tournaments. Their glory was vain and as unstable as the wind.[90] In Chrétien's chivalric universe the chief opportunity for displaying largesse was, of course, the great Arthurian feasts on the high church holidays when the king lavished boundless gifts on his knights and other attendants. Unlike his predecessor Jean Renart, Gerbert de Montreuil neglects to show the king indulging in conspicuous generosity. (Perhaps, like his father Philip Augustus, Louis retained the Capetian reputation for stinginess toward jongleurs and writers like Gerbert de Montreuil.)[91] During the week of celebration of Gerart and Eurïaut's wedding, however, the festivities were so sumptuous that no jongleur arrived on foot who did not depart on horse or with a fur mantle. Never since the Pentecost or Christmas feasts of King Arthur in Wales was there such generous hospitality (*Violette*, vv. 6578–90). And Gerbert recalls Chrétien's often-remembered pun: "*Pentecouste* was in fact so named because it *couste* so much" (vv. 6285–86).[92]

The journeys of itinerant knights offered to romance writers the frequent opportunity to describe hospitality and largesse. In Chrétien's hands, largesse was usually assigned to a highborn maiden in need of the knight's services (both with arms and in bed) and occurred so often that it was formulated. Although Jean Renart's hero did not travel frequently, Gerbert de Montreuil's heroes profited abundantly from the services of maidens. In the *Continuation*, for example, Perceval received such hospitality on at least a score of occasions.[93] In the *Violette*, Gerart made stops at the castles of Vergy (v. 2169), Bien Assis (v. 4686), and Monglai (v. 4950), where he too was received by maidens in difficulty. At Cologne Duke Milon served the hero a dinner so sumptuous that Gerbert could only compare it with the hospitality of his patron Marie, countess of Ponthieu (vv. 3206–8). When Chrétien de Troyes dedicated his *Conte du Graal* to Philippe, count of Flanders, he not only compared his patron to the great Alexander who was the epitome of largesse, but he also considered the count *larges* in the Gospel sense. His left hand did not know what his right hand was doing.[94] In sending his *Roman de la Violette* to Countess Marie, Gerbert de Montreuil praises her as the finest woman of the world whose manifold virtues included *largeté*. However Chrétien or Gerbert saw themselves benefiting from this virtue, by recommending this ideal to historical patrons, they attempted to extend the practice to their contemporaries. For this reason it is also noteworthy that *larguesce* like *proesce* is not a word found in Gace Brulé's vocabulary. The poet is so absorbed with his subject *amors* as to make him oblivious to other norms, but the author of the *Histoire* opines, "If only King Henry [of his own time] could rule his own land in peace, then chivalry, prowess, nobility, and largesse would emerge from its gates" (vv. 4313–17).

The Absent Clergy

In the thousands of lines of the *Histoire du Guillaume le Maréchal*, the clergy were scarcer than women. The monk who was obscured by his cowl and who abducted a noble lady was certainly not the most laudable of monks (vv. 6689–864). Another cleric rescued Philip Augustus from drowning in the Epte at the disaster of Courcelles-lès-Gisors (vv. 11031–56). Otherwise, the clergy, both monks and secular clerics, were virtually absent from the scene. Nowhere do they appear at the tournaments to sing masses before the conflict as they do in the romances. On his deathbed, the Marshal reproaches clerics like Pierre the Chanter for demanding restitution of the five hundred horses he had won during a lifetime of tourneying: "Churchmen are too hard on us, they shave us too closely.... Either their argument is false ... or no man (*hom*, i.e., faithful knight) can find salvation" (vv. 18476–96). Religion played little visible role in Guillaume's life in France. We find him making a single pilgrimage to the shrine of the Three Kings in Cologne to thank God the Father and the holy mother Mary (vv. 6583–91); later he took the cross in behalf of his patron the young King Henry and spent two years in the Holy Land displaying his usual feats of prowess and largesse, but since his biographer did not accompany him, only a score of lines were devoted to the episode (vv. 7275–301). Neither do the clergy play a large role on the romance scene. The principal exception is Chrétien's *Conte du Graal* in which the hero Perceval's quest for the Grail bears heavy religious overtones. Although Gerbert de Montreuil's *Continuation* perpetuates this tradition, his *Roman de la Violette* follows Chrétien's other romances and those of Jean Renart in relegating clerics and their activities to the periphery of their narratives.

The absence of clergy is most evident at the tournaments of Chrétien (with one ambiguous exception) and those of the *Histoire*.[95] Since from 1130 through 1215 church councils had solemnly prohibited these activities to knights, it is not surprising that the clergy were conspicuous by their absence in the *Histoire* or even in the romances of Chrétien. A generation later, the situation changes markedly, however. Jean Renart in the *Rose* has the knights parade ceremoniously to church to hear mass before the tournament of Saint-Trond (vv. 2432–45). Likewise, Gerbert in the *Violette* brings his knights to church early in the morning to hear the mass of the Holy Spirit so that they can go to battle without fraternal hatred (*malvaistiés*), the chief sin against the Holy Spirit (vv. 5867–72). At the final trial by battle on Pentecost as well, the contestants appear before the king, enter church to make offerings, and are led to a meadow where they swear their oaths on relics provided by the clergy before they begin to fight (vv. 6300–302, 6348–51). Thereafter throughout the thirteenth century attendance at mass before tournaments or judicial combats became obligatory both in romance literature and eventually in practice as well. This is one of those examples where life began to imitate art.

Throughout romance literature the conventional practices of the Christian calendar were maintained. The great church festivals of Christmas, Easter, and Pentecost were duly celebrated, which, in turn, implied the clergy's presence even when they are not visible. At Montargis King Louis hears mass in the royal chapel while the knights attend services in another church (*Violette*, vv. 6127–29). When Euriaut learns of Lisïart's false accusation, she immediately crosses herself, the appropriate Christian reflex (v. 970). Saints are invoked at crucial moments, although at times the reader may feel that they have been inserted to fill the needs of the rhyme. Gerbert de Montreuil employed ten different saints in the *Violette*, double his repertoire in his *Continuation*. For example, Gerart offers his oath by Saint Clement (v. 6367) before the last trial by battle to prove Eurïaut's innocence. Prayers to God in times of danger also play an important role throughout Gerart's journeys. When a lady is about to be raped by three knights, she calls upon Jesus for help and Gerart providentially comes to her rescue (vv. 4494–500). His battle against the giant at the castle of Bien-Assis is waged with repeated calls for divine help (vv. 4493–848), and his own search for his *amie* is actually accomplished in direct answer to prayer (vv. 5110–11). The most extraordinary prayer, however, was offered by Eurïaut herself when she is bound to the stake and about to be consumed by flames. Inspired by the *chanson de geste Le Couronnement de Louis*, Gerbert composed a prayer that recited biblical history from Creation to Pentecost and developed the doctrines of Creation, the Fall, and Incarnation in 150 verses. In this passage, unusual in romance literature, Gerbert's ostensible intent is not to display theological learning but to buy time for his hero to arrive at her defense (vv. 5182–334).

If conventional religious observance provides the backdrop of romance narrative, rarely were ecclesiastical personages named. Throughout the entire *Histoire* only one bishop is mentioned—Philippe de Dreux, the bellicose bishop of Beauvais. He is identified only as the bishop of Beauvais whom the mercenary captain Mercadier captured along with Guillaume de Mello (vv. 11264–69). Although Gerbert de Montreuil is careful to identify a score of aristocratic participants at the tournament of Montargis as *effets de réel*, when he approaches the last judicial duel on Pentecost he simply notes that the affair was attended by the bourgeois, knights, vicomtes, counts, dukes, and an archbishop, who is not named; nor is a bishop provided to perform Gerart's and Eurïaut's wedding at Nevers (vv. 6292–94).

Vernacular Speech

If we perceive conventional religious routines practiced in the background of the romances, we can also hear them speaking a language that was permeated with religion.[96] The Latin medium naturally hindered ecclesiastical writers from conveying the language of the aristocracy who spoke only French. While the vernacular authors wrote octosyllabic verse with rhymed couplets, which was not intended to reproduce ordinary discourse, they did introduce, however, long passages of direct dialogue in which both the name of God and the saints thoroughly saturated oral speech. From Chrétien de Troyes through Jean Renart not only were "adieu" and "farewell" standard parlance, but countless phrases like "by God," "in God's name," "if God pleases," "God grant you," "thank God," and "God help me" punctuate their sentences. Even if some of this linguistic seasoning was added to facilitate meter and rhyme, its universality remains unescapable. Throughout both the *Histoire de Guillaume le Maréchal* and the *Roman de la Violette*, not to speak of the *Continuation*, this pattern of speech abounded. The *Histoire* resounded with *Si Dex plaist* (v. 1401), *Si m'eït Deus* (v. 1769), *Par Diu* (v. 13077), and *Dex me beneie* (v. 13082). Gerbert continued with *Dex me gart* (*Violette*, v. 589), *Ja Diu ne plache* (v. 606), and *doinst Dex* (v. 805). As a writer of lyrics, Gace Brulé naturally shared the language of romance and seasoned his verses with frequent invocations of the Deity: *Deu vos comant* (no. 3, p. 10), *Deus me voie* (no. 14, p. 42), and *qui Dieus maleïe* (no. 60, p. 194). While God is called upon chiefly to reinforce his *fine amors* and may even, on occasion, be confused with the god of love (*Li deus d'amors malement nos consoille*, no. 23, p. 82), at times the references were specifically Christian, as for instance a mention of judgment day (*jusqu'au juïse*, no. 31, p. 110) and the encouragement to "pray to Jesus, son of Mary" (*Se prïerai Jhesu lou fil Marie*, no. 63, p. 208).

It is legitimate to question how much this vernacular verse echoes oral diction, but it is equally worthy of note that Pierre the Chanter and his theological colleagues at Paris took seriously these frequent invocations of divinity.[97] Recalling the second commandment, "You should not take the name of God in vain," and Jesus's injunction "Do not swear . . . but let your yes be yes and your no be no," they discussed the habit of invoking God in the context of oaths (*iuramenta*). They concluded that although such parlance was not equivalent to a solemn oath that resulted in perjury, and neither was it equivalent to an ignominious oath, such as swearing by the bodily members of God, Jesus, or Mary (as the Angevin kings were reputed to do), both of which were mortal sins, nonetheless invoking the name of God lightly was a venial sin, especially if it became habitual. This discussion, which took notice of the practice in vernacular literature, strongly suggests that it was also prevalent in oral discourse at the time. It also demonstrates that although the clergy, God's ministers on earth, were removed to the peripheries of vernacular narratives, the presence of God, even though a banality, was central to aristocratic oral discourse.

The interaction between the aristocracy and the clergy was not a simple process in the Parisian region or elsewhere during the reign of Philip Augustus. To be sure, aristocrats massively funded churches and monasteries in which they were often buried and to which they occasionally sought entrance as members. They fought for the church's causes in the crusades overseas and against the heretics in the South. For all their services, they were promised entrance into the kingdom of heaven, but most of their engagement with the church was expressed in Latin documentation written down by the clerics and monks themselves. The vernacular literature, however, composed for the aristocracy's amusement and instruction, was remarkably different. It is true that the language recited in the vernacular reverberated with the ubiquity of the Deity and saints, but with the notable exception of the romances of the Holy Grail, religion remained far from the center of preoccupation in vernacular writing. Clergy and monks were virtually absent. Uninhibited delight was indulged not only in warfare but especially in the frequent tournaments that the clergy had proscribed as seeking vain glory and as avaricious quests for booty. Vernacular romances were obsessed with women and earthly love (albeit not necessarily sexual) and glorified the sensuality of feminine beauty. Crusades were deplored particularly because they caused absence between lovers. New knights received their swords not in churches as the clergy desired but in the field. To encapsulate his image the aristocrat represented himself on his seal fully armed, galloping on his steed, and brandishing his sword, the high symbol of his vocation.

Both our Latin and our vernacular sources contain evident fictions. The massive corpus of Latin chronicles, charters, and administrative documents is thoroughly impregnated with the churchmen's ideology and program and to a lesser degree, the king's. The vernacular writings voice the ideals, conventions, and even the fantasies of the aristocrats to whom they were directed. In them alone we meet the beautiful woman, romantic love, and the solitary knight exercising bravery in countless single combats. Only in Latin charters can we measure the immense wealth that passed from the aristocrats to the church. Only in the vernacular writings do we have a glimpse of the aristocratic pleasures of singing, dancing, hunting, and winning at tournaments. The two kinds of sources do not so much compete with one another as interact with each other. Both must be accepted, kept in context, and kept always subject to interpretation. Neither gives the complete picture; each corrects the other. Taken together they expand our horizon in viewing the aristocracy around Paris at this brief moment during the reign of Philip Augustus. Any picture without the two is incomplete.

Chapter 10

Knights at the Cathedral of Chartres

If aristocrats gave massively to the church and defended its interests at home and abroad, nearly the only visual evidence of their contribution was their tombs, usually in monasteries where they were relegated to the chapter house.[1] Neither were they more visible in the sculpture of the cathedrals at Paris, Senlis, Soissons, and Chartres, where the imagery was devoted largely to the themes of the Bible and saints' lives. Only in the scene of the resurrection at the Last Judgment on the central western portal at Paris does a solitary knight emerge from his tomb clad in chain mail and wearing an iron helmet. The cathedral of Chartres, to be sure, lies on the western limits of the Paris region. However, a devastating fire there in 1194 provided an opportunity to introduce a radical change in a major church. The resulting reconstruction was a new Gothic edifice that placed special emphasis on the stained-glass windows, thus enabling the artists to make a fresh start. Although the tradition of biblical and hagiographical imagery was maintained, the stained-glass windows in the choir, the most sacred center of the edifice, introduced a radically new feature—a squadron of knights, fully armed, on horseback and in procession. Who were they and why were they there?

The Rebirth of the Cathedral

On 10 June 1194 the venerable Romanesque cathedral of Bishop Fulbert (d. 1028) caught fire.[2] It was not the first time the church at Chartres had burned—it had occurred every century since the 700s. In 1134 the cathedral had been saved from the flames that consumed the town, but once again in 1194 the church was in flames. The origins of the conflagration are not known: perhaps it was an accident during construction, perhaps it was a fire provoked by a dispute. Nor can the extent of damage be assessed. The entire west front, which had been remodeled in the twelfth century, was saved as well as the crypt under the altar. Without doubt, however, the most important survival was the tunic of the Virgin Mary, certainly the church's most precious relic. It was this tunic that inspired the reconstruction of the magnificent cathedral fashioned in the new Gothic architecture, and which remains the glory of Chartres to this day. Nearly two decades after the fire, the seemingly miraculous survival of the Virgin's tunic also inspired a body of writings recounting not only the miracles performed by the Virgin after the fire, but also the popular enthusiasm for the construction.[3] We are permitted skepticism over the tales about countless peasants who harnessed themselves to carts to transport blocks of stone to the building site, producing this immense and technically sophisticated edifice. What is undeniable, of course, is that the resulting monument was both extraordinarily costly and erected in record time.

From 1194 through the Revolution and culminating in the bombing of 1944, the historical documentation at Chartres has suffered severely. What fragments that have survived are insufficient to explain the financing of the new construction. The occasional donations recorded in the cartulary and obituary—a gift of 200 *livres* from Philip Augustus, the donation of the bishop's and the cathedral chapter's revenues for three years, or two-thirds of a fine of 3,000 *livres* levied on the bourgeoisie of Chartres in 1210 (the other third was to go to the king)—were mere pittances in comparison to the total cost. Although pilgrimages to Chartres played a role, pilgrims nonetheless contributed mainly in kind, which does not account for the immense sums required. What is again clear is that the financing and construction of the new church was chiefly the responsibility of the bishop and the chapter.[4] Beyond their initial contribution of three years' revenues, they had to find other funds. From 1183 to 1217 the bishop was Renaud, a highborn aristocrat from the family of the counts of Bar and the lords of Mouçon.[5] Through his mother Agnès, he was a cousin of both Philip Augustus and Thibaut VI, count of Blois and Chartres. Doubtlessly he was wealthy. Many of the canons of the chapter likewise came from wealthy families, and the chapter itself was well endowed with property, revenue, and tithes. Since the building was effectively finished in the 1220s and 1230s, the clergy evidently succeeded in obtaining the necessary financing both from their own resources and from the bourgeoisie of the town.[6]

The speed of construction was also remarkable. Retaining the surviving west facade with its lancet windows intact, the master builder proceeded from the west to the east and, of course, from the lower levels to the upper clerestories and vaults. The progress of construction can be dated with new precision thanks to recently developed techniques of dendrochronology. Holes have been uncovered in the walls that contain the remains of wooden scaffolding. The trees for the scaffolding were felled in 1195 just after the fire. From the nave through the choir the lower level was under construction between 1210 and 1215. After the ground floor, the clerestories in the choir were erected as early as 1213–18. By January

1221 the canons of the chapter had moved their stalls into the choir.[7] Presumably both the windows and the vaults of the choir protected the new furniture from the weather. Work proceeded into the clerestories of the transepts in the twenties and early thirties. Guillaume le Breton, the royal historian, who expressed admiration for the church throughout his *Philippidos*, noted as he was writing between 1222 and 1226 that the edifice that had suffered so severely from the fire was today (*hodie*) shining with new stones in full glory, thus proving that God permits evil only to result in greater good. Apparently the building looked complete to him.[8] Accomplished in three decades, this amazing speed of construction was accompanied by a pronounced cohesion of style.[9]

As the walls rose, the windows were installed simultaneously, beginning at the ground level and proceeding to the clerestories. The builders of Chartres assembled the largest collection of stained-glass windows to their day, and most of it has survived to our time. It was also assembled at great cost since glass was more expensive than stone for constructing walls. The pattern of fenestration for the clerestories consisted of two lancets surmounted by a rose. The windows were produced in small workshops that worked rapidly, but they did not fashion more than four windows each. Laying out the stained glass on an underlying pattern superimposed on a table, the glassmakers proceeded as if they were assembling a puzzle. From 1200 to 1230 the interior of the church was covered with plaster and painted ochre while the columns were rendered white. False joints were traced on the smooth surface to give the illusion of an interior wall composed of masonry blocks. The soft hues of ochre and white further enhanced the luminosity of the windows.[10]

Four windows of the twelfth century—the three lancets of the western facade and the Belle Verrière—survived the 1194 conflagration. The vast expanse of thirteenth-century glass that was installed during the succeeding decades remained intact until 1757 when the canons of Chartres, like those of Paris, began to tire of the somber atmosphere imposed by the colored windows and replaced several of them with grisailles, that is, windows of semiopaque, mostly noncolored glass. Out of a total of 176 windows some 12 were destroyed, mainly in the clerestories, to allow more light into the choir. Since then individual parts of windows have been restored or replaced as damages occurred. Around 1700, however, before these replacements, the antiquarian genealogist Roger de Gaignières, as he had done for tombstones, commissioned watercolor sketches of many of the windows at Chartres, thus recording those that were subsequently destroyed.[11]

From the 1970s, a vast campaign was launched to clean and restore all the glass at Chartres, beginning with the west front, then passing to the lower lancet windows of the nave and to the northern rose. From 2006 to the present the project was intensified by concentrating on the clerestories of the choir and the southern transept. In this final phase each window was dismantled, each piece of glass studied, cleaned or replaced, photographed, and finally remounted in its restored tracery behind a protective second window. This minute examination has led to the conclusion that most of the surviving glass is original, thus assuring us that we now enjoy the extraordinary experience of seeing the glass of Chartres as it was seen by its contemporaries in the second decade of the thirteenth century.[12]

The rebuilt Gothic cathedral of Chartres with its vast expanse of decorated windows provides an unusual opportunity for assessing the status of the aristocracy around Paris during the reign of Philip Augustus. In the clerestory of the choir we find a remarkable procession of knights on horseback. They are placed within the upper roses, the highest and most honorific part of the clerestory windows (Figure 15). The choir was the most holy place of the church, completely enclosed and containing the main altar, the most precious relics, and the seats of the bishop and the cathedral canons who conducted the divine services. Fully armed with helmet, mail armor, and sword at their belt, each knight proceeded solemnly on horseback carrying his shield and lance to which was attached his banner. His shield, banner, and occasionally his garments and his horse's trappings bear the distinctive heraldry of his family. This is the first time in France that such a warrior was so honored in the most sacred center of a church.

Knights in the Stained-Glass Windows and Sculpture of the Cathedral

Unusual as these mounted knights are, we might not be surprised that they were actually not the first aristocrats to appear in the artwork of Chartres. On the ground level in the legendary windows that surround the church, two families are identified as patrons. A window in a southern apsidal chapel dedicated to Saints Marguerite and Catherine (window no. 16) shows Marguerite de Lèves and her husband Guérin de Friaize along with another figure, Geoffroi de Mezlay. Marguerite, who is kneeling before the Virgin and Christ, was the vidame of Chartres and a member of a powerful Chartrean family that had produced a former bishop. The two men, identified by the heraldry on their shields, are standing clad in chain mail, the one holding a sword, the other a lance. The window can now be dated to around 1201 in conformity with the early chronology of the ground floor.[13] Not far away in the southern ambulatory around the choir is the count of Blois and Chartres. In the Zodiac lancet (no. 28a), the count is pictured on horseback with his heraldic shield and lance and is being greeted

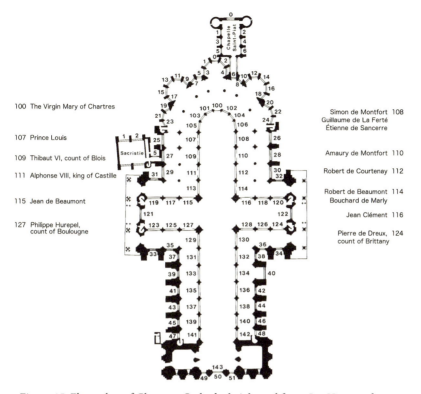

100 The Virgin Mary of Chartres

Simon de Montfort 108
Guillaume de La Ferté
Étienne de Sancerre

107 Prince Louis

109 Thibaut VI, count of Blois

Amaury de Montfort 110

111 Alphonse VIII, king of Castille

Robert de Courtenay 112

Robert de Beaumont 114
Bouchard de Marly

115 Jean de Beaumont

Jean Clément 116

127 Philippe Hurepel,
     count of Boulougne

Pierre de Dreux, 124
count of Brittany

Figure 15. Floor plan of Chartres Cathedral. Adapted from *Les Vitraux du Centre et des Pays de la Loire*, Corpus vitrearum, France, Recensement des vitraux anciens de la France, vol. 2 (Paris: CNRS, 1981), 26 (fig. 10).

by three peasants who are identified in the preceding panel as vine-dressers. This motif is repeated in the adjoining lancet (no. 28b), which is dedicated to the life of the Virgin. The first lancet bears a legend that appears to read, "Count Thibaut gives . . . to the vine-dressers at the request of the count of Perche."[14] This may refer to an unrecorded incident involving Count Thibaut VI (d. 1218) and Count Thomas of Perche who accompanied Prince Louis to England and was killed in the battle of Lincoln in 1217, or the iconography may echo a popular story of the earlier count Thibaut IV of Blois who was celebrated for his alms-giving to the poor.[15] These chapels, however, were not actually part of the choir where the canons worshipped but part of the ambulatory that surrounded the choir where pilgrims circulated.

In addition to these historical families, other images of knights can be found throughout the church serving as exemplary figures within the great profusion of saints and biblical personages. For example, a window in a southern ambulatory chapel (no. 18) dedicated to the recent martyr Thomas Becket, archbishop of Canterbury, depicts two knights clad in chain mail assaulting the archbishop with their swords while the archbishop is praying before the altar, but this is certainly not a scene to honor the chivalric profession. In the Charlemagne window in the north ambulatory (no. 7) is pictured the epic hero Roland and the Saracen Ferragant confronting each other on horseback in a scene inspired by the *Chanson de Roland*. Like the knights in the clerestory, both are armed with helmet, shield, and lance. As in romance literature, Ferragant's lance breaks from the force of the initial joust and both combatants fall to the ground where they fight on foot, but Roland dispatches the Saracen with his sword in the next panel. In this last scene the glassmakers endow Roland with the halo of sainthood, which he wears in succeeding panels where he sounds his horn, breaks his sword Durendal, and confers with Count Baudouin. In other scenes mounted knights in full armor accompany the emperor, battle the Saracens, and besiege Pampeluna. Thus the legends of Charlemagne and his faithful knight Roland were duly memorialized. Elsewhere in the ambulatory and nave are knights who were saints, identified by their halos, and who perform warlike tasks fully armed. For example, Saint Julien the Hospitaler is depicted riding off on horseback and fighting with other knights (no. 21), and Saint Theodore, clad in chain mail from head to knees, holds his lance as he sets fire to a pagan temple (no. 9). And there are occasional depictions of the practical side of chivalric life. On one panel of the Zodiac lancet (no. 28a), a knight has dismounted so that his horse can forage—it is the month of May; on another, blacksmiths are pounding out spurs and shields on their anvils (no. 48).[16]

Crowned kings abound on the exterior sculpture (for example, in the kings' galleries on the western and southern portals),[17] but with the exception of the Becket martyrdom, all the knights on the outside of the edifice are saints. In the left portal of the south transept, for example, the holy martyrs honoring the protomartyr, Saint Stephen, are flanked once again by Saint Theodore and Saint George. With a halo behind their helmetless heads, both wear tunics over their chain mail and are belted with swords and carry lances and shields.[18] It was only appropriate that the cathedral should honor the bellicose profession with the sanctity of martyrdom. The chief virtue of knighthood, bravery (*fortitudo*), is likewise found on the north side of the cathedral among the virtues personified by female figures. At the apex of the left portal of the northern transept, *Fortitudo* is dressed in armor, bearing a sword and shield decorated with a lion, but her gender is obscured by the trappings of the masculine profession. Both on the inside and outside of the church, therefore, these scattered images of knights were immediately accessible to the public who stood before them. Their function was clearly didactic, to teach lessons from good and bad examples of knighthood. And with the exceptions of the families of Friaize, Mezlay, and Blois, none of the knights are contemporaneously identifiable figures. Rather than heraldry their shields bear decorative designs. Neither Roland's shield nor the new shield fashioned by the blacksmith portrays family heraldry.

Knights in the Clerestories of the Choir

In the clerestories of the choir, however, the mounted knights who line both sides toward the eastern apse can, for the most part, be quickly identified from their heraldry.[19] Each of these clerestories consists of a rose window atop two lancets. Heading the procession of the clerestory rose windows on the north side is Prince Louis (no. 107, Plate 2A). Here, before 1223 when he became king, Louis is clearly designated by the fleurs-de-lis and the absence of a crown. In the lancets below (now disappeared but sketched in the Gaignières collection) he reappeared twice as kneeling in prayer before a candle and offering a window.[20] Following him is Thibaut VI, count of Chartres and Blois (no. 109, Plate 3A), bearing his heraldry on his banner. He too is depicted twice below, at prayer before an altar. Next in procession is Alfonso VIII, king of Castile (no. 111, Plate 4), the father of Blanche of Castile, the wife of Prince Louis. A crown surmounts his helmet, and his heraldry of a castle is clearly recognized on his shield. In one of the lancets below (now lost), the same heraldry was depicted, surrounded by the shells of Saint Jacques.[21] The next clerestory window (no. 113) is devoted to a Christological theme, but behind it in the northern transept, at the corner of the nave, the procession is brought up by Philippe Hurepel (no. 127), the legitimated son of Philip Augustus, half brother of Prince Louis, and count of Boulogne. He carries only his heraldic shield and also reappears in the right lancet below; his wife Mahaut and daughter Jeanne appear in the adjacent lancets (no. 125), both in the attitude of prayer and with their blazons.

On the south side of the choir heading toward the apse, the procession is led by two identical knights, differentiated only by the color of their horses, both bearing the heraldry of the lords of Montfort. They are Simon and Amaury de Montfort (nos. 108 and 110, Plates 5A and 6A), father and son from the powerful lordship located between Paris and Chartres, and celebrated leaders of the Albigensian Crusade.[22] The third in line is Robert de Courtenay (no. 112, Plate 7A), lord of Champignelles, cousin of the royal family and later butler of the royal court. Below in a lancet, now disappeared, he prays before an altar with his heraldic shield.[23] The procession on the south side of the choir is brought up by the enigmatic Robert de Beaumont (no. 114, Plate 8A) who may be identified as belonging to the family of Beaumont-les-Autels near Nogent-le-Rotrou.[24] One other important chivalric figure, however, joins the procession on the south side at the highest level, but he is in the south transept where he is close to other representatives of his family. This is Pierre de Dreux, duke of Brittany and royal cousin, who appears in the rose of the clerestory on the west side of the southern transept (no. 124, Plate 9A).[25] The lancets below contain his heraldry and his wife, Alix de Thouars, at prayer. To their right is the magnificent rose of the southern transept, below which the Dreux family is represented prominently as donors.

If the mounted knights found in the highest rose windows of the clerestories represented a superior register, the lancets below formed a secondary register. We have seen that occasionally the aforementioned personages depicted in the rose windows also appeared below in the lancets. In addition, we find at this lower level, on the south side of the choir in a lancet beneath the first Montfort (no. 108), Guillaume de La Ferté, now recoverable only in a Gaignières sketch (Plate 10).[26] Étienne de Sancerre follows in the next lancet (right lancet of no. 108) represented by his heraldry, again surviving in a Gaignières sketch (Plate 11A).[27] He was lord of Châtillon-sur-Loing (now Châtillon-Coligny), son of Étienne, count of Sancerre, and also a royal cousin. Similarly, below the rose of Robert de Beaumont-les-Autels (no. 114) is the figure of Bouchard de Marly of the Montmorency-Marly family (Plate 12A). In the north transept at the corner of the choir is Jean de Beaumont (no. 115 left lancet, Plate 13A), pictured on horseback like the personages in the roses, although he is in the second register. He is accompanied by his wife who is standing in the adjoining lancet (no. 115 right lancet). Both are identified by the distinctive heraldry of the subsidiary branches of the counts of Beaumont-sur-Oise, in this case, Beaumont-du-Gâtinais. A final figure in the secondary register is Jean Clément, a royal marshal, who is placed in a clerestory lancet in the southern transept at the corner of the choir (no. 116, Plate 14A).

If these fourteen knights can be quickly identified, their reason for being so honored is less readily apparent. Canon law, the fundamental law of the clergy, was totally silent on who was responsible for decorating a church and how the images were to be chosen. The artisans who worked in small groups and on a limited number of projects naturally lacked oversight over the entire program, and donors, of course, could express their wishes only on the individual projects they sponsored. In the absence of documentation and of plausible alternatives we are left to conclude that the bishop and canons of the church were responsible for the overall planning and execution of the decoration, as they were for financing and constructing the cathedral.[28] Unfortunately no record has survived of their deliberations nor any treatise elucidating their program. Such handicaps, however, have not prevented modern art historians from deducing programs of iconography by comparing patterns of existing imagery with the liturgical and theological texts available to the clergy at the time. In recent years art historians have benefited from an impressive arsenal of tools including dictionaries, concordances, and numerous texts not only available in critical editions but also searchable by electronic techniques. The result is that today art historians are better equipped to assemble medieval texts to justify iconographic programs than any past medieval cleric, no matter the strength of his memory or the resources of his library. Their researches have resulted in bold and all-encompassing iconographical explanations, but occasionally their ingenuity exceeds plausibility.[29]

The Virgin Presides over the Choir

If there is one iconographic program that emerges beyond doubt, it is found in the five clerestory windows of the apse, situated at the end of the choir toward which the two processions of knights converge. These windows were the focal point of the entire interior of Chartres and can be viewed without obstruction throughout the choir and the nave. In the central panel (no. 100, Plate 1A) is enthroned the Virgin Mary, the mother of Christ, who is seated on her lap. She is the queen of heaven, the supreme patroness of the church, and she wears the tunic in which she gave birth to Jesus. The tunic had been offered to Chartres by the emperor Charles the Bald in 876 and had miraculously survived the fire of 1194. She also wears an imperial crown, perhaps recalling the emperor who had bequeathed the sacred relic. Beneath her are depicted the scenes of the Visitation and Annunciation, the principal episodes preparatory to her miraculous delivery of the Savior. On the four surrounding panels to the left (nos. 101, 103) and right (nos. 102, 104) are adoring seraphim and cherubim along with Moses, Aaron, and David and the prophets Isaiah, Jeremiah, Ezekiel, and Daniel, all of whom prophesied the birth of the Messiah. The simple biblical basis of this iconographic program was therefore apparent not only to the canons of the chapter but also to all the faithful versed in Scripture.[30] Below are found money changers, butchers, bakers, furriers, and perhaps a hosier who is named Gaufridus—all tradesmen who appear as donors of the windows. While the particular crafts are self-evident, their relationship to Mary and the above prophets of the virgin birth has again challenged the ingenuity of art historians. The relevance of bread to the ceremony of the Eucharist is indeed plausible, but the double presence of money changers, who were equated with usurers and Jews, remains puzzling except for their evident wealth with which they financed the windows. Gaufridus, too, remains unidentified.[31]

The appearance of knights in the clerestory windows of the apse, however, does not require ingenuity because a simple and obvious solution is at hand that could be apprehended both by the canons below and the knights above. The sacred choir was presided over by the Virgin crowned with the imperial crown of heaven. On her lap is Christ, not an infant but a diminutive, mature ruler who holds the imperial orb in his hand. Toward this throne file two columns of knights, armed with their banners unfurled. They are an honor guard befitting the sacred court. As the knights approach the Virgin's throne, they also pass over the high altar of the Virgin at the center of the choir below.[32] It was never forgotten that Chartres possessed the most famous of all Mary's relics, the *sancta camisa*, the holy tunic that she wears in the apse clerestory. It was preserved behind the high altar in a wooden chest covered with plaques of gold and elevated on a tribune so that one could pass under it. Ordinarily the chest could not be seen from outside the choir, but on special occasions princes, nobility, and, at times, pilgrims were allowed access. It was, moreover, constantly in view of the knights in the clerestories. Not only were the knights honored to serve as the Virgin's guard, she too reciprocated a useful service. At a date difficult to determine, a legend surfaced that those intending to engage in war, having donned their armor and having passed close to the chest to touch the holy tunic, would thus receive protection from swords and lances, even from amputation. Perhaps this custom was as ancient as the ninth century when the tunic was used to defend the city of Chartres against the siege of the Viking Rollo.[33] No tendentious theories involving the Ark of the Covenant and the crusade need be extracted from the apse windows. The knights of the clerestories simply enjoyed the honor of escorting their queen, the blessed Virgin, who wore her crown and sacred tunic.

Which Knights Were Chosen?

What qualified a knight to serve in this honor guard? Obviously the immediate justification was the intention and wealth to bestow a window. Of the fourteen knights, six acknowledged that they donated the entire bay—the rose plus the two lancets below—because they are explicitly represented as donors in the lower lancets beneath the rose in which they also appeared. The remaining were donors only in the windows where they appeared. Such displays, however, offer little indication of what the windows cost. Only four of the knights appear as donors in the obituary of the cathedral, and the sums they had contributed were minor: four *livres* from Prince Louis, for example, ten *livres* from Count Thibaut, and five *livres* from Simon de Montfort.[34] Scholars have therefore searched for more comprehensive factors to explain their composition.

The leaders on each side of the choir, Prince Louis to the left (no. 107, Plate 2A) and the Montforts to the right (nos. 108 and 110, Plates 5A and 6A), are responsible for an early hypothesis that the Albigensian Crusade, of which they were the principal leaders, determined the group's membership. It is true that nine out of fourteen were known to have actually participated at one time or another, but a closer analysis of chronology raises questions about this hypothesis.[35] The decision at Chartres as to who would be selected for the windows must have been made well before 1218 when the clerestories were completed. Three who participated in the crusade, however, did not arrive until 1218 or after. Five, including King Alfonso of Castile and the royal brother Count Philippe de Boulogne, left no trace of participation. That eight of fourteen had not participated in the crusade before 1218 indicates that departure on the Albigensian Crusade was not the unique qualification for inclusion. A reconsideration of the fourteen knights therefore reopens the question and suggests that association with the royal prince was more likely to be the ultimate criterion.

Prince Louis was not only an enthusiastic crusader, but he had also developed a deep loyalty to the Virgin of Chartres. After the crusade against the heretics was first preached in 1209, he enthusiastically took the cross in February of 1213, but when the pope urged his departure, at Soissons in April his father Philip Augustus prevented him from departing because more urgent threats had appeared in the north from the English and Flemish, threats that culminated in the battle of Bouvines in 1214. While still prince, Louis's ventures in the Midi were therefore limited to the marginally successful campaigns of 1215 and 1219.[36] In contrast, Simon de Montfort was the outstanding leader of the movement until his death in 1218; Louis's most effective contributions came after he became king in 1223, after the clerestory windows were already completed. His expedition of 1226 brought about his premature death. The prince's devotion to the Virgin, however, had begun literally before birth. His panegyrist Guillaume le Breton declared that his mother Elisabeth (Isabelle) de Hainaut had felt the embryonic prince stirring in her womb as she was praying to the Virgin at Chartres, just as the Annunciation window in the apse portrays Elizabeth, the mother of John the Baptist, feeling her son move when she met Mary.[37] As a regalian bishopric Chartres had long enjoyed royal protection, but Louis declared in 1225 that the church remained under his special care.[38] Emblematic of this protection, he assembled an entourage of knights whom he led in the procession of the clerestory windows. He had begun to collect them almost a decade earlier, but their cohesion becomes most evident in the documentation after Louis became king and the windows were installed. The composition of this entourage can best be seen in Table 12.

According to the chance survival of a fiscal account from the prince's household in 1213, we can see that it already included not only his brother Philippe, who was still a boy, but also three of his most faithful familiars, Robert de

Courtenay, Étienne de Sancerre, and Adam de Beaumont, the last of whom closely associated with his brother Jean de Beaumont.[39] Thibaut VI, count of Blois and Chartres (Plate 3A), who immediately follows Louis on the north side, merits his position simply by the right of his lordship exercised from his castle, which lay a hundred meters to the south, but he also may have had other ties with the prince. Like others, he participated in the Albigensian Crusade and traveled farther south into Spain where he contributed to the Christian victory over the Muslims at Las Navas de Tolosa. While in Spain he contracted leprosy and nearly disappeared from the historical record, but it is possible that he joined Louis's expedition to England in 1217, because the *Histoire de Guillaume le Maréchal*, which was both contemporary and well informed about the venture, briefly places him there with the castellan of Saint-Omer.[40] Louis was also accompanied on the 1217 expedition by his close familiars Robert de Courtenay, Étienne de Sancerre, and the brothers Adam and Jean de Beaumont, abundantly attested by the contemporary chroniclers.[41]

The contemporary king of Castile (no. 111, Plate 4), the figure who follows Count Thibaut, was Ferdinand III who took office in 1217, but born in 1194 he would still be young and without notable accomplishments by 1218, although he was the nephew of Blanche of Castile, Louis's wife. Alfonso VIII, however, who had died in 1214, was Blanche's father and Louis's father-in-law. Although he never visited the Capetian realm, he was celebrated in Spain as the victor of Las Navas de Tolosa against the Muslims and the first to bear the heraldry of Castile, which both he and his daughter display proudly at Chartres. Family ties also determine the eligibility of two other knights who appear in the clerestories of the transepts. In the north transept, bringing up the rear of the procession headed by Louis, was Philippe Hurepel, count of Boulogne (no. 127), Louis's half brother. He occupies the whole bay on the western corner of the transept. Born in 1200 to Agnès de Méran while Philip Augustus was estranged from his legal wife, Ingeborg of Denmark, Philippe was technically a bastard, but Pope Innocent legitimated him in 1202 in order to win favor with the French king. Since he was officially knighted in May of 1222, his inclusion in the chivalric ranks in the windows of Chartres may well have been intended to celebrate this event.[42] In any case, he fully merited that position because from 1223 through Louis's death in 1226 he was a loyal participant at all of his brother's major assemblies. He is not found among the Albigensian crusaders. Across the cathedral in the southwest corner of the southern transept was installed Pierre, duke of Brittany, of the royal cousins from Dreux (no. 124, Plate 9A). Not only did he and his wife Alix de Thouars occupy a whole bay, but they were the patrons of the entire facade of the southern transept as well. This impressive display of power was installed before the transept rose (lancets, ca. 1219–25; rose, ca. 1225–30) and occurred when Pierre still loyally supported his cousin the king and attended his assemblies.

Robert de Courtenay (no. 112, Plate 7A), who follows the Montforts in the rose on the south side of the choir, was the second son of a family of royal cousins. He belonged to that close circle of Louis's entourage who appeared with the prince as early as 1213. After Louis became king, he was named butler of the royal court and was thereafter a regular witness to the king's charters.[43] Robert's career was closely duplicated by Étienne de Sancerre (no. 108, Plate 11A) whose heraldry appears in the lancet below the rose of Simon de Montfort. He was a younger son of the counts of Sancerre; he joined the crusade in 1226, but, like Robert de Courtenay, had been Louis's faithful companion since 1213.[44] A third member of this group was Jean de Beaumont (no. 115, Plate 13A) who was consigned to a lancet in the eastern corner of the northern transept. His wife occupied the adjacent lancet. From their heraldry it is clear that they belonged not to the family of the counts of Beaumont-sur-Oise but to a collateral line. Jean's lordship can be identified as Beaumont-du-Gâtinais.[45] In the documentation he is frequently associated with Adam, his brother, who also accompanied Louis on the English expedition of 1217. The two were assiduous in attending Louis's assemblies. Less frequently present was Bouchard de Marly, who is found in a lancet on the south side of the choir (no. 114, Plate 12A). From the prominent family of Montmorency-Marly, he was active in the Albigensian Crusade from 1210, but is recorded in only two of Louis's charters inventoried in Table 12 (1221, 1226).[46]

Another member of Louis's entourage was Jean Clément who was placed in a lancet in the eastern corner of the southern transept (no. 116, Plate 14A).[47] Unlike the other images of knights, Jean is depicted here as standing, clad in full mail armor, without helmet, belted with a sword, and, most important, receiving the banner of the oriflamme from the hand of Saint Denis who is standing next to him. On his *surcot* is depicted the heraldry of the Clément family. Jean was the son of Henri Clément, royal marshal, close counselor and favorite of Philip Augustus. Henri served with Prince Louis at the battle of La Roche-aux-Moines and died a hero from the wounds received there. Although the post of marshal was not considered hereditary, Philip conferred it on Henri's infant son Jean.[48] In October 1223 when Louis became king, Jean acknowledged the office was not hereditary by swearing that he would not claim as his own possessions the horses, palfreys, and rouncies that he had received for his work as royal marshal and that he and his heirs would respect the proviso that the office of marshal was not hereditary.[49] In the clerestory window, however, Jean accepts from the hand of Saint Denis the oriflamme, the prestigious banner of the abbey of Saint-Denis, which the Capetians, to invoke the blessing of the saint, had long

242

carried into battle, most recently at Bouvines in 1214. (Jean's brother Eudes became abbot of Saint-Denis in 1228, a date that may help to date the window.) It is difficult to say, however, whether Jean was thereby attempting to exalt the position of his family, because the royal marshal normally carried the banner as part of his duties and he had already renounced his hereditary claim to the post. In fact, Robert de Courtenay, who would become the royal butler, was likewise carrying a red banner like the oriflamme. Nonetheless, from 1224, Jean, now confirmed as royal marshal, attended King Louis's assemblies.

It remains to elucidate the relations between Prince Louis and the lords of Montfort, Simon and his son Amaury (nos. 108 and 110, Plates 5A and 6A), which are not immediately apparent in the documentary record. The reason is simple: from 1209 when the prince came to his majority at his knighting, Simon and Amaury had already taken the cross and were deeply involved in the Albigensian Crusade far from Paris, thus reducing opportunity for interchange. Only after Simon's death at the siege of Toulouse in 1218 did Amaury begin to frequent Louis's entourage. Louis's willingness to participate in the enterprise was impeded by his father in 1213, but his involvement after the victory at Bouvines in 1214 is ample confirmation of their common interests.

The relative obscurity of two knights in the clerestory windows, however, makes their presence more difficult to explain. In a rose window on the south side of the choir (no. 114, Plate 8A) is represented a knight with the heraldry of two leopards *passants* on his shield and banner, but he is not otherwise identified in the rose or in the lancets below. In the seventeenth century Gaignières identified him by comparing his heraldry with the seal of a Robert de Beaumont found in a charter of Saint-Père de Chartres of 1226 (Plate 8B).[50] Although Beaumont is one of the most common place-names in France, this one is most probably Beaumont-les-Autels (dép. Eure-et-Loir), which contained both a castle, now ruined, and a Benedictine priory.[51] The family was active from the eleventh century and favored the names of Robert and Geoffroy.[52] In 1202 a Geoffroy de Beaumont departed on the Fourth Crusade; both his father and his son were named Robert.[53] A Robert de Beaumont made a gift to the abbey of Josaphat around 1212, and a Robert de Beaumont was enrolled in the obituary of Chartres for the date 25 January.[54] These brief fragments do not form a recognizable portrait of a knight who was given an honored position in the rose windows riding behind Robert de Courtenay. Perhaps a clue is provided by the anonymous historian of the Albigensian Crusade who mentioned a certain Robert de Beaumont engaged with Simon de Montfort at the siege of Toulouse in 1218.[55] If this is the Chartrean Robert, it would explain why he rode behind the Montforts on the south side of the choir, but as yet it offers little connection with Prince Louis.

The second enigmatic knight, found on the south side of the choir in a lancet now destroyed but sketched by Gaignières (no. 108 left lancet, Plate 10), was a more elaborated image than the usual kneeling patron. To the left is a knight half kneeling in prayer who is garbed in chain mail, without helmet, but with a sword at his belt. Behind him is a valet holding a banner in one hand and the reins of a horse in the other. In the center is a shield bearing the heraldry of three silver circles on a red background, which is replicated on the banner. Except for the fact that he is not riding and is helmetless, the knight bears the same attributes as the other mounted knights. Fortunately the figure in the lancet was identified by an inscription, WILLERMUS DE FERIT, which Gaignières matched with a seal, inscribed SIGILLUM WILLERMI DE FERITATE. Gaignières also attributed to Guillaume de La Ferté two charters of Saint-Père de Chartres dated 1207.[56] He can also be found in charters of 1208 and 1212 from the abbey of Vaux-de-Cernay.[57] Like Beaumont, Ferté is a common place-name, but in the feudal inventory of the lords of Montfort, under the castellany of Montfort, the lord *de Ferrate* is listed as a liege vassal. His service of castle-guard is noted, as are five subvassals and his holdings.[58] If this lord of La Ferté is, in fact, the Guillaume in the window, he was an important vassal of the lords of Montfort and appropriately placed in a lancet beneath Simon de Montfort. No record survives, however, of his service in the Albigensian Crusade. Since we know little about him, he is another knight who cannot yet be assigned to Prince Louis's entourage. Nonetheless, eleven out of thirteen knights in Chartres's clerestories have left evidence of association with the royal prince, which, of course, does not exclude their participation in the crusade as well.[59] It is true that this coterie of knights whom Prince Louis assembled to do guard duty at Chartres was recruited at the western borders of our region. Nonetheless, the families of Montfort, Marly, Dreux, Clément (at Mez-le-Maréchal), Beaumont-du-Gâtinais, and La Ferté provide substantial representation of the aristocracy of the Paris region.

The "Sealing" of the Cathedral:
A New Representation of Knights

High above the sanctuary of the choir the knights in the clerestory windows not only provided an honor guard for the queen of heaven, they also represented themselves in an entirely new manner. As fully armed on horseback, they display themselves as they did on their seals. Now the rose window of each bay becomes a colorful seal, transforming those in yellow wax that authenticated their documents. At Chartres the seal of the chapter of canons had enthroned the crowned Virgin queen, robed in her tunic with the Christ-child on her lap

(Plate 1). The counterseal proclaimed the benediction of the angel of the Annunciation: "Ave Maria, gracia plena, dominus tecum, benedicta."[60] In the twelfth
century this image of the Virgin had been faithfully replicated on the central
portal of the west facade and in the Belle Verrière lancet, likely located in the
apse of the original church and then installed in the ambulatory of the choir of
the new church (no. 30).[61] Now the image was once again emblazoned high on
the central window of the apse for all to see in both the choir and nave (no. 100).
Not to be left out, Bishop Renaud de Mouçon placed in a clerestory lancet on
the north side of the choir (no. 113) not his episcopal seal, but the personal seal
of his family.[62]

When we compare the knights' actual seals with the stained-glass windows,
we can see that the model that was adopted for the windows was not the warlike "equestrian seal with sword" but the earlier "equestrian seal with banner
(gonfalon)," like that of Robert de Vitry (Plate 15).[63] The knights have therefore
exchanged the warlike pose for the peaceful posture more appropriate to guard
service. The horses do not charge into battle at a gallop; they amble solemnly in
procession (à l'amble). Nor do the knights raise their swords to attack, but with
swords at their belts they parade with banners streaming from their lances.
Moreover, unlike the other images of knights scattered throughout the windows
and sculpture at Chartres, all fourteen knights of the clerestories, whether in
the rose windows or in the lancets, were careful not to omit their family heraldry. Prince Louis was the first Capetian to place the heraldry of the fleur-de-
lis on his seal; the rose window at Chartres was the first to portray it in color
(Plate 2).[64] More important, family lineage is now emphasized. Five of the knights
were younger brothers or secondary members of the family lineage. Beginning
with the royal brother Philippe, and continuing with Robert de Courtenay (Plate
7), Jean de Beaumont (Plate 13), and Étienne de Sancerre (Plate 11), they bear
their family heraldry "broken" with a lambel to indicate their status both on their
seals and on the windows. Jean Clément, the marshal, has "broken" his seal with
a diagonal band (Plate 14). On the battle and tournament fields the heraldry
was doubtlessly portrayed in color on their shields, trappings, and banners, but
the wax seals are totally devoid of color. At Chartres the Virgin permitted her
honor guard to display their decorations. We can admire their heraldry here
in all of its brilliant hues for the first time. Finally, by sealing the clerestories
with their equestrian image, the knights at Chartres emphasized the solidarity of
the chivalric class. They included not only lesser knights such as Robert de
Beaumont, as yet unidentified, Robert de Courtenay, a second son of a lordly
family, and Jean de Beaumont-du-Gâtinais, from a subsidiary family of the counts,
but also two barons, Simon and Amaury de Montfort, a count, Thibaut de Blois,
a duke, Pierre de Dreux, two royal princes, Louis and Philippe Hurepel, and a

crowned king, Alfonso VIII of Castile. Despite the disparities of rank, all were united under the single image of an armed knight on horseback. Before the Virgin, all knights were equal. The clerestories of Chartres therefore dramatically epitomize the rapid ascension of the knightly class. The first equestrian seals bearing family heraldry appeared in the 1130s and 1140s. Before 1180 there was only a scattering throughout northern France, but the last two decades of the twelfth century witnessed a veritable explosion of heraldic seals between the Loire and Meuse rivers.[65] Few knights could be found without them. By 1218, these seals had ascended to the clerestories of Chartres, expanded their dimensions, and occupied the highest position in the cathedral.

Admittedly, it is difficult to distinguish between the knights who participated in the Albigensian Crusade and those who formed the entourage of Prince Louis because the two groups overlapped. It is also true that crusaders identified by the cross affixed to their garment are rarely depicted in churches; nonetheless this sign of the cross was essential to the knight in historical practice, to distinguish him as a crusader and to signify both the protection and the benefits that he gained from his status. It is perilous to employ the argument from silence in the medieval period when documentation was always scarce, but it remains clear that the knights of the clerestories at Chartres do not, in fact, represent themselves as crusaders against the Albigensian heretics but as a chivalric class, proud of their family heritage portrayed fully by their heraldry.[66]

This "sealing" of the cathedral was to become a permanent feature at Chartres. When the Gothic church was officially consecrated on 17 October 1260, those who attended the service could lift their eyes to recognize the heraldry displayed not only in the clerestory windows but also on the crossing of the ribs of the vaults high above the choir, where the heraldry of five great families was emblazoned in brilliant colors. The families were represented by Louis IX (d. 1270), king of France (Plate 16); Ferdinand III (d. 1252) or Alfonso X (d. 1284), king of Castile; Hugues IV (d. 1272), duke of Burgundy; Charles (d. 1285), count of Anjou and Maine; and Henry III (d. 1261), duke of Brabant, or one of Henry's successors.[67] The kings of France and Castile were already present in the choir clerestories in 1218. Now by attaching their heraldry to the highest vaults of the church these families could rise no higher in exalting their status at Chartres.

Appendixes

Appendix 1. Tables

Table 1. Hierarchical List

	Fam. no.	Name	Nomina castellany	Scripta castellany
Counts	1	Mathieu de Beaumont	Paris	x
		Jean		
	2	Aliénor de Vermandois, countess of Saint-Quentin		
	3	Robert I de Dreux		
		Robert II		
		Robert III		
		Pierre, duke of Brittany		
Barons	4	Simon V de Montfort		
		Amaury V		
	5	Mathieu de Montmorency	Paris	
	6	Guy de Garlande, lord of Tournan		
		Anseau (Rance)		
	6	Guillaume de Garlande (Idoine), lord of Livry and Neufmarché		
		Guillaume (Alix)		
	7	Guy II, butler of Senlis	Senlis	
		Guy III		
		Guy IV		
	8	Jean de Nesle		Montdidier, x
Vicomtes	9	Adam, vicomte of Melun	Melun	Melun
	10	Payen, vicomte of Corbeil	Corbeil	
Castellans	11	Mathieu de Marly	Paris	
		Bouchard		
		Thibaut		
	12	Roger de Meulan, lord of La Queue	Paris, Meulan	
	13	Simon de Neauphle		
	14	Guy de Chevreuse (Aveline)		Melun
		Guy (Helisende)		
	15	Adam de l'Île		
		Anseau (d. 1219)		
		Anseau (d. 1252)		
	16	Hugues de Chaumont		Chaumont
		Guillaume		
	17	Jean de Gisors		Gisors, x
		Hugues		
	18	Dreux de Mello, lord of Loches		

	Fam. no.	Name	Nomina castellany	Scripta castellany
	19	Gautier the Chamberlain, lord of Nemours		
		Philippe		
		Gautier/Gauteron, lord of Nemours		
		Ours, lord of Méréville		
		Gautier the Young, lord of Villebéon		
	20	Aubert de Hangest		Chauny and
		Florence		Montdidier
Vavassores	21	Gace de Poissy (Jacqueline)	Poissy	
		Gace		
		Robert		
		Amaury		
		Gace (Aelidis)		
	21	Simon de Poissy (Mathilde)	Paris, Poissy	
		Simon (Agnès)		
		Simon (Agnès d'Andresel)		
	22	Guillaume Mauvoisin	Mantes	
		Manasses		
		Pierre		
		Guy		
	22	Robert Mauvoisin	Mantes	
	23	Pierre de Richebourg	Paris	Mantes
	24	Philippe de Nanteuil	Béthisy	
Other names	25	Guillaume des Barres	Dammartin	
not in the	26	Hugues de Pomponne	Dammartin	
hierarchical		Renaud	Senlis	
lists	27	Guillaume Pastez	Corbeil	
	28	Jean de Corbeil	Corbeil	
		Baudouin		
	29	Aubert d'Andresel	Melun	
		Jean		
	30	Philippe de Lévis		
		Milon		
		Guy		
	31	Barthélemy de Roye		
	32	Pierre de Béthisy		
		Renaud		
	33	Pierre du Thillay		

x—In the *Scripta de feodis*, surveys of the fiefs and vassals of Jean, count of Beaumont, Jean de Nesle, and Jean de Gisors were done separately from the eleven surveys of the castellanies of the Paris region.

Table 2. Monastic Charters

	Percentage of 1,729 monastic charters
TRANSACTION TYPE	
Gift	65%
Sale	22%
Gift-countergift	8%
Exchange	3%
Pledge	2%
Litigation	14%
WEALTH TYPE	
Property	45%
Revenue—total	55%
Cens and revenues in kind	33%
Tithes	17%
Forest usage	2%
Money	3%
Jurisdiction	10%
PRINCIPALS	
Transactions between laity	2%
Women	15%
OTHER PARTIES	
Laudatio parentum (983 charters)	57%
Husband or wife	38%
Son or daughter	22%
Brother or sister	21%
Father or mother	4%
Only husband or wife	19%
Only immediate family (spouse, son, daughter)	13%
Laudatio domini	22%

Note: All percentages are percentages of the total number of charters. Some charters record more than one transaction type or the transfer of more than one type of wealth.

Table 3. *Laudationes Parentum*

	Percentage of 983 monastic charters
Laudatio parentum	100%
Husband or wife	66%
Son or daughter	39%
Brother or sister	37%
Father or mother	7%
Only husband or wife	34%
Only immediate family (spouse, son, daughter)	24%

Table 4. Castles and Residences

| Castle or Residence | Family | Donjon | | | | | | | Courtine enclosure | | Exterior |
		Shape	Fp (m²)	WTh (m)	IGS (m²)	Height (m)	Floors	TFS (m²)	EFp (m²)	Towers (no., diam.)	Moats
Chevreuse	Chevreuse	R	318	1.2, 1.8	197	19	4	788	3,000		X
Beaumont-sur-Oise	Beaumont	R	508	3	270		3?	810?	7,000	8	X
Luzarches	Beaumont	Tr	271	2.4, 3.8	117	11	2	234			
Conflans[-Sainte-Honorine]	Beaumont	R	194	1.65	111	15	3	333			
Rochefort-en-Yvelines	Montfort	R	224	3	80				1,500–1,800		
Montfort[-l'Amaury]	Montfort	C	357	2.8	191		3	573			
Beynes	Montfort	C	115	2.2	40		3	120	1,380		
Houdan	Montfort	C	237	3	75	25	3	225	1,380		
Nemours	Chamberlains	R	209	1.7–2.3	109	16	4	436			
Louvre	Ph. Aug.	C	191	4.2	41	32	4	164	5,700	6×8.5 m	X
Yèvre-le-Châtel	Ph. Aug.	x							374	4×9.5 m and 10.2 m	
Dourdan	Ph. Aug.	C (ext)	145	3.8	28	25	3	84	4.800	8×9 m	X
Brie-Comte-Robert	Dreux	x							3,360	8×7.6–8.6 m	X
Nesles-en-Tardenois	Dreux	C (ext)	227	4.4	44	23	3	132	3,500	8×10.5 m	X
Mez-le-Maréchal (Dordives)	Clément	R		2.5	50		3	150	3,170	4×8.5 m, 2×6.5 m	
Diant	Barres	x							3,600	4×10 m, 3×7 m	X
Roissy (I)		R	210								
Roissy (II)		R	150								
Roissy (III)		R	130	1.4	73		3?	219?			X

Donjon shape: C (cylindrical), R (rectangular), Tr (trapezoidal), ext (exterior; donjon is outside the courtine enclosure), x (castles without donjons).

Other columns: Fp (footprint), WTh (wall thickness), IGS (interior ground space), TFS (total floor space), EFp (enclosure footprint).

Note: Of the castles on the Philippine model (the Louvre, Yèvre-le-Châtel, Dourdan, Brie-Comte-Robert, Nesles-en-Tardenois, Mez-le-Maréchal, Diant), an estimation of the space of the living quarters inside the courtines can be made only for Brie-Comte-Robert (1,126 m²).

Table 5. Vassals and Subvassals

	Paris environs					Vexin					South of Paris				Vermandois				Row Total	Section Total	Grand Total
	Paris	Senlis	Dammartin	Béthisy	Poissy	Mantes	Meulan	Pontoise	Chaumont	Gisors	Étampes	Corbeil	Melun	Montlhéry	La Ferté-Milon	Crépy-en-Valois	Chauny	Montdidier			
A	18	22	19	6	5	7					12	15	19	15					138		
B						9	20	12	9	13			12	71	10	24	40	27	247	*351	
Ca						59	16	64	15	12			153	72	33	94	93	48	659		
Cb																			90		
Cc																			149		
Cd																			25		
D	12				9	7					13	25	57	5					128	1,051	
Ea																			38+43		
Eb																			4+54		
Ec																			59		
Ed																			45		
Ee																			255	498	
F																			951	951	
G																			378	378	
																					3,229

* In overlapping castellanies of rows A and B I have taken the higher figure for the section total (351).

A   King's direct vassals, Nomina
B   King's direct vassals, Scripta
C   Subvassals, Scripta
   Ca   Subvassals by castellany
   Cb   Subvassals of Jean, count of Beaumont
   Cc   Subvassals of Jean de Nesle
   Cd   Subvassals of Jean de Gisors
D   Vassals of lords besides the king, Nomina
E   Other surveys
   Ea   Mathieu le Bel
   Eb   Gautier the Chamberlain
   Ec   Saint-Germain-des-Prés
   Ed   Bishop of Paris
   Ee   Amaury de Montfort
F   Principals of monastic charters not named among the king's direct vassals in the Scripta and Nomina surveys
G   Feudal lords in monastic charters (in laudationes domini)

Table 6. Liege Homage, Castle-Guard, and Host and Chevauchée

	Paris environs						Vexin				South of Paris				Vermandois				Row Total or Avg.
	Paris	Senlis	Dammartin	Béthisy	Poissy	Mantes	Meulan	Pontoise	Chaumont	Gisors	Étampes	Corbeil	Melun	Montlhéry	La Ferté-Milon	Crépy-en-Valois	Chauny	Montdidier	
Nomina																			
Total	30	22	19	6	14	14					25	40	76	20					266
DV	18	—	—	—	5	7					12	15	19	15					91/219
DV%	60%				36%	50%					48%	38%	25%	75%					42%
Scripta																			
DV						9	20	12	9	13			12	71	10	24	40	27	247
LH						—	10	3	—	—			1	25	5	13	18	10	85/216
LH%						—	50%	25%	—	—			8%	35%	50%	54%	45%	37%	39%
H						—	1	0	—	—			0	22	5	11	20	15	74/216
H%						—	5%	0%	—	—			0%	31%	50%	46%	50%	56%	34%
CGK						1	10	—	2	5			—	63	8	12	8	6	115/235
CGM						var.	47	—	4	27			—	130	34.5	27	44	7	320.5
k/m						var.	3.9	—	.33	2.25			—	10.8	2.9	2.25	3.7	.6	3.3
H&C						8	16	12	8	1			—	9	10	23	35	20	142/235
H&C%						89%	80%	100%	89%	8%			—	13%	100%	96%	88%	74%	60%

DV   Direct vassals of the king (holding from the king)
LH   Knights owing liege homage to the king
H   Knights owing homage to the king
CGK   Knights owing castle-guard
CGM   Total months of castle-guard owed (var., variable duration:
      castle-guard owed in time of war only)
k/m   Knights per month owing castle-guard
H&C   Knights owing host and *chevauchée*

—*Nomina*: In the castellanies of Senlis, Dammartin, and Béthisy, the bailli registered only the names of those who were direct vassals, omitting names of those who did not hold from the king.

—*Scripta*: Where it appears that the bailli did not inquire about homage or services owed, the cell is marked with a dash.

Table 7. Knights' Quotas

	Quota	Banneret	Nomina	Scripta
VEXIN				
Jean, count of Beaumont	20	Coucy	Paris tr	90 vassals
Mathieu de Montmorency	20	Vexin	Paris tr	
Guillaume de Garlande	20	Vexin		
Guy, butler of Senlis	10	Vexin	Senlis tr	
Guy de la Roche	10	Vexin		
Robert de Picquigny	5	Vexin		
Pierre de Richebourg	5	Vexin	Paris ntr; Mantes tr	27 vassals
Castellan of Neauphle	5	Vexin	Poissy tr	240 *livres*
Gilles d'Aci	5	Vexin	Melun tr	
Robert de Poissy, le Riche	5	Vexin	Poissy tr	2,000 *livres*
Amaury de Poissy	3	Vexin	Paris ntr; Poissy ntr	300 *livres*
Pierre Mauvoisin	5	Norm.		
Guy de Thourotte	5		Paris ntr; Senlis tr	
Philippe de Nanteuil		Vexin	Béthisy tr	Crépy, 32 vassals, lh, ee
SUBTOTAL of 14 knights	118			
Knights of the Vexin	30			
Knights of Dammartin	10			
Knights of Pierrefonds	20			
SUBTOTAL	60			
TOTAL VEXIN	178			
VERMANDOIS				
Jean de Nesle and brother	40	Flanders		Montdidier, 149 vassals, lh
Aubert de Hangest		Coucy		Montdidier, Coucy, 6 vassals, h, ee
Jean de Montgobert		Coucy		
Raoul Flamenc		Verm.		Montdidier, h, ee
Gilles de Pleissis		Verm.		Chauny, h
Robert de la Tournelle		Verm.		Crépy, lh, ee
Gilles de Marquaix		Verm.		Péronne, 30 vassals, lh
Raoul de Clermont		Verm.		
Guy de Choisy	5			
Renaud de Magny	5			Chauny, h, ee
Raoul d'Estrées	5	Verm.		
Baudouin de Rom	5	Coucy		
SUBTOTAL of 12 knights	60			
Knights of Chauny, Valois, and Senlis	50			
Knights of Montdidier	50			
SUBTOTAL	100			
TOTAL VERMANDOIS	160			
GRAND TOTAL	338			334 vassals

tr—holding from the king (*tenens de rege*); ntr—not holding from the king; lh—liege homage; h—homage; ee—host and *chevauchée* (*exercitum et equitatum*)

Table 8. Landed Wealth in the Scripta Survey and Monastic Charters

	pt	pd	pc	pn	pm	pp	pf	rc	rk	ru	rt	rf	rm	jj	jh	jp	jd	Total p	Total r	Total j	Total p, r, j
A - Scripta (652 items)	342	59	11	39	26	4	4	65	27	6	6	4		9	26	14	2	485	108	51	644
A - Scripta, %	52%	9%	2%	6%	4%	1%	1%	10%	4%	1%	1%	1%		1%	4%	2%		74%	17%	8%	99%
B - Scr & Nom, %	66%	9%	4%	4%	7%			1%								1%	4%				99%
C - 1,729 MCs, %																					
D - 610 MCs (832 items)	228	24	9	49	11	8		146	104	27	78		28	10	25	39	40	329	383	114	826
D - 610 MCs, %	27%	3%	1%	6%	1%	1%		18%	13%	3%	9%		3%	1%	3%	5%	5%	40%	46%	14%	99%
Da - Gifts	146	17		36	6	8		132	81	24	58		13	8	18	35	30	213	308	91	612
Da - Gifts, %	18%	2%		4%	1%	1%		16%	10%	3%	7%		2%	1%	2%	4%	4%	26%	37%	11%	74%
Db - S, CG, Ex	82	7	9	13	5			14	23	3	20		15*	2	7	4	10	116	75	23	214
Db - S, CG, Ex, %	10%	1%	1%	2%				2%	3%		2%		2%		1%		1%	14%	9%	3%	26%

Retained wealth (rows A and B)

A The data is derived from the holdings of 272 persons, including the 247 vassals of Table 5, row B, plus vassals in nos. 98–103 of the Scripta survey (feoda quae Johannes de Gisorcio tenet de rege)

B Figures for twenty-five persons in the Scripta survey who are also listed in the Nomina survey

Alienated wealth (rows C, D, Da, and Db)

C Figures for the 1,729 monastic charters (MCs) are taken from Table 2
D The 610 monastic charters are a subset of the 1,729 monastic charters
Da Gifts in the 610 monastic charters
Db Sales, countergifts, and exchanges in the 610 monastic charters
* Transactions tallied here (row Db, column rm) include purchases by aristocrats and transactions between laity.

p – landed property
pt terra, land
pd domus, house
pc castellum, castle
pn nemus, forest
pm molendinum, mill
pp pressorium, winepress
pf furnum, oven

r – landed revenues
rc cens, regular payments in money
rk regular payments in kind
ru forest usage, forest customs
rt tithes
rf fief-rente
rm money, cash sums

j – jurisdictions
jj justicia, justice
jh hospites, hôtes, serfs
jp pedagium, toll
jd dowry or dower

Table 9. Gifts from Men and Women Compared

	pt	pn	p other	rc	rk	rt	r other	j all	Total p	Total r	Total j	Total p, r, j
Gifts, men	128	31	26	107	68	54	28	81	185	257	81	523
Percentage of 523 items	24%	6%	5%	20%	13%	10%	5%	15%	35%	49%	15%	100%
Gifts, women	18	5	5	25	13	4	9	10	28	51	10	89
Percentage of 89 items	20%	6%	6%	28%	15%	4%	10%	11%	31%	57%	11%	100%
Gifts, total	146	36	31	132	81	58	37	91	213	308	91	612
Percentage of 612 items, men												85%
Percentage of 612 items, women												15%

Statistics are derived from the sample of 610 monastic charters referred to in Table 8, row Da.
See Table 8 for types of landed property, landed revenues, and jurisdictions not specified here.

p—landed property; pt—*terra*, land; pn—*nemus*, forest
r—landed revenues; rc—*census*, *cens*; rk—revenues in kind
j—jurisdictions

Table 10. Revenues in Kind

	Scripta	Scr. %	Charters	Ch. %	Total	Tot. %
Wheat types						
Bladum, frumentum, wheat	10	32%	65	59%	75	53%
Annona, wheat and rye	—	—	6	5%	6	4%
Hibernagium, winter wheat	—	—	2	2%	2	1%
Wheat—total of all types	10	32%	73	66%	83	59%
Méteil, mixed grain	—	—	1	1%	1	1%
Segetis, rye	—	—	2	2%	2	1%
Avena, oats	4	13%	8	7%	12	9%
Vinum, wine	5	16%	7	6%	12	9%
Panes, bread loaves	3	10%	1	1%	4	3%
Capones, chickens	5	16%	—	—	5	4%
Gallina, cocks	2	6%	1	1%	3	2%
Ova, eggs	1	3%	—	—	1	1%
Porcum, pigs	—	—	1	1%	1	1%
Salum, salt	—	—	4	4%	4	3%
Castanea, chestnuts	—	—	2	2%	2	1%
Allecium, herring	1	3%	1	1%	2	1%
Champart, tax on produce	—	—	9	8%	9	6%
Total no. of items owed as revenue in kind	31	100%	110	100%	141	100%

As in Table 8, the sections of the *Scripta* survey tabulated include the eleven castellanies, plus nos. 98–103 of the *Scripta* survey. The charters tabulated are the same 610 monastic charters referred to in Table 8, row D.

Table 11. Crusader Finances (Transaction Types and Wealth Types)

TRANSACTION TYPE (82 transactions)	No. of transactions in charters of crusaders	Percentage
Gift	57	70%
Sale	7	9%
Gift-countergift	11	13%
Pledge	2	2%
Subvention	3	4%
Loan	2	2%
Total	82	

WEALTH ALIENATED (58 transactions)	No. of transactions in charters of crusaders	Percentage
Property	18	31%
Revenue—total of all types	30	51%
cens	10	17%
revenues in kind	13	22%
forest usage	4	7%
tithes	3	5%
Jurisdiction	10	17%
Total	58	

The data is derived from 107 of the 1,729 charters that contained mentions of crusaders.

Table 12. Knights at Chartres

	Rose no.	Lancet no.	Obit. donor	Albig. Crus.	Acct. of 1213	Exped. of 1217	1221[1]	1223[2]	1223[3]	1224[4]	1224[5]	1224[6]	1225[7]	1225[8]	1226[9]	1226[10]	1226[11]
Prince (King) Louis	107	107	4 lb.	1215 1219 1226	X	X	X	X	X	X	X	X	X	X	X	X	
Thibaut VI, count of Blois and Chartres	109	109	10 lb.	before 1212?		X?											
Alfonso VIII, king of Castile	111	111															
Philippe, count of Boulogne	127	127			X			X	X			X	X	X	X	X	X
Simon de Montfort		108	5 lb.	1209				X	X						X		X
Amaury de Montfort		110		1212											X	X	
Robert de Courtenay		112		1211	X	X	X	X	X				X	X	X		
Robert de Beaumont		114	2 lb.	1218							X						
Pierre, duke of Brittany		124		1219 1226		X	X	X	X				X				
Guillaume de La Ferté	108				X	X	X				X	X	X	X			
Étienne de Sancerre	108			1226	X	X	X	X		X	X	X	X	X	X	X	X
Bouchard de Marly	114			1210 1218			X						X		X		X
Jean de Beaumont-du-Gâtinais (Adam de Beaumont)	115				X	X		X		X	X	X	X			X	X
Jean Clément	116				X	X								X	X	X	X

1 *Layettes*, vol. 1, no. 1439 (March 1221).
2 *Registres*, 535–36 (August 1223).
3 *Layettes*, vol. 1, no. 1610 (November 1223).
4 *Layettes*, vol. 2, no. 1639 (March 1224).
5 *RHF*, 23:637, no. 133 (June 1224).
6 Newman, *Seigneurs de Nesle*, 2:233 (October 1224).
7 *Registres*, 538 (1225?).
8 *Layettes*, vol 2, no. 1713 (July 1225).
9 *Layettes*, vol. 2, no. 1742 (January 1226).
10 *Layettes*. vol. 2, no. 1749 (March 1226).
11 *Layettes*, vol. 2, no. 1811 (November 1226).

Appendix 2. Genealogies

Below are simplified genealogies for seventeen of the thirty-three aristocratic families introduced in Chapter 2, plus the counts of Flanders. The first genealogy in Appendix 2, for the counts of Beaumont-sur-Oise, was prepared by Professor Baldwin. The others, with whatever errors they might contain, are editorial additions and were made as a supplement to Chapter 2. The genealogies are given in the order in which the families are introduced in Chapter 2. Individuals in bold in Chapter 2 are also in bold here. Many spouses, siblings and children are not shown in the genealogies; the order of siblings, left to right, does not always represent their order of birth; many dates of death are approximate. Sources used are listed in the notes for Appendix 2.

1. Beaumont
2. Vermandois and Valois
3. Flanders
4. Dreux
5. Montfort
6. Montmorency and Montmorency-Marly
7. Garlande (Tournan)
8. Garlande (Livry)
9. Nesle
10. Chevreuse
11. Île-Adam
12. Gisors
13. Dreux de Mello
14. Chamberlains (Nemours and Méréville)
15. Poissy
16. Mauvoisin
17. Corbeil
18. Andresel

Abbreviations: ct. (count), ctess. (countess), vct. (vicomte), ld. (lord, *dominus*), bp. (bishop), archbp. (archbishop).

1. Beaumont

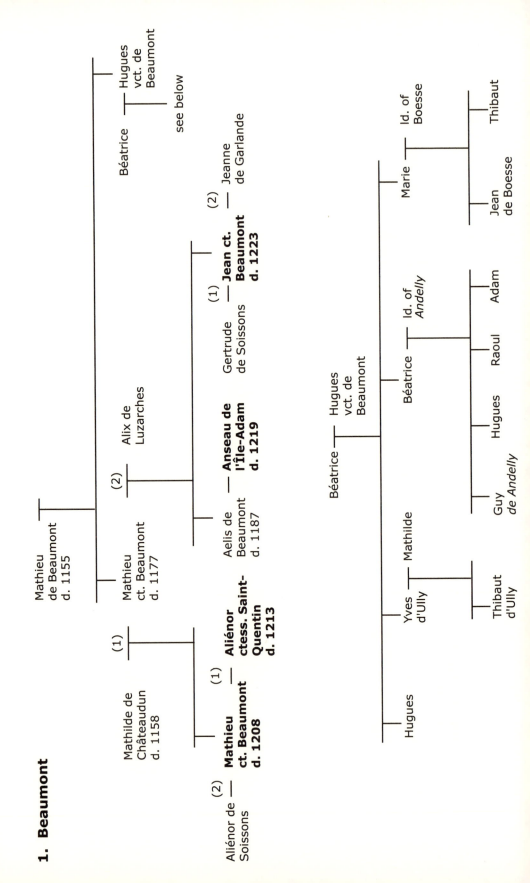

2. Vermandois and Valois (and the Capetians)

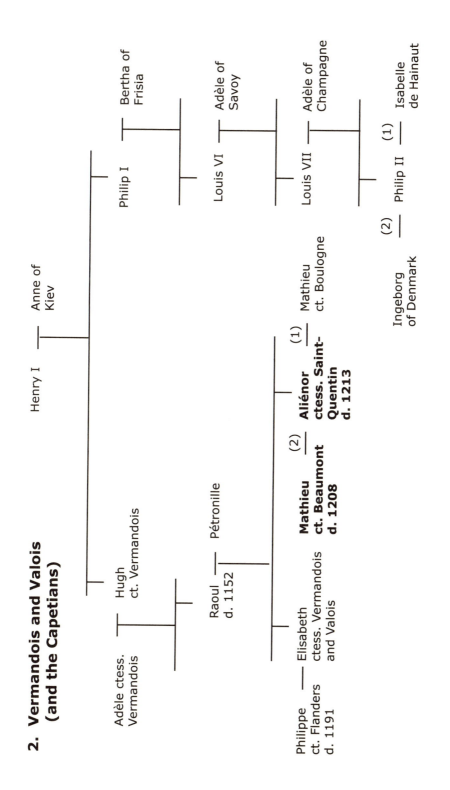

3. Flanders

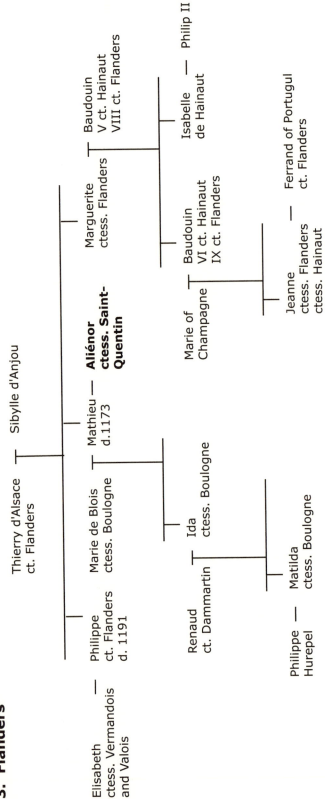

4. Dreux

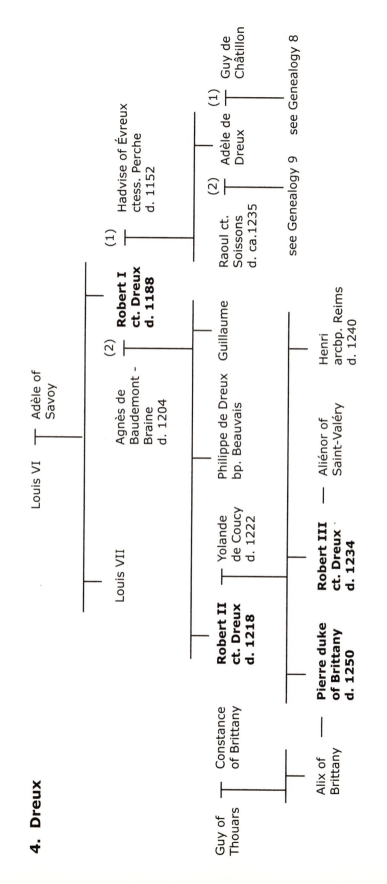

Louis VI — Adèle of Savoy

(1) Hadvise of Évreux ctess. Perche d. 1152

(2) Agnès de Baudemont - Braine d. 1204

Louis VII

Robert I ct. Dreux d. 1188

Raoul ct. Soissons d. ca.1235

(1) Guy de Châtillon

Adèle de Dreux

(2) see Genealogy 9   see Genealogy 8

Guillaume

Philippe de Dreux bp. Beauvais

Yolande de Coucy d. 1222

Robert II ct. Dreux d. 1218

Henri arcbp. Reims d. 1240

Aliénor of Saint-Valéry

Robert III ct. Dreux d. 1234

Guy of Thouars

Constance of Brittany

Alix of Brittany

Pierre duke of Brittany d. 1250

5. Montfort

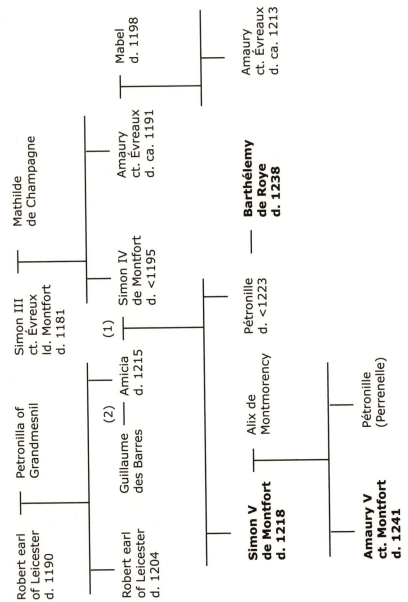

6. Montmorency and Montmorency-Marly

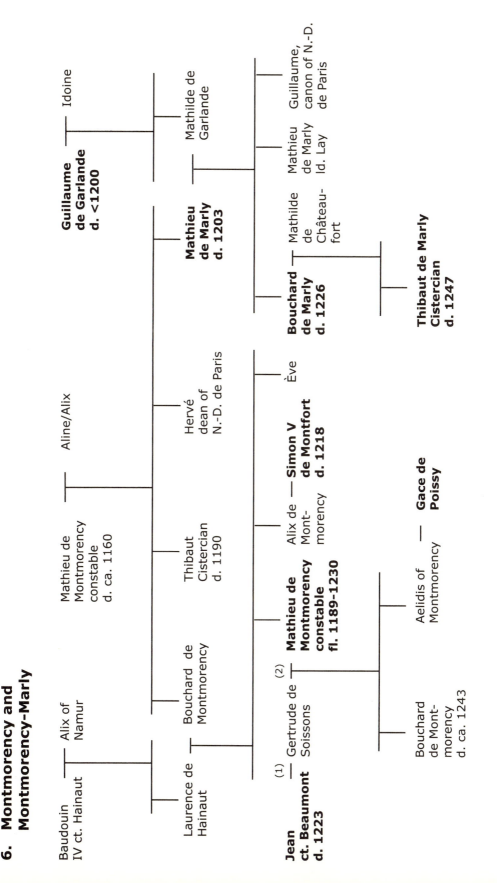

7. Garlande (Tournan)

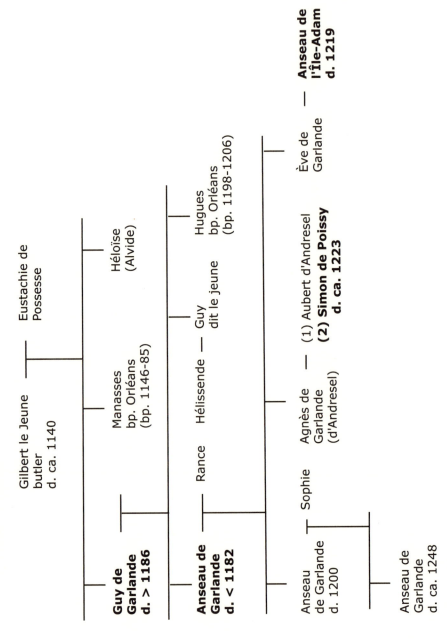

Gilbert le Jeune
butler
d. ca. 1140
— Eustachie de
Possesse

**Guy de
Garlande
d. > 1186**

Manasses
bp. Orléans
(bp. 1146-85)

Héloïse
(Alvide)

**Anseau de
Garlande
d. < 1182**
— Rance

Hélissende — Guy
dit le jeune

Hugues
bp. Orléans
(bp. 1198-1206)

Sophie

Agnès de
Garlande
(d'Andresel)
— (1) Aubert d'Andresel
**(2) Simon de Poissy
d. ca. 1223**

Ève de
Garlande
— **Anseau de
l'Île-Adam
d. 1219**

Anseau
de Garlande
d. 1200

Anseau de
Garlande
d. ca. 1248

8. Garlande (Livry)

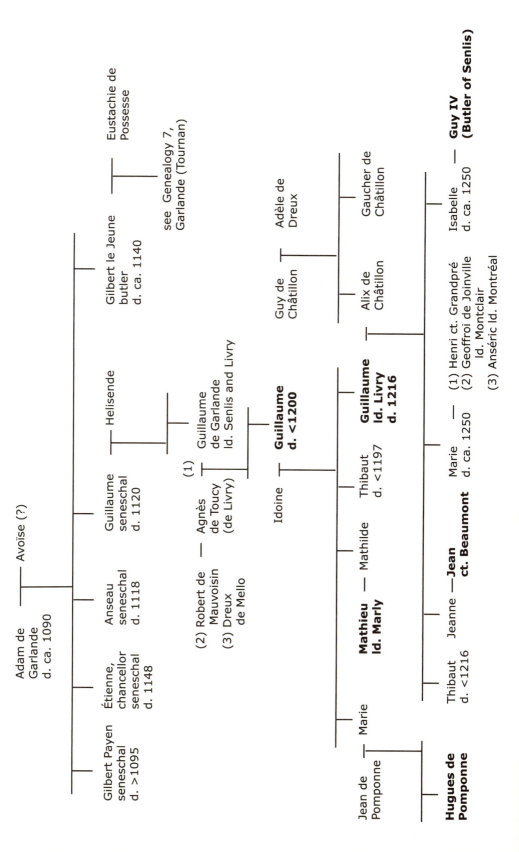

9. Nesle

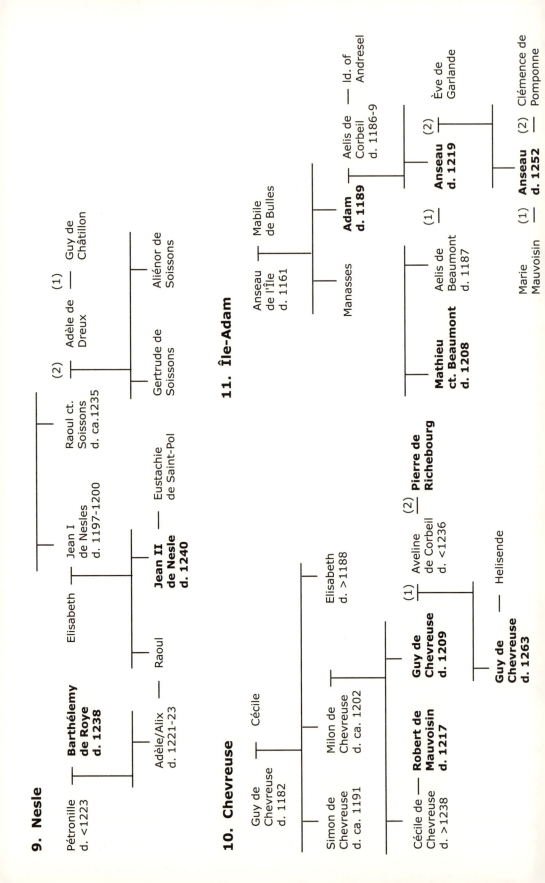

Pétronille
d. <1223

Barthélemy
de Roye
d. 1238

Adèle/Alix
d. 1221-23 — Raoul

Elisabeth

Jean I
de Nesles
d. 1197-1200

Jean II
de Nesle
d. 1240 — Eustachie
de Saint-Pol

Raoul ct.
Soissons
d. ca.1235

(2)
Adèle de
Dreux

(1)
Guy de
Châtillon

Gertrude de
Soissons

Aliénor de
Soissons

10. Chevreuse

Guy de
Chevreuse
d. 1182

Cécile

Simon de
Chevreuse
d. ca. 1191

Milon de
Chevreuse
d. ca. 1202

Elisabeth
d. >1188

Cécile de
Chevreuse
d. >1238 — **Robert de**
Mauvoisin
d. 1217

Guy de
Chevreuse
d. 1209

(1)
Aveline
de Corbeil
d. <1236

(2)
Pierre de
Richebourg

Guy de
Chevreuse
d. 1263 — Helisende

11. Île-Adam

Anseau
de l'île
d. 1161 — Mabile
de Bulles

Manasses

Adam
d. 1189 — Aelis de
Corbeil
d. 1186-9 — Id. of
Andresel

Mathieu
ct. Beaumont
d. 1208 — Aelis de
Beaumont
d. 1187

(1)

Anseau
d. 1219 — Ève de
Garlande

(2)

(1)
Marie
Mauvoisin — **Anseau**
d. 1252 — **(2)** Clémence de
Pomponne

12. Gisors

13. Dreux de Mello

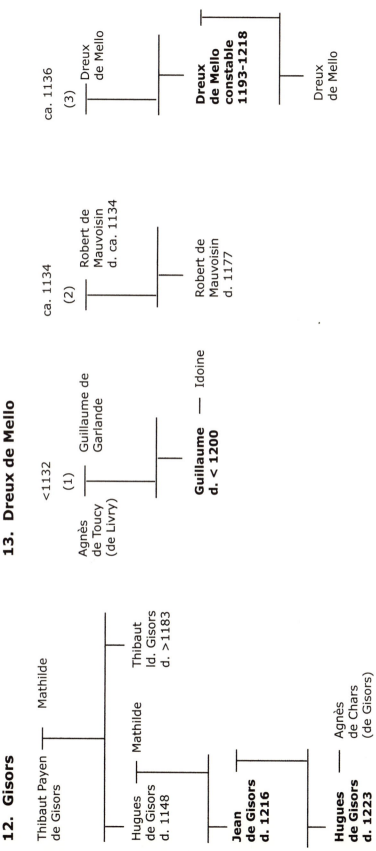

Thibaut Payen de Gisors — Mathilde

Hugues de Gisors d. 1148 — Mathilde

Thibaut ld. Gisors d. >1183

Jean de Gisors d. 1216 — Agnès de Chars (de Gisors)

Hugues de Gisors d. 1223

Agnès de Toucy (de Livry) (1) <1132 — Guillaume de Garlande

Robert de Mauvoisin (2) ca. 1134 d. ca. 1134

Dreux de Mello (3) ca. 1136

Guillaume d. < 1200 — Idoine

Robert de Mauvoisin d. 1177

Dreux de Mello constable 1193-1218

Dreux de Mello

14. Chamberlains (Nemours and Méréville)

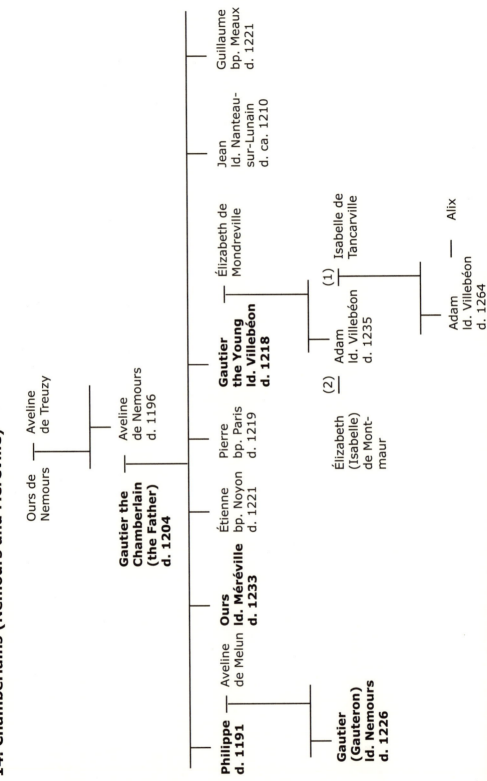

15. Poissy (two branches)

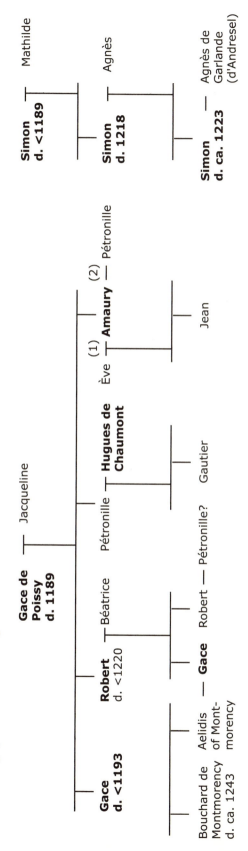

16. Mauvoisin

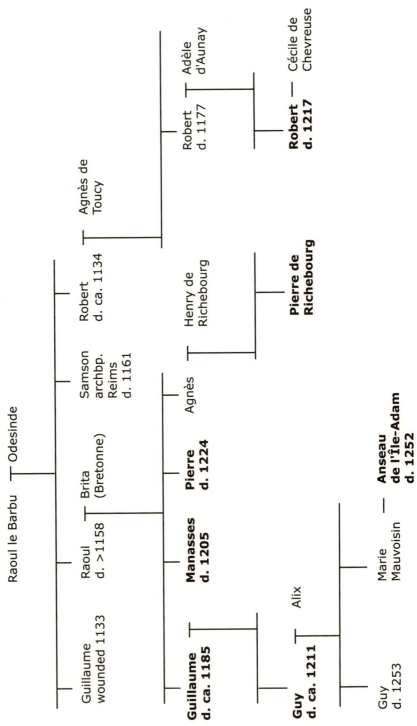

Raoul le Barbu — Odesinde

Guillaume wounded 1133

Raoul d. >1158 — Brita (Bretonne)

Samson archbp. Reims d. 1161

Robert d. ca. 1134 — Agnès de Toucy

Robert d. 1177 — Adèle d'Aunay

Robert d. 1217 — Cécile de Chevreuse

Henry de Richebourg

Pierre de Richebourg

Manasses d. 1205

Pierre d. 1224 — Agnès

Guillaume d. ca. 1185 — Alix

Guy d. ca. 1211

Guy d. 1253

Marie Mauvoisin — **Anseau de l'Île-Adam d. 1252**

17. Corbeil

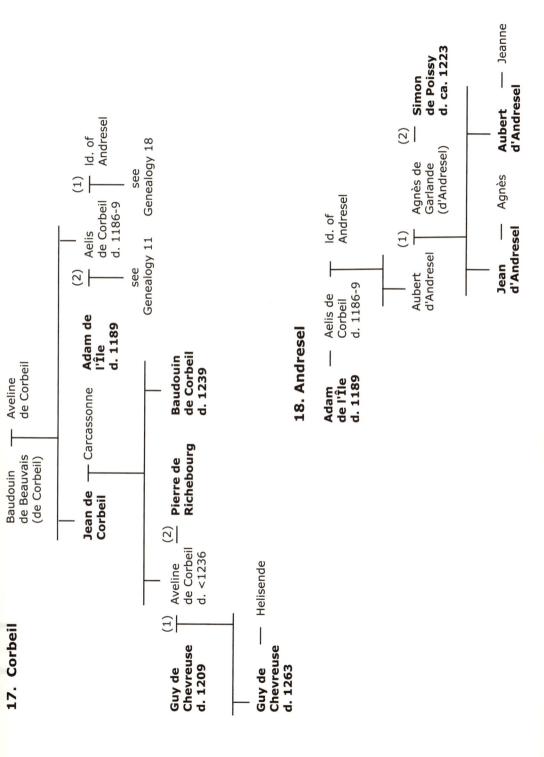

Baudouin de Beauvais (de Corbeil) — Aveline de Corbeil

(1) Id. of Andresel

Aelis de Corbeil d. 1186-9

see Genealogy 18

(2)

see Genealogy 11

Jean de Corbeil — Carcassonne

Adam de l'Île d. 1189

Guy de Chevreuse d. 1209

(1) Aveline de Corbeil d. <1236

(2) **Pierre de Richebourg**

Baudouin de Corbeil d. 1239

Guy de Chevreuse d. 1263 — Helisende

18. Andresel

Adam de l'Île d. 1189 — Aelis de Corbeil d. 1186-9

Id. of Andresel

(1) Aubert d'Andresel

Agnès de Garlande (d'Andresel)

(2) **Simon de Poissy d. ca. 1223**

Jean d'Andresel — Agnès

Aubert d'Andresel — Jeanne

Notes

Chapter 1

1. Suger, *Vie de Louis VI le Gros*, ed. Waquet (1964). A thorough examination of the evidence for Suger's narrative is Civel, *La Fleur de France* (2006), 227–52. The seigneurial anarchy of the period is the leitmotif of Thomas Bisson's *The Crisis of the Twelfth Century* (2009); on Suger and Louis VI, see pp. 229–33.

2. These themes are the subject of my *The Government of Philip Augustus* (1986); and, with Walter Simons, "The Consequences of Bouvines" (2014).

3. Crouch, *The Birth of Nobility* (2005), p. 3 and chap. 7. As might be anticipated, the word *aristocratie* apparently first appeared in Nicolas Oresme's translations of Aristotle's *Ethics* and *Politics* (ca. 1370), where he invented thousands of neologisms passing from the Greek through Latin into French: "Aristocratie," *Dictionnaire du moyen français*, www.atilf.fr/dmf.

4. Bloch, "L'Île-de-France (les pays autour de Paris)" (2011; first published 1913), 692–787, esp. 692, 716, 729, 754, 758, 786.

5. Duby, *La Société aux XIe et XIIe siècles dans la région Mâconnaise* (1953); Barthélemy, *La Société dans le comté de Vendôme de l'an mil au XIVe siècle* (1993); Lemesle, *La Société aristocratique dans le Haut-Maine* (1999); Evergates, *The Aristocracy in the County of Champagne* (2007).

6. Baldwin, *Paris, 1200* (2006 and 2010).

7. Bloch, "L'Île-de-France," 699.

8. "Similiter francia particularis circa parisius et francia generalis." Pierre the Chanter, Oxford, Balliol Coll. MS 23, fol. 22ra, cited in Baldwin, *Masters, Princes and Merchants* (1970), 2:109 n. 1.

9. On the surveys of fief-holders, see this chapter, 10–11; on the cartularies, see 7.

10. This factor explains the success of the studies of the Mâconnais, the Vendômois, and of Anjou and Champagne. Normandy under the Capetians awaits its study.

11. Baldwin, *Government*, 396–99.

12. I have supplemented the cartulary of Ourscamp (OurPD) with charters from Ourscamp copied by Gaignières (OurBN). The thirty-two cartularies (plus OurBN) are marked with an asterisk in the "Cartularies and Charter Collections" section of the bibliography.

13. On these 610 charters, see below, Chapter 6, 125–26; Chapter 7, 135–36; and Table 8.

14. Six are published in *Obituaires de la province de Sens*, tomes 1 and 2, ed. Molinier (1901–6): Notre-Dame de Paris, Saint-Victor de Paris, Saint-Martin-des-Champs, Val-Notre-Dame, Porrois, Joyenval. The other is published in Depoin, "Manuscrits funèbres de Saint-Léonor de Beaumont" (1918). On the obituaries, see below, Chapter 8, 148–50.

15. "Rouleau mortuaire de Guillaume des Barres," ed. Dufour (2006).

16. Maquet, *Les Seigneurs de Marly* (1882), 148–55.

17. Dimier, "Le Bienheureux Jean de Montmirail" (1960–61).

18. Barthélemy, *La Société dans le comté de Vendôme*, 365–439; Lemesle, *La Société aristocratique dans le Haut-Maine*, 49–83; Civel, *La Fleur de France*, 295–336; Duby, *La Société aux XIe et XIIe siècles dans la région Mâconnaise*.

19. Baldwin, "The Aristocracy in the Paris Region During the Reign of Philip Augustus, 1179–1223: A Quantitative Approach," 2 parts (2012 and 2013). An earlier essay introduces the church charters and presents my earliest research on them: Baldwin, "Les Chevaliers dans les cartulaires monastiques de la région parisienne" (2011).

20. For a preliminary treatment of this ecclesiastical bias, see Baldwin, "Les Chevaliers dans les cartulaires monastiques," 52–53.

21. For recent work on the canonists at Paris, see the studies of Anne Lefebvre-Teillard: "L'École parisienne et la formation 'politique' des clercs au début du XIIIe siècle" (2008); and "Petrus Brito, auteur de l'apparat 'Ecce vicit leo'?" (2010).

22. Bernard of Pavia, *Summa decretalium*, ed. Laspeyres (1860); Brundage, *Medieval Canon Law* (1995), 210–11; Le Bras, Lefebvre, and Rambaud, *L'Âge classique (1140–1378): Sources et théorie du droit* (1965), 294.

23. Parts of Register E are edited in *RHF*, vol. 23 (Paris, 1894); and in *Les Registres de Philippe Auguste* (1992); and elsewhere (see *Registres*, "Avant-Propos," 6). On the creation of the registers, see Baldwin, *Government*, 412–18. The names of Registers B, D, and F were assigned to later copies of the preceding volumes.

24. *Registres*, 327–35, for dukes, counts, barons, castellans, and knights.

25. Ibid., 308–24.

26. Ibid., 267–76.

27. *Nomina militum LX libratas redditus habentium*, ed. Delisle, in *RHF*, 23:686–89, nos. 369–93. The castellanies I have selected from the *Nomina* survey, roughly from north to south, are Béthisy, Senlis, Dammartin, Paris, Mantes-la-Jolie, Poissy, Montlhéry, Corbeil, Melun, and Étampes.

28. Under the title *Scripta de feodis*, the editors of volume 23 of the *RHF* published a variety of documents found in the registers of Philip Augustus and divided the documents into two sections, a *pars prior* (pp. 608–81, section nos. 1–342) and a *pars posterior* (pp. 681–723, section nos. 343–561). In the present book, the title *Scripta de feodis* refers to the *pars prior* (*Scripta de feodis*, ed. Delisle, in *RHF*, 23:608–81). Documents cited from the *pars posterior* are cited by the subtitles assigned by the editors of *RHF*, volume 23. The castellanies I have selected from the *Scripta de feodis* are the following, grouped by region: Vexin castellanies, pp. 621–33 (Gisors, nos. 61–62; Mantes-la-Jolie, nos. 68–69; Meulan, nos. 72–76; Chaumont, nos. 77–79; Pontoise, nos. 92–96); Vermandois castellanies, pp. 646–58 (Crépy-en-Valois, nos. 194–200; Chauny, nos. 201–11; La Ferté-Milon, nos. 220–22; Montdidier, nos. 227–35); two castellanies south of Paris, pp. 669–75 (Melun, nos. 289–99; Montlhéry, nos. 300–313).

29. Nieus, "Des seigneurs sans chancellerie? Pratiques de l'écrit documentaire chez les comtes et les barons du nord de la France aux XIIe–XIIIe siècles" (2010).

30. For the inventory, see Register E (AN JJ 26), fol. 15r.

31. *Le Livre de terres et de revenus de Pierre du Thillay, fondateur de l'Hôtel-Dieu de Gonesse, bailli de Caen de 1205 à 1224: Ses terres en Île-de-France et en Basse-Normandie*, ed. Baldwin (2002), 13–23. For a survey of contemporary landbooks, see Baldwin, "Pierre du Thillay, Knight and Lord: The Landed Resources of the Lower Aristocracy in the Early Thirteenth Century" (2003), 18–22.

32. VND, fols. 63r–68r.

33. Higounet, *La Grange de Vaulerent* (1965), 66–69.

34. *Registres*, 207–28.

35. On seals, see Bedos-Rezak, "Les Sceaux au temps de Philippe Auguste" (1982).

36. For example, "Et ut hoc ratum et inconcussum in posterum perseveret, presentes litteras feci sigilli mei munimine roborari." AN S 1354, no. 1; and the copy of this charter in the cartulary of Saint-Martin-des-Champs, SMCps, 3:342.

37. Civel, *La Fleur de France*, 253.

38. See the reflections of Bedos-Rezak, *When Ego Was Imago* (2011), 109–12.

39. Aurell, *Le Chevalier lettré* (2011), 21–38.

40. Gerbert de Montreuil, *La Continuation de Perceval*, ed. Williams and Oswald (1922–75).

41. *Registres*, 203, no. 120; Fawtier, "Un fragment du compte de l'hôtel du prince Louis de France pour le terme de la purification 1213" (1933), 243.

42. Guilhiermoz, "Une charte de Gace Brulé" (1893).

43. This is the thesis of Grossel, *Le Milieu littéraire en Champagne sous les Thibaudiens (1200–1270)* (1997), 1:313–22.

44. Aurell, *Des chrétiens contre les croisades, XIIe–XIIIe siècle* (2013), 120–22.

45. Raoul de Hodenc, *Le Roman des Eles*, ed. Busby (1983). Raoul was also the author of the Arthurian romance *Meraugis de Portleguez*, which, because of its idiosyncratic characteristics, is less useful for my purposes.

46. See above, 7–8, for Saint Thibaut.

47. *Les Vers de Thibaud de Marly*, ed. Stone (1932), 36–57; Maquet, *Les Seigneurs de Marly*, 86–87.

48. On Hélinand, see Baldwin, *Government*, 570–71 n. 28. His career as a jongleur at the royal court probably preceded the period when the king took an aversion to the profession.

49. I have wrestled with these hermeneutic problems in *The Language of Sex* (1994), xxi–xxv; and *Aristocratic Life in Medieval France* (2000), 19–21, 265–67.

50. The reports of explorations around Paris are conveniently archived and open to consultation at DRAC (Direction régionale des Affaires culturelles), Île-de-France, located at 47 rue Le Peletier, 75009 Paris.

51. On this fiction see Chênerie, *Le Chevalier errant dans les romans arthuriens en vers des XIIe et XIIIe siècles* (1986).

52. Bautier and Bautier, "Contribution à l'histoire du cheval au moyen âge" (1980), explores the literature in Latin; see pp. 28, 30, 38.

53. MSM, fol. 15r–v (1200).

54. Bar 5466, fols. 853–54 (1222), in Lefèvre, "Les Dîmes novales dans la région parisienne du XIIe au XIIIe siècle" (1985), 727 and n. 37.

55. The monastery of Saint-Yved was raising horses in its forests in 1210, and the fairs of Champagne included horse markets; see Bautier and Bautier, "Contribution," 43, 44. The *Histoire de Guillaume le Maréchal* identified a horse market at the fair of Lagny; see *Histoire de Guillaume le Maréchal*, ed. Holden (2002–6), vol. 1, vv. 5962–65. Draft horses were plentiful in contemporary England; see Langdon, "Horse Hauling" (1984). The evidence is based on the abundance of domanial and administrative documents from both the monasteries and the monarchy beginning with the Domesday Book. Evidence from archaeology is not offered.

56. Guillaume le Breton, *Gesta*, ed. Delaborde (1882), 266–90.

57. Guillaume le Breton, *Philippidos*, ed. Delaborde (1885), 310–49.

58. See Arbogast et al., *Archéologie du cheval* (2002); horses make up less than 2 percent in the bone collections from the thirteenth century (12). Two horseshoes and assorted buckles for harnesses were found at Roissy-en-France, apparently made for riding horses and not for agricultural draft animals; see *Le Château de Roissy-en-France (Val d'Oise)*, ed. Dufour (2014), 91, 101, 161, 162.

59. My speculations on the absence of the horse in archaeological remains have benefited from discussions with Benoît Clavel on 23 May 2013.

Chapter 2

1. Baldwin, *Government*, 31–34, 104–14; for their court service, see pp. 426–27.

2. Ibid., 81, 91–92, 200–202, 217–18, 342, 382.

3. Guillaume le Breton, *Gesta*, ed. Delaborde, 266–91; and *Philippidos*, ed. Delaborde, 296–347. For a list of the knights, see Baldwin, *Government*, 450–53.

4. On these three, and the elusive identity of "Benedict," see Baldwin, *Government*, 400.

5. Roger of Howden, *Chronica*, ed. Stubbs (1868–71), 4:56–57.

6. For example, at the tournament of Lagny in 1180; see *Histoire de Guillaume le Maréchal*, ed. Holden, vol. 1, vv. 4457–970.

7. The most successful example of this approach is Cartellieri, *Philipp II. August, König von Frankreich* (1899–1922), 4 vols.

8. On the chroniclers and Philip's armies, see Baldwin, *Government*, 279–80.

9. See above, 10–11.

10. *Registres*, 327–35.

11. "Roi, conte, duc et prince, chastelein, vavassor." *Les Vers de Thibaud de Marly*, ed. Stone, v. 486; see also v. 664.

12. *Registres*, 308–24; see pp. 317–20 for Vermandois and the Vexin.

13. *Nomina militum*, ed. Delisle, 686–89, nos. 369–93.

14. On the early counties, see Civel, *La Fleur de France*, 151–52.

15. Power, *The Norman Frontier in the Twelfth and Early Thirteenth Centuries* (2004), 288–95.

16. Civel, *La Fleur de France*, 172–79; Baldwin, *Government*, 87–100.

17. Baldwin, *Government*, 81, 91–92, 200–202, 382, 517.

18. Mathieu, *Recherches sur les premiers comtes de Dammartin: Un nouvel éclairage* (1995), 34; see *Layettes du Trésor des Chartes*, ed. Teulet (1863–65), vol. 1, no. 613, for the agreement accompanying the marriage of Renaud's daughter, Mathilde, to Philippe.

19. The neighboring county of Soissons was omitted from my study.

20. Rigord, *Gesta*, ed. Carpentier (2006), 246; Rigord, *Gesta*, ed. Delaborde (1882), 84.

21. NDP, 1:21–22 (1206); Douët d'Arcq, *Recherches historiques et critiques sur les anciens comtes de Beaumont-sur-Oise* (1855), pp. 46–47, nos. 54–56 (1206–7); *Layettes*, vol. 1, nos. 455, 814 (both preserved in the Beaumont archives). For the rubric of Innocent III's letter from 1201 (only the rubric has survived), see *Vetera monumenta Slavorum meridionalium*, ed. Theiner (1863–75), 1:63, no. 264. Mathieu has not been found among the crusaders: see Longnon, *Les Compagnons de Villehardouin* (1978). On the church, see Friedmann, *Paris, ses rues, ses paroisses* (1959), 64–65.

22. *Layettes*, vol. 1, no. 829 (1207).

23. Borrelli de Serres, *La Réunion des provinces septentrionales à la couronne par Philippe Auguste* (1899), lviii–lx, cxxix–cxxx; Newman, *Les Seigneurs de Nesle en Picardie* (1971), 1:66 n. 26.

24. Saint-Léonor: Douët d'Arcq, *Recherches historiques*, pp. 30–31, no. 29 (1184), p. 33, no. 32 (1199). Val-Notre-Dame: VND, fols. 28r (1190), 33r–v (1190), 51r–v (1192); and Douët d'Arcq, *Recherches historiques*, pp. 37–38, no. 42 (1192), pp. 38–39, no. 43 (1194), p. 87, no. 119 (1220), pp. 87–88, no. 120 (1221).

25. The claim to Luzarches went back to the early twelfth century; see Suger, *Vie de Louis VI le Gros*, ed. Waquet, 18–20; Civel, *La Fleur de France*, 67–68.

26. *Layettes*, vol. 1, nos. 1235–37. On the succession, see below, Chapter 3, 66.

27. RHF, 23:693, no. 415 (*Servitia nonnullorum feodorum*, ed. Delisle); Guillaume le Breton, *Gesta*, ed. Delaborde, 276, 279; Guillaume le Breton, *Philippidos*, ed. Delaborde, 320, 322.

28. *The Cartulary of Countess Blanche of Champagne*, ed. Evergates (2009), no. 40, among others.

29. *Registres*, 510; *Actes*, vol. 4, no. 1446 (1216).

30. *Registres*, 531–32. See below, Chapter 3, 67, for fuller discussion.

31. *Scripta de feodis*, pp. 675–76, nos. 316–17.

32. AN J 168 (Beaumont archives).

33. The most recent and comprehensive studies of Aliénor and the Vermandois are Carolus-Barré, "Une arrière petite-fille de Hugues Capet, Aliénor de Vermandois" (1996); and Duval-Arnould, "Les Aumônes d'Aliénor" (1984). On Philippe, Aliénor, and the Vermandois in the context of the first decade of Philip's reign, see Baldwin, *Government*, 8, 15, 17–19, 22–26, 81, 200.

34. Borrelli de Serres, *La Réunion*, xxxv–xxxix.

35. *Actes*, vol. 1, no. 399 (1191–92).

36. Texts and full treatment in Duval-Arnould, "Les Aumônes d'Aliénor," 431–46.

37. For example, *Actes*, vol. 2, no. 496.

38. Mor, 19.

39. *Registres*, 61, 88–93, 119–29.

40. *Scripta de feodis*, pp. 646–55, nos. 178–222; pp. 657–58, nos. 227–35. The castellanies of Vermandois surveyed included Saint-Quentin, Péronne, Crépy-en-Valois, Chauny, Ribemont, La Ferté-Milon, and Montdidier. See also Baldwin, "Les Chevaliers dans les cartulaires monastiques de la région parisienne," 59.

41. *RHF*, 23:693, nos. 415–16 (*Servitia nonnullorum feodorum*). Her contingents are those of Saint-Quentin, Montdidier, Péronne, Chauny, Valois, and Senlis. See also Baldwin, *Government*, "Appendix E: Knight Service at Bouvines," the column for Register C.

42. Register C (AN JJ 7), fols. 134r–137v.

43. *Registres*, 550–51.

44. Huon d'Oisi, *Tournoiement des dames*, ed. Pulega (1970), pp. 3–9, at v. 8; for the identification of the poem's "La contesse de Crespi" as Aliénor, p. 91.

45. OurBN, fol. 105 (dated 1191).

46. The fundamental collection of sources for the family of Dreux remains Duchesne, *Histoire généalogique de la maison royale de Dreux* (1631), now only partially replaced by recent editions.

47. Guillaume le Breton, *Philippidos*, ed. Delaborde, 251, 301.

48. Lewis, *Royal Succession in Capetian France* (1981), 60–63; Evergates, *The Aristocracy in the County of Champagne*, 216.

49. Baldwin, *Government*, 426.

50. *Registres*, 328.

51. Baldwin, *Government*, 426; see also Guillaume le Breton, *Philippidos*, ed. Delaborde, 256.

52. *The Cartulary of Countess Blanche*, ed. Evergates, no. 383 (1206), no. 384 (1209).

53. Rigord, *Gesta*, ed. Delaborde, 84, 136; ed. Carpentier, 245, 342; Guillaume le Breton, ed. Delaborde, *Philippidos*, 182.

54. *Budget*, CCV (1); *Actes*, vol. 2, no. 827; *Registres*, 199; Baldwin, *Government*, 538 n. 79, 539 n. 81.

55. Guillaume le Breton, *Gesta*, ed. Delaborde, 226; Anonymous of Béthune, *Extrait d'une chronique française des rois de France*, ed. Delisle (1904), 763.

56. Guillaume le Breton, *Philippidos*, ed. Delaborde, 256.

57. Guillaume le Breton, *Gesta*, ed. Delaborde, 255, 293; Guillaume le Breton, *Philippidos*, ed. Delaborde, 353; Anonymous of Béthune, *Histoire des ducs de Normandie et des rois d'Angleterre*, ed. Michel (1840), 143–45.

58. Petit-Dutaillis, *Étude sur la vie et le règne de Louis VIII* (1894), 98, 121, 122, 146, 239. Louis offered him the castle of Marlborough and later in 1227 promised compensation in Normandy if it was not delivered; see Duchesne, *Dreux*, 269–70.

59. For example, see *The Cartulary of Countess Blanche*, ed. Evergates, no. 385; Duchesne, *Dreux*, 268.

60. The most comprehensive study of Pierre de Dreux remains Painter, *The Scourge of the Clergy* (1937). Pierre de Dreux's charters have been collected and edited by Lémeillat, *Actes de Pierre de Dreux* (2013).

61. SMCps, 3:82–83 (1187); SGM (1184) in Duchesne, *Dreux*, 238; priory of Gournay-sur-Marne (1184, 1187) in Duchesne, *Dreux*, 238, 239; abbey of Saint-Vincent-au-Bois (1184) in Duchesne, *Dreux*, 238; Douët d'Arcq I, no. 720 (1184), where both titles are included.

62. Abbey of Igny (1205) in Duchesne, *Dreux*, 252; SYB, 178–80 (1209); Douët d'Arcq I, no. 722 (1215).

63. Duchesne, *Dreux*, 267 (1220, 1222); Douët d'Arcq I, no. 728 (1225).

64. SYB, 189 (1202), 195 (1208), 196 (1208), 197 (1218), 308 (1222), 372–77 (obituary of Saint-Yved de Braine).

65. *Chartularium universitatis Parisiensis*, ed. Denifle and Châtelain (1884), vol. 1, no. 14 (1186–87); *Actes*, vol. 1, no. 146 (1185); no. 423 (1192). The gifts included incomes on lands at Villeneuve-Saint-Georges and Torcy.

66. SGM in Duchesne, *Dreux*, 250 (1195); SVP in Duchesne, *Dreux*, 253 (1211); SGP, 2:96 (1202), 213–14 (1215). Lands and rents at Montlhéry, Paray (Paray-Vielle-Poste), Rungis, and Villeneuve-Saint-Georges were among those involved in the transactions. The family also held land in Gournay-sur-Marne: Duchesne, *Dreux*, 253 (1207).

67. *Layettes*, vol. 1, nos. 1581 (1223), 1582 (1223). Little remains of the ruins.

68. *Littere Baronum: The Earliest Cartulary of the Counts of Champagne*, ed. Evergates (2003), no. 4.

69. *The Cartulary of Countess Blanche*, ed. Evergates, no. 384.

70. *Layettes*, vol. 2, no. 1708. Bonneuil is identified by its proximity to Haute-Fontaine.

71. *The Cartulary of Countess Blanche*, ed. Evergates, no. 385.

72. Duchesne, *Dreux*, 268.

73. Guillaume's inheritance is mentioned in *Actes*, vol. 1, no. 423 (1192). Guillaume and Robert-Yolande served together in the Norman campaign of 1203, where Guillaume is identified as lord of Brie: *Budget*, CCV (1). Robert-Yolande's rights in Brie were recognized in 1208: NDP, 1:299–304 (1208) and 2:248–53 (1209).

74. Duchesne, *Dreux*, 273–75 (1227). On Brie-Comte-Robert, see below, Chapter 4, 84–88.

75. Power, *The Norman Frontier*, 291. On the early Montforts, see Civel, *La Fleur de France*, 181–82.

76. *Layettes*, vol. 1, no. 588.

77. Ibid., nos. 438, 815.

78. For example, CSH, 97 (1207); STÉ, 17 (1207), 18 (1208), 19 (1208).

79. *Registres*, 51–52 (ca. 1200–1202). This position may have been created by King Henri II in 1160: *Recueil des actes de Henri II*, ed. Delisle and Berger (1909–27), 1:251–53. See also Dor, "Seigneurs en Île-de-France occidentale et en Haute Normandie" (1992), 242.

80. AN L 850, no. 6; Dor, "Seigneurs en Île-de-France," 156–59; SD, vol. 1, pp. 389–90 (1208).

81. Longnon, *Les Compagnons de Villehardouin*, 113–14.

82. The *Scriptum feodorum de Monteforti* is edited in Dor, "Seigneurs en Île-de-France" (1992), vol. 2.

83. The donation charters are numerous but the principal collections are in Rhein, "La Seigneurie de Montfort en Iveline" (1910), 124–246, 297–360; and Molinier, "Catalogue des actes de Simon et d'Amauri de Montfort" (1873).

84. SGP, 2:208 (ca. 1215).

85. VdC, 1:71–72 (1179), 72 (1170–95), 140 (ca. 1202), 168 (1208), 190 (ca. 1222), 225 (1222).

86. For example, Molinier, "Catalogue des actes de Simon et d'Amauri de Montfort," p. 448, no. 7 (1202, Hautes-Bruyères); Yer, 204 (1207), 225–26 (1219); Por, 34 (1208).

87. See also the gift of Amicia to the cathedral: NDC, 2:35–36 (1206).

88. Bedos[-Rezak], *La Châtellenie de Montmorency* (1980), is the authoritative study of the family. See also Civel, *La Fleur de France*, 189–90.

89. Newman, *Les Seigneurs de Nesle*, 1:65 n. 25.

90. SD, vol. 1, pp. 387–88 (1200); Bedos[-Rezak], *La Châtellenie de Montmorency*, 58. For other examples of disputes, see SD, vol. 1, pp. 388 (1204), 388–89 (1205), 389–90 (1208), 390–91 (1219), 395–96 (1221).

91. *Layettes*, vol. 1, no. 660 (1202).

92. For example, VND, fols. 43v–45r (1193).

93. Rigord, *Gesta*, ed. Carpentier, 286; ed. Delaborde, 106–7. He was also a guarantor of the privileges granted by Philip to the Genoese, at Genoa (1190); see *Actes*, vol. 1, no. 365.

94. Guillaume le Breton, *Philippidos*, ed. Delaborde, 187.

95. RHF, 23:693, no. 415 (*Servitia nonnullorum feodorum*); Guillaume le Breton, *Gesta*, ed. Delaborde, 276, 279.

96. Pierre des Vaux-de-Cernay, *Hystoria Albigensis*, ed. Guébin and Lyon (1926–39), 2:244; Pierre des Vaux-de-Cernay, *The History of the Albigensian Crusade*, trans. by Sibly and Sibly (1998), 246.

97. *The Cartulary of Countess Blanche*, ed. Evergates, nos. 39–47.

98. *Layettes*, vol. 1, no. 1439; *Registres*, 531–32.

99. Douët d'Arcq I, nos. 2942 (1193), 2943 (1203), 2950 (1194).

100. Ibid., nos. 192 (1224) and 193 (1230).

101. *Recueil des actes de Louis VI*, ed. Dufour (1992), 3:152–67. On the early history of the Garlandes, see Civel, *La Fleur de France*, 192–98.

102. See the genealogies in Civel, *La Fleur de France*, 436–37; and Evergates, *The Aristocracy in the County of Champagne*, 255.

103. AN Supp. seals, no. 0126 (1208).

104. SMCps, 3:68–70 (1185–86); *Layettes*, vol. 1, nos. 1311, 1406.

105. *Actes*, vol. 1, no. 164 (1186); NDP 1:7.

106. On these families, see below.

107. For Saint-Denis de Tournan, see AN S 1175, nos. 19, 20, 22, 38, 40 (1215, 1216, 1197, 1192); for Saint-Maur-des-Fossés, AN L 460, nos. 16, 27 (1190–92). For an edition of AN S 1175, no. 40 (1192), which gives notice of gifts of Anseau de Garlande and his family to the church of Saint-Denis de Tournan, see Stein, "Un sénéchal du XIIIe siècle, Guillaume de Combreux" (1933), 333–34.

108. *Histoire de Guillaume le Maréchal*, ed. Holden, vol. 1, vv. 7475–77.

109. Baldwin, *Government*, 113–14; SMCps 3:107 (1190–1191); Guillaume le Breton, *Gesta*, ed. Delaborde, 272.

110. *Actes*, vol. 1, no. 451; vol. 2, no. 501.

111. Douët d'Arcq I, no. 2265; AN J 394, no. 31 (1211).

112. *Gallia christiana* (1739–1877), vol. 7, Instrumenta, cols. 273–74 (1186); *Actes*, vol. 2, no. 699 (1201–8); SMCps, 3:306–7 (1212). For donations to this church, see also below, Chapter 3, 68.

113. HDP, 47 (1212); SMCps, 3:226–27 (1204), 266–67 (1208), 332–33 (1216).

114. On the Montmorency-Marly clan and Guy, butler of Senlis, see below.

115. For the settlement, see below, Chapter 3, 66.

116. Register C (AN JJ 7), fol. 116.

117. See below, Chapter 9, 198–99.

118. *Recueil des actes de Louis VI*, ed. Dufour, 3:158–68; Civel, *La Fleur de France*, 202–5.

119. Duchesne, "Histoire de la maison des bouteillers de Senlis" (1878), 170–81. Despite its age this remains the major study of the family.

120. Ibid., 175–77 (1190); SGM, pp. 183–84 (1220).

121. *Registres*, 197.

122. For example, Douët d'Arcq I, nos. 272 (1186) and 273 (1203).

123. The definitive study of the family is Newman, *Les Seigneurs de Nesle*, 1:36–50, and the attached genealogy.

124. Douët d'Arcq II, no. 3052 (1232); AN Supp. seals, nos. 4260 and 4260 bis (1223–24).

125. Geoffroi de Villehardouin, *La Conquête de Constantinople*, ed. Faral (1973), 1:12. Longnon, *Les Compagnons de Villehardouin*, 149–50, claims that it was not Jean II but Jean I who participated in the Fourth Crusade. Longnon and Newman agree that the father went on the Third Crusade.

126. "Miles quidem procerus corpore et forme venustissime" (Guillaume le Breton, *Gesta*, ed. Delaborde, 288). See also Guillaume le Breton, *Philippidos*, ed. Delaborde, 340.

127. For the identification of Blondel as Jean de Nesle, see *Gace Brulé, trouvère champenois*, ed. Dyggve (1951), 100–101. Newman's exhaustive research has not produced evidence for this identification. He cites without further comment the conjecture of Arthur Cullmann that the "seigneur de neele" in the songs of Audefroi le Batard is Jean de Nesle. See Newman, *Les Seigneurs de Nesle*, 1:44.

128. Newman, *Les Seigneurs de Nesle*, 1:72 n. 41.

129. Ibid., 1:40–41.

130. Ibid., 48–50; for the many donations, see AB (the nunnery is also known as the Abbaye-aux-Bois).

131. *Scripta de feodis*, pp. 656–57, nos. 223–25; Newman, *Les Seigneurs de Nesle*, 1:46–49.

132. *RHF*, 23:693, no. 415 (*Servitia nonnullorum feodorum*).

133. *Registres*, 319.

134. *Actes*, vol. 3, no. 960.

135. Roger of Wendover, *Flores historiarum*, ed. Hewlett (1886–89), 2:194–95.

136. *Scripta de feodis*, p. 669, no. 289.

137. Ibid., p. 671, no. 299.

138. *Nomina militum*, p. 687, no. 371.

139. Douët d'Arcq I, nos. 695 (Adam, 1204) and 701 (Payen, 1199).

140. *Registres*, 331 (*Dominus Marliaci, Dominus de Cauda*); Power, *The Norman Frontier*, 222 n. 106.

141. Maquet, *Les Seigneurs de Marly*, is a comprehensive study.

142. For example, compare Bouchard de Marly, Douët d'Arcq I, no. 2714 (1224), with Mathieu de Montmorency, Douët d'Arcq I, no. 192 (1224). The legends on both seals carry the name of Montmorency. Plate 12B, below, shows the seal of Bouchard de Marly.

143. Roger of Howden, *Chronica*, 4:56–57, identified him as Mathieu Montmorency, but to Rigord he was Mathieu de Marly; see Rigord, *Gesta*, ed. Carpentier, 354; ed. Delaborde, 142.

144. See Longnon, *Les Compagnons de Villehardouin*, 116–18, though Longnon misidentifies him as Mathieu de Montmorency.

145. SGM, pp. 190–91 (1202); VdC, 1:76 (1180–1202), 130 (1199), 204 (1216); Por, 25 (before 1204), 29 (1206), 36–37 (1209), 84 (1223–24).

146. *Les Vers de Thibaud de Marly*, ed. Stone; Hasenohr, "Thibaut de Marly" (1992); Maquet, *Les Seigneurs de Marly*, 86–87.

147. Woehl, *Volo vincere* (2001), 144–48.

148. Por, 36–37 (1209), 38 (1209), 41 (1210), 44–46 (1214), 61 (1218), 88 (1224). Gifts from other members of the family include Por, 76 (1223), 77 (1223), and 83 (1223).

149. "Église Cathédrale de Paris: Obituaire du XIIIe siècle," in *Obituaires de la province de Sens*, 1.1:113–14; NDP 1:297–98 (1221).

150. Maquet, *Les Seigneurs de Marly*, 148–55. In addition to the donations to Vaux-de-Cernay above (note 145), see VdC, 1:213–14 (1218).

151. *Actes*, vol. 3, no. 1255 (1212). On the window at Chartres, see below, Chapter 10.

152. Power, *The Norman Frontier*, 259–61. He appears in the list of castellans as *Dominus de Cauda* (*Registres*, 331); for the identification of *Cauda* as La Queue-en-Brie, see Power, *The Norman Frontier*, 222 n. 106. Three charters concerning lands or rights of Roger near or at La Queue-en-Brie are SMCps, 3:175 (1189–1201) and 372 (1221); HDP, 33 (1204). For genealogies, see Civel, *La Fleur de France*, 448; and Power, *The Norman Frontier*, 509.

153. Roger of Howden, *Chronica*, 4:56, 57; *Registres*, 198.

154. SMCps, 3:83–84 (1187), 243 (1205); VND, fol. 39r–v (1192).

155. SVP, fol. 76r (1190); *Actes*, vol. 1, no. 312 (1190), and vol. 2, no. 667 (1200).

156. *Layettes*, vol. 1, nos. 438–40; Power, *The Norman Frontier*, 259.

157. SMCps, 3:277–78 (1209).

158. Power, *The Norman Frontier*, 509.

159. Douët d'Arcq I, nos. 2833 (1195) and 2834 (1204); AN Supp. seals, no. 0418 (1205).

160. *Registres*, 331 (*Dominus Nialphe*).

161. Longnon, *Les Compagnons de Villehardouin*, 128; *Registres*, 199. For examples of gifts, see VdC, 1:75 (1180), 152 (1206), 156 (1206), 189 (1213), 209 (1218), 218 (1220). On the early history of Neauphle, see Civel, *La Fleur de France*, 30, 247, 248, 325, 326, 338–40.

162. AN Supp. seals, no. 3042 (1206).

163. Civel, *La Fleur de France*, 34–42, 452; Moutié, *Chevreuse* (1874–76), 2:109–81.

164. NDR, 431 (1191). The king intervened when these arrangements were disputed: *Actes*, vol. 1, no. 418 (1192).

165. NDM, 7.

166. VdC, 1:84 (1182–96), 149 (before 1206), 153 (1206), 154 (1206), 157–58 (1207), 163 (1208), 165 (two charters from 1208), 180 (1205); 163 (1208) was a gift from his sister Cécile.

167. VdC, 1:173 (1208–10). This is a rare example of a letter from a lay lord (*dominus* or *domina*) to the king.

168. Yer, 19–20 (1207). For donations of the Chevreuse family to Yerres, see also Moutié, *Chevreuse*, 2:125 (1188), 133 (1208), 137 (1225).

169. Por, 33 (1208), 69–70 (1220), 74–75 (1221).

170. *Scripta de feodis*, p. 670, no. 291.

171. *Scriptum feodorum de Monteforti*, ed. Dor, in his "Seigneurs en Île-de-France," no. 6.

172. AN Supp. seals, nos. 2696 (1208) and 3040 (1202).

173. On the castle, see below, Chapter 4.

174. *Registres*, 331. The term *Castellanus Insule* may designate the castellan of Lille, since it is placed near those of Gand and Arras, but it is also followed by the lord of Mello near Senlis, which would accommodate Île-Adam. For the family, see Darras, *Les Seigneurs-châtelains de l'Île-Adam* (1939). The Amis de l'Île-Adam are engaged in collecting the charters that concern the family. See their "Les Chartes latines concernant l'Isle-Adam et sa région" (2006).

175. *Layettes*, vol. 1, nos. 792 (1205) and 816 (1206). The originals are AN J 168, nos. 13 and 15.

176. VND, fols. 31v–32r (before 1189), 27v (1190); AN S 4197, no. 3 (1208); AN S 4201, no. 5 (1219).

177. SMCps 3:76 (1186).

178. Vincent, *Norman Charters from English Sources* (2013), pp. 227–28, no. 101.

179. Douët d'Arcq I, no. 2449 (1205).

180. Roger of Howden, *Chronica*, 4:14–15.

181. SGP, 2:116 (1192–1204), 58 (1195), 84 (1200); VND, fols. 56v–57r (1193), 58r–v (1193).

182. *Scripta de feodis*, p. 625, no. 79 (*Petronilla*); p. 624, no. 77 (*Willelmus de Calvo Monte*). Hugues was the son of Galo de Chaumont and his wife Mathilde: AN L 944, no. 35 (n.d.); VND, fols. 15v, 16r (n.d.). For Galo, Mathilde, and Hugues, see also Civel, *La Fleur de France*, 53, 428. Guillaume was a witness to Hugues and Pétronille in 1193: VND, fols. 56v–57r, 58r–v. In 1190 and 1210 a Helisent, lady of Chaumont, and her son Eudes des Barres gave to the abbey of Saint-Victor: SVP, fols. 152r (1190), 156v (1210). The relationship of Helisent and Eudes to Hugues, Pétronille, and Guillaume is not yet clear.

183. Douët d'Arcq I, nos. 1807 (1182), 1808 (1200).

184. Baldwin, *Government*, 88–90, 298–99, and illustration 9 (Gisors, Tour du Prisonnier).

185. Powicke, *The Loss of Normandy* (1961), 176, 340; Power, *The Norman Frontier*, 221–22, 243; Civel, *La Fleur de France*, 53–54.

186. *Scripta de feodis*, pp. 630–31, nos. 98–103 (a section originating in the earlier Register C and likewise included in Register E).

187. SD, vol. 1, pp. 668 (1201) and 668–669 (1206); VdC, 1:127 (1197); SMPo, 168 (1199); SMPoCh, 10 (1216).

188. Douët d'Arcq I, no. 2276 (end of twelfth century).

189. SMPo, 156–57 (1183), 168 (1199); SMPoCh, 10 (1216), 16–17 (1218); SD, vol. 1, pp. 668–69 (1206).

190. *Scripta de feodis*, p. 621, no. 61.

191. See the thorough study of this family by Newman, *Les Seigneurs de Nesle*, 1:81–88. It is not clear that this family had the status of castellan.

192. See the genealogy in Newman, *Les Seigneurs de Nesle*, 1:264; and the conclusion of Power, *The Norman Frontier*, 358 n. 111, and 406. For various hypotheses about these marriages, see Brière, "Une alliance familiale entre les Garlande, les Mauvoisin et les Mello au XIIe siècle" (1961).

193. *Actes*, vol. 2, nos. 554 (1197), 699 (1201). See below, Chapter 3, 68, for the patronage of the abbey of Livry.

194. *Layettes*, vol. 1, nos. 996–1001. Among the pledges, G. de Trainel is identified as Dreux junior's brother, and Manasses de Mello is also listed, possibly as a relative.

195. *Gesta Regis Henrici Secundi Benedicti Abbatis*, ed. Stubbs (1867), 2:179.

196. Rigord, *Gesta*, ed, Carpentier, 391; ed. Delaborde, 162. Dreux the constable was active in the Auxerrois region. See, for example, SGAux (cartulary of Saint-Germain d'Auxerre), fol. 47v (1201); and Lespinasse, *Le Nivernais et les comtes de Nevers* (1909–14), 1:472–74.

197. Baldwin, *Government*, 104–5, 426.

198. *Layettes*, vol. 1, no. 804.

199. Douët d'Arcq I, no. 191 (1211).

200. Richemond, *Recherches généalogiques sur la famille des seigneurs de Nemours* (1907–8), is the standard history of the family.

201. Aubry de Trois-Fontaines, *Chronica*, ed. Scheffer-Boichorst (1874), 884.

202. Richemond, *Recherches généalogiques*, 1:21–24, 76–77.

203. Guillaume le Breton, *Gesta*, ed. Delaborde, 257; Baldwin, *Government*, 107–9.

204. *Actes*, vol. 2, no. 587.

205. *Actes*, vol. 2, no. 888; vol. 4, no. 1516.

206. Jean received, among other lands, the domain of Combs (Richemond, *Recherches généalogiques*, 2:220); Guillaume, who would become bishop of Meaux, was provided with land and various revenues until his ecclesiastical revenus reached two hundred *livres* (ibid., 1:139–40).

207. The cartulary of Barbeau (Bar) contains charters from the family too numerous to cite. See an early confirmation by King Philip: *Actes*, vol. 1, no. 173 (1186).

208. Richmond, *Recherches généalogiques*, 1:x–xiii, xxi–xxiv (Hôtel-Dieu de Nemours); SVP, fols. 114r (1174), 43r (1222); SD, vol. 1, pp. 425 (1207), 66 (1216), 335 (1216); NDC, 2:62–63 (1212).

209. Douët d'Arcq I, nos. 231 (1174), 236 (1203).

210. *Registres*, 331 (*Dominus de Hangest*); *Scripta de feodis*, p. 657, no. 227 and p. 651, no. 203. Aubert was also listed among the *vavassores*: *Registres*, 334 (*Aubertus de Hangest*).

211. *Actes*, vol. 2, no. 854; RHF, 23:693, no. 415 (*Servitia nonnullorum feodorum*).

212. *Budget*, CLXIX; see Baldwin, *Government*, 112, for details.

213. *Scripta de feodis*, p. 657, no. 227.

214. For example, SCC, 1:368 (1202); Mor, 24–25 (1213); and charters dating from 1189, 1202, 1210, 1224, 1225 from the archives of Saint-Quentin, Saint-Prix de Saint-Quentin, and Picquigny. (I owe this information to Robert Fossier.)

215. *Histoire de Guillaume le Maréchal*, ed. Holden, vol. 1, vv. 4016–20.

216. Douët d'Arcq I, nos. 2357 (Aubert, 1220) and 2358 (Florence, 1223).

217. *Registres*, 333–35.

218. On Aubert, see above.

219. Depoin, in SMPo, 430–39. On their origins, see Civel, *La Fleur de France*, 199, 333.

220. Woehl, *Volo vincere*, 137–39; RHF, 23:693, no. 416 (*Servitia nonnullorum feodorum*).

221. RHF, 23:633, no. 110 (*Inquisitio valoris feodorum castellaniae Pissiaci . . . anno Domini 1217*). Robert's fiefs were also given a separate chapter by the bailli Guillaume de Ville-Thierri: *Scripta de feodis*, pp. 631–32, no. 104.

222. RHF, 23:693, no. 416 (*Servitia nonnullorum feodorum*).

223. *Scriptum feodorum de Monteforti*, ed. Dor, in his "Seigneurs en Île-de-France," no. 2.

224. *Actes*, vol. 1, no. 206 (1187).

225. Vincent, *Norman Charters*, pp. 226–27, no. 100; Abb, 23–24 (1184), 29 (1191–92), 37 (1207), 48 (1224); *Actes*, vol. 1, nos. 419 (1192) and 420 (1192); Civel, *La Fleur de France*, 333.

226. VND, fol. 40v (1180); VdC, 1:100 (1189), 103 (1190), 139 (1202), 219 (1220); Joy, 94 (1227); OurPD, 466–67 (n.d.); *Actes*, vol. 1, no. 288 (before 1190).

227. Douët d'Arcq II, nos. 3250 (Gace, 1225), 3249 (Amaury, 1225), 3255 (Robert, 1226); AN Supp. seals, no. 2826 (Robert, 1227).

228. SJVa, 79–80 (1208).

229. Woehl, *Volo vincere*, 127–39; RHF, 23:693, no. 416 (*Servitia nonnullorum feodorum*).

230. Guillaume le Breton, *Gesta*, ed. Delaborde, 313–14.

231. *Actes*, vol. 3, no. 960 (1206).

232. Ibid., no. 1265 (1212).

233. RHF, 23:633, no. 110 (*Inquisitio valoris feodorum castellaniae Pissiaci*).

234. *Registres*, 529 (1223). The fortress was near Poissy, between the abbeys of Joyenval and Abbecourt.

235. *Actes*, vol. 1, no. 251, and vol 4, nos. 1625 and 1568; Petit-Dutaillis, *Étude sur la vie et le règne de Louis VIII*, appendix "Catalogue des actes de Louis VIII," p. 465, no. 118 (1224).

236. *Actes*, vol. 1, no. 250 (1189); VdC, 1:139 (1202), 187 (1212).

237. "Ego Simon de Pisciaco notum facio . . . quod ego de consensu et concessu Agnetis uxoris meae et heredum meorum concessi et dedi magistro Johanni regis clerico et amico meo XVI denarios in censu, quos habui ante ecclesiam sancti Stephani Parisius cum omni libertate et dominio et justitia ejusdem censive ad opus domus Dei hospitalis, videlicet sancti Jacobi, quod idem Johannes ibidem construere proponit in perpetuum libere possidendos . . . Rogo etiam dilectissimum dominum meum Philippum Francorum regem, quatenus amore Dei et meo ipsi hoc factum placeat confirmare. Actum apud Egremont . . . MCCIX." Quétif and Échard, *Scriptores ordinis praedicatorum* (1721), 1:17a. The editors found this charter in the archives of Saint-Jacques and identified Master Jean as Jean de Barastre. (I wish to thank William Courtenay for this information.) Denifle and Châtelain likewise identified Master Jean as Jean de Barastre but more recently scholars have argued that Master Jean, the dean of Saint-Quentin, was Jean de Saint-Albans. See *Chartularium universitatis Parisiensis*, vol. 1, ed. Denifle and Châtelain, 100–102, nos. 43 and 44; and Gorochov, *Naissance de l'université* (2012), 80–81, 326, 361, 401. [On the identity of Master Jean, see now William Courtenay, "The Donation of St. Jacques at Paris to the 'Dominicans'," *Archivum Fratrum Praedicatorum* 83 (2013), 107–23, which appeared after Prof. Baldwin's death.]

238. Joy, 74 (1203); *Actes*, vol. 2, no. 745 (1203).

239. "Ego Guyer cognomento Malus-Vicinus . . . ," Jos, 1:351 (1200).

240. *Gallia christiana*, vol. 8, Instrumenta, col. 328; "De Guillelmo Malevicino monacho facto," in *RHF*, vol. 14 (Paris, 1806), 245–46; Kaeuper, *Holy Warriors* (2009), 131–33.

241. Depoin, in SMPo, 250–69. For genealogies, see Civel, *La Fleur de France*, 441; Power, *The Norman Frontier*, 507.

242. *Histoire de Guillaume le Maréchal*, ed. Holden, vol. 1, vv. 5019–20.

243. *RHF*, 23:693, no. 416 (*Servitia nonnullorum feodorum*).

244. *Actes*, vol. 2, nos. 548 (1196–1202) and 560 (1197), and vol. 3, no. 1305 (1213); *Registres*, 198, 200.

245. SGP, 2:105 (1204), 149 (1204–8); Jos, 1:351–52 (1200); NDC, 1:252–53 (1195); see also *Actes*, vol. 2, no. 745 (1203), and vol. 3, no. 1146 (1210).

246. Vincent, *Norman Charters*, pp. 236–37, no. 109 (1190–1200).

247. *Actes*, vol. 2, no. 871 (1204).

248. *Registres*, 301.

249. *Actes*, vol. 2, no. 554 (1197); VdC, 1:162 (ca. 1208), 197 (1215); Por, 39 (1209), 75–76 (1221); SGM, p. 138 (1202); SD, vol. 1, p. 544 (1217); Cha, fol. 208r (1214).

250. Longnon, *Les Compagnons de Villehardouin*, 121–22; Woehl, *Volo vincere*, 153–56.

251. Douët d'Arcq I, nos. 2770 (Robert, n.d.) and 2766 (Guy, 1202).

252. Pierre de Richebourg was the nephew of the brothers Guillaume, Manasses, and Pierre Mauvoisin. See Power, *The Norman Frontier*, 254–55, 507.

253. *Scripta de feodis*, p. 623, no. 68 (Mantes), p. 626, no. 84 (Nogent); *Nomina militum*, p. 689, no. 390 (Paris), p. 688, no. 386 (Mantes).

254. Jos, 1:360–62 (1205); Dor, "Seigneurs en Île-de-France," 371.

255. *Layettes*, vol. 1, no. 594; *Budget*, CCVII (1); Power, *The Norman Frontier*, 254–55.

256. *Registres*, 334; for a genealogy, see Newman, *Les Seigneurs de Nesle*, 2:71.

257. On Philippe in royal documents, see Baldwin, *Government*, 112–13, 426, 486 n. 107.

258. For Courcelles, see Roger of Howden, *Chronica*, 4:56–57; for Bouvines, Rigord, *Gesta*, ed. Carpentier, 355; ed. Delaborde, 142; and *RHF*, 23:693, no. 415 (*Servitia nonnullorum feodorum*).

259. *Nomina militum*, p. 687, no. 374 (Béthisy); *Scripta de feodis*, pp. 650–51, no. 200 (Crépy).

260. *Registres*, 97–98; *Actes*, vol. 4, no. 1774 (1222).

261. Cha, fol. 271v (1206); NLH, fols. 2v–4r.

262. *Nomina militum*, p. 689, no. 389 (Guillaume de Cornillon); Senlis, Bibl. mun., MS Afforty, vol. 15, p. 51 (copy of charter from the archives of Chaalis, dated 1202); Baldwin, *Government*, 429, 433 (Renaud de Cornillon).

263. *Nomina militum*, p. 689, no. 389 (*Federicus de Maciaco* and *Gilebertus de Neela*); SVP, fol. 197 (1214); *Actes*, vol. 4, no. 1614, vol. 1, no. 140, and vol. 2, no. 931.

264. *Nomina militum*, p. 689, no. 388; Baldwin, *Government*, 114; "Rouleau mortuaire de Guillaume des Barres," ed. Dufour, 208–10. For the family name, taken from the defensive wall of the Right Bank of Paris, see Baldwin, *Government*, 487 n. 120.

265. *Histoire de Guillaume le Maréchal*, ed. Holden, vol. 1, vv. 4042–43, 4083–99, 4192–94, 7751–52; vol. 2, vv. 12277–320, 17146–51, 17408–12, 19113–39.

266. Ibid., vol. 1, vv. 2905–27.

267. Ibid., vol. 2, vv. 19125–52.

268. *Gesta Regis Henrici Secundi*, ed. Stubbs, 2:155–57.

269. Guillaume le Breton, *Philippidos*, ed. Delaborde, 81.

270. Guillaume le Breton, *Gesta*, ed. Delaborde, 284.

271. Douët d'Arcq I, no. 1295 (1200).

272. SMCps, 3:385–86 (1222); SGAux, fol. 41r (1210). See also *Registres*, 319, where the following bannerets were listed from the Vexin: *Guillelmus de Barris, Johannes de Barris, Odo de Barris, Petrus de Barris, Guillelmus de Barris juvenis.*

273. SVP, fol. 154r (1214).

274. *Actes*, vol. 2, no. 669; *Registres*, 199. It was given to his daughter as a dowry when she married Raoul du Sart. Later he participated in an inquest on Raoul's lands (*Registres*, 146–47).

275. Baldwin, *Government*, 426–27.

276. FLN, fol. 117r–v (1182); AN S 4185, no. 1 (Val-Notre-Dame, 1200); AN S 1186/B, fol. 5v (donation to Saint-Éloi, a priory of Saint-Maur-des-Fossés, 1190); Cha, fol. 229v (1201), fol. 254r (1203, 1206); Yer, 188–89 (1205); SVP, fol. 154r (1214); SMCps, 3:385–86 (1222). For others, see "Rouleau mortuaire de Guillaume des Barres," ed. Dufour, 208. For the donation to Saint-Éloi, see also *Actes*, vol. 5, no. 1839 (1190).

277. *Nomina militum*, p. 689, no. 388.

278. SMCps, 3:226–27 (1204).

279. *Actes*, vol. 2, no. 929.

280. Cha, fols. 228r (1207), 216r (1209), 192r–v (1213), 233r–v (1219).

281. *Nomina militum*, p. 687, no. 373; *Registres*, 197.

282. Douët d'Arcq II, no. 3267 (1212).

283. *Nomina militum*, p. 687, no. 371; Baldwin, *Government*, 127–34; Delisle, "Chronologie des baillis et des sénéchaux royaux," in *RHF*, vol. 24 (1904), *57.

284. VdC, 1:191 (1214), 246 (1225); Yer, 20–29 (1214), 224 (1218). The former *prévôt* of Bapaume was Baudouin Pastez (Baldwin, *Government*, 134, 148).

285. NDP, 1:9; Cha, fol. 284r (1217); SD, vol. 1, pp. 388–89 (1205), 736–37 (1207), 825–26 (1211).

286. Cha, fol. 248r (1217).

287. *Nomina militum*, p. 687, no. 371.

288. *Scripta de feodis*, p. 671, no. 300. For his donations, see VdC, 1:78 (181); Bar, fol. 229r (1201); Yer, 125–27 (1208). For the donation to Yerres, see also Depoin, "Les Vicomtes de Corbeil" (1899), 68. For a genealogy with both Jean de Corbeil and the vicomtes of Corbeil, see Civel, *La Fleur de France*, 429.

289. Douët d'Arcq I, nos. 1888 (Jean, 1196), 1889 (Carcassonne, 1210), 1887 (Baudouin, 1200–1250).

290. *Nomina militum*, p. 686, no. 369.

291. Ibid., p. 688, no. 385.

292. SMCux, 81–84 (1222); Bar, fols. 320v, 315r–316r (1222); *Actes*, vol. 4, no. 1786; *Layettes*, vol. 1, no. 1543 (1222). Jean's wife Agnès and Aubert's wife Jeanne also gave their consent.

293. SMCux, 126 (1218), 84–86 (1221), 127 (1224); Bar, fols. 191r (1182), 310v–311r (1197), 275r–v (1222), 191r–v (1222); *Actes*, vol. 1, no. 100 (a gift to Barbeau). For the testament, see Bar, fol. 309r–v (1226).

294. *Scriptum feodorum de Monteforti*, ed. Dor, in his "Seigneurs en Île-de-France," no. 13.

295. Moutié, "Notes historiques et généalogiques sur les seigneurs de Lévis et leur famille," in NDR, 313–428; Civel, *La Fleur de France*, 137–38. Philippe held fiefs in the castellany of Montlhéry; see *Scripta de feodis*, p. 673, no. 308. For a genealogy, see Richemond, *Recherches généalogiques*, 2:241.

296. Baldwin, *Government*, 426–27.

297. Ibid., 111–12; *Actes*, vol. 2, no. 644.

298. SD, vol. 1, p. 540 (1203).

299. Baldwin, *Government*, 112, 132, 433; Woehl, *Volo vincere*, 123–32.

300. Baldwin, *Government*, 109–11; Daon, "Barthélemy de Roye, chambrier de France" (1943).

301. *Layettes*, vol. 1, no. 412.

302. *Actes*, vol. 2, nos. 745, 866, and vol. 3, no. 959.

303. OurPD, 5–6 (1218); Joy, 74–114; Daon, "Barthélemy de Roye," 51–53, provides a list of his donations.

304. NDC, 2:74 (1214).

305. Delisle, *Littérature latine et histoire du moyen âge* (1890), 65–67.

306. Douët d'Arcq I, nos. 234 (1205) and 235 (1220).

307. Baldwin, *Government*, 127–31, 134; Delisle, "Chronologie des baillis et des sénéchaux royaux," *53–*57, *77, *84. Guy de Béthisy, a third member of the team may not be related to this family. On Guy, see Delisle, "Chronologie," *58; and Baldwin, *Government*, 496 n. 284.

308. SCC, 1:388 (1206) and 2:25–26 (1221), 35 (1222), 36–37 (1222); Cha, fols. 283v–284r (1221), 147 (1221), 141r (1222); OurPD, 473 (1223); Noy, fols. 126v–127r, 129r (1209), 184v–185r (1210).

309. Douët d'Arcq I, no. 1418 (1219).

310. For Pierre du Thillay, see Delisle, "Fragments de l'histoire de Gonesse" (1859); and Baldwin, "Pierre du Thillay," 9–15.

311. HDP, 24 (1200); *Budget*, CLXXIX (2).

312. SD, vol. 1, p. 240; AN S 2309 (1195). For the dating of the charter (AN S 2309), which recorded what he and others held from Mathieu le Bel, see below, Chapter 5, 105–6.

313. *Le Livre de terres et de revenus de Pierre du Thillay*, ed. Baldwin, 13.

314. An inquest of 1247 reveals that when an accused usurer had sought redress from Pierre du Thillay, when Pierre was bailli of Caen (1205–ca. 1224), the accused had intended to find Pierre at the Temple of Paris: *Querimoniae Normannorum, anno 1247*, ed. Delisle, in RHF, 24:15, no. 96.

315. *Actes*, vol. 4, nos. 1576, 1577, 1584 (all dated 1219).

316. *Le Livre de terres et de revenus de Pierre du Thillay*, ed. Baldwin.

317. *Registres*, 308–24. The exceptions include, of course, a woman (the countess of Vermandois) and two administrative families (Béthisy and Pastez). The others not appearing in the list were the lords of Île-Adam, Andresel, Lévis, and Le Thillay.

318. The feudal surveys include both the *Nomina militum*, used above to supplement the meager list of *vavassores* in the *Registres*, and the *Scripta de feodis*.

319. *Registres*, 196–204.

320. For the royal policy on *fief-rentes* prior to Bouvines, see Baldwin, *Government*, 272–77.

321. For the following numbers and for sources, see below, Chapter 5, 104–5, and Table 5.

322. *Nomina militum*, p. 689, no. 389, and p. 687, no. 373; VdC, 1:191 (1214); SLP, 112 (1222).

323. See the discussion in Civel, *La Fleur de France*, 147, 153–57.

324. For examples of *domicellus*, see SVP, fol. 169r (Foulque Courcelles, 1217); and Bar, fol. 181v (Milo *de Savegniaco*, 1221). For examples of *armiger*, see HDP, 50 (Baudouin, 1213); SJVi, fol. 106r (Robert *de Molendinis*, 1205).

325. An early but rare example is Guérin, son of Renaud *de Grangiis*, who pledged to give to Vaux-de-Cernay a domain and justice in the year in which he became a knight (*anno quo miles fiet*): VdC, 1:74 (ca. 1180). On dubbing, see below, Chapter 9, 212–15.

326. RHF, 23:691, nos. 402 and 404 (*Nomina militum, viduarum et valletorum*, ed. Delisle).

327. For the appearance of seals before our period, see the discussion of Civel, *La Fleur de France*, 253–64. On seals in our period, see Bedos-Rezak, "Les Sceaux au temps de Philippe Auguste." For an interpretive introduction to the seal, see her important *When Ego Was Imago*.

328. For one example, see above, Chapter 1, note 36.

329. Bedos-Rezak, "Les Sceaux," 721; Civel, *La Fleur de France*, 253.

330. *Histoire de Guillaume le Maréchal*, ed. Holden, vol. 2, vv. 18329–30.

331. Bedos-Rezak, "Les Sceaux," 735; Bedos-Rezak, *When Ego Was Imago*, 30, 31, 56.

332. See the reflections of Brigitte Bedos-Rezak, *When Ego Was Imago*, 109–12.

333. Douët d'Arcq I, no. 2265 (1211).

334. Robert II, count of Dreux, Douët d'Arcq I, no. 721 (1202); Robert III, Douët d'Arcq I, no. 726 (1212). No seal is available for a count of Beaumont, but Aliénor styled herself countess of Beaumont (*Sigillum Helienore comitisse Bomonte*) when she was married to Count Mathieu: Douët d'Arcq I, no. 1053 (1177). After 1193, her legend read *Sigillum Elienor Comitisse sci Quintini et Valesie*; see Douët d'Arcq I, no. 1032 (1212); and Carolus-Barré, "Une arrière petite-fille de Hugues Capet, Aliénor de Vermandois," 204.

335. Douët d'Arcq I, nos. 701 (Payen, 1199), 695 (Adam, 1204), 271 (Guy, butler, 1186), and 273 (Guy, butler, 1203).

336. Douët d'Arcq I, nos. 231 (Gautier the Father, 1174, 1202), 233 (Ours, 1220), 192 (Mathieu, 1224).

337. Douët d'Arcq II, no. 3052 (Jean de Nesle, 1232); vol. 1, no. 2358 (Florence de Hangest, 1223); AN Supp. seals, no. 0126 (Anseau de Garlande, 1208).

338. Douët d'Arcq I, nos. 708 (Simon, 1211) and 710 (Amaury, 1230).

339. Bedos-Rezak, "Les Sceaux," 727, observes that *miles* does not appear before 1219.

340. For an example of Raoul's seal, see Douët d'Arcq I, no. 1010 (ca. 1135); Robert de Vitry's seal is Douët d'Arcq II, no. 3928 (1161). See also Bedos-Rezak, "Les Sceaux," 726.

341. Douët d'Arcq I, no. 708 (1211).

342. For examples of the conical helmet, see Douët d'Arcq I, nos. 2929 (1169, Montmorency) and 1888 (1192, Corbeil). For examples of the cylindrical helmet, Douët d'Arcq I, no. 2942 (1193, Montmorency), and II, no. 3036 (1220, Nanteuil); and AN Supp. seals, nos. 4260 (1223, Nesle) and 2826 (1227, Poissy). See also Bedos-Rezak, "Les Sceaux," 732.

343. Douët d'Arcq I, nos. 2266 (Alix de Garlande, 1208), 2277 (Agnès de Gisors, 1225), 1057 (Jeanne de Garlande, 1220).

344. Douët d'Arcq I, no. 1889 (1210).

345. From at least two thousand charters, I have found the following exceptions. In 1199, Conon, son of "nobilis quondam viri" Hugues, lord of Coudun, was involved in a controversy with Saint-Yved de Braine (SYB, 285). In 1210, Robert, lord of Rosay and "nobiles viri Gaucherus de Rumigniaco, Renaldus et Oderdus de Braio" conveyed woods to Saint-Denis (SD, vol. 1, p. 95). In 1212, at the request of "nobilium virorum domini Mathei de Montemorenciaco, domini Guillelmi de Garlanda, domini Manesse de Melleto et domini Roberti de Pissiaco et aliorum," Jean, count of Beaumont, deferred litigation with the abbot of Saint-Denis (SD, vol. 1, p. 703). In 1216, Simon de Montfort confirmed the gift that the "nobilis vir Theobaldus de Gallanda" made to Notre-Dame de Livry (Cartularium vetus Livriaci, fol. 17, in Dor, "Seigneurs en Île-de-France," 179–80; the cartulary is lost but copies or summaries of some charters are preserved in MS 676 of the Bibliothèque Sainte-Geneviève). In 1219, "Reginaldus de Orrevilla, miles, et Gaufridus de Orrevilla, canonicus Carnotensis," attested that "nobilis vir Goerius de Lanereto" gave tithes to Saint-Martin des Champs (SMCps, 3:356).

346. Following are a few examples among many of abbots, bishops, and popes using the terms *vir nobilis* and *mulier nobilis*: Raoul, abbot of Saint-Maur-des-Fossés, "nobili viro Ansello de Gallanda" in 1216 (*Layettes*, vol. 1, no. 1205); Mathilde, abbess of Chelles, "domino Willelmo de Garlanda, viro nobili" in 1219 (SMPoCh, 15); Maurice, bishop of Paris, declared the terms of a donation made by "dominus Symon, vir nobilis de Pissiaco" in 1193 (HDP, 18); Pierre, bishop of Paris, mentioned a gift of "nobilis viri quodam domini Caprasii" in 1210 (NDP, 2:75–76); Renaud, bishop of Chartres, referred to the "vir nobilis Symon dominus Montis Fortis" in 1200 (Arch. dép. Yvelines, 47 H 1, in Dor, "Seigneurs en Île-de-France," 134); R[ogerius], bishop elect of Laon, referred to the "nobilis mulier domina Juliana de Rancigniaco" in 1208 (SD, vol. 2, p. 94); Lucius III, referred to the

"nobilem virum de Melloto" in 1183 (SD, vol. 2, p. 515, and *Regesta Pontificum Romanorum*, ed. Jaffé and Loewenfeld, 2:446, no. 14744); Innocent III referred to the "nobilis vir R. de Malo-Vicino et mater eius" in 1209 (Por, 39).

347. That Guillaume le Maréchal was said to have led a pleasant, noble life in France does not suggest hereditary nobility. "Li Mareschals molt richement e molt bel et molt noblement demorra cel termine en France," *Histoire de Guillaume le Maréchal*, ed. Holden, vol. 1, vv. 6299–301.

348. Baldwin, *Aristocratic Life*, 69–70.

349. For example, Andreas Capellanus, *De amore* 1.6.17: "Ad hoc imprimis istam tibi trado doctrinam, quod mulierum alia est plebeia, alia nobilis, alia nobilior. Item masculus alius est plebeius, alius est nobilis, alius nobilior, alius nobilissimus." *Andreas Capellanus on Love*, ed. and trans. Walsh (1982), 44.

Chapter 3

1. For a historiographical overview, see Crouch, *The Birth of Nobility*, 99–116.

2. Bernard of Pavia, *Summa decretalium*, 3.20 (pp. 90–92), 3.22 (pp. 96–99). On Roman law and canon law on testaments, see Sheehan, *The Will in Medieval England* (1963), 119–35.

3. Bernard of Pavia, *Summa decretalium*, 4.21 (pp. 190–93). See below, 76–77.

4. Bernard of Pavia, *Summa decretalium*, 3.23 (pp. 99–101); Buckland, *A Manual of Roman Private Law* (1947), 226–34; Helmholz, *Canon Law and the Law of England* (1987), 247–50.

5. The authoritative and exhaustive study of the *laudatio parentum* based on sources from western France is White, *Custom, Kinship and Gifts to Saints: The* Laudatio parentum *in Western France, 1050–1150* (1988); for his complex conclusions, see pp. 189–209. See also Barthélemy, *La Société dans le comté de Vendôme*, 519–25; Lemesle, *La Société aristocratique dans le Haut-Maine*, 111–17; Evergates, *The Aristocracy in the County of Champagne*, 91–93.

6. Baldwin, *Government*, 82–86; Baldwin, *Paris, 1200* (2010), 2–3; *Histoire de Guillaume le Maréchal*, ed. Holden, vol. 1, v. 372.

7. Many of these genealogies are most conveniently found in Civel, *La Fleur de France*, 424–57.

8. See, for example, SMCps, 3:333–34, "secundum consuetudines et usus Francie," concerning the sale of a property (1217); and SGA, fol. 18, "secundum ius commune et consuetudinem civitatis Parisiensis," also concerning the sale of property (1192). (The custom of this last text may have been limited to the city of Paris.)

9. "Item tam inter barones et milites quam inter burgenses et rurales succedant heredes in hereditatibus suis secundum morem et usum Francie circa Parisius. Item maritagia mulierum revertantur ad heredes ipsarum et possint inde condere testamentum si voluerint." Vic and Vaissette, *Histoire générale de Languedoc*, ed. Molinier et al. (1872–1904), vol. 8, col. 633.

10. *Layettes*, vol. 1, no. 337 (1185).

11. Evergates, *The Aristocracy in the County of Champagne*, 122; text in *The Cartulary of Countess Blanche of Champagne*, ed. Evergates, 408. In 1224 Count Thibaut issued an ordinance that decreed the rules of patrilineal succession: Evergates, *The Aristocracy in the County of Champagne*, 122; text in *The Cartulary of Countess Blanche*, 197–98.

12. See below, 75.

13. *Layettes*, vol. 1, nos. 1235–37 (1217).

14. *Actes*, vol. 4, no. 1600 (1219).

15. *Registres*, 530–31 (1223), 531–532 (1223). See Appendix 2 for a genealogy of the Beaumont family.

16. *Gallia christiana*, vol. 7, Instrumenta, cols. 273–74 (1186); *Actes*, vol. 2, no. 554 (1197) and no. 699 (1201–8). See Newman, *Les Seigneurs de Nesle*, 1:196, for Jean de Pomponne's relation to the Garlandes; and Civel, *La Fleur de France*, 436, for a genealogy of the Garlandes. See also above, Chapter 2, 38, on the donations of the Garlande family.

17. Joy, 88–89 (1224), 91–92 (1224), 92 (1224), 92–93 (1224), 94 (1227).

18. See above, Chapter 2, for the donations of the families. See the genealogies in Civel, *La Fleur de France*, 424–57, for the family connections.

19. Civel, *La Fleur de France*, 158–65. His samples are based on the cartularies of Saint-Magloire in Paris and Vaux-de-Cernay to the southwest.

20. This survey is based on the sample of 1,729 monastic charters, which yielded 1,910 aristocratic males and 638 females drawn from the principal actors in each transaction, plus the consenters of the *laudationes parentum* and the *laudationes domini*. Scholars interested in anthroponymy have made comparisons over time, between places and between classes. See, for example, Bourin, "France du Midi et France du Nord" (1996); and Barthélemy, *La Société dans le comté de Vendôme*, 623–51. The scope of my sample does not allow such comparisons.

21. For the etymological origin of the names I have relied on Gravelaine, *Encyclopédie des prénoms* (1989).

22. On the Mauvoisin family and their name, see above, Chapter 2, 49–50.

23. The fundamental works on heraldry for our purposes remain those of Michel Pastoureau: "La Diffusion des armoiries et les débuts de l'héraldique" (1982); and *Traité d'héraldique* (1979). His *L'Art héraldique au moyen âge* (2009) is a recent adaptation of the previous work. Civel has devoted an extensive chapter to the phenomenon with much supporting material from the Paris region in our period: Civel, *La Fleur de France*, 253–90. For a comprehensive survey of the heraldry in the Paris region, see Bedos-Rezak, "L'Apparition des armoiries sur les sceaux" (1993).

24. Pastoureau, "La Diffusion," 737, 738, 743; and Pastoureau, *Traité d'héraldique*, 303.

25. Jean Renart, *L'Escoufle*, ed. Sweetser (1974), vv. 1136–37; Pastoureau, *Traité d'héraldique*, 199.

26. *Histoire de Guillaume le Maréchal*, ed. Holden, vol. 1, vv. 977, 3486.

27. See below, Chapter 10, 243–45.

28. See the conclusions of Pastoureau, "La Diffusion," 747, 749.

29. Douët d'Arcq I, nos. 2929 (1169), 2930 (1177), 2942 (1193), 2943 (1203), 2714 (1224).

30. Ibid., no. 272 (1186).

31. Ibid., no. 707 (1195).

32. AN Supp. seals, no. 0126 (1208).

33. Douët d'Arcq I, no. 2834 (1204).

34. AN Supp. seals, no. 2673 (1215).

35. Ibid., no. 3042 (1206).

36. Douët d'Arcq I, no. 2449 (1205).

37. Ibid., nos. 191 (1211), 2781 (1221).

38. AN Supp. seals, no. 3042 (1206).

39. Douët d'Arcq II, no. 3250 (1225).

40. Douët d'Arcq I, no. 186 (1214); Pastoureau, "La Diffusion," 756; Pastoureau, *Traité d'héraldique*, 160–61; Civel, *La Fleur de France*, 270–71.

41. Douët d'Arcq I, no. 1418 (1219).

42. Ibid., no. 2265 (1211).

43. Douët d'Arcq II, no. 3036 (1220).

44. Douët d'Arcq I, no. 712 (1234).

45. Ibid., nos. 1295 (1200), 1296 (1214).

46. Douët d'Arcq II, nos. 3250 (1225), 3251 (1202), 3249 (1225), 3258 (1229); AN Supp. seals, no. 2826 (1227).

47. Douët d'Arcq I, nos. 710 (Amaury, 1230), 708 (Simon, 1211 and 1215).

48. Pastoureau, "La Diffusion," 750.

49. Douët d'Arcq I, no. 709 (Guy de Montfort, 1226), and II, no. 3255 (Robert de Poissy, 1226).

50. See below, Chapter 10, 244–45.

51. *RHF*, 23:691, nos. 402–6 (*Nomina militum, viduarum et valletorum*, ed. Delisle). Another survey of widows was made for the bailliage of Bourges in 1212: *Actes*, vol. 3, no. 1276.

52. The figure of 15 percent in Table 2 is the sum of 10 percent of the transactions in which women were the principals and 5 percent of the transactions that concerned dowries and dowers. See also below, Chapter 7, 142.

53. For the statistical basis of this section, see Baldwin, "The Aristocracy in the Paris Region," part 1, 40–43.

54. OurPD, 384.

55. Yer, 78–79; HDP, 21–22.

56. OurPD, 492–93 (1198).

57. Hér, 27–28 (1202).

58. NDP, 1:431 (1200); SLP, 107 (1220).

59. OurBN, fol. 103v (1212); OurPD, 129 (1222).

60. Noy, fols. 150v–151r (1201); see also Hér, 26 (1201); SYB, 234–35 (1208).

61. Noy, fol. 150 (1212). For other examples of the dower as half of the husband's property, see OurBN, fols. 64r–v (1184) and 63r (1202); OurPD, 229–30 (1206); Jos, 2:28–30 (1220); Actes, vol. 3, no. 1399 (1215).

62. SD, vol. 1, p. 59 (1124).

63. Actes, vol. 2, no. 666 (ca. 1200).

64. The genealogy is constructed from Arch. dép. 93/70B (1160–96) and 70B no. 2 (1201).

65. Nomina militum, no. 390. See below, Chapter 4, 94.

66. Actes, vol. 1, no. 451 (1193).

67. Ibid., no. 452 (1193).

68. Actes, vol 2, no. 500 (1195). For an early example (1182) of the king's involvement in dowry and dower arrangements, see Actes, vol. 1, no. 64.

69. Actes, vol. 3, no. 1380 (1215). The conquest of Normandy allowed the king to reward his familiar knights and their children with advantageous marriages, involving dowries and dowers. See Actes, vol. 2, no. 888 (1205), for Adam, son of Gautier the Young, the chamberlain; Actes, vol. 2, no. 905 (1205), and vol. 3, no. 1348 (1214), for Alix, daughter of Barthélemy de Roye; and Actes, vol. 3, no. 1376 (1215), for Amicie, likewise daughter of Barthélemy. Although these negotiations bore similarities to those of the Paris region, they were fundamentally governed by the Norman custom of apportioning one-third for the wife.

70. See above, note 61.

71. Philippe de Beaumanoir, Coutumes de Beauvaisis, ed. Salmon (1899–1900), 1:212–13, no. 445; Green, The Aristocracy of Norman England (1997), 368; Tabuteau, Transfers of Property in Eleventh-Century Norman Law (1988), 176; Lemesle, La Société aristocratique dans le Haute-Maine, 125.

72. Bernard of Pavia, Summa decretalium, 4.21 (pp. 190–93); Martinus, De iure dotium, in Kantorowicz, Studies in the Glossators of Roman Law (1938), 255–66; Berger, Encyclopedic Dictionary of Roman Law (1953), s.v. dos (p. 444), donatio ante nuptias (p. 443); Sheehan, "The Influence of Canon Law on the Property Rights of Married Women in England" (1963), 109–13.

Chapter 4

1. "Erat enim instar ac si mundus ipse excutiendo semet, reiecta uetustate, passim candidam ecclesiarum vestem indueret." Raoul Glaber, Historiarum libri quinque, ed. France (1989), 114–16, 126.

2. Suger, Vie de Louis VI le Gros, ed. Waquet, 16–19 (Montmorency), 18 (Luzarches), 36–122 (Montlhéry), 255–57 (Livry), 128–36 (Le Puiset), 174, 250–52 (Crécy, Nouvion, Coucy). For Louis VI's policy toward castles, see Civel, La Fleur de France, 99–113.

3. For a list of the castles with a map, see Registres, 338–42, 602.

4. The most comprehensive inventory of French medieval castles is Salch, L'Atlas des châteaux forts en France (1977). For a survey of the aristocratic castles during Philip's reign, see Civel, La Fleur de France, 131–39.

5. On the Clément family, see Baldwin, *Government*, 33–34.

6. Before 1150: Beaumont-sur-Oise, Luzarches, Conflans-Sainte-Honorine, Rochefort-en-Yvelines, Montfort-l'Amaury, Beynes, Houdan. 1150–1200: Chevreuse, Nemours, Brie-Comte-Robert. After 1200: Nesles-en-Tardenois, Mez-le-Maréchal, Diant, Fère-en-Tardenois, Blandy-les-Tours. The square donjon at Mez-le-Maréchal was built before 1200, while the courtines were an addition of the early thirteenth century. For dates of construction, see Châtelain, *Châteaux forts et féodalité en Île-de-France du XIe au XIIIe siècle* (1983).

7. The basic dimensions of seventeen castles and residences mentioned below have been tabulated in Table 4 ("Castles and Residences") for comparative purposes. The selection is based on the availability of information.

8. NDP, 1:7–8. The homage was renewed in 1226 and 1270: NDP, 1:148, 158.

9. Dufaÿ, "Histoire du donjon de La Madeleine à Chevreuse" (1990); Barat, Debout, and Langlois, "Chevreuse (Yvelines), Donjon du château de la Madeleine, Rapport de sondage archéologique" (2010); Châtelain, *Châteaux forts*, 56–64.

10. Langlois, "Beaumont-sur-Oise (Val-d'Oise), site du château" (1984); Châtelain, *Châteaux forts*, 157–61, 164–69.

11. NDP, 1:7.

12. Châtelain, *Châteaux forts*, 46–49.

13. Dufaÿ, "Le Château de Beynes (Yvelines) du XIIe au XVIe siècle" (2001); Châtelain, *Châteaux forts*, 70–72.

14. Baldwin, *Government*, 297–301.

15. Châtelain, *Châteaux forts*, 297–300.

16. For the early castles of the counts of Dreux, see Civel, *La Fleur de France*, 131–32.

17. Piechaczyk, "Le Château de Brie-Comte-Robert, un château de Robert Ier de Dreux" (2013); Châtelain, *Châteaux forts*, 335–39.

18. From the abundant literature on *archères*, see Mesqui, *La Résidence et les éléments d'architecture* (1993), 251–74.

19. Mesqui, *Les Demeures seigneuriales* (1988), 376–81; Châtelain, *Châteaux forts*, 311–17.

20. Mesqui, *Les Demeures seigneuriales*, 180–86; Châtelain, *Châteaux forts*, 318–26.

21. Mesqui, *Les Demeures seigneuriales*, 256–61; Châtelain, *Châteaux forts*, 354–59.

22. Stein, "Le Mez-le-Maréchal" (1931); Mesqui, *Les Demeures seigneuriales*, 220–25, 387–88; Châtelain, *Châteaux forts*, 257–62.

23. For extensive discussion of the amenities of residential castles in France, see Mesqui, *La Résidence et les éléments d'architecture*, 135–36 (kitchens), 149–64 (hallways and stairs), 169–80 (latrines).

24. Dufaÿ, "Histoire du donjon de la Madeleine à Chevreuse." I am particularly grateful for a visit to the site on 23 May 2013 conducted by Étienne Lallau and Nicholas Girault, archaeologists in charge.

25. Châtelain, *Châteaux forts*, 159–61, 164–69, 329–30.

26. Flambard Héricher, "Le Château des comtes de Meulan à Vatteville-la-Rue" (2001).

27. Harmand, "Houdan et l'évolution des donjons au XIIe siècle" (1969); Harmand, "Le Donjon de Houdan: Études complémentaires" (1972); Châtelain, *Châteaux forts*, 73–77.

28. Langlois, "Le Donjon de Montfort-l'Amaury" (1990); Châtelain, *Châteaux forts*, 69–72.

29. Viré, "Rapport de synthèse diagnostic archéologique entrepris dans le château de Blandy-les-Tours en 1995;" Châtelain, *Châteaux forts*, 468–73.

30. Châtelain, *Châteaux forts*, 263–68.

31. Archaeological reports published by Les Amis du vieux château de Brie-Comte-Robert include "Le Château de Brie-Comte-Robert: Rapport de synthèse provisoire, 1996," "Le Château de Brie-Comte-Robert, Seine-et-Marne: Bilan des recherches archéologiques, 2004," "Bilan des recherches archéologiques de 2008–2010." See also Aymard, Dumont, and Piechaczyk, *Le Château de Brie-Comte-Robert et ses seigneurs* (2004). I am grateful to Michel Piechaczyk and his colleagues for a visit to the site on 12 April 2013 and for furnishing archaeological reports published by Les Amis du vieux château de Brie-Comte-Robert.

32. See above, Chapter 1, 22–23.

33. For Aliénor, see Noy, fol. 120r (1195); the transaction also involved a stone house. For Guy IV, see Duchesne, "Histoire de la maison des bouteillers de Senlis," 179 (1222); the charter concerned the establishment of a chapel at Ermenonville and mentioned as well a castle there. Another example is Anseau de Garlande, who promised the abbot of Saint-Denis that he would not fortify his house; see SD, vol. 1, p. 824 (1195).

34. See Table 8, row D, columns pd and pc; row D reports data from 610 ecclesiastical charters, which are a subset of the 1,729 ecclesiastical charters introduced in Chapter 1. On Table 8, see below, Chapter 6, 123–25.

35. Anseau de Garlande, in an exchange with Saint-Maur-des-Fossés: AN S 1175, no. 18 (1220).

36. See Table 8, row A, columns pd and pc. For examples of a *domus fortis* and a *firmitas*, see *Scripta de feodis*, p. 670, no. 293 (Melun), and p. 673, no. 309 (Montlhéry).

37. Statistics are derived from Dor, "Seigneurs en Île-de-France," 380–445.

38. Civel, *La Fleur de France*, 139–42, provides a list of the houses in the castellany of Montfort; Civel lists eighty-one houses located on around fifty square kilometers.

39. The final and definitive report on the excavation is *Le Château de Roissy-en-France*, ed. Dufour. Thanks to Jean-Yves Dufour for making this publication available to me upon its appearance.

40. *Le Château de Roissy-en-France*, ed. Dufour, 35–40, 61.

41. Ibid., 62–76, 78–87, 99–102.

42. Ibid., 103–7, 111–16.

43. The château d'Orville at the neighboring village of Louvres and the château du Bois Chaland at Lisses (dép. Essonne) offer two similar complexes that have not been sufficiently explored to offer fruitful comparisons.

44. A useful synthesis of the following developments can be found in Chapelot and Fossier, *Le Village et la maison au Moyen Âge* (1980), 217–328.

45. Ibid., 329–31.

46. Lambert d'Ardres, *Historia comitum Ghisnensium*, ed. Heller (1889), p. 624, chap. 127; Lambert of Ardres, *The History of the Counts of Guines and Lords of Ardres*, trans. Shopkow (2001), 160–61.

47. For regional studies, see *La Maison forte au Moyen Âge*, ed. Bur (1986); Mesqui, *Les Demeures seigneuriales*; Sirot, *Noble et forte maison* (2007).

48. I wish to thank Annick Pegeon of the Archives nationales for sharing with me her dossier of charters on the Roissy and Montfermeil families.

49. Bedos[-Rezak], *La Châtellenie de Montmorency*, 179; Duchesne, *Preuves de l'histoire de la maison de Montmorency* (1624), 55–56 (1174).

50. For example, Aubry de Mareuil rented his holdings at Roissy to Roger la Pie, a royal *sergent*: *Actes*, vol. 2, no. 565 (1197). Yolande d'Aulnay and Gautier her son gave to Notre-Dame de l'Île-Adam her *griage* at Roissy: SMCps, 3:348 (1218). Thibaut Rosel de Morienval and his wife and sons gave their tithes at Roissy to Morienval: Mor, 26–27 (1220).

51. *Le Château de Roissy*, ed. Dufour, 34, and Bedos[-Rezak], *La Châtellenie de Montmorency*, 179–81. Bedos-Rezak uses the transmission of the property of Roissy to identify the descendants of Guy and Richilde. If, as Bedos-Rezak posits, Agnès, daughter of Guy de Groslay and Richilde de Roissy, married Guillaume de Montfermeil, Roissy property would have been transferred to the Montfermeils. In fact, however, Guillaume de Montfermeil married Agnès de Clacy. See below, note 56.

52. AN S 1570, no. 14 (1225). Philippe de Roissy's seal has also survived: AN S 2402, no. 15; Douët d'Arcq II, no. 3435 (1226). In 1226 Philippe is identified as possessing a *censive* at Roissy. At the same time a Richilde is identified either as his wife, *mulier*, or mother, *mater* (the manuscript reads *mr*): AN S 2402, no. 13 (1226). If the latter, which is the most likely, Richilde would be the wife of Reric.

53. AN S 1570, no. 19 (1238); AN T 269-14, no. 29 (1253). In 1257 Philippe's sons, Pierre and Jean, also employed the title: AN S 1570, no. 5 (1257).

54. *Actes*, vol. 2, no. 666. For the judgment and the family genealogy, see above, Chapter 3, 75.

55. *Nomina*, no. 390.

56. Bibliothèque Sainte-Geneviève, MS 351, fol. 65r (70r), for Guillaume's marriage to Agnès de Clacy, and not to Agnès de Groslay. See also SGM, pp. 107-108 (1209) and p. 373 (1211). On MS 351 of the Bibliothèque Sainte-Geneviève, see Pegeon, "Le Château de Roissy-en-France et l'histoire" (2014), 402–4.

57. AN S 2127, no. 20 (1205); SGM, pp. 107–8 (1209); AN L 1014 (1211); SGM, p. 373 (1211); AN L 887, nos. 4 (1218) and 5 (1228).

58. AN S 1570, no. 10 (1256–57); AN L 887, no. 14 (1254).

59. AN S 1570, no. 5 (1257).

60. "Nobilis vir Adam dominus ville quae dicitur Mons Firmoilus" (Arch. dép. 93/70B).

61. These appear in his gifts to the abbey of Livry; see Arch. dép. 93/67(1) (1208), 93/70A no. 2 (1208), 93/70B no. 3 (1223).

62. SVP, fol. 33v (1234).

63. Delisle, "Fragments de l'histoire de Gonesse," 249, 252–54.

64. HDP, 42 (1212).

65. See above, Chapter 2, 48–49.

66. *Layettes*, vol. 1, nos. 455, 814 (1206); NDP, 1:21, 22 (1206); Friedmann, *Paris, ses rues, ses paroisses*, 64–65.

67. SVP, fols. 149v–150r.

68. Joy, 77 (1209).

69. SVP, fol. 29v (1182).

70. SMCps, 3:245 (1206).

71. Piechaczyk, "Le Château de Brie-Comte-Robert, un château de Robert Ier de Dreux," 141–53. Tiles, fireplaces, and many other objects are preserved in the on-site museum.

72. *Le Château de Roissy-en-France*, ed. Dufour, 107–9.

73. Piechaczyk, Piechaczyk, and Coindre-Béon, *Le Château de Brie-Comte-Robert* (2004), photograph p. 32.

74. Barat, Debout, and Langlois, "Chevreuse (Yvelines), Donjon du château de la Madeleine," 24. The final report on ceramics, by Fabienne Ravoire, is awaited, but see Lallau and Debout, *Le Château de Chevreuse* (2014), 46–59, for photographs. Similar but more extensive findings at Montmorency stem from the second half of the thirteenth century; see Caillot and André, "Vieux château, Lycée Turgot, Montmorency (95): Rapport final d'opération archéologique" (2012), 1:117–49.

75. *Le Château de Roissy-en-France*, ed. Dufour, 58–60, 96–98.

76. Ibid., 116–29.

77. Chrétien de Troyes, *Erec et Enide*, ed. Roques (1970).

78. Jean Renart, *Le Roman de la Rose*, ed. Lecoy (1979).

79. Gerbert de Montreuil, *Le Roman de lâ Violette*, ed. Buffum (1928). For Chrétien, Jean, and Gerbert on food, see Baldwin, *Aristocratic Life*, 174–83.

80. *Histoire de Guillaume le Maréchal*, ed. Holden, vol. 1, vv. 3041–49.

81. Gentili, Caillot, and Viré, "Louvres (Val-d'Oise), château d'Orville, Rapport d'activité 2005," 18. See also Gentili et al., "Le Site du château d'Orville à Louvres (Val-d'Oise)" (2011).

82. Hallavant, "Étude carpologique du château de la Madeleine (Chevreuse, 78)" (2007).

83. The following paragraphs sum up the abundant data on cereals and meat reported in *Le Château de Roissy-en-France*, ed. Dufour, 42–47, 54, 61, 76–78, 87–89, 154–60.

84. Barat, Debout, and Langlois, "Chevreuse (Yvelines), Donjon du château de la Madeleine," 21.

85. In 1223 Guillaume made an agreement with the monks of Livry over his hunting rights and the boundaries of his park: Arch. dép. 93/70B no. 3 (1228).

86. Table 8, row A, column rk. The baillis noted twenty-seven revenues in kind (with thirty-one specified items received as revenue in kind; see Table 10) among 652 total items possessed by aristocrats.

87. See Table 8, row D, column rk. No specific charters exist from Chevreuse or Roissy.

88. See below, Chapter 6, 125-27, for further comparison of aristocrats' gifts versus retained wealth.

89. See the summary in Baldwin, "Pierre du Thillay," 21 (table 1); by comparison, Pierre's Norman lands, for example, brought him 474 loaves of bread, 561 capons and hens, and 5,416 eggs (ibid., 24–25).

Chapter 5

1. *Documents relatifs au comté de Champagne et de Brie*, ed. Longnon (1901–4), 1:1–74; Evergates, *Feudal Society in the Bailliage of Troyes* (1975), 61–69.

2. *The Red Book of the Exchequer*, ed. Hall (1896), 2:624–47.

3. *Registres*, 267–76.

4. Ibid., 279–305.

5. *Scripta de feodis*, in *RHF*, 23:608–81, nos. 1–60, nos. 112–77.

6. Ibid., nos. 61–109.

7. Ibid., nos. 178–235 and 238–312. On the surveys, see Baldwin, *Government*, 286–93 (Normandy) and 293–94 (the old Capetian domain).

8. *Nomina militum*, in *RHF*, 23:686–89, nos. 369–93.

9. SGP, 1:309–12. The abbey's cartulary also contains a list of twelve vassals of Geoffroy Pooz who himself was presumably a vassal of the abbey since the list is found in the cartulary. Each vassal declared his holdings and his own subvassals. Five vassals acknowledged Geoffroy as liege lord; six acknowledged him as lord (SGP, 1:313–14).

10. NDP, 1:5–11.

11. *Scriptum feodorum de Monteforti*, ed. Dor.

12. *Nomina militum*, no. 386 (Mantes), no. 390 (Paris).

13. "Petrus de Richeborc tenet hoc quod habet apud Medontam de domino rege excepto molendino de subtus turre, et omne hoc quod habet apud Guerrevillam, except vico in quo manet prepositus de Guerrevilla, unde debet exercitum et equitatum ad suum custum; preterea tenet de rege XXVII feoda militum citra Secanam et ultra." *Scripta de feodis*, p. 623, no. 68.

14. "Dominus Petrus de Divite Burgo tenet centum solidos de reditu in prepositura Nongenti die festi sancti Johannis Baptiste, de quibus ipse fuit homo comitis defuncti, et tenet feodum de Chenoie quod dominus Willelmus de Nigele, miles, tenet de ipso, et feodum de Levainfontainne quod Henricus de Poncellis, miles, tenet de ipso, et unum aliud feodum apud Levainfontainne quod dominus Amauricus de Probato Monte tenet de ipso, et feodum quod Simon de Merroles, miles, tenet de ipso, et debet inde exercitum et equitatum." Register C, fol. 122v; *Scripta de feodis*, p. 626, no. 84, from Register E. The text here is a collation of the two versions.

15. Table 5, rows A and B. These names have been alphabetized to avoid duplication. In these surveys the scribes omitted on rare occasions the reference to holding from the king, but the rubrics and the service demanded leave no doubt that direct tenants are involved. The differing figures in the three overlapping castellanies are best explained by differing methods and the different dates of the surveys.

16. Table 5, rows Ca, Cb, Cc, and Cd. Since these names are too numerous to be alphabetized, they contain duplicates. For the surveys of the fiefs and vassals of the additional individuals mentioned here and tabulated in Table 5, rows Cb, Cc, and Cd, see *Scripta de feodis*, nos. 98–103 (Jean de Gisors), nos. 223–26 (Jean de Nesle), and nos. 316–17 (Jean, count of Beaumont).

17. Table 5, row D.

18. See Table 7.

19. Table 5, row F. I have alphabetized these names along with the names of the 351 direct vassals of rows A and B in order to eliminate duplicates.

20. Table 5, row G. These names have not been alphabetized.

21. Table 5, rows Ea, Eb, Ec, Ed, Ee. For Mathieu le Bel, see AN S 2309 and SD, vol. 1, p. 240; for Gautier the Chamberlain, *Actes*, vol. 2, no. 587; for Saint-Germain-des-Prés, SGP, 1:309–12; for the bishop of Paris, NDP, 1:5–11; for Amaury de Montfort, *Scriptum feodorum de Monteforti*, ed. Dor.

22. For example, see SD, vol. 1, pp. 65–66, 242, and vol. 2, p. 29; VND, fols. 32v–33r; Mon, 128; SVP, fol. 118r; SMCps, 3:211; SMF, fol. 41v; Por, 27; NDP, 2:253.

23. I have found only three cases. For example, Alberic, knight of Guignecourt, gave to Chaalis four and a half arpents of land *de allodiis* in the territory of Montlognon (near Chaalis, to the north): Cha, fol. 117v (1187). For the other two, see OurPD, 282 (1221); SJVi, fol. 58v (1223).

24. SD, vol. 1, pp. 239–72. In 1221, for example, Philippe d'Estrées contested the abbey, claiming that he held his lands in fief from the king and not from the abbey (SD, vol. 1, p. 788).

25. Suger, *Vie de Louis VI le Gros*, ed. Waquet, 238–41.

26. AN S 2309.

27. SD, vol. 1, p. 240. On redating the charter to 1195, see Baldwin, "Pierre du Thillay," 11–14; Baldwin, "The Aristocracy in the Paris Region," part 1, 46–47. For works accepting the date of 1125 and situating the charter in the context of Abbot Suger, see Constable, "Suger's Monastic Administration" (1986), 25; Grant, *Abbot Suger of St-Denis* (1998), 218–20; and Berkhofer, *Day of Reckoning* (2004), 85, 106.

28. *Scripta de feodis*, no. 200.

29. Table 5, rows Cb, Cc, Ee.

30. *Actes*, vol. 3, no. 1083; Petot, "L'Ordonnance du 1er mai 1209" (1955); Evergates, *The Aristocracy in the County of Champagne*, 35; Baldwin, *Government*, 262–63.

31. For the exceptions, see CSH, 85 (1185); SGM, p. 188 (1200); SGA, fol. xxiv (1213); SJVi, fol. 103r (1216); SMPo, 18 (1218, 1220); Bar, fols. 138v, 325r, 181v (1217, 1220, 1221); SD, vol. 1, p. 409 (1221).

32. SD, vol. 1, pp. 91 ("ad usus et consuetudines francie," 1234), 634 ("ad usus et consuetudines Vulcassini," 1220); OurBN, fol. 47v; AB, 117. For further examples of insistence on liege homage from the abbot of Saint-Denis, see SD, vol. 1, pp. 240, 243–45.

33. *Layettes*, vol. 1, no. 792.

34. SD, vol. 1, p. 245 (1224).

35. NDP, 1:5–11.

36. *Actes*, vol. 2, no. 587.

37. Statistics are taken from Dor, "Seigneurs en Île-de-France," vol. 2.

38. Baldwin, *Government*, 265–66. The counts of Troyes may be a rare exception; see Evergates, *The Aristocracy in the County of Champagne*, 84.

39. For a few examples among many, see *Layettes*, vol. 1, no. 336; *Actes*, vol. 2, nos. 762, 937, 947, 950, and vol. 3, no. 1365.

40. *Layettes*, vol. 1, no. 792; SD, vol. 1, p. 245.

41. SD, vol. 1, pp. 242–44.

42. See Table 6 for the totals of those owing homage or liege homage in the castellanies surveyed in the *Scripta de feodis*. In the *Scripta* survey, some knights listed as holding lands or revenues from the king were identified as owing homage or liege homage, and some knights listed as holding land or revenues from the king were not identified as owing either kind of homage. For Table 6, these latter knights are not counted as owing either kind of homage, despite holding from the king. Almost all of these knights did owe military service of some variety, however. Only 6 of the 247 vassals of the king in the eleven castellanies of the Scripta survey were listed with their holdings and without mention of either homage or of any military services owed to the king.

43. See Table 6. The *Nomina* survey made no mention of homage owed for any of the knights. However, most of the knights who held from the king, if not all, undoubtedly held substantial lands or revenues from the king. Accordingly, those listed as vassals of the king (holding from the king) in the *Nomina* survey have been counted as owing liege homage. The total of 266 knights in ten castellanies of the *Nomina* survey includes 138 knights who held from the king and 128 knights who did not hold from the king. For three castellanies (Senlis, Dammartin, and Béthisy), only knights holding from the king were listed. In Table 6, for the calculation of the percentage of *Nomina* knights who were direct vassals of the king, I have not counted these three castellanies and their 47 knights. If, however, we include these knights in the calculation of the percentage of knights who were direct

vassals, the figure would be 52 percent (138 knights of 266 total knights) instead of 42 percent (91 knights of 219 total).

44. Evergates, *The Aristocracy in the County of Champagne*, 19.

45. *Actes*, vol. 3, no. 1309; Baldwin, *Government*, 261–62.

46. NDP, 1:7, 182–83; *Layettes*, vol. 1, no. 1572; Douët d'Arcq, *Recherches historiques*, 108.

47. *Registres*, 338–42; for a map of the 110 castles, see ibid., 602.

48. Coulson, "Fortress-Policy in Capetian Tradition and Angevin Practice" (1983), especially 23, 32–38; Baldwin, *Government*, 301.

49. For examples of castles in Normandy assigned with the requirement that they be rendered on request, see *Actes*, vol. 2, no. 761 (Radepont, 1203); *Layettes*, vol. 1, no. 747, and vol. 2, no. 875 (Conches and Nonancourt, 1205); *Layettes*, vol. 1, no. 1304 (Saint-Rémy-du-Plain, 1218). For examples of pledges for the rendering of castles, see *Layettes*, vol. 1, no. 594 (Ivry-la-Bataille and Avrilly, 1200), and nos. 1262–69 (Conches and Nonancourt, 1217).

50. *Actes*, vol. 1, no. 164 (1186); NDP, 1:7.

51. *Layettes*, vol. 1, no. 410 (1193).

52. *Actes*, vol. 2, no. 603 (1199).

53. *Layettes*, vol. 1, no. 1372 (1219).

54. *Actes*, vol. 4, no. 1638 (1220).

55. See Table 6. Curiously, the scribe who compiled the list of 110 castles in Register A roughly a decade earlier omitted mention of La Ferté-Milon and Chauny. While the fortifications at La Ferté-Milon are well attested by documentary and archaeological evidence, there is no trace of fortifications at Chauny; see Salch, *L'Atlas des châteaux forts en France*, 37, 529. Paris and Senlis also were not included in the list in Register A. However, the chancery clerics placed both of these in the list of episcopal cities in the king's domain: *Registres*, 336–37 ("Civitates et castra que rex habet in domanio"); Baldwin, *Government*, 311–12. The other castellanies surveyed in the *Scripta de feodis* were included in the list of Register A. The identification of *Crespeium* in the edition of this list (*Registres*, p. 341, no. 68) should be changed from Crépy-en-Laonnois to Crépy-en-Valois.

56. Coulson, "Fortress-Policy," 27 (Mantes); *Actes*, vol. 2, no. 59 (Chaumont), no. 233 (Pontoise), no. 234 (Poissy); *Registres*, 460–62 (Meulan).

57. *Actes*, vol. 2, no. 491 (item no. 38), and vol. 3, nos. 1295 and 1389; Coulson, "Fortress-Policy," 27.

58. In the survey of the castellany of Montlhéry, the bailli listed fifty-one knights as owing two months of *custodia* per year and two knights owing four months of *custodia* per year. Nine knights owed *stacio* and another owed *custodia*, without a term specified. These latter ten knights have been counted as owing two months of castle-guard per year, the typical term of service in the castellany of Montlhéry. In the survey of the castellany of Montdidier, five knights who acknowledged owing castle-guard, but who did not know how much they owed, have been counted in Table 6 as owing one month per year.

59. Dor, "Seigneurs en Île-de-France," vol. 2.

60. The authoritative study of the roll is now Nieus, "Le Château au cœur du réseau vassalique" (2011). The roll, titled *Super militibus*, is AN R^1 675/1 (formerly AN R^1 34), and is dated to 1192–1202 by Nieus.

61. Baldwin, *Government*, 293–95; Jean, sire de Joinville, *Histoire de Saint Louis*, ed. Wailly (1874), 28.

62. Nieus draws this conclusion from subsequent documentation at Picquigny: Nieus, "Le Château au cœur du réseau vassalique," 103–7.

63. SGM, pp. 130–31: "Dominus castri et milites feodati qui tenentur ratione feodorum suorum facere stagium pro custodia castri, necnon et familie tam domini quam dictorum militum erunt plene de cura sancti Wlgisi." For Aliénor, see SNR, 56–57.

64. For example, see *Actes*, vol. 1, nos. 59 (Chaumont) and 233 (Pontoise).

65. *Actes*, vol. 2, no. 616.

66. *Actes*, vol. 2, no. 491 (Saint-Quentin); vol. 3, nos. 1295 (Chauny) and 1389 (Crépy-en-Valois); *Actes*, vol. 2, no. 540 (Roye).

67. NDP, 1:303 (1209).

68. SFP, 81–82 (1187–1209).

69. SLS, 115.

70. SD, vol. 1, p. 785 (1183): "Volumus etiam quod si praedicto comiti guerra acciderit in exercitu et equitatu et gerris suis tornamentis exceptiis homines praescripte ville vocati veniant"; SD, vol. 2, p. 201 (1211): "monachi in querimoniam deduxerunt quod dictus R[enaudus] homines ville Beati Dyonisii que dicitur Ut. super tallia touta et aliis consuetudinibus scilicet exercitu equitatu inquietabat et ad guerras et ad torneamenta eos ducabat et mittebat quod ei facere non licebat"; SCC, 1:437–38 (1215): "dicti homines ibunt de cetero ad torneamenta et equitationes domini Johannis, sicut ire solent."

71. This was clearly the function of the Pipe Rolls at the English Exchequer of Westminster.

72. Baldwin, *Aristocratic Life*, 109–10.

73. *Histoire de Guillaume le Maréchal*, ed. Holden, vol. 1, vv. 1232–46.

74. For the accounts, see *Budget*.

75. For the details of the mercenary army and the campaign of 1202–3, see Baldwin, *Government*, 166–73, 191–94.

76. *Registres*, 259–62 (1194, modified in 1204).

77. The war tax was still functioning in the mid-thirteenth century. For an example from Saint-Maur-des-Fossés, see SMF, fol. 295: "Quociens que rex facit exercitum contra hostes regni et petit auxilium pro exercitu ab universis ecclesiis regni . . ." The cartulary records the amounts due to the king (e.g., "XVII lb. pro uno sumerio") as well as the villages that the abbey taxed to furnish the sum. Earlier, in 1194, the abbey gave ninety *sergents* and two wagons (*Registres*, 260). In 1202 it gave 267 lb. (*Budget*, CXLIX).

78. For the details of the following, see Baldwin, *Government*, 272–77.

79. *Registres*, 196–204 (1204–20).

80. *Histoire de Guillaume le Maréchal*, ed. Holden, vol. 1, vv. 6160–61, 6163–69, 6267–68.

81. Roger of Howden, *Chronica*, ed. Stubbs, 4:56–57. Another captive, Alain de Roucy, was listed as a banneret for Coucy, but he also appears twice in the *Scripta* surveys of the castellanies of the Paris region on account of his fiefs at Étampes and Chauny.

82. Baldwin, *Government*, 280–81.

83. *Registres*, 308–24; for Vermandois, see 317–18; for the Vexin, 318–20.

84. By comparing individuals, thirty of fifty-six, or 54 percent, were identical with names in the two feudal surveys. Since at least a decade passed between the compilation of the bannerets list and the two feudal surveys, the comparison of families is more realistic.

85. Transcribed on fol. 89v of Register C, it is preceded by a list of hostages from the Lowlands campaign in May–June of 1213 (fols. 87–88r). See RHF, 23:693, nos. 415–16 (*Servitia nonnullorum feodorum*).

86. Baldwin, *Government*, 218, 285–86, 450–53.

87. Individuals who are listed but not assigned a quota have not been counted in the quota totals of Table 7.

88. *Scripta*, nos. 223–26 (Jean de Nesle), nos. 316–17 (Jean de Beaumont), no. 68 (Pierre de Richebourg).

89. *Registres*, 104–5; RHF, 23:633, nos. 110–11 (*Inquisitio valoris feodorum castellaniae Pissiaci . . . anno Domini 1217*).

90. For the figures in this paragraph, see Tables 5, 6, and 7.

91. Guillaume de Garlande was positioned in the center of the field and Mathieu de Montmorency and Jean de Beaumont were on the right wing; see Guillaume le Breton, *Gesta*, ed. Delaborde, 272, 276, 279, 284.

92. Guillaume le Breton, *Philippidos*, ed. Delaborde, 286. It is also possible that Louis's army contained knights from the localities.

93. Transcribed on fols. 4r–5v of Register C, it is preceded by pledges from Flemish knights dating from 1213 to 1215.

94. See Baldwin, *Government*, 412–18, on the three royal registers; and pp. 262, 285, 289–93, and 547 n. 162 on the feudal surveys and their dating.

95. For the fiefs of Jean de Gisors, see Register C, fol. 8v; *Scripta de feodis*, pp. 630–31, nos. 98–103. For Robert de Poissy, see Register C, fol. 9r; *Scripta*, pp. 631–32, no. 104. For Montlhéry, Register C, fols. 25v, 142r–143r; *Scripta*, pp. 671–75, nos. 300–313.

96. On Bonneuil, see *Scripta*, pp. 649–50, no. 195.

97. Brown, "The Tyranny of a Construct" (1974); Reynolds, *Fiefs and Vassals* (1994); Crouch, *The Birth of Nobility*, 261–78.

Chapter 6

1. *Scripta*, p. 621, no. 61.

2. The 272 tenants include the 247 vassals of the eleven castellanies of the Paris region surveyed in the *Scripta de feodis* (see Table 5, row B), plus the vassals of another inventory in the *Scripta de feodis*, a survey of the lands and vassals of Jean de Gisors entitled *feoda quae Johannes de Gisorcio tenet de rege* (*Scripta de feodis*, pp. 630–31, nos. 98–103). I have counted Jean de Gisors and his vassals and their properties with the five Vexin castellanies.

3. *RHF*, 23:633, no. 110; and *Registres*, 104–5 (*Inquisitio valoris feodorum castellaniae Pissiaci*). Assessments of the fiefs of twenty-two valets (*domicelli*) follow the assessments of the knights' fiefs in Register E.

4. *Scripta*, pp. 631–32, no. 104, and p. 631, note 8. Of the two versions in Register C and E, I have followed that of Register C.

5. *Registres*, 74–75; *Actes*, vol. 3, no. 1265. Béthemont (between Poissy and Orgeval) was included among the villages of the castellany of Poissy (*Registres*, 179).

6. See *RHF*, 23:693, no. 416 (*Servitia nonnullorum feodorum*); and Table 7.

7. For examples, see *Scripta*, p. 623, no. 68, and p. 653, no. 211; Bar, fol. 191r (1182); SD, vol. 1, p. 500 (1209).

8. Since only 44 out of 247 individuals in the *Scripta* survey (or 18 percent of the individuals) were identified in the monastic charters, it is clear that, because of chronological disparities between the survey conducted ca. 1218–20 and the particular charters, families are a better basis for comparison than individuals.

9. *Galterus de Marinis* (Marines), *Scripta*, p. 629, no. 94; SD, vol. 1, p. 649 (1218). Naturally, alienations of whole properties done before 1218 would not be declared in an inventory prepared in the years ca. 1218–20. Since my selection of charters is concentrated on the years 1180–1220, this sample of properties captures few alienations of whole properties.

10. *Albericus de Choi*, *Scripta*, p. 655, no. 220; SMS, fol. 29v (1217). *Odardus Turcus*, *Scripta*, p. 655 no. 220; SJVi, fol. 48v (1214). *Girardus de Valle Enguejardi* (Vallangoujard), *Scripta*, p. 629, no. 95; SMPoCh, 9 (1214).

11. *Teoinus de Ruelio* (Ruel, *cens*), *Scripta*, p. 624, no. 75; SMPoCh, 8 (1212). *Petrus de Munellis* (produce), *Scripta*, p. 672, no. 304; HDP, 67 (1222). *Renaldus de Cicingni* (Sinceny, produce), *Scripta*, p. 652, no. 205; Hér, 32 (1212). *Girardus de Valle Enguejardi* (tithes), *Scripta*, p. 629, no. 95; SMPoCh, 4 (1207). *Guido de Alneto* (tithes), *Scripta*, p. 673, no. 309; SGM, p. 62 (n.d.). *Guillelmus de Orceio* (Orsay, tithes), *Scripta*, p. 674, no. 311; NDP, 1:85 (1205). *Guido de Val Grinosa* (Vaugrigneuse, tithes), *Scripta*, p. 672, no. 305; HDP, 13 (1188). *Renaldus de Cheziaco* (Chézy-en-Orxois, tithes), *Scripta*, p. 655, no. 222; Arch. dép. 60 (Oise), H 2850/2 (1223). *Johannes li Bougres* (tithes), *Scripta*, p. 649, no. 194; Mor, 26–27 (1220).

12. Baldwin, "Pierre du Thillay," 9–15, 21–26, 36–37. The charters of 1208 and 1215 are published in Delisle, "Fragments de l'histoire de Gonesse," 248–49 and 252–54. For Pierre's landbook, see *Le Livre de terres et de revenus de Pierre du Thillay*, ed. Baldwin, 13–31.

13. In the twenty-seven instances in the *Scripta* survey in which revenues in kind were noted (Table 8), thirty-one specific items received as revenue were recorded (Table 10).

14. Baldwin, "Pierre du Thillay," 21.

15. For an overarching study of the French economy in the thirteenth century, see Sivéry, *L'Économie du royaume de France au siècle de Saint Louis* (1984). Sivéry avers that the sources do not become sufficient for such a study before the second half of the thirteenth century (p. 37). The standard study for the following centuries is Fourquin, *Les Campagnes de la région parisienne à la fin du moyen âge* (1964).

16. Rigord, *Gesta*, ed. Carpentier, 330, 334, 338, 352; ed. Delaborde, 128, 130, 132, 134. Among the numerous prices in the budget of 1202–3, the most frequently cited prices for a *setier* of wheat are five *sous* (for example, *Budget*, CXLVII, col. 1) and six *sous*, eight *deniers* (*Budget*, CLXXIII, cols. 1 and 2). See also Sivéry, *L'Économie*, 63.

17. Baldwin, "Pierre du Thillay," 22–23. The *grange de Vaulerent* is situated outside the village of Villeron.

18. Sivéry, *L'Économie*, 257–60, confesses that it is difficult to measure the economic impact of Paris on the surrounding region.

Chapter 7

1. This theme has been developed in Bedos-Rezak, *When Ego Was Imago*, 23–26.

2. On the early development of cartularies, see Berkhofer, *Day of Reckoning*. For the cartularies of Saint-Denis, see Grosse, "Remarques sur les cartulaires de Saint-Denis aux XIIIe et XIVe siècles" (1993).

3. For a study that concentrates on the ecclesiastical side, see in particular Bouchard, *Holy Entrepreneurs* (1991).

4. See, for example, Duby, *Guerriers et paysans, VII–XIIe siècle* (1973); Rosenwein, *To Be the Neighbor of Saint Peter* (1989); and McLaughlin, *Consorting with Saints* (1994).

5. Keyser, "La Transformation de l'échange des dons pieux" (2003). Keyser takes account of parallel studies as well.

6. In addition to contracts of gifts, sale, and exchange, Keyser also includes contracts of quittance (*quitare*). I have omitted this last category from my analysis because it is rarely identified in the Parisian region. I have considered the effects of a quittance to be the same as a gift and have included whatever examples I have found in the category of gifts.

7. "Quicquid ad honorem et communem utilitatem et ad quietem pauperum ecclesie spectat, recta intentione querentibus, unum maxime necessarium sollicite procurandum est, ne operam et impensam silentio perdant, et que pro pace et concordia tam presentium quam futurorum viriliter elaboraverint, per negligentiam et oblivionem, discordie postmodum et contentionis seminarium fiant. Quapropter nos omnes Carnotensis capituli fratres notum fieri volumus, et presentibus et posteris, quod dominus Ursio de Merlaio injuste accipiebat pedagium, in quadam parte terre Beate Marie, de Belsia. Summonitus a canonicis, ad justiciam venire noluit et ad ultimum excommunicatus fuit. Tandem Deo miserante et inspirante, rediens ad cor, venit in capitulum, ibi culpam suam cognovit et vadimonium rectitudinis, primum in manu decani, postea vero, multis tam clericis quam laicis adstantibus et videntibus, super altare Beate Marie humiliter posuit." *Chartes Vendômoises*, ed. Métais (1905), 106–7; and NDC, 1:146–47. For other early examples, see Rosenwein, *To Be the Neighbor of Saint Peter*, 38, 137–38, 144, 149; Livingstone, *Out of Love for My Kin* (2010), 101–2.

8. "Ego Ferricus de Gentilliaco, miles, notum facio universis Christi fidelibus ad quos presentes littere pervenerint, quod ego [dedi] in perpetuam elemosinam ecclesie Beati Martini de Campis totam decimam tam in blado quam in vino et in aliis rebus, quas habebam apud Gentiliacum, et quicquid juris habebam in territorio de Tour, et pressoragium, et censum quem Galterius Cent Mars et frater ejus Revenuz de Lovecines, et Petronilla la Bigote de Vitriaco mihi debebant singulis annis in festo Sancti Remigii. Et ut hoc ratum et inconcussum in posterum perseveret, presentes litteras feci sigilli mei munimine roborari. Actum anno gracie M°CC° septimo decimo, mense octobri." AN S 1354, no. 1; SMCps 3:342. Louveciennes (*Lovecines*) is adjacent to Marly-le-Roi, to the east. On the abbreviated, standardized charter, see Berkhofer, *Day of Reckoning*, 95, 168.

9. Bernard of Pavia, *Summa decretalium*, ed. Laspeyres, 3.15 (pp. 81–82); Berger, *Encyclopedic Dictionary of Roman Law*, 452–53; Baldwin, *The Medieval Theories of the Just Price* (1959), 19, 42–43.

10. SD, vol. 1, p. 410 (1211); NDP, 2:17 (1201).

11. SVP, fol. 55v (n.d.). See also Yer, 192 (1207). However, land measures varied. See Baldwin, "Pierre du Thillay," 34–41.

12. SMCux, 106 (1217).

13. SGP, 2:86 (1200) and 1:93 (1223).

14. NDP, 2:258 (1220–21).

15. For examples of sums of 200 *livres*, see HDP, 31 (1202), 33 (1209); SLP, 94 (1211); SJVi, fol. 55r (1219); for 300 *livres*, see NDP, 2:521 (1205); Noy, fol. 119v (1210); for 400 *livres*, NDP, 1:429.

16. NDP, 1:45 (1181).

17. SJVi, fol. 57r (1223); also, see Noy, fol. 157v (1213), for an offer of seventy *livres* for seven *muids* of wheat.

18. OurPD, 133 (1205); SLP, 91 (1209).

19. NDP, 2:229 (1212–13).

20. Bernard of Pavia, *Summa decretalium*, 3.16 (pp. 82–83); Berger, *Encyclopedic Dictionary*, 268.

21. SMCps, 3:241 (1205); SJVi, fol. 42v (1195); SGM, p. 192 (1195).

22. Bernard of Pavia, *Summa decretalium*, 3.17 (pp. 84–86); Berger, *Encyclopedic Dictionary*, 630.

23. SCCha, fol. 34r (1210); SMCps, 3:142 (1186–93).

24. HDP, 42 (1209); SJVi, fol. 106r (1205); SVP, fols. 181v–182r (1219); SMF, fol. 58r (1219); SMCps, 3:147–48 (1195).

25. SD, vol. 1, p. 491 (1221) and vol. 2, p. 342 (1186); Abb, 46 (1220).

26. Table 8, row Db, column rm, tallies transactions involving sums of money that were not gifts to churches or monasteries. These were mainly transactions between laity, hence they are not included in the figures given here. Purchases by aristocrats from churches or monasteries were rare. For two examples, see 141 of this chapter, and note 58 below.

27. Keyser, "La Transformation," 796.

28. *Vita B. Joannis de Monte-Mirabili* (1865), 220F.

29. See the graphs in Keyser, "La Transformation," 797.

30. SVP, fol. 139r (1210); Cha, fol. 198v (1209); NDP, 2:265 (1218).

31. "Donatio est datio ex liberalitate procedens, dicta donatio, quasi dono datio . . . Duae sunt species donationis, scilicet inter vivos et causa mortis; donatio inter vivos est, quando rem quam dono malo alium habere, quam me ipsum, donatio vero causa mortis, quando malo me habere, quam alium, sed magis alium, quam heredem meum." Bernard of Pavia, *Summa decretalium*, 3.20 (p. 90).

32. "Tractavimus de donationibus inter vivos et causa mortis; sed quoniam donatio causa mortis solet fieri in testamentis, de testamentis dicamus." Bernard of Pavia, *Summa decretalium*, 3.22 (p. 96).

33. "Item illud notandum quod ea, quae donantur clerico intuitu ecclesiae, ecclesiae acquiruntur, quae vero intuitu personae, in bonis ipsius clerici computantur." Bernard of Pavia, *Summa decretalium*, 3.20 (p. 92).

34. *Actes*, vol. 1, no. 345, and vol. 4, no. 1796.

35. *Layettes*, vol. 2, no. 1710.

36. *Histoire de Guillaume le Maréchal*, ed. Holden, vol. 1, vv. 6891–98; vol. 2, vv. 18136–69, 18598–608, 18652–64, 18685–732.

37. *Actes*, vol. 1, no. 392 (Aveline, wife of Philippe, the son of Gautier the Chamberlain, 1191); Joy, 84–85 (Alix, daughter of Barthélemy de Roye, 1223).

38. VdC, 1:173 (1208–10).

39. HVND, 132 (1221); SMPoCh, 2 (ca. 1223); Douët d'Arcq, *Recherches historiques et critiques sur les anciens comtes de Beaumont-sur-Oise*, 87 (1221), 87–88 (1221).

40. Preuilly, 94 (1211), 97 (1201).

41. OurBN, fols. 91v–92r (1200–1228).

42. HDP, 46 (1211), 47 (1212).

43. VdC, 1:106–7 (1190).

44. Yer, 20 (n.d.).

45. SVP, fol. 54r–v (1220–23). Mathieu de Marly, lord of Lay, was the brother of Bouchard de Marly (d. 1226).

46. Bar, fol. 309r–v (1226).

47. Constable, *Monastic Tithes from Their Origins to the Twelfth Century* (1964), 57–136. For the difficulties in recovering tithes, see Baldwin, *Masters, Princes, and Merchants*, 1:229–35.

48. SGM, p. 62; Lebeuf, *Histoire de la ville et de tout le diocèse de Paris* (1883–93), 4:211. For other examples, see AB, 136–37 (1223); SCC, 1:279 (1189). In the former case, Gautier, knight of Vendeuil (dép. Aisne), recognized that he held tithes at Marché-Allouarde (dép. Somme) illegally. In the latter, a knight confessed that he held tithes at Cuisles (dép. Marne) unjustly.

49. *Scripta*, p. 673, no. 309.

50. SVP, fol. 41v (1198). The tithes were likely at Fontenay-sous-Bois (dép. Val-de-Marne).

51. SJVi, fol. 55r (1219).

52. Baldwin, *Masters, Princes, and Merchants*, 1:275–77.

53. For examples of pledged rents, see Abb, 46 (1220); SD, vol. 1, p. 491 (1221).

54. SMCps, 3:370 (1221), 372 (1221), 374–76 (1221). See also Vincent, *Norman Charters from English Sources*, 97–101.

55. "Debitorum onore gravatus et necessitate compulsus." Noy, fol. 170r–v (1209).

56. *Actes*, vol. 3, no. 1236, and vol. 4, no. 1710.

57. Table 8, row Da.

58. SD, vol. 1, pp. 539–40 (1201), 825 (1207).

59. SGM, pp. 129–30 (1220).

60. NDP, 1:399–400 (1219).

61. Table 8, row Da, provides the aggregate numbers (men and women) for donations in the 610 charters.

62. The few extant cases come from Vermandois. For example, see OurPD, 40 (1201), 34 (1209); SJVi, fol. 53 (1208); Hér, 23 (1197). Guarantors are treated in Bernard of Pavia, *Summa decretalium*, 3.18 (pp. 86–88). They were common in Normandy; see Tabuteau, *Transfers of Property in Eleventh-Century Norman Law*, 196–204.

63. The charters rarely mention such objections, but see the cases of Dreux Buffe and others below.

64. See above, Chapter 3, 63–65.

65. VND, fols. 31r–32v (n.d.); fols. 45v–48r (1193). *Guarreria* likely refers to a quarry belonging to Val-Notre-Dame, the forest in question being adjacent to the quarry.

66. Jos, 2:2–3 (1217).

67. *Vita B. Joannis de Monte-Mirabili*, 200F, 228A.

68. SJVa, 73–74 (1206).

69. SNR, 147–48 (1219).

70. For the deployment of these legal procedures in the royal court, see Baldwin, *Government*, 41–43, 141–44.

71. Mori, 156–57 (1192).

72. OurPD, 545–46 (1214).

73. Bedos[-Rezak], *La Châtellenie de Montmorency*, 57–60.

74. During Philip's reign the royal chancery issued 323 charters containing transactions involving the aristocracy of the Paris region. Of these, 173 have survived only in ecclesiastical archives, and 108 are preserved in the chancery registers, while the rest have survived elsewhere. Of the 173 in the ecclesiastical archives, 27 percent involved litigation. Of the 108 in the chancery registers, 7 percent involved litigation. See Baldwin, "The Aristocracy in the Paris Region," part 1, pp. 33, 60.

75. SGM, pp. 189–90 (1194).

76. SLE, 96–97 (1202); Longnon, *Les Compagnons de Villehardouin*, 123.

Chapter 8

1. For religious beliefs as they pertained to the aristocracy, see Baldwin, *Aristocratic Life in Medieval France*, 194–247.

2. Le Goff, *La Naissance du purgatoire* (1981), 209–40, 283–316.

3. See above, Chapter 7, 132–33.

4. SJVa, 56 (1181). The unfinished business in the transaction, confirmed by the additional gift of eleven *livres*, involved the consent of the lord of the fief (the *laudatio domini*).

5. See above, Chapter 7, 133.

6. SVP, fol. 164v, "cum Parisius egretudine laborem de hac vita misera et mortali ad vitam vitalem pervenire desiderans"; Bar, fol. 104r–v, "in dolore pareret filium et iam in extremis posite laboraret"; Pré, fol. 109v, "tanquam iuvenis et inique ductus"; SYB, 309, "emendare forisfacta."

7. SNR, 74–5, "in mea viduitate et in plena vita mea, mei compos et sane mentis existens, pro remedio et salute anime mee et meorum antecessorum divine pietatis intuita."

8. SCC, 1:401; VdC, 1:95.

9. NDP, 1:122 and 3:229; SMCux, 104.

10. SJVi, fol. 109r.

11. NDP, 1:119–20 (Guillaume de Garlande, 1212), 121–22 (Guy de Chevreuse, 1204); SNR, 56 (Aliénor, countess of Saint-Quentin, 1200).

12. See above the examples of the Beaumonts (a church at Paris), Garlandes (the abbey Notre-Dame de Livry), and Royes (the abbey of Joyenval), Chapter 2, 28, 38, 54.

13. The charters of these donations I owe to the generosity of Professor Nicholas Vincent who made them available to me electronically and which are now published. See Vincent, *Norman Charters from English Sources*, 226–27 (Gace de Poissy, 1179–89), 227–28 (Adam de l'Île-Adam, 1179–89), 236–37 (Guy Mauvoisin, 1190–1200).

14. See Chapter 7, 133.

15. The expressions prefaced 124 of the sample of 610 charters surveyed in Table 8, rows D, Da, and Db.

16. A comprehensive survey and introduction to French obituaries is provided by Lemaître, *Répertoire des documents nécrologiques français* (1980–92). The seven obituaries are from Notre-Dame de Paris, Saint-Victor de Paris, Saint-Martin-des-Champs, Val-Notre-Dame, Porrois, Joyenval, and Saint-Léonor de Beaumont. See above, Chapter 1, note 14.

17. Donations in a foundation's cartulary from the family of the individual remembered in the foundation's obituary are noted below by reference to the cartulary in parentheses.

18. *Obituaires*, 1.1:113–14, 124. On Geoffroi de Chevreuse and Guy de Chevreuse, see Moutié, *Chevreuse*, 2:101.

19. *Obituaires*, 1.1:95–96, 128–29.

20. Ibid., 192 (Gautier), 96–97 (Barthélemy), 111 (Guillaume de Garlande), 115 (Guillaume des Barres).

21. Ibid., 202 (Adam); 209, 232 (Pierre).

22. For donations of Pierre du Thillay, see NDP, 1:404–5 and 2:445–46.

23. *Obituaires*, 1.1:579 (Marly); 576, 594 (Chamberlains; SVP, fol. 43r); 535–36 (Roye; SVP, fol. 33v); 608 (Garlande); 545, 555 (Barres; SVP, fol. 156v); 581 (Chevreuse; SVP in Moutié, *Chevreuse*, 2:129); 544, 556, 567 (Montfort); 576 (butlers of Senlis); 555, 595 (Montmorency; SVP, fol. 18v).

24. *Obituaires*, 1.1:591 (Mathieu le Bel; SVP, fol. 186r); 589 (Palaiseau); 543, 558 (Massy; SVP, fol. 197).

25. *Obituaires*, 1.1:444 (Montforts; SMCps, 3:182); 464 (Chamberlains); 421 (Royes); 464 (Montmorency; SMCps, 3:181).

26. *Obituaires*, 1.1:430 (Beaumont; SMCps, 3:368, 374); 431 (Île-Adam; SMCps, 3:67, 76).

27. *Obituaires*, 1.1:428 (Nanterre); 450 (Aulnay-sous-Bois; SMCps, 3:122); 454 (*Cornellon*); 462 (Andilly, dép. Val-d'Oise; 464 (Gentilly, dép. Val-de-Marne; SMCps, 3:342); 465 (Chennevières; SMCps, 3:357).

28. *Obituaires*, 1.1:628, 629 (Beaumont; VND, fol. 51r–v); 626, 630–32 (Montmorency; VND, fols. 43v–50r); 628–32 (Île-Adam; VND, fol. 27v); 629 (Montfort; AN L 944, no. 39); 628, 631 (Garlande).

29. *Obituaires*, 1.1:626 (Thourotte, dép. Oise); 626 (*Fresnes*); 626 (Trie-Château; VND, fol. 13r); 628 (*Montecaprino*; AN L 944, no. 9); 629 (Pierrefonds; VND, fol. 42); 629 (Franconville; VND, fol. 53v); 631 (Vallangoujard; AN S 2071, no. 90).

30. *Obituaires*, 1.2:637, 638–39 (Montfort); 637 (Chevreuse; Por, 1:69); 638 (Marly; Por, 1:38, 41); 640 (Lévis).

31. *Obituaires*, 2:283–309.

32. Depoin, "Manuscrits funèbres de Saint-Léonor de Beaumont," 18, 23, 28, 29, 33, 38.

33. For the donations, see above, Chapter 2, n. 276, and "Rouleau mortuaire de Guillaume des Barres," ed. Dufour, 208.

34. *Obituaires*, 1.1:115.

35. FLN, fol. 117r–v.

36. Jean Dufour has published the edition with introduction and maps of the itinerary: "Rouleau mortuaire de Guillaume des Barres," ed. Dufour, 206–43, 696–701. The following discussion benefits from this material.

37. Ibid., 210–11, for the illumination and the Parisian workshops.

38. Ibid., 212–14.

39. See the maps, ibid., 698–701.

40. Ibid., 213.

41. Of the foundations producing the thirty-two cartularies, the four houses with female religious were the Hôtel-Dieu of Paris and the abbeys of Porrois, Saint-Antoine, and Yerres.

42. OurPD, 269–70 (Pierre *li Vermaus* and Renaud de Coucy, 1186); SJVi, fol. 48r (Manasses, *miles de Escencuz*, 1217); SNR, 128–29 (Robert, knight of Mézières, and his wife, 1203). From outside the sample of thirty-two cartularies, another example of conversion is Hugues le Loup, brother of Guy, butler of Senlis: Mon, 134 (n.d.).

43. Rhein, "La Seigneurie de Montfort en Iveline," 322 (1222). For the two other cases of oblates, see Yer, 74 (n.d.); SNM, 44 (1186). See also Lynch, *Simoniacal Entry into Religious Life from 1000 to 1260* (1976), 36–40.

44. VND, fol. 48r–50r (1193); HDP, 23 (1199).

45. Yer, 153 (1183); Por, 57 (1217).

46. Por, 48 (1216).

47. For the sole exception to this, see OurPD, 269–70 (1186). See also Lynch, *Simoniacal Entry*, 83–224.

48. OurPD, 385 (1198).

49. Brundage, *Medieval Canon Law and the Crusader* (1969), 139–90.

50. Fifteen of the mentions cannot be associated with designated campaigns. Prominent figures from the Paris region whose crusade cannot be identified include Thibaut de Marly (NDP, 2:200, a charter from 1173) and Gace de Poissy (VND, fol. 38v, a charter from 1184).

51. Geoffroi de Villehardouin, *La Conquête de Constantinople*, 1:5.

52. Montfort, STÉ, 13–15 (1202–3); Beaumont, NDP, 1:21 (1206); Coucy, OurPD, 115–18 (1201–4); Marly, Por, 25 (before 1204) and 29–30 (1206); Mauvoisin, SLP, 75 (1202); Boves, SLE, 96–98 (1206); Marly, Por, 30 (1204).

53. Geoffroi de Villehardouin, *La Conquête de Constantinople*, 1:11; Longnon, *Les Compagnons de Villehardouin*, 13. Ferry and Jean accompanied their father Baudouin d'Yerres; see Yer, 229 (1203).

54. *Petrus Choiseaus*, Cha, fol. 122r (1202); *Petrus de Vilers*, OurPD, 154–55 (1202).

55. "Volumus insuper ut ipsorum haereticorum bona omnia publicentur, et tam tibi vel in persona propria laboranti, vel necessarium auxilium impendenti, quam hominibus terrae tuae qui contra perfidos arma susceperint expugnandos, illa valeat remissio peccatorum quam his qui laborant pro terre sancte subsidio duximus indulgendam." *Die Register Innocenz' III., 10. Pontifikatsjahr,*

1207/1208, ed. Murauer and Sommerlechner (2007), 256; PL, vol. 215, col. 1247; Pierre des Vaux-de-Cernay, *Hystoria Albigensis*, ed. Guébin and Lyon, 1:74.

56. SD, vol. 1, p. 388 (Mathieu de Montmorency, 1214).

57. *Scripta*, p. 652, no. 206 (Simon de Chavigny); pp. 631–32, nos. 104–7 (Robert de Poissy). Simon de Chavigny confirmed the donation of revenues to Saint-Crépin-en-Chaye just before his departure for crusade against the Albigensians: SCCha, fol. 114r (1210).

58. Pierre des Vaux-de-Cernay, *Hystoria Albigensis*, 2:244 (Mathieu de Montmorency).

59. The cartulary does contain a charter from Simon *de la Gleiserei* pertaining to the Third Crusade: VdC, 1:122 (1194). However, the charters of the region are surprisingly silent about the Albigensian Crusade. Other sources, such as Pierre des Vaux-de-Cernay, note that Simon de Montfort's retinue for the Albigensian Crusade included such prominent participants as Guy de Lévis, Guy de Montfort, Simon and Geoffroi de Neauphle, Simon and Robert de Poissy, Pierre de Richebourg, Roger d'Andilly, Bouchard and Mathieu de Marly, Guillaume de Garlande, and Robert Mauvoisin. On them, see Woehl, *Volo vincere cum meis vel occumbere cum eisdem*, 123–56.

60. STÉ, 13. For another subvention from the priory of Saint-Arnoult near Rochefort-en-Yvelines, see Rhein, "La Seigneurie de Montfort en Iveline," 313 (1200).

61. VND, fols. 43v–45v.

62. VND, fols. 68v–69v (n.d.), reports an elaborate scheme of lending ten *livres* to Robert, chamberlain of Montmorency, with guarantees of repayment when he left for Jerusalem.

63. SSC, 55 (1190), 55–56 (1192).

64. For example, OurPD, 228 (1203), 237 (1202).

65. SMCps, 3:107 (1191); see also SCC, 1:279 (1189); SLE, 96–98 (1202).

66. Confirmation by his brother Robert de Poissy in 1213: Abb, 42.

67. For example, SCCha, fol. 44v (Guy, castellan of Coucy, 1190); Bar fol. 139r (1195).

68. Por, 25 (before 1204).

69. SCC, 1:279 (1189).

70. SD, vol. 1, p. 595 (1216).

71. VND, fol. 32r (1189); SYB, 254 (1189); NDP, 1:21 (1206).

72. Schenk, *Templar Families* (2012), 2–6.

73. Brunel, "The Knights Templar and Money" (2012).

74. *Actes*, vol. 1, no. 378.

75. De Curzon, *La Maison du Temple de Paris* (1888), 12, 15, 16; Léonard, *Introduction au cartulaire manuscrit du Temple (1150–1317)* (1930), 119.

76. Léonard, *Introduction au cartulaire manuscrit du Temple*, 119–20.

77. *Cartulaire général de l'ordre des Hospitaliers de S. Jean de Jérusalem*, ed. Le Roulx (1894–1906), 1:409–10 (1181), 482–83 (1185), 524 (1188), 574 (1191), and 2:48 (1214).

78. Léonard, *Introduction au cartulaire manuscrit du Temple*, 119: "Possessiones Templi in Insula Franciae sitae plurimae erant sed de plerisque paucae habentur notitiae." See also de Curzon, *La Maison du Temple de Paris*, 12–16.

79. Leroy, "Commanderies of Champagne and of Brie" (2012), 196.

80. "Ego itaque Radulfus de Risuns . . . transmitto quod mea prospera [*sic*] voluntate, ob anime mee parentumque meorum remedium, Deo et domui milicie templi viginti aissinos terre in perpetuam helemosinam tribui et eidem libere quiete in perpetuum possidendos concessi. Deinde maiorem anime mee considerans profectum, relictis secularibus et ejusdem domus suscepto habitu, me eidem mancipavi serviturum. Ut autem hoc donum meum ratum et incussum permaneat, et ne quolibet modo calupnia [*sic*] emergat, subscriptione testium et sigillo domini Radulfi, comitis Suessionis, presentem feci pag[i]nam roborari. Hujus enim rei testes sunt Johannes de Nigella, frater comitis predicti, Robertus Cosset, frater Willelmus de Risuns. Data Accon, menses aprilis, anno M° C° LXXXX° II° dominice incarnationis." AN S 4952, liasse 2, no. 5; photograph by Ghislain Brunel and the Archives nationales in *The Knights Templar*, ed. Baudin et al. (2012), 251; transcription in Brunel, "Les Rois de France et l'Orient" (2000), 47.

81. Schenk, *Templar Families*, 10, map.

82. For "contritionism" in Latin theology and vernacular romance, see Baldwin, "From the Ordeal to Confession" (1998); Baldwin, *Aristocratic Life*, 194–247. For the application of "contritionism" to aristocrats, ibid., 223–34.

83. For "attritionism," see Payen, *Le Motif du repentir dans la littérature française médiévale* (1967), 489–97.

84. NDP, 2:200 (1173), 202–3 (1223).

85. On Thibaut's life, see *Les Vers de Thibaud de Marly*, ed. Stone, 36–57; Civel, *La Fleur de France*, 395–97. For the Montmorency-Marly family, see above, Chapter 2, 41–42.

86. Thibaud de Marly, *Les Vers*, 57–76. From internal evidence, he composed *Les Vers* between 1170 (the assassination of Thomas Becket) and 1189 (the death of King Henry II), but it is unlikely that he began this work of monastic inspiration before his conversion in the years 1182–85. On the *Quinze signes*, see Labie-Leurquin and James, "Quinze signes du jugement dernier" (1992).

87. Alexandre de Paris, *Le Roman d'Alexandre*, trans. Harf-Lancner (1994), vv. 56–57; Pierre the Chanter, *Verbum abbreviatum: Textus conflatus*, ed. Boutry (2004), 195; *Textus prior*, ed. Boutry (2012), 175; *Textus alter*, ed. Boutry (2012), 121; Gerald of Wales, *Gemma ecclesiastica*, ed. Brewer (1862), 290; Baldwin, *Masters, Princes, and Merchants*, 1:203–4 and 2:143–44.

88. Montigny is a common name but a family of that name may be found in the castellany of Senlis; see *Nomina*, no. 373; Newman, *Les Seigneurs de Nesle*, 2:164.

89. Thibaud de Marly, *Les Vers*, 78–80; Lauwers, "Du pacte seigneurial à l'idéal de conversion: Les Légendes hagiographiques de Simon de Crépy" (2002); Iogna-Prat, "La Place idéale du laïc à Cluny" (2002), 307–12.

90. Thibaud de Marly, *Les Vers*, 77–78; Payen, *Le Motif du repentir*, 490–92. A Guichard de Beaujeu also married into the family of Montlhéry from the Paris region; see Duby, *La Société aux XIe et XIIe siècles dans la région Mâconnaise*, 466.

91. SD, vol. 1, p. 245 (1224); *Nomina*, no. 373. For a *fief-rente* from the king, see *Registres*, 197.

92. Thibaud de Marly, *Les Vers*, ed. Stone, v. 100, alternate reading of MS B: "Se il ne lest le siecle ne siecle ne lest lui."

93. On Hélinand and his works, see Baldwin, *Government*, 570–71 n. 28; Civel, *La Fleur de France*, 394–99. All references below are to the stanzas in Hélinand de Froidmont, *Les Vers de la mort*, trans. Boyer and Santucci (1983). For an English translation, see "The *Verses on Death* by Hélinant de Froidmont," trans. Paden (1978). Translations below are my own.

94. "Rouleau mortuaire de Guillaume des Barres," ed. Dufour, 213, 221.

95. These have been collected and published in Adhémar, "Les Tombeaux de la Collection Gaignières" (pt. 1, 1974; pt. 2, 1976; pt. 3, 1977).

96. See above, 153.

97. SCC, 1:401 (1207); CSH, 99 (1207–17).

98. VdC, 1:95–97 (1186); Rhein, "La Seigneurie de Montfort en Iveline," 323–24 (1223).

99. Bernard of Pavia, *Summa decretalium*, ed. Laspeyres, 3.24 (pp. 101–3).

100. Baldwin, *Aristocratic Life*, 87–88; Baldwin, *Masters, Princes, and Merchants*, 1:224–26.

101. Adhémar, "Les Tombeaux," pt. 1, no. 85; Bouchot I, no. 3670; BnF Est., Rés. Pe 1o, fol. 45. He is identified by that name in charters from 1182–92. See above, Chapter 2, 37–38, for the Garlande family at Tournan.

102. Adhémar, "Les Tombeaux," pt. 1, nos. 69, 70; Bouchot I, nos. 3643 and 3644; BnF Est., Rés. Pe 1o, fols. 18 and 19; Bar, fols. 315r–316r (1222); *Layettes*, vol. 1, no. 1543 (1222); *Actes*, vol 4., no. 1786 (1222).

103. Adhémar, "Les Tombeaux," pt. 1, no. 90; Bouchot I, no. 3659; BnF Est., Rés. Pe 1o, fol. 34. An Eudes des Barres is found in the charters of Preuilly from 1202 to 1220: Preuilly, 98, 119, 122, 141, 144. *Pleisseto de Buneis* is likely Le Plessis (formerly Le Plessis de Bunes), located southwest of the abbey of Preuilly, between Châtenay-sur-Seine and Courcelles-en-Bassée.

104. Adhémar, "Les Tombeaux," pt. 1, no. 161; Bouchot II, no. 4550; BnF Est., Rés. Pe 11a, fol. 43.

105. Douët d'Arcq II, no. 3258 (Simon de Poissy, 1229); Bouchot II, no. 4550 (heraldry of Guillaume de Poissy's shield). The identity of this Guillaume de Poissy and his relationship to Simon de

Poissy is not clear. Among the charters of Abbecourt and Saint-Victor from the late twelfth and early thirteenth centuries containing references to Guillaume de Poissy (likely two different Guillaumes) are Abb, 29 (1191–92); SVP, fols. 54r–56v (n.d.).

106. Adhémar, "Les Tombeaux," pt. 1, no. 187; Bouchot I, no. 2263; BnF Est., Rés. Pe 1c, fol. 128.

107. Douët d'Arcq II, no. 3809 (1214); SMPoCh, 4–5 (1207), 9 (1214). He is accompanied in the charters by his brother Gérard de Vallangoujard (de Valle Enguejardi), whose heraldry is "une croix pattée" (Douët d'Arcq II, no. 3804, from the year 1235).

108. Adhémar, "Les Tombeaux," pt. 1, no. 128; Bouchot I, no. 2067; BnF Est., Rés. Pe 1b, fol. 35. Gaucher appears in charters from 1215 to 1221: SCC, 1:441 (1215), 2:21 (1221). The fleur-de-lis also appears on the family seal: Douët d'Arcq II, no. 3036 (Philippe de Nanteuil, 1220). For similar tombs of the Nanteuil family, see Adhémar, "Les Tombeaux," pt. 1, nos. 129, 130, 296.

109. Adhémar, "Les Tombeaux," pt. 3, no. 1963; Bouchot II, no. 4713; BnF Est., Rés. Pe 11a, fol. 205; Douët d'Arcq I, no. 1296 (Guillaume des Barres).

110. Adhémar, "Les Tombeaux," pt. 1, no.155; Bouchot II, no. 3988; BnF Est., Rés. Pe 5, fol. 27; Douët d'Arcq I, nos. 234, 235. At his feet is a further inscription, *Hugo de Plalili me fecit*, which is also found on Queen Ingeborg's tomb at Corbeil. See below for her tomb.

111. Adhémar, "Les Tombeaux," pt. 1, no. 290; Bouchot II, no. 4090; BnF Est., Rés. Pe 6, fol. 26; Douët d'Arcq I, no. 233 (Ours, 1220, with heraldry "trois jumelles en fasce").

112. Adhémar, "Les Tombeaux," pt. 1, no. 65; Bouchot I, no. 1937; BnF Est., Rés. Pe 1, fol. 75; inscription in Duchesne, *Histoire généalogique de la maison royale de Dreux*, 255; Douët d'Arcq I, no. 721 (1202).

113. Adhémar, "Les Tombeaux," pt. 1, no. 230; Bouchot I, no. 1960; BnF Est., Rés. Pe 1, fol. 98; Douët d'Arcq I, no. 534 (1220).

114. Adhémar, "Les Tombeaux," pt. 1, no. 45; Bouchot I, no. 1993; BnF Est., Rés. Pe 1a, fol. 21.

115. Adhémar, "Les Tombeaux," pt. 1, no. 166; Bouchot I, no. 1994; BnF Est., Rés. Pe 1a, fol. 22. Inscribed on the tomb is *Magister Hugo de Placliago me fecit*. On her problems with clothing early in her marriage, see Baldwin, *Aristocratic Life*, 191 and 323 n. 71.

116. Adhémar, "Les Tombeaux," pt. 1, no. 296; Bouchot I, no. 2068; BnF Est., Rés. Pe 1b, fol. 36.

117. Adhémar, "Les Tombeaux," pt. 1, no. 323; Bouchot I, no. 1961; BnF Est., Rés. Pe 1, fol. 99.

118. Adhémar, "Les Tombeaux," pt. 1, no. 233; Bouchot II, no. 4089; BnF Est., Rés. Pe 6, fol. 25. This effigy, including the heraldry, bears strong resemblances to that of Adam the Chamberlain, lord of Villebéon (d. 1264), described above. On the two Adams de Villebéon, see Richemond, *Recherches généalogiques sur la famille des seigneurs de Nemours*, 2:72–82, 125–30.

119. Lauwers, "La 'Vie du seigneur Bouchard, comte vénérable'" (2002).

120. On Simon de Crépy, see above, 160–62.

121. See the collection of charters in Vincent, *Norman Charters*.

122. *Gallia christiana*, vol. 7, cols. 889–90. See also Maquet, *Les Seigneurs de Marly*, 148–55.

123. Evergates, *The Aristocracy in the County of Champagne*, 236–37, 259, 374 n. 141; *Documents relatifs au comté de Champagne et de Brie, 1172–1361*, ed. Longnon, 1:40 (*Feoda Campanie*, pt. 1, no. 1037), 92 (*Feoda Campanie*, pt. 2, no. 2454); Dimier, "Le Bienheureux Jean de Montmirail." Dimier, p. 183, adds to the list of Jean's inheritances La Ferté-sous-Jouarre, Tresmes, Gandelu, and Condé-en-Brie. See also Civel, *La Fleur de France*, 400–402.

124. *Actes.* vol. 2, no. 581.

125. SJVi, fols. 44r (1195), 107r (n.d.); MSM, fol. 15v (1206).

126. For Jean, see SMCps, 3:271–72 (1208); for Helvide, SJVi, fol. 106r (1208). Philip Augustus confirmed an agreement between Jean and Saint-Martin-des-Champs in 1217; see *Actes*, vol. 4, no. 1497.

127. *Gallia christiana*, vol. 9, cols. 475–76, claims that the author was Gaucher, abbot of Longpont (1201–19). The *Vita* was probably finished before 1236 when the abbey proposed Jean's canonization.

128. *Vita B. Joannis de Monte-Mirabili*, 218–35, at 219A.

129. Ibid., 224F, 225A–B. This may refer to the siege of Gisors, 12 April 1193, which Rigord reported as a victory; see Rigord, *Gesta*, ed. Carpentier, 319; ed. Delaborde, 123.

130. *Itinerarium peregrinorum et gesta regis Ricardi*, ed. Stubbs (1864), 93.

131. *Vita B. Joannis de Monte-Mirabili*, 219C.

132. Ibid., 219C; *Littere Baronum*, ed. Evergates, 55 (no. 11); Evergates, *The Aristocracy in the County of Champagne*, 110.

133. The anecdotes are reported throughout chapters 1 and 2, *Vita B. Joannis de Monte-Mirabili*, 219C–221E, 222D–225C.

134. Ibid., 219E–F; Jordan, *The French Monarchy and the Jews* (1989), 30–32; Baldwin, *Government*, 51–53.

135. In 1206 at Crèvecoeur, for his soul and for the souls of Helvide, his wife, and their children, he gave a measure of land in the Cambrésis (MSM, fol. 15v).

136. *Vita B. Joannis de Monte-Mirabili*, 220E–221B.

137. Ibid., 221B–E. For commentary, see Gorochov, *Naissance de l'université*, 72–82.

138. *Vita B. Joannis de Monte-Mirabili*, 226B–D; Dimier, "Le Bienheureux Jean de Montmirail," 184–85.

139. *Vita B. Joannis de Monte-Mirabili*, 226D–F.

140. Ibid., 228D.

141. Ibid., 227D–F; Dimier, "Le Bienheureux Jean de Montmirail," 186.

142. *Vita B. Joannis de Monte-Mirabili*, 228E–F.

143. Ibid., 228B–C, 229A.

144. SJVi, fol. 37r (1225), f. 37r (1236).

145. *Vita B. Joannis de Monte-Mirabili*, 229B–C.

146. "Cujus forma talis esse videbatur, qualis a pictoribus in vitro depingi solet Domini nostri imago." *Vita B. Joannis de Monte-Mirabili*, 230C–D.

147. "Deo disponente, per triduum solummodo fuit in purgatorio." *Vita B. Joannis de Monte-Mirabili*, 234A.

148. Ibid., 230E–231A.

149. On the construction of Longpont, see Bruzelius, "Cistercian High Gothic" (1979).

150. Adhémar, "Les Tombeaux," pt. 1, no. 64; Bouchot I, no. 2513; BnF Est., Rés. Pe 1e, fol. 92; Dimier, "Le Bienheureux Jean de Montmirail," 187–88; Duval-Arnould, "Quelques inscriptions funéraires de l'abbaye de Longpont" (1984), 689–91. A wooden box covered with copper and decorated with the heraldry of the royal family and great nobles was made in the mid-thirteenth century to conserve Jean's bones. For his daughter Marie's tomb, also at Longpont, see Adhémar, "Les Tombeaux," pt. 1, no. 327.

Chapter 9

1. Hue de Rotelande, *Ipomedon*, ed. Holden (1979), vv. 27–29.

2. Aurell, *Le Chevalier lettré*, 21–38.

3. *Vie de saint Eustache* (excerpts), ed. Meyer (1891), 227. See also Bourgain, "L'Emploi de la langue vulgaire dans la littérature au temps de Philippe Auguste" (1982), 769.

4. I have experimented with vernacular literature as a historical source for the aristocracy in my *Aristocratic Life in Medieval France*.

5. This is not to overlook the importance of the Anonymous of Béthune who wrote a contemporary history in French, but he was located in the Flemish not the Paris region, and he deals primarily with the Anglo-Norman lands. He compiled his history in two versions, the *Histoire des ducs de Normandie et des rois d'Angleterre* and the *Chronique des rois de France*. For editions of the two versions, see Anonymous of Béthune, *Histoire des ducs de Normandie et des rois d'Angleterre*, ed. Michel; and *Extrait d'une chronique française des rois de France par un anonyme de Béthune*, ed. Delisle.

6. *L'Histoire de Guillaume le Maréchal*, ed. Meyer (1891–1901), with helpful notes and summaries; Painter, *William Marshal* (1933); Duby, *Guillaume le Maréchal* (1984); Crouch, *William Marshal* (1990); *History of William Marshal*, ed. Holden, trans. Gregory, historical notes Crouch.

7. This standard literary French of the Middle Ages used to be called Francien, but since it has been recognized that so few manuscripts originated from the Paris region, it has become inappropriate.

8. References to verses of the *Histoire* below are to Holden's edition.

9. Conon de Béthune, *Les Chansons de Conon de Béthune*, ed. Wallensköld (1921), chanson 3, p. 5.

10. Jean Renart, *L'Escoufle*, ed. Sweetser; Jean Renart, *Le Roman de la Rose*, ed. Lecoy. For an introduction to Jean Renart, see Baldwin, *Aristocratic Life*, 1–21, 32–49.

11. Gerbert de Montreuil, *La Continuation de Perceval*, ed. Williams and Oswald; Gerbert de Montreuil, *Le Roman de la Violette*, ed. Buffum. For an introduction to Gerbert de Montreuil, see Baldwin, *Aristocratic Life*, 1–21, 58–67.

12. For Philip Augustus's residences, see Baldwin, *Government*, 40.

13. On Gerbert's tournament at Montargis, see Baldwin, *Aristocratic Life*, 63–66.

14. For Renaud, Marie, and Simon, see above, Chapter 2, 25–26, 28.

15. On lyric insertions in Jean Renart and Gerbert de Montreuil, see Baldwin, *Aristocratic Life*, 11–19.

16. Lecoy has calendared them in his edition of Jean's *Roman de la Rose*, xxii–xxix.

17. Buffum included forty in his edition and found four more in the manuscript variants. See Gerbert de Montreuil, *Le Roman de la Violette*, ed. Buffum, lxxxii–xci; and Buffum, "The Songs of the *Roman de la Violette*" (1911).

18. On Gace, see Gace Brulé, *The Lyrics and Melodies*, ed. Rosenberg, Danon, and Van der Werf (1985), xiii–xl; Baldwin, "The Image of the Jongleur in Northern France Around 1200" (1997), 653–58. The lyrics are cited by number and page from the edition of Rosenberg, Danon, and Van der Werf.

19. Gace Brulé, *Lyrics and Melodies*, no. 2, pp. 4–9; no. 50, p. 170.

20. Ibid., frontispiece (Vatican City, Biblioteca Apostolica Vaticana, Regina lat. 1490, fol. 18r).

21. Ibid., nos. 4, 27, 38, 82 (pp. 14, 96, 133, 338) for Geoffroy, duke of Brittany; nos. 12, 34, 49, 75, 77 (pp. 36, 122, 166, 252, 260) for the count of Blois; no. 45 (p. 150) for the countess of Brie.

22. *Registres*, 203; Fawtier, "Un fragment du compte de l'hôtel du prince Louis de France," 243.

23. Guilhiermoz, "Une charte de Gace Brulé," 127.

24. *Gace Brulé, trouvère champenois*, ed. Dyggve, 175; Grossel, *Le Milieu littéraire en Champagne sous les Thibaudiens*, 1:313–22.

25. Bécam, *Rhyme in Gace Brulé's Lyric* (1998), 1, 29, 186.

26. Gace Brulé, *Lyrics and Melodies*, no. 77, p. 61 (Nanteuil); no. 63, p. 208 ("sweet lady"); no. 66, p. 216, and no. 62, p. 204 (French king).

27. Gace Brulé, *Lyrics and Melodies*, no. 6, p. 18.

28. Roach, "*Bruslez amis* and the Battle of Bouvines" (1979).

29. Holger Petersen Dyggve is the indefatigable sleuth for playing the game; see *Gace Brulé, trouvère champenois*, ed. Dyggve.

30. Ibid., 45–48. Aubry de Trois-Fontaines, in one of his genealogies, claims that Alix de Châtillon had as husband "Guilelmus qui Noblez appellatus est" (*Chronica*, ed. Scheffer-Boichorst, 909).

31. *Gace Brulé, trouvère champenois*, ed. Dyggve, 42–45. Guillaume des Barres is my guess.

32. *Gace Brulé, trouvère champenois*, ed. Dyggve, 74–84.

33. Ibid., 70–74.

34. Ibid., 100–102. Newman, in his exhaustive research on the genealogies of the families of Nesle (*Les Seigneurs de Nesle*, 1:36–50) and Dargies (1:89–93), makes no mention of literary careers, save for a reference (1:44) to prior conjectures that the trouvère Blondel de Nesle was Jean II de Nesle. See also above, Chapter 2, 39–40.

35. See above, Chapter 8, 150.

36. For the most recent history, see Zink, *Les Troubadours* (2013).

37. Raoul de Hodenc, *Le Roman des Eles*, ed. Busby.

38. Sandauer, *L'Élement scolastique dans l'œuvre de Raoul de Houdenc* (1922), discusses the elements of syllogism, opposition, and allegory to demonstrate the influence of the schools on Raoul's works. On Raoul's identity, see Fourrier, "Raoul de Hodenc: Est-ce lui?" (1964).

39. Baumgartner, "Remarques sur la poésie de Gace Brulé" (1984).

40. The image is also adopted in Jean Renart's *Lai de l'ombre*, ed. Lecoy (1979), v. 456.

41. Aurell, *Des chrétiens contre les croisades, XIIe–XIIIe siècle*, 120–22.

42. *Chansons attribuées au Chastelain de Couci*, ed. Lerond (1964), chanson 5, pp. 76–78; *Les Chansons de croisade avec leurs mélodies*, ed. Bédier and Aubry (1909), 92–96.

43. *Chansons attribuées au Chastelain de Couci*, ed. Lerond, chanson 1, pp. 57–60; *Les Chansons de croisade*, ed. Bédier and Aubry, 101–6.

44. Barthélemy, *Les Deux Âges de la seigneurie banale* (1984), 179, 313, 509, genealogy 504–5; Longnon, *Les Compagnons de Villehardouin*, 118.

45. *Actes*, vol. 2, nos. 645 (Saint-Vincent, 1200) and 712 (Ourscamp, 1202). For other donations, see below, notes 48 and 49.

46. Geoffroi de Villehardouin, *La Conquête de Constantinople*, ed. Faral, 1:116, 126.

47. LonA, pp. 63–64 (1202); OurPD, 118 (1204).

48. OurPD, 113–14 (1190); SCCha, fol. 44v (1190).

49. OurPD, 115–16 (1201).

50. *Le Roman du castelain de Couci et de la dame de Fayel par Jakemes*, ed. Matzke and Delbouille (1936).

51. Boulton, *The Song in the Story* (1993), 35–42.

52. Buffum, "The Songs of the *Roman de la Violette*," 134–37.

53. For the melodies, see Hendrik van der Werf, "About the Melodies," in Gace Brulé, *The Lyrics and Melodies*, 341–46; Boulton, *The Song in the Story*, 5–9.

54. Baldwin, *Aristocratic Life*, 21–30; Baldwin, "The Image of the Jongleur in Northern France around 1200," 636–37, 639–44.

55. Chrétien de Troyes, *Le Chevalier de la charrette*, ed. Roques (1983), vv. 1634–38.

56. Baldwin, *Aristocratic Life*, 171–72; Mehl, *Les Jeux au royaume de France du XIIIe au début du XVIe siècle* (1990), 13–25, 76–90, 113–34, 135–48.

57. Chrétien de Troyes, *Le Chevalier au lion (Yvain)*, ed. Roques (1982), v. 2470.

58. Baldwin, *Aristocratic Life*, 172–74.

59. Anonymous of Béthune, *Histoire des ducs de Normandie et des rois d'Angleterre*, ed. Michel, 143–45.

60. Table 8, row D.

61. SVP, fol. 78r–v (1196); OurPD, 137–38 (1194).

62. Bar, fol. 277v (1218); Duchesne, "Histoire de la maison des bouteillers de Senlis," 179 (1223).

63. *Registres*, 74–75.

64. Guillaume le Breton, *Philippidos*, ed. Delaborde, 54.

65. Among the many studies, see, for example, Flori, *L'Essor de la chevalerie, XIe–XIIe siècles* (1986).

66. VdC, 1:74 (ca. 1180).

67. SD, vol. 1, p. 243 (1210). A clear distinction between minor children and children who had reached majority was made in a charter of Jean de Corbeil and his wife Carcassonne involving the consent of their heirs to a donation to Saint-Victor: SVP, fol. 78r–v (1196).

68. Chrétien de Troyes, *Le Conte du Graal (Perceval)*, ed. Lecoy (1990), vv. 1635–38, 1692–96.

69. Guillaume le Breton, *Gesta*, ed. Delaborde, 222. See also Anonymous of Béthune, *Extrait d'une chronique française des rois de France*, ed. Delisle, 763; Roger of Wendover in Matthew Paris, *Chronica majora*, ed. Luard (1872–1993), 2:524. The king had knighted Philippe, son of Baudouin IV, count of Hainaut, in 1195: *La Chronique de Gislebert de Mons*, ed. Vanderkindere (1904), 305.

From 1168 to 1195 Gislebert recorded at least nine dubbings; see, for example, *La Chronique de Gislebert de Mons*, 95, 237, 292.

70. *Budget*, CCI (1), records the expenses of three robes for new knights at Pentecost.

71. Chrétien de Troyes, *Le Chevalier au lion (Yvain)*, ed. Roques, vv. 5–6.

72. *Registres*, 502, 533.

73. For the confusion over the knighting of young Henry, see *Histoire de Guillaume le Maréchal*, ed. Holden, 3:69–70. It is likely that Louis VII belted Count Richard of Poitou (later King Richard I), also in 1173; see *Gesta Regis Henrici Secundi Benedicti Abbatis*, ed. Stubbs, 1:63.

74. Pierre des Vaux-de-Cernay, *Hystoria Albigensis*, ed. Guébin and Lyon, 1:124.

75. The mention of tournaments in the ecclesiastical charters is limited to grants of exemption to nonaristocratic classes. For example, Hervé, lord of Alluyes, granted to the inhabitants of Saint-Jean de Brou that they would be "immunes ab omni exactioni . . . nec me sequi debent in tornamento," SJVa, 65–66 (ca. 1197). Saint-Denis sought exemptions for its communities: "in exercitu et equitatu et guerris suis tornamentis exceptiis," SD, vol. 1, pp. 784–85 (1183); "aliis consuetudinibus scilicet exercitu equitatu inquietabat et ad guerras et ad tornamenta eos ducabat," SD, vol. 2, p. 201 (1211). For other examples, see SCC, 1:437, 438; SMPoCh, 13.

76. Duby, *Guillaume le Maréchal*.

77. *La Chronique de Gislebert de Mons*, ed. Vanderkindere, 95–160.

78. The tournament sites closest to Paris included (1) Gournay-sur-Aronde and Ressons-sur-Matz, located between Compiègne and Montdidier; (2) Lagny-sur-Marne, near Pomponne; (3) Pleurs, dép. Marne; (4) Joigny, south of Sens; and three sites north of Chartres—(5) Anet and Sorel, (6) Maintenon and Nogent-le-Roi, and (7) Épernon.

79. Simon de Montfort (d. 1218) and the younger Guillaume des Barres may have been half brothers through their mother; see *L'Histoire de Guillaume le Maréchal*, ed. Meyer, 3:52.

80. Baldwin, "Jean Renart et le tournoi de Saint-Trond" (1990); Baldwin, *Aristocratic Life*, 70–86.

81. Baldwin, *Aristocratic Life*, 64–66.

82. Ibid., 60–61.

83. Huon d'Oisi, *Tournoiement des dames*, ed. Pulega; Jeanroy, "Notes sur le tournoiement des dames" (1899).

84. Aliénor later identified herself as the countess of Saint-Quentin. Alix de Dreux was the daughter of Robert I, count of Dreux (d. 1188), and Agnès de Baudemont-Braine.

85. Anonymous of Béthune, *Extrait d'une chronique française des rois de France*, ed. Delisle, 769.

86. Ibid.

87. On largesse, see Baldwin, *Aristocratic Life*, 98–104.

88. Chrétien de Troyes, *Cligès*, ed. Micha (1978), vv. 197–208.

89. Chrétien de Troyes, *Erec et Enide*, ed. Roques, vv. 2213–14.

90. *Vita B. Joannis de Monte-Mirabili*, 291C–D.

91. Rigord, *Gesta*, ed. Carpentier, 224–26; ed. Delaborde, 71–72.

92. Chrétien de Troyes, *Le Chevalier au lion (Yvain)*, ed. Roques, vv. 5–6.

93. Baldwin, *Aristocratic Life*, 110–12.

94. Chrétien de Troyes, *Le Conte de Graal (Perceval)*, ed. Lecoy, vv. 13–33.

95. Ibid., vv. 6854–65; Baldwin, *Aristocratic Life*, 86–90.

96. Baldwin, *Aristocratic Life*, 199.

97. Ibid., 199–202.

Chapter 10

1. A version of this chapter appeared as "Les Chevaliers à Chartres" (2014). I wish to thank Karine Boulanger of the Centre André Chastel and Clément Blanc-Riehl, director of the Centre de sigillographie et d'héraldique at the Archives nationales, for providing photographs of the windows and seals accompanying this chapter.

2. The literature on Chartres is immense. The most recent and authoritative work on the cathedral is *La Grâce d'une cathédrale: Chartres*, ed. Pansard (2013). For its history before 1194, see most recently Fassler, *The Virgin of Chartres* (2010). Although concentrating on the bakers, vintners, and money changers, Williams, *Bread, Wine, and Money* (1993), is valuable for the historical context; see especially pp. 3–36. Manhes-Deremble, *Les Vitraux narratifs de la cathédrale de Chartres* (1993), is a fundamental work on the lancet glass. Lautier, "La Royauté française dans le décor de la cathédrale de Chartres" (2012), provides the most recent research on this subject. I also want to thank Claudine Lautier for her personal and indispensable help with the windows at Chartres.

3. "Les Miracles de Notre-Dame de Chartres," ed. Thomas (1881).

4. Lautier, "The Canons of Chartres" (2013).

5. Bar-le-Duc, dép. Meuse; Mousson, dép. Meurthe-et-Moselle.

6. Williams, *Bread, Wine, and Money*, 30–36; Mazel, "Pouvoirs locaux et acteurs du chantier" (2013).

7. NDC, 2:95–96 (1221). The most recent dating of the phases of construction is in Lautier, "La Royauté française dans le décor de la cathédrale de Chartres," 240.

8. Guillaume le Breton, *Philippidos*, ed. Delaborde, 55; Baldwin, *Government*, 397–98; Manhes-Deremble, *Les Vitraux narratifs*, 12–15; Williams, *Bread, Wine, and Money*, 15–17.

9. Timbert, "La Construction de la cathédrale gothique" (2013).

10. Lautier, "La Diversité des ateliers de peintres-verriers du XIIIe siècle" (2013).

11. The sketches are preserved mainly at Paris at the BnF, Département des estampes et de la photographie. See the inventory of Bouchot, *Inventaire des dessins exécutés pour Roger de Gaignières* (1891). Images of many of these drawings are available on the BnF's website for digitized materials, Gallica.

12. Lautier, "Les Restaurations de vitraux du moyen âge à nos jours" (2013); Lautier, "Restaurations récentes à la cathédrale de Chartres et nouvelles recherches" (2011).

13. Deremble and Deremble, "Les Vitraux médiévaux, un patrimoine exceptionnel" (2013), 189–90; Manhes-Deremble, *Les Vitraux narratifs*, 15–17. Earlier studies have argued for the dates of 1220–27.

14. The legend is smudged and what can be read mixes Latin and the vernacular (VINERŪS, *vignerons*): COMES TEOBALD DAT . . . VINERŪS AD PRECES COMITIS [PER]TICE.ENSIS.

15. Manhes-Deremble, *Les Vitraux narratifs*, 107; Robert d'Auxerre, *Chronicon*, ed. Holder-Egger (1882), 233; Ernald of Bonneval, *S. Bernardi Vita prima*, PL, vol. 185 (1879), col. 300; Pierre the Chanter in Baldwin, *Masters, Princes, and Merchants*, 1:255–56 and 2:182. The windows are dated to 1225 but only tentatively.

16. Manhes-Deremble, *Les Vitraux narratifs*, 336–37, 372–73.

17. Lautier, "Les Deux Galeries des rois" (2013).

18. Katzenellenbogen, *The Sculptural Program of Chartres Cathedral* (1959), 135 n. 1 and plates 68, 69. The figure identified here as Saint Theodore could also be Saint Maurice or Saint Eustache, other military saints; see Bugslag, "Ideology and Iconography in Chartres Cathedral" (1998), 502–3. The biblical figure of Gideon was also clad in mail in the right bay of the north transept. Work on the sculpture of the south transept was begun in 1220 and on the sculpture of the north transept in 1224; see Katzenellenbogen, *Sculptural Program*, 54.

19. This identification has been undertaken by Perrot, "Le Vitrail, la croisade et la Champagne" (1989); Brenk, "Bildprogrammatik und Geschichtsverständnis der Kapetinger im Querhaus der Kathedrale von Chartres" (1991); Grant, "Representing Dynasty: The Transept Windows at Chartres Cathedral" (2010); and Deremble and Deremble, "Les Vitraux médiévaux," 151, 198–206.

20. For the two lancets of window 107, see Bouchot I, no. 82; BnF Est., Rés. Oa 9, fol. 68; and Bouchot I, no. 75; BnF Est., Rés. Oa 9 fol. 56.

21. Bouchot I, no. 1726; BnF Est., Rés. Pc 18, fol. 8.

22. The possibility that Guy de Montfort, brother of Simon, might be depicted is eliminated by the heraldry of the second knight, which is not *brisé* as would be necessary for Guy. See Guy de Montfort's heraldry in Douët d'Arcq I, no. 709.

23. For the two lancets of window 112, see Bouchot I, no. 99; BnF Est., Rés. Oa 9, fol. 85; and Bouchot I, no. 145; BnF Est., Rés. Oa 10, fol. 15.

24. See below, 242.

25. Bouchot I, no. 94; BnF Est., Rés. Oa 9, fol. 80.

26. Bouchot I, no. 65; BnF Est., Rés. Oa 9, fol. 45.

27. Bouchot I, no. 1746; BnF Est., Rés. Pc 18, fol. 28.

28. Deremble and Deremble, "Les Vitraux médiévaux," 154. Even the *Manuale de mysteriis ecclesie* composed by Pierre de Roissy, chancellor of the cathedral in the first decade of the thirteenth century, is of little help in resolving the problem; see Manhes-Deremble, *Les Vitraux narratifs*, 22–26.

29. Most recently Ivo Rauch has argued that the Virgin Mary of the apse represents the Ark of the Covenant before which the children of Israel were numbered in the desert, and that they, in turn, represent the crusaders against the Albigensians. This would then explain the obvious presence of Prince Louis and Simon and Amaury de Montfort; see Rauch, "Die Bundeslade und die wahren Israeliten" (2004). See my doubts about these iconographical arguments in Baldwin, "Les Chevaliers à Chartres," 702–3. Another attempt to interpret the ensemble of choir clerestories typologically is Deremble and Deremble, *Vitraux de Chartres* (2003), 71–81.

30. Deremble and Deremble, "Les Vitraux médiévaux," 194–98.

31. Williams, *Bread, Wine, and Money*, 37–63, 103–38, has intensively explicated the historical and iconographical meaning of these trades.

32. It can now be determined that before the Revolution the chapter possessed relics of at least two-thirds of the saints who were represented in the windows; see Lautier, "Échos et correspondances iconographiques" (2013), 211–12.

33. "Les Miracles de Notre-Dame de Chartres," ed. Thomas, 526–28, 549–50; *Jean le Marchant: Miracles de Notre-Dame de Chartres*, ed. Kunstmann (1973), 162–69; *Vielle chronique* (end of fourteenth century) in NDC, 1:58–59. See also Bugslag, "Pilgrimage to Chartres: The Visual Evidence" (2005); and Lautier, "The Sacred Topography of Chartres Cathedral" (2009).

34. *Obituaires*, 2:119, 124 (Louis); 61, 121 (Thibaut); 92 (Simon de Montfort). Robert de Beaumont also gave two *livres* (ibid., 116).

35. Those participating in the Albigensian Crusade with the earliest recorded date: Prince Louis (1215), Count Thibaut de Blois (before 1212?), Simon de Montfort (1209), Amaury de Montfort (1212), Robert de Courtenay (1211), Robert de Beaumont (1218), Pierre de Dreux (1219), Étienne de Sancerre (1226), and Bouchard de Marly (1210). See Table 12.

36. Petit-Dutaillis, *Étude sur la vie et le règne de Louis VIII*, 184, 186.

37. Guillaume le Breton, *Philippidos*, ed. Delaborde, 382.

38. NDC, 2:105. On Chartres as a regalian bishopric, see Baldwin, *Government*, 442.

39. Fawtier, "Un fragment du compte de l'hôtel du prince Louis de France," 240–45.

40. *Histoire de Guillaume le Maréchal*, ed. Holden, vol. 2, vv. 17374–75. This participation was reiterated by the continuator of Guillaume de Tyr and by the Ménestrel of Reims: *L'Estoire de Eracles empereur et la conqueste de la terre d'outremer* (1859), 321; *Recits d'un ménestrel de Reims au treizième siècle*, ed. de Wailly (1876), 154. The Count Thibaut in the legendary window of the south ambulatory (no. 28a) probably dates after the Thibaut of the choir clerestory (no. 109). See above, 232–33.

41. Anonymous of Béthune, *Extrait d'une chronique française des rois de France*, ed. Delisle, 771, 772, 774; Anonymous of Béthune, *Histoire des ducs de Normandie et des rois d'Angleterre*, ed. Michel, 172, 174, 177, 179, 188, 190, 195, 198, 201, 202; Matthew Paris, *Chronica majora*, ed. Luard, 3:28; Matthew Paris, *Historia Anglorum*, ed. Madden (1866–69), 2:221.

42. Van Kerrebrouck, *Les Capétiens* (2000), 111; *Registres*, 533. Lautier, "La Royauté française dans le décor de la cathédrale de Chartres," 245, dates this window ca. 1225.

43. Van Kerrebrouck, *Les Capétiens*, 470–71, 481.

44. Gouget and Le Hête, *Les Comtes de Blois et de Champagne* (2004), 162–63.

45. Douët d'Arcq, *Recherches historiques et critiques sur les anciens comtes de Beaumont-sur-Oise*, cxxviii–cxxxi; Newman, *Seigneurs de Nesle*, 1:217, 220–21.

46. Woehl, *Volo vincere*, 144–48. Also, in 1226 he acquitted to the king his hunting rights in the forest of Cuise (near Compiègne); see *Registres*, 539.

47. Bugslag, "Ideology and Iconography in Chartres Cathedral."

48. Guillaume le Breton, *Gesta*, ed. Delaborde, 264–65; Guillaume le Breton, *Philippidos*, ed. Delaborde, 295; Baldwin, *Government*, 113.

49. Register E (AN JJ 26), fol. 223vb: "Ego Johannes marescallus domini Ludovici regis Francorum notum facio . . . me super sacrosancta iurasse . . . quod non retinebo equos nec palefridos nec roncinos redditos ad opus meum ratione ministerii mei quod habeo de dono ipsius domini regis nec ego neque heredes reclamabimus marescalciam iure hereditario tenendam et habendam. . . . Actum apud Suessionem . . . 1223 mense augusto."

50. Gaignières drawing with seal of Robert de Beaumont, Paris, BnF Est., Rés. Pe 1p, fol. 70; Bouchot I, no. 3780. He was also identified in a charter of Saint-Chéron de Chartres of 1239: SChé, fol. 207.

51. Salch, *L'Atlas des châteaux forts en France*, 284; Cottineau, *Répertoire topo-bibliographique des abbayes et prieurés* (1936–39), 1:306 (Beaumont-les-Autels). Unfortunately the archives of the priory do not provide clues to the identity of Robert.

52. Thompson, *Power and Border Lordship in Medieval France* (2002), 70–71, 146. Their activities and names can be found in the cartularies of Saint-Père de Chartres (SPC), Sainte-Trinité de Tiron (STri) and Saint-Denis de Nogent-le-Rotrou (*Saint-Denis de Nogent-le-Rotrou, 1031–1789*, ed. Métais).

53. Jos, 1:358 (1202); STri, 2:117–18 (1202); Longnon, *Les Compagnons de Villehardouin*, 107.

54. Jos, 1:373 (1211–19); *Obituaires*, 2:116; a Reginald de Beaumont, canon of Chartres, was listed as a "vir siquidem nobilis genere, de nobilioribus castellanis dyocesis Carnotensis" (ibid., 101).

55. *La Chanson de la croisade Albigeoise*, ed. Gougaud (1989), 397, 413, 423, 425, 455. See also Woehl, *Volo vincere*, 174–75, who links him with a brother named Ponce.

56. SPCBN (cartulary of Saint-Père de Chartres assembled by Gaignières), pp. 80, 236.

57. VdC, 1:171, 186 (1208, 1212).

58. *Scriptum feodorum de Monteforti*, ed. Dor, no. 79.

59. In the *Violette* Gerbert de Montreuil creates a fictional tournament at Montargis convoked by Louis VIII, as we have seen. Among the royal party were found the counts of Montfort (v. 5912), Brittany (v. 5914), and Boulogne (v. 5921), all of whom were represented at Chartres; see Baldwin, *Aristocratic Life*, 63–64.

60. Douët d'Arcq II, no. 7150.

61. Lautier, "Les Vitraux de la cathédrale de Chartres" (2003), 31–32.

62. Compare with the seal of Henri II, count of Bar, nephew of Bishop Renaud, Douët d'Arcq I, no. 796 (1230); for Bishop Renaud's episcopal seal, which depicted him standing with a crozier, in the act of blessing, see Douët d'Arcq II, no. 6567. Renaud and his father Renaud, count of Bar, and his mother Agnès, and his brother Henri I, count of Bar, appear in the chapter's obituary: *Obituaires*, 2:77, 177. See above, note 19, on the heraldry in the windows.

63. Douët d'Arcq II, no. 3928 (Robert de Vitry, 1161).

64. Pastoureau, *Les Emblèmes de la France* (1998), 32–33, 121–29.

65. Pastoureau, *Traité d'héraldique*, 303. See also above, Chapter 2, 60–62, and Chapter 3, 70–73.

66. The only crusader to appear as such in the windows of Chartres is Charlemagne who fought the Saracens in Spain (no. 7), but he also is without a cross.

67. Pastoureau, "Le Décor héraldique des clefs de voûte de la cathédrale de Chartres" (2011).

Appendix 2. Genealogies

1. Beaumont: Douët d'Arcq, *Recherches historiques et critiques sur les anciens comtes de Beaumont-sur-Oise*, lxiv–cxxx; *Registres*, 530–32; Baldwin, "The Aristocracy in the Paris Region," pt. 1, p. 64; Civel, *La Fleur de France*, 127–28, 375, 425.

2. Vermandois and Valois: Carolus-Barré, "Une arrière petite-fille de Hugues Capet, Aliénor de Vermandois"; Borrelli de Serres, *La Réunion des provinces septentrionales à la couronne par Philippe Auguste*; Civel, *La Fleur*, 432–33.

3. Flanders: Nicholas, *Medieval Flanders* (1992), 441; Gilbert of Mons, *Chronicle of Hainaut*, trans. Napran (Woodbridge, 2005), 52–53; Baldwin, *Government*, 200–202, 269–70.

4. Dreux: Duchesne, *Dreux*, 13–82; Civel, *La Fleur*, 434.

5. Montfort: Power, *The Norman Frontier*, 498; Maddicott, *Simon de Montfort* (1996), xxiv–xxv, 3; Baldwin, *Government*, 110; Civel, *La Fleur*, 185, 450–51.

6. Montmorency and Montmorency-Marly: Duchesne, *Histoire généalogique de la maison de Montmorency et de Laval* (1624), 105–11, 118–20, 145–60, 661–66; Maquet, *Les Seigneurs de Marly*; Abb, nos. 45 (1224), 79 (1236), 86 (1238); Civel, *La Fleur*, 455–56.

7. Garlande (Tournan): Mathieu, "La Famille de Garlande à Possesse" (1993); Bournazel, *Le Gouvernement Capétien* (1975), 39–40; Civel, *La Fleur*, 436–37. Mathieu's schema is shown here. For Agnès de Garlande's husbands, see the notes on genealogies 15 (Poissy) and 18 (Andresel).

8. Garlande (Livry): Brière, "Une alliance familial entre les Garlande, les Mauvoisin et les Mello au XIIe siècle;" Newman, *Les Seigneurs de Nesle*, 1:193–97, 217–20, 264–66; Bournazel, *Le Gouvernement Capétien*, 35–40; Civel, *La Fleur*, 192–96, 330, 436–37. In addition, see the sources cited above in note 16 of Chapter 3, and SMCps, vol. 3, no. 621. There is disagreement on the generation between Guillaume-Helisende and Guillaume-Idoine. The conclusions of Brière are shown here in preference over Bournazel's. On Idoine, the wife of Guillaume de Garlande (d. <1200), see the note on Genealogy 12.

9. Nesle: Newman, *Les Seigneurs de Nesle*, 1:33–50, 59–80, chart following p. 287.

10. Chevreuse: Moutié, *Chevreuse*, 2:99–181; Civel, *La Fleur*, 34–42, 452.

11. Île-Adam: Depoin, in SMPo, 418–22; Darras, *Les Seigneurs-châtelains de l'Île-Adam*; Civel, *La Fleur*, 439. Clémence de Pomponne was the daughter of Hugues de Pomponne (see Genealogy 8).

12. Gisors: Depoin, in SMPo, 407–17; Le Père Anselme, *Histoire généalogique et chronologique de la maison royale de France* (Paris, 1712), 1:506; Civel, *La Fleur*, 438. Depoin and Civel consider Idoine, the wife of Guillaume de Garlande (d. <1200), to be the sister of Jean de Gisors (d. 1216). Le Père Anselme considered Idoine, the wife of Guillaume de Garlande, to be the daughter of Marguerite de Gisors, who was the sister of Hugues (d. 1148) and Thibaut (d. >1183) de Gisors.

13. Dreux de Mello: Brière, "Une alliance familiale entre les Garlande, les Máuvoisin et les Mello au XIIe siècle;" Newman, *Les Seigneurs de Nesle*, 1:264–66; Power, *The Norman Frontier*, 358 n. 111. Power entertains the possibility that the half-brother of Guillaume-Idoine and Robert de Mauvoisin (d. 1177) was not Dreux the constable, as shown here, but Dreux the constable's father. As mentioned above (note 8), Bournazel, *Le Gouvernement Capétien*, 35–40, presents an alternative to the schema of Brière and Newman.

14. The Chamberlains (Nemours and Méréville): Richemond, *Recherches généalogiques sur la famille des seigneurs de Nemours*.

15. Poissy: The genealogy of the Gace branch of the Poissy family is based on Abb, nos. 5, 10, 11, 17, 24, 32, 40, 45, 50, 65, 83, 85, 86 (1184–1238); Joy, no. 34 (1227); Depoin, in SMPo, 355–58, 437, 439. See also Civel, *La Fleur*, 198–99, 333–34, 428. A Guillaume de Poissy (above, Chapter 7, 134 and 139), not shown in the genealogy, appears to have been the youngest son of Gace and Jacqueline: Abb, no. 28 (1208); no. 80 (1226 or 1236); SVP, fols. 54r–56v. The Guillaume de Poissy buried at Notre-Dame de Poissy, however (above, Chapter 8, 166–68), appears to have belonged to the Simon branch of the Poissy family, given his heraldry. The Simon branch of the Poissy family follows Depoin, in SMPo, 420, 429–39, with one difference. Depoin numbered the succession of the three Simons as Simon II, III and IV and believed Simon IV married Agnès de Garlande (d'Andresel) and died shortly after making his testament in 1243. However, it is likely that Simon de Poissy who married Agnès de Garlande died ca. 1223, and his son authored the testament of 1243. On Simon II (d. <1189) and his wife Mathilde, see *Actes*, vol. 2, nos. 250 and 251 (1189). For Simon III and his wife Agnès, see for example NDP, 2:13 (1201); SJVa, 77–78 (1208); above, 48–49 and note 237 of Chapter 2 (1209). Two charters of Philip Augustus likely followed shortly after Simon III's death: *Actes*, vol. 4, no. 1568 (1219) and no. 1625 (1220). On Simon IV and Agnès de Garlande (d'Andresel), see SMCux, no. 31 (1218); Abb, no. 41 (1220); SMCux, nos. 1–4 (1222); and *Registres*, 529 (Simon's liege homage to Philip Augustus for the fortress of Aigremont, 1223). Between 1218 and 1222 Agnès de Garlande

(d'Andresel) appeared in charters with Simon de Poissy. Thereafter, she acted without Simon (e.g., SJVa, no. 214, a gift to the church at Aigremont, 1224).

16. Mauvoisin: Power, *The Norman Frontier*, 254–55, 507; Newman, *Les Seigneurs de Nesle*, 1:264–66; Depoin, in SMPo, 250–69; Civel, *La Fleur*, 441. See also Brière, "Une alliance familiale entre les Garlande, les Mauvoisin et les Mello au XIIe siècle," 9–12, who argues that the paternal grandfather of Robert Mauvoisin (married Cécile de Chevreuse, d. 1217) was Raoul (d. >1158) and not Raoul's brother Robert (d. ca. 1134). On Pierre Mauvoisin's date of death, see Power, 507.

17. Corbeil: Depoin, "Les Vicomtes de Corbeil et les chevaliers d'Étampes au XIIe siècle," 23, 29–35, and *pièces justificatives*, 61–69, nos. 23–40; Moutié, *Chevreuse*, 136; Civel, *La Fleur*, 429. For Aelis de Corbeil in genealogies 17 and 18, see Depoin, in SMPo, 420; Depoin, "Les Vicomtes de Corbeil," 30–31 and *pièce justificative* no. 32 (1196); NDBP, no. 1 (1190); SSC, 156; and SMPo, no. 157 (ca. 1166).

18. Andresel: For Aelis de Corbeil and her son Aubert d'Andresel, see above, note 17; for Agnès de Garlande (d'Andresel) and Simon de Poissy (d. ca. 1223), see above, note 15; for Agnès and her husband Aubert d'Andresel, see Leroy, "Le Refuge de Barbeau" (1865), 194 (charter dated 1183), and Lebeuf, *Histoire de la ville et de tout le diocèse de Paris*, 5:323, 423; for Agnès and Aubert's sons and their wives, see SMCux, nos. 1–4, 31, 38, 39 (1218–1224), and Abb, no. 48 (1224). The identification of Agnès d'Andresel (*Agnes domina de Andesello*) as Agnès de Garlande, daughter of Anseau-Rance de Garlande, is based in part on Agnès d'Andresel's mentions of Anseau de Garlande as her nephew (*nepos*) in various of the above charters. The nephew of Agnès de Garlande was Anseau, son of Anseau (d. 1200) and Sophie (Genealogy 7).

Bibliography

Cartularies and Charter Collections of Monasteries and Churches

Asterisks indicate the thirty-two cartularies (plus OurBN as a supplement to OurPD) from which the sample of 1,729 charters is taken. Foundations are abbeys of monks unless noted otherwise.

AB — Abbaye-aux-Bois (Cistercian nuns): *Le Chartrier de l'Abbaye-aux-Bois (1202–1311)*. Ed. Brigitte Pipon. Mémoires et documents de l'École des chartes 46. Paris, 1996.

*Abb — Abbecourt (Premonstratensian regular canons): *Abbecourt-en-Pinserais, monastère de l'orde de Prémontré*. Ed. Joseph Depoin. Pontoise, 1913.

*Bar — Barbeau (Cistercian): Cartulary of the abbey of Barbeau. Paris, BnF lat. 10943.

Bar 5466 — Barbeau: Cartulary of the abbey of Barbeau. Paris, BnF lat. 5466.

*Cha — Chaalis (Cistercian): Cartulary of the abbey of Chaalis. Paris, BnF lat. 11003.

CSH — Conflans-Sainte-Honorine (Benedictine priory): "Les Comtes de Beaumont-sur-Oise et le prieuré de Conflans-Sainte-Honorine." Ed. Joseph Depoin. *Mémoires de la Société historique et archéologique de Pontoise et du Vexin* 33 (1915): 1–262.

FLN — Fontaines-les-Nonnes (priory of Fontevraud, nuns): Cartulary of the priory Notre-Dame de Fontaines-les-Nonnes. Bibl. mun. de Meaux, MS 68 (62).

*HDP — Hôtel-Dieu de Paris: *Archives de l'Hôtel-Dieu de Paris (1157–1300)*. Ed. Léon Brièle. Paris, 1894.

Hér — Héronval (Cistercian priory of Longpont): *Cartulaire d'Héronval publié par le Comité archéologique de Noyon*. Noyon, 1883.

HVND — Hôpital de l'abbaye du Val-Notre-Dame: "Cartulaire de l'hôpital de l'abbaye du Val-Notre-Dame au diocèse de Paris (XIIIe siècle)." Ed. Henri Omont. *Mémoires de la Société de l'histoire de Paris et de l'Ile-de-France* 30 (1903): 127–74.

Jos — Notre-Dame de Josaphat (north of Chartres, Benedictine): *Cartulaire de Notre-Dame de Josaphat*. Ed. Charles Métais. 2 vols. Chartres, 1911–12.

Joy — Joyenval (Premonstratensian regular canons): "Recueil des principales chartes de l'abbaye de Joyenval." Ed. Adolphe Dutilleux. *Mémoires de la Société historique et archéologique de l'arrondissement de Pontoise et du Vexin* 13 (1890): 74–114.

*LonA — Longpont (dép. Aisne, Cistercian): Cartulary of the abbey of Longpont. Paris, BnF lat. 11005.

Mon — Montmartre (north of Paris, Benedictine nuns): *Recueil des chartes de l'abbaye royale de Montmartre*. Ed. Edouard de Barthélemy. Paris, 1883.

Mor — Morienval (Benedictine nuns): *Cartulaire de l'abbaye de Morienval*. Ed. A. Peigné-Delacourt. Senlis, 1879.

Mori   Morigny (Benedictine): *Morigny: Son abbaye, sa chronique et son cartulaire.* Ed. Ernest Menault. Paris, 1867.

*MSM   Mont-Saint-Martin (Premonstratensian regular canons): Cartulary of the abbey of Mont-Saint-Martin. Paris, BnF lat. 5478.

NDBP   Notre-Dame de Bon-Port (Pont-de-l'Arche, Cistercian): *Cartulaire de l'abbaye royale de Notre-Dame de Bon-Port.* Ed. J. Andrieux. Évreux, 1862.

NDC   Notre-Dame de Chartres (cathedral church): *Cartulaire de Notre-Dame de Chartres.* Ed. E. de Lépinois and Lucien Merlet. 3 vols. Chartres, 1862–65.

NDM   Notre-Dame des Moulineaux (Grandmontine priory): *Recueil de chartes et pièces relatives au prieuré Notre-Dame des Moulineaux.* Ed. Auguste Moutié. Paris, 1846.

*NDP   Notre-Dame de Paris (cathedral church): *Cartulaire de l'église de Notre-Dame de Paris.* Ed. Benjamin Guérard. 4 vols. Paris, 1850.

*NDR   Notre-Dame de la Roche (regular canons): *Cartulaire de l'abbaye de Notre-Dame de la Roche.* Ed. Auguste Moutié. Paris, 1862.

NLH   Nanteuil-le-Haudouin (priory of Cluny): Cartulary of the priory of Nanteuil-le-Haudouin. Arch. dép. 60 (Beauvais, dép. Oise), H 2650.

*Noy   Noyon (cathedral church): Cartulary of the chapter of Noyon. Arch. dép. 60 (Beauvais, dép. Oise), G 1984.

*OurBN   Ourscamp (Cistercian): Cartulary of the abbey of Notre-Dame d'Ourscamp assembled by Roger de Gaignières. Paris, BnF lat. 5473.

*OurPD   Ourscamp: *Cartulaire de l'abbaye de Notre-Dame d'Ourscamp.* Ed. A. Peigné-Delacourt. Documents inédits de la Société des antiquaires de Picardie 6. Amiens, 1865.

*Por   Porrois (Cistercian nuns): *Cartulaire de l'abbaye de Porrois au diocèse de Paris, plus connue sous son nom mystique Port-Royal.* Vol. 1, *1204–1280.* Ed. Adolphe de Dion. Paris, 1903.

Pré   Prémontré (regular canons): Cartulary of the abbey of Notre-Dame et Saint-Jean-Baptiste de Prémontré. Bibl. mun. de Soissons, MS 7.

Preuilly *Chartes et documents de l'abbaye cistercienne de Preuilly.* Ed. Albert Catel and Maurice Lecomte. Montereau, 1927.

*SA   Saint-Antoine (Paris, Cistercian nuns): Cartulary of the abbey of Saint-Antoine. Paris, AN LL 1595.

*SCC   Saint-Corneille de Compiègne (Benedictine): *Cartulaire de l'abbaye de Saint-Corneille de Compiègne,* vol. 1, *877–1216,* and vol. 2, *1218–1260.* Ed. Émile Morel. Montdidier and Paris, 1904 and 1909.

*SCCha   Saint-Crépin-en-Chaye (Soissons, Arrouaisian regular canons): Cartulary of the abbey of Saint-Crépin-en-Chaye. Paris, BnF lat. 18372.

SChé   Saint-Chéron de Chartres (regular canons): Copies of charters and other documents pertaining to the abbey of Saint-Chéron de Chartres, assembled in 1860 by E. Lefèvre. Paris, BnF Nouv. acq. lat. 1409.

*SD   Saint-Denis (Benedictine): Cartulaire blanc of the abbey of Saint-Denis. Paris, AN LL 1157 (vol. 1), LL 1158 (vol. 2).

SFP   Saint-Fursy de Péronne (collegiate church): *Charters of St. Fursy of Péronne.* Ed. William Mendel Newman and Mary Rouse. Cambridge, Mass., 1977.

SGA   Saint-Germain l'Auxerrois (Paris, collegiate church): Cartulary of the chapter of Saint-Germain-l'Auxerrois. Paris, AN LL 387.

SGAux   Saint-Germain d'Auxerre (Benedictine): Grand cartulaire of the abbey of Saint-Germain d'Auxerre. Auxerre, Bibl. mun., MS 161.

*SGM   Sainte-Geneviève-du-Mont (Paris, regular canons): Cartulary of the abbey of Sainte-Geneviève de Paris. Paris, Bibliothèque Sainte-Geneviève MS 356.

*SGP Saint-Germain-des-Prés (Paris, Benedictine): *Recueil des chartes de l'abbaye de Saint-Germain-des-Prés des origines au début du XIIIe siècle*, vol. 1, *558–1182*, and vol. 2, *1183–1216*. Ed. René Poupardin. Paris, 1909, 1932.

SJVa Saint-Jean-en-Vallée (regular canons): *Cartulaire de Saint-Jean-en-Vallée de Chartres*. Ed. René Merlet. Collection de cartulaires chartrains 1. Chartres, 1906.

*SJVi Saint-Jean-des-Vignes (regular canons, Soissons): Cartulary of the abbey of Saint-Jean-des-Vignes. Paris, BnF lat. 11004.

*SLE Saint-Leu d'Esserent (Benedictine priory): *Le Prieuré de Saint-Leu d'Esserent: Cartulaire (1080–1538)*. Ed. Eugène Müller. Pontoise, 1901.

*SLP Saint-Lazare de Paris (leprosarium, priory of regular canons): *Recueil d'actes de Saint-Lazare de Paris (1124–1254)*. Ed. Simone Lefèvre and Lucie Fossier. Documents, études et répertoires publiés par l'Institut de recherche et d'histoire des textes 75. Paris, 2005.

SLS Saint-Léger de Soissons (regular canons): *Cartulaire de l'abbaye de Saint-Léger de Soissons*. Ed. l'Abbé Pécheur. Soissons, 1870.

*SMCps Saint-Martin-des-Champs (priory of Cluny): *Recueil de chartes et documents de Saint-Martin-des-Champs, monastère parisien*. Ed. Joseph Depoin. 5 vols. Paris, 1912–21.

*SMCux Saint-Martin de Champeaux (collegiate church): *Le Chartrier de la collégiale de Saint-Martin de Champeaux*. Ed. Jean Dufour. Hautes études médiévales et modernes 94. Geneva, 2009.

*SMF Saint-Maur-des-Fossés (Benedictine): Livre noir of the abbey of Notre-Dame de Saint-Maur-des-Fossés. Paris, AN LL 46.

SMPo Saint-Martin de Pontoise (Benedictine): *Cartulaire de l'abbaye de Saint-Martin de Pontoise*. Ed. Joseph Depoin. Sociéte historique du Vexin. Pontoise, 1895–1909.

SMPoCh Saint-Martin de Pontoise: *Chartrier de l'abbaye de Saint-Martin de Pontoise (1200–1250)*. Ed. Joseph Depoin. Société historique du Vexin. Pontoise, 1911.

*SMS Saint-Médard de Soissons (Benedictine): Cartulary of the abbey of Saint-Médard de Soissons, *Cartularium novum*. Paris, BnF lat. 9986.

SNM Saint-Nicaise de Meulan (Benedictine priory): *Recueil des chartes de Saint-Nicaise de Meulan, prieuré de l'ordre du Bec*. Ed. Emile Houth. Paris, Pontoise, 1924.

*SNR Saint-Nicolas de Ribemont (Benedictine): *Cartulaire de l'ancienne abbaye de Saint-Nicolas-des-Prés sous Ribemont*. Ed. Henri Stein. Saint-Quentin, 1884.

SPC Saint-Père de Chartres (Benedictine): *Cartulaire de l'abbaye de Saint-Père de Chartres*. Ed. Benjamin Guérard. 2 vols. Paris, 1840.

SPCBN Saint-Père de Chartres: Cartulary of the abbey of Saint-Père de Chartres assembled by Roger de Gaignières. Paris, BnF lat. 5417.

*SQ Saint-Quentin (collegiate church): Livre rouge of the collegiate church of Saint-Quentin. Paris, AN LL 985B.

SSC Saint-Spire de Corbeil (collegiate church): *Cartulaire de Saint-Spire de Corbeil au diocèse de Paris*. Ed. Émile Coüard-Luys. Rambouillet, 1882.

*STÉ Saint-Thomas d'Épernon (Benedictine priory): *Cartulaires de Saint-Thomas d'Épernon et de Notre-Dame de Maintenon, prieurés dépendant de l'abbaye de Marmoutier*. Ed. Auguste Moutié and Adolphe de Dion. Rambouillet, 1878.

STri Sainte-Trinité de Tiron (Thiron-Gardais, Benedictine): *Cartulaire de l'abbaye de la Sainte-Trinité de Tiron*. Ed. Lucien Merlet. 2 vols. Chartres, 1883.

*SVP Saint-Victor de Paris (regular canons): Cartulary of Saint-Victor de Paris. Paris, AN LL 1450A.

*SYB   Saint-Yved de Braine (Premonstratensian regular canons): *Le Chartrier de l'abbaye prémontrée de Saint-Yved de Braine, 1134–1250.* Ed. Olivier Guyotjeannin. Mémoires et documents de l'École des Chartes 49. Paris, 2000.

*VdC   Vaux-de-Cernay (Cistercian): *Cartulaire de l'abbaye de Notre-Dame des Vaux de Cernay de l'ordre de Cîteaux au diocèse de Paris.* Ed. Lucien Merlet and Auguste Moutié. 2 vols. Paris, 1857–58.

*VND   Val-Notre-Dame (Cistercian): Cartulary of the abbey of Val-Notre-Dame. Paris, AN LL 1541.

*Yer   Yerres (Benedictine nuns): Cartulary of the abbey of Notre-Dame d'Yerres. Paris, AN LL 1599B.

Cartularies and charter collections consulted but not cited specifically include the following:

Beaupré (Cistercian): Cartulary of the abbey of Beaupré. Paris, BnF lat. 9973.

Étampes (collegiate church): *Cartulaire de Notre-Dame d'Étampes.* Ed. J. M. Alliot. Documents publié par la Société historique et archéologique du Gâtinais 3. Paris, 1888.

Hôtel-Dieu de Beauvais: *Cartulaire de l'Hôtel-Dieu de Beauvais.* Ed. Victor Leblond. Publications de la Société académique de l'Oise 4. Paris, 1919.

Hôtel-Dieu de Pontoise: *Cartulaire de l'Hôtel-Dieu de Pontoise.* Ed. Joseph Depoin. Pontoise, 1886.

Longpont (dép. Essonne, east of Montlhéry, priory of Cluny): Cartulary of the priory of Longpont. Paris, BnF nouv. acq. lat. 932.

Saint-Christophe-en-Halatte (north of Senlis, priory of Cluny): *Cartulaire du prieuré de Saint-Christophe-en-Halatte.* Ed. A. Vattier. Senlis, 1876.

Saint-Germain-en-Laye (north of Marly-le-Roi, Benedictine priory): "Le Prieuré de Saint-Germain-en-Laye. Origines et cartulaire." Ed. Joseph Depoin. *Bulletin de la Commission des antiquités et des arts de Seine-et-Oise* 15 (1895): 102–29.

Saint-Jean-en-l'Isle à Corbeil (Hospitaler commandery): "Le Prieuré de Saint-Jean-en-l'Île-lez-Corbeil." Ed. Jean-Marc Roger. *Paris et Ile-de-France, Mémoires* 60 (2009): 177–291.

Saint-Laurent de Montfort-l'Amaury (Benedictine priory): "Le Prieuré de Saint-Laurent de Montfort-l'Amaury." Ed. Adolphe de Dion, *Mémoires et documents publiés par la Société archéologique de Rambouillet* 8 (1887–88): 127–259.

Saint-Magloire (Benedictine, Paris): *Chartes et documents de l'abbaye de Saint-Magloire.* Tome 1, *Fin du Xe siècle–1280.* Ed. Anne Terroine, Lucie Fossier, and Yvonne de Montenon. Documents, études et répertoires publiés par l'Institut de recherche et d'histoire des textes. Paris, 1998.

Saint-Merry de Paris (collegiate church): "Cartulaire et censier de Saint-Merry de Paris." Ed. Léon Cadier and Camille Couderc. *Mémoires de la Société de l'histoire de Paris et de l'Ile-de-France* 18 (1891): 101–271.

Saint-Remy-lès-Senlis (Benedictine nuns): Cartulary of the abbey of Saint-Remy-lès-Senlis. Paris, BnF lat. 11002.

Other Manuscripts and Archival Documents

Beauvais, Arch. dép. 60 (dép. Oise), H 2850 (materials from the priory of Saint-Arnoul de Crépy-en-Valois regarding Chézy-en-Orxois).

Bobigny, Arch. dép. 93 (dép. Seine-Saint-Denis), cotes 93/67–72. Fonds de Livry.

Paris, Archives nationales

Série J, Trésor des chartes, Layettes: J 168 (Beaumont-sur-Oise); J 394 (*Securitates*).

Série JJ, Trésor des chartes, Registres: JJ 7 (Register C); JJ 26 (Register E).

Série L, Monuments ecclésiastiques, cartons: L 460 (Saint-Maur-des-Fossés); L 850 (materials from Saint-Denis regarding Montmorency); L 887 (materials from Sainte-Geneviève de Paris regarding Roissy-en-France); L 944 (Val-Notre-Dame); L 1014 (Abbaye Saint-Antoine).

Série S, Biens des établissements religieux supprimés: S 1175 (Saint-Maur-des-Fossés); S 1186 (Saint-Éloi, priory of Saint-Maur-des-Fossés); S 1354 (Saint-Martin-des-Champs); S 1570 (Sainte-Geneviève-du-Mont); S 2071, S 2127 (Saint-Victor de Paris); S 2309, S 2402 (Saint-Denis); S 4185, S 4197, S 4201 (Val-Notre-Dame); S 4952 (Knights Hospitalers).

Série T, Papiers privés tombés dans le domaine public: T 269 (Roissy).

Paris, Bibliothèque Sainte-Geneviève, MS 351.

Paris, BnF, Département des estampes et de la photographie, Collection Gaignières. Drawings of tombs, seals and windows in volumes Oa 9, Pc 18, Pe 1, Pe 1a, Pe 1b, Pe 1c, Pe 1e, Pe 1o, Pe 1p, Pe 5, Pe 6, and Pe 11a.

Senlis, Bibl. mun., Collection Afforty, vol. 15.

Vatican City, Biblioteca Apostolica Vaticana, Ottoboni lat. 2796. Register A.

Other Primary Sources

Actes de Pierre de Dreux, duc de Bretagne (1213–1237). Ed. Marjolaine Lémeillat. Rennes, 2013.

Alexandre de Paris. *Le Roman d'Alexandre*. Trans. Laurence Harf-Lancner, ed. E. C. Armstrong et al. Paris, 1994.

Andreas Capellanus. *Andreas Capellanus on Love*. Ed. and trans. P. G. Walsh. London, 1982.

Anonymous of Béthune. *Extrait d'une chronique française des rois de France par un anonyme de Béthune*. Ed. Léopold Delisle. In *RHF* 24:750–75. Paris, 1904.

———. *Histoire des ducs de Normandie et des rois d'Angleterre*. Ed. Francisque Michel. Paris, 1840.

Aubry de Trois-Fontaines. *Chronica*. Ed. P. Scheffer-Boichorst. In MGH, Scriptores, 23:631–950. Hannover, 1874.

Bernard of Pavia. *Summa decretalium*. Ed. E. A. T. Laspeyres. Regensburg, 1860.

Cartulaire général de l'ordre des Hospitaliers de S. Jean de Jérusalem. Ed. Joseph Delaville Le Roulx. 4 vols. Paris, 1894–1906.

The Cartulary of Countess Blanche of Champagne. Ed. Theodore Evergates. Medieval Academy Books 112. Toronto, 2009.

La Chanson de la croisade Albigeoise. Ed. and trans. Henri Gougaud. Lettres gothiques. Paris, 1989.

Chansons attribuées au Chastelain de Couci (fin du XIIe–début du XIIIe siècle). Ed. Alain Lerond. Paris, 1964.

Les Chansons de croisade avec leurs mélodies. Ed. Joseph Bédier and Pierre Aubry. Paris, 1909.

Chartes Vendômoises. Ed. Charles Métais. Société archéologique, scientifique et littéraire du Vendômois. Vendôme, 1905.

Chartularium universitatis Parisiensis. Vol. 1. Ed. Heinrich Denifle and Émile Châtelain. Paris, 1889.

Chrétien de Troyes. *Le Chevalier au lion (Yvain)*. Ed. Mario Roques. Les Classiques français du Moyen Âge, no. 89. Paris, 1982.

———. *Le Chevalier de la charrette*. Ed. Mario Roques. Les Classiques français du Moyen Âge, no. 86. Paris, 1983.

———. *Cligès*. Ed. Alexandre Micha. Les Classiques français du Moyen Âge, no. 84. Paris, 1978.

———. *Le Conte du Graal (Perceval)*. Ed. Félix Lecoy. 2 vols. Les Classiques français du Moyen Âge, nos. 100 and 103. Paris, 1984, 1990.

———. *Erec et Enide*. Ed. Mario Roques. Les Classiques français du Moyen Âge, no. 80. Paris, 1970.

Conon de Béthune. *Les Chansons de Conon de Béthune*. Ed. Axel Wallensköld. Paris, 1921.

Documents relatifs au comté de Champagne et de Brie, 1172–1361. Ed. Auguste Longnon. 3 vols. Paris, 1901–14.

Ernald of Bonneval. *S. Bernardi Vita prima: Liber secundus*. In PL, vol. 185, cols. 267–302. Paris, 1879.

L'Estoire de Eracles empereur et la conqueste de la terre d'outremer. Recueil des historiens des croisades, Historiens occidentaux, 2:1–481. Paris, 1859.

Gace Brulé. *Gace Brulé, trouvère champenois: Édition des chansons et étude historique.* Ed. Holger
Petersen Dyggve. Mémoires de la Société Néophilologique de Helsinki 16. Helsinki, 1951.

———. *The Lyrics and Melodies of Gace Brulé.* Ed. and trans. Samuel Rosenberg and Samuel Danon;
music ed. Hendrik van der Werf. Garland Library of Medieval Literature, vol. 39, ser. A. New
York, 1985.

Geoffroi de Villehardouin. *La Conquête de Constantinople.* Ed. Edmond Faral. 2 vols. Paris, 1973.

Gerald of Wales. *Gemma ecclesiastica.* Ed. J. S. Brewer. In *Giraldi Cambrensis Opera,* vol. 2. London,
1862.

Gerbert de Montreuil. *La Continuation de Perceval.* Ed. Mary Williams and Marguerite Oswald. 3
vols. Les Classiques français du Moyen Âge, nos. 28, 50, 101. Paris, 1922, 1925, 1975.

———. *Le Roman de la Violette ou de Gerart de Nevers.* Ed. Douglas Labaree Buffum. Société des
anciens textes français. Paris, 1928.

*Gesta Regis Henrici Secundi Benedicti Abbatis: Chronicle of the Reigns of Henry II and Richard I,
A.D. 1169-1192, Known Commonly Under the Name of Benedict of Peterborough.* Ed. William
Stubbs. 2 vols. London, 1867.

Gislebert de Mons [Gilbert of Mons]. *Chronicle of Hainaut.* Trans. Laura Napran. Woodbridge, 2005.

———. *La Chronique de Gislebert de Mons.* Ed. Léon Vanderkindere. Brussels, 1904.

Guillaume le Breton. *Gesta.* In *Œuvres de Rigord et de Guillaume le Breton,* ed. Henri-François
Delaborde, 1:168–333. Paris, 1882.

———. *Philippidos.* In *Œuvres de Rigord et de Guillaume le Breton,* ed. Henri-François Delaborde,
vol. 2. Paris, 1885.

Hélinand de Froidmont. *Les Vers de la mort: Poème du XIIe siècle.* Trans. Michel Boyer and Monique Santucci. Paris, 1983.

———. "The *Verses on Death* by Hélinant de Froidmont." Trans. William D. Paden, Jr. *Allegorica* 3,
no. 2 (1978): 63–103.

Histoire de Guillaume le Maréchal. Ed. A. J. Holden, with English translation by S. Gregory and
historical notes by D. Couch, as *History of William Marshal.* 3 vols. Anglo-Norman Text Society, Occasional Publications, nos. 4–6. London, 2002–6.

*L'Histoire de Guillaume le Maréchal, comte de Striguil et de Pembroke, régent d'Angleterre de 1216 à
1219.* Ed. Paul Meyer. 3 vols. Paris, 1891–1901.

Hue de Rotelande. *Ipomedon: Poème de Hue de Rotelande, fin du XIIe siècle.* Ed. A. J. Holden. Paris,
1979.

Huon d'Oisi. *Tournoiement des dames.* In *Ludi e spettacoli nel medioevo: I tornei di dame,* ed. Andrea
Pulega, 3–9. Milan, 1970.

Itinerarium peregrinorum et gesta regis Ricardi. Ed. William Stubbs. Chronicles and Memorials of
the Reign of Richard I, vol. 1. London, 1864.

Jean le Marchant: Miracles de Notre-Dame de Chartres. Ed. Pierre Kunstmann. Ottawa, 1973.

Jean Renart. *L'Escoufle: Roman d'aventure.* Ed. Franklin Sweetser. Textes littéraires français 211.
Geneva, 1974.

———. *Le Lai de l'ombre.* Ed. Félix Lecoy. Les Classiques français du Moyen Âge, no. 104. Paris, 1979.

———. *Le Roman de la Rose; ou, Guillaume de Dole.* Ed. Félix Lecoy. Les Classiques français du
Moyen Âge, no. 91. Paris, 1979.

Jean, sire de Joinville. *Histoire de Saint Louis, Credo, et Lettre à Louis X.* Ed. Natalis de Wailly. Paris,
1874.

Lambert d'Ardres. *Historia comitum Ghisnensium.* Ed. J. Heller. In MGH, Scriptores, 24:550–642.
Hannover, 1889.

———. *The History of the Counts of Guines and Lords of Ardres.* Trans. Leah Shopkow. Philadelphia, 2001.

Layettes du Trésor des Chartes. Ed. Alexandre Teulet. Vols. 1 and 2. Paris, 1863–66.

Littere Baronum: The Earliest Cartulary of the Counts of Champagne. Ed. Theodore Evergates. Medieval Academy Books 107. Toronto, 2003.

Le Livre de terres et de revenus de Pierre du Thillay, fondateur de l'Hôtel-Dieu de Gonesse, bailli de Caen de 1205 à 1224: Ses terres en Île-de-France et en Basse-Normandie. Ed. John W. Baldwin. Cahiers Léopold Delisle 51, fascs. 1–2. Paris, 2002.

Martinus. *De iure dotium tractatus.* In Hermann Kantorowicz, *Studies in the Glossators of Roman Law,* 255–66. Oxford, 1938.

Matthew Paris. *Chronica majora.* Ed. Henry Richards Luard. 7 vols. Rerum Brittanicarum Medii Aevi Scriptores. London, 1872–83.

———. *Historia Anglorum.* Ed. Frederic Madden. 3 vols. Rerum Brittanicarum Medii Aevi Scriptores. London, 1866–69.

"Les Miracles de Notre-Dame de Chartres: Texte Latin inédit." Ed. Antoine Thomas. *Bibliothèque de l'École des Chartes* 42 (1881): 505–50.

Nomina militum LX libratas redditus habentium. Ed. Léopold Delisle. In *RHF* 23:686–89 (nos. 369–93). Paris, 1894.

Obituaires de la province de Sens. Tome 1 (Diocèse de Sens et de Paris, 2 vols.) and tome 2 (Diocèse de Chartres), ed. Auguste Molinier. Recueil des historiens de la France, Obituaires. Paris, 1901–6.

Philippe de Beaumanoir. *Coutumes de Beauvaisis.* Ed. Amédée Salmon. 2 vols. Paris, 1899–1900.

Pierre des Vaux-de-Cernay. *The History of the Albigensian Crusade: Peter of les Vaux-de-Cernay's "Historia Albigensis."* Trans. W. A. Sibly and M. D. Sibly. Woodbridge, 1998.

———. *Petri Vallium Sarnaii monachi Hystoria Albigensis.* Ed. Pascal Guébin and Ernest Lyon. 3 vols. Paris, 1926–39.

Pierre the Chanter. *Petri Cantoris Parisiensis Verbum adbreviatum.*
Textus conflatus. Ed. Monique Boutry. CCCM 196. Turnhout, 2004.
Textus prior. Ed. Monique Boutry. CCCM 196A. Turnhout, 2012.
Textus alter. Ed. Monique Boutry. CCCM 196B. Turnhout, 2012.

Le Premier Budget de la monarchie française: Le Compte général de 1202–1203. Ed. Ferdinand Lot and Robert Fawtier. Bibliothèque de l'École des Hautes Études. Sciences historiques et philologiques, no. 259. Paris 1932.

Querimoniae Normannorum, anno 1247. Ed. Léopold Delisle. In *RHF* 24:1–73. Paris, 1904.

Raoul de Hodenc. *Le Roman des Eles.* In *Le Roman des Eles; The Anonymous Ordene de Chevalerie,* ed. Keith Busby. Utrecht Publications in General and Comparative Literature 17. Amsterdam, 1983.

Raoul Glaber. *Historiarum libri quinque.* Ed. and trans. John France, as *Rodulfi Glabri Historiarum libri quinque/The Five Books of the Histories.* Oxford, 1989.

Recits d'un ménestrel de Reims au treizième siècle. Ed. Natalis de Wailly. Paris, 1876.

Recueil des actes de Henri II, roi d'Angleterre et duc de Normandie, concernant les provinces françaises et les affaires de France. Ed. Léopold Delisle and Élie Berger. 3 vols. Paris, 1909–27.

Recueil des actes de Louis VI, roi de France (1108–1137). Ed. Jean Dufour. 4 vols. Paris, 1992.

Recueil des actes de Philippe Auguste. Ed. Henri-François Delaborde, Charles Petit-Dutaillis, Jacques Boussard, and Michel Nortier. 6 vols. Paris, 1916–2005.

Recueil des historiens des Gaules et de la France. 24 vols. Paris, 1734–1904.

The Red Book of the Exchequer. Ed. Hubert Hall. 3 vols. London, 1896.

Regesta Pontificum Romanorum ab condita ecclesia ad annum post Christum natum MCXCVIII. Ed. Philipp Jaffé et al. 2nd ed. 2 vols. Leipzig, 1885–88.

Die Register Innocenz' III., 10. Pontifikatsjahr, 1207/1208. Ed. Rainer Murauer and Andrea Sommerlechner. Publikationen des Historischen Instituts beim Österreichischen Kulturinstitut in Rom, II. Abteilung, 1. Reihe, Band 10. Vienna, 2007.

Les Registres de Philippe Auguste. Ed. John W. Baldwin, with Françoise Gasparri, Michel Nortier, and Elisabeth Lalou. Recueil des historiens de la France, Documents financiers et administratifs 7. Paris, 1992.

Rigord. *Gesta.* In *Histoire de Philippe Auguste,* ed. Élisabeth Carpentier, Georges Pon, and Yves Chauvin. Sources d'histoire médiévale 33. Paris, 2006.

——. *Gesta*. In *Œuvres de Rigord et Guillaume le Breton*, ed. Henri-François Delaborde, 1:1–167. Paris, 1882.

Robert d'Auxerre. *Chronicon*. Ed. O. Holder-Egger. In MGH, Scriptores, 26:219–76. Hannover, 1882.

Roger of Howden. *Chronica magistri Rogeri de Houedene*. Ed. William Stubbs. 4 vols. London, 1868–71.

Roger of Wendover. *Rogeri de Wendover Liber qui dicitur Flores historiarum*. Ed. Henry G. Hewlett. 3 vols. London, 1886–89.

Le Roman du castelain de Couci et de la dame de Fayel par Jakemes. Ed. John E. Matzke and Maurice Delbouille. Paris, 1936.

"Rouleau mortuaire de Guillaume des Barres." In *Recueil des rouleaux des morts (VIIIe siècle—vers 1536)*, vol. 2, *1181–1399*, ed. Jean Dufour, 206–43, 696–701. Recueil des historiens de la France, Obituaires. Paris, 2006.

Saint-Denis de Nogent-le-Rotrou (1031–1789). Ed. Charles Métais. Vannes, 1895.

Scripta de feodis ad regem spectantibus et de militibus ad exercitum vocandis, e Philippi Augusti regestis excerpta. Ed. Léopold Delisle. In *RHF* 23:608–81 (*Pars prior*), 681–723 (*Pars posterior*). Paris, 1894.

Scriptum feodorum de Monteforti. Ed. Marc-Antoine Dor. In Dor's "Seigneurs en Île-de-France," vol. 2. 1992.

Suger. *Vie de Louis VI le Gros*. Ed. Henri Waquet. Les Classiques de l'Histoire de France au Moyen Âge. Paris, 1964.

Thibaud de Marly. *Les Vers de Thibaud de Marly: Poème didactique du XIIe siècle*. Ed. Herbert King Stone. Paris, 1932.

Vetera monumenta Slavorum meridionalium historiam illustrantia. Ed. Augustine Theiner. 2 vols. Rome and Zagreb, 1863–75.

Vie de saint Eustache [excerpts]. Ed. Paul Meyer. In "Notices sur quelques manuscrits français de la Bibliothèque Phillips à Cheltenham," *Notices et extraits des manuscrits de la Bibliothèque nationale* 34, no. 1 (1891): 224–28.

Vita B. Joannis de Monte-Mirabili. Acta sanctorum, September, 8:218–35. Paris and Rome, 1865.

Secondary Sources

Adhémar, Jean. "Les Tombeaux de la Collection Gaignières: Dessins d'archéologie du XVIIe siècle." 3 parts. *Gazette des Beaux-Arts* 84 (1974), 87 (1976), 90 (1977).

Les Amis de l'Île-Adam. "Les Chartes latines concernant l'Isle-Adam et sa région." *Mémoires de la Société historique et archéologique de Pontoise, du Val-d'Oise et du Vexin* 88 (2006): 177–88.

Les Amis du vieux château de Brie-Comte-Robert.
   "Le Château de Brie-Comte-Robert. Rapport de synthèse provisoire, 1996."
   "Le Château de Brie-Comte-Robert. Bilan des recherches archéologiques, 2004."
   "Bilan des recherches archéologiques de 2008-2010."
   (Archaeological reports can be ordered directly from Les Amis du vieux château, www.amisduvieuxchateau.org.)

Anselme, Le Père. *Histoire généalogique et chronologique de la maison royale de France*. Vol. 1. Paris, 1712.

Arbogast, R.-M., B. Clavel, S. Lepetz, P. Méniel, and J.-H. Yvinec. *Archéologie du cheval: Des origines à la période moderne en France*. Paris, 2002.

Aurell, Martin. *Le Chevalier lettré: Savoir et conduite de l'aristocratie aux XIIe et XIIIe siècles*. Paris, 2011.

——. *Des chrétiens contre les croisades, XIIe–XIIIe siècle*. Paris, 2013.

Aymard, Jérôme, Daniel Dumont, and Michel Piechaczyk. *Le Château de Brie-Comte-Robert et ses seigneurs*. Les amis du vieux château, 2004.

Baldwin, John W. "The Aristocracy in the Paris Region During the Reign of Philip Augustus, 1179–1223: A Quantitative Approach." 2 parts. *Francia: Forschungen zur westeuropäischen Geschichte* 39, no. 1 (2012): 29–68; *Francia* 40, no. 1 (2013): 27–55.

——. *Aristocratic Life in Medieval France: The Romances of Jean Renart and Gerbert de Montreuil, 1190–1230.* Baltimore, 2000.

——. "Les Chevaliers à Chartres: Les Fenêtres hautes de la cathédrale." *Comptes rendus des séances de l'Académie des Inscriptions et Belles-Lettres*, April–June 2014, 693–726.

——. "Les Chevaliers dans les cartulaires monastiques de la région parisienne." In *Chevalerie et christianisme aux XIIe et XIIIe siècles*, ed. Martin Aurell and Catalina Girbea, 51–65. Rennes, 2011.

——. "From the Ordeal to Confession: In Search of Lay Religion in Early Thirteenth-Century France." In *Handling Sin: Confession in the Middle Ages*, ed. Peter Biller and A. J. Minnis, 191–209. York Studies in Medieval Theology 2. York, 1998.

——. *The Government of Philip Augustus: Foundations of French Royal Power in the Middle Ages.* Berkeley, Calif., 1986.

——. "Jean Renart et le tournoi de Saint-Trond: Une conjonction de l'histoire et de la littérature." *Annales. Économies, Sociétés, Civilisations* 45 (1990): 565–88.

——. "The Image of the Jongleur in Northern France Around 1200." *Speculum* 72 (1997): 635–63.

——. *The Language of Sex: Five Voices from Northern France Around 1200.* Chicago, 1994.

——. *Masters, Princes, and Merchants: The Social Views of Peter the Chanter and His Circle.* 2 vols. Princeton, N.J., 1970.

——. *The Medieval Theories of the Just Price: Romanists, Canonists, and Theologians in the Twelfth and Thirteenth Centuries.* Transactions of the American Philosophical Society, n.s., vol. 49, no. 4. Philadelphia, 1959.

——. *Paris, 1200.* Paris, 2006; Stanford, Calif., 2010.

——. "Pierre du Thillay, Knight and Lord: The Landed Resources of the Lower Aristocracy in the Early Thirteenth Century." *Francia: Forschungen zur westeuropäischen Geschichte* 30, no. 1 (2003): 9–41.

Baldwin, John W., and Walter Simons. "The Consequences of Bouvines." *French Historical Studies* 37 (2014): 243–69.

Barat, Yvan, Grégory Debout, and Marc Langlois. "Chevreuse (Yvelines), Donjon du château de la Madeleine, Rapport de sondage archéologique." Montigny-le-Bretonneux: Service archéologique départemental des Yvelines, 2010.

Barthélemy, Dominique. *Les Deux Âges de la seigneurie banale: Pouvoir et société dans la terre des sires de Coucy (milieu XIe–milieu XIIIe s.).* Paris, 1984.

——. *La Société dans le comté de Vendôme de l'an mil au XIVe siècle.* Paris, 1993.

Baudin, Arnaud, Ghislain Brunel, and Nicolas Dohrmann, eds. *The Knights Templar: From the Days of Jerusalem to the Commanderies of Champagne.* Paris, 2012.

Baumgartner, Emmanuèle. "Remarques sur la poésie de Gace Brulé." *Revue des langues romanes* 88 (1984): 1–13.

Bautier, Robert-Henri, ed. *La France de Philippe Auguste: Le Temps des mutations.* Colloques internationaux du Centre National de la Recherche Scientifique, 602. Paris, 1982.

Bautier, Robert-Henri, and Anne-Marie Bautier. "Contribution à l'histoire du cheval au moyen âge: L'Élevage du cheval." *Bulletin philologique et historique (jusqu'à 1610) du Comité des travaux historiques et scientifiques*, année 1978 (1980): 9–75.

Bécam, Susan E. *Rhyme in Gace Brulé's Lyric: Formal and Semantic Interplay.* Studies in the Humanities 34. New York, 1998.

Bedos-[Rezak], Brigitte. *La Châtellenie de Montmorency des origines à 1368: Aspects féodaux, sociaux et économiques.* Pontoise, 1980.

Bedos-Rezak, Brigitte. "L'Apparition des armoiries sur les sceaux en Île-de-France et en Picardie (v. 1130–1230)." In *Form and Order in Medieval France: Studies in Social and Quantitative Sigillography*, 23–41. Aldershot, 1993.

———. "Les Sceaux au temps de Philippe Auguste." In *La France de Philippe Auguste*, ed. R.-H. Bautier, 721–35. Paris, 1982.

———. *When Ego Was Imago: Signs of Identity in the Middle Ages*. Leiden, 2011.

Berger, Adolf. *Encyclopedic Dictionary of Roman Law*. Transactions of the American Philosophical Society, n.s., vol. 43, no. 2. Philadelphia, 1953.

Berkhofer, Robert F., III. *Day of Reckoning: Power and Accountability in Medieval France*. Philadelphia, 2004.

Bisson, Thomas. *The Crisis of the Twelfth Century: Power, Lordship, and the Origins of European Government of the Twelfth Century*. Princeton, N.J., 2009.

Bloch, Marc. "L'Île-de-France (les pays autour de Paris)." In Marc Bloch, *Mélanges historiques*, 692–787. Paris, 2011. First published 1913.

Borrelli de Serres, Léon-Louis. *La Réunion des provinces septentrionales à la couronne par Philippe Auguste: Amiénois, Artois, Vermandois, Valois*. Paris, 1899.

Bouchard, Constance Brittain. *Holy Entrepreneurs: Cistercians, Knights, and Economic Exchange in Twelfth-Century Burgundy*. Ithaca, N.Y., 1991.

Bouchot, Henri. *Inventaire des dessins exécutés pour Roger de Gaignières et conservés aux départements des estampes et des manuscrits*. 2 vols. Paris, 1891.

Boulton, Maureen B. M. *The Song in the Story: Lyric Insertions in French Narrative Fiction, 1200–1400*. Philadelphia, 1993.

Bourgain, Pascale. "L'Emploi de la langue vulgaire dans la littérature au temps de Philippe Auguste." In *La France de Philippe Auguste: Le temps des mutations*, ed. Robert-Henri Bautier, 765–84. Paris, 1982.

Bourin, Monique. "France du Midi et France du Nord: Deux systèmes anthroponymiques?" In *L'Anthroponymie: Document de l'histoire sociale des mondes méditerranéens médiévaux*, 179–202. Collection de l'École française de Rome 226. Rome, 1996.

Bournazel, Eric. *Le Gouvernement Capétien au XIIe siècle, 1108–1180: Structures sociales et mutations institutionnelles*. Paris, 1975.

Brenk, Beat. "Bildprogrammatik und Geschichtsverständnis der Kapetinger im Querhaus der Kathedrale von Chartres." *Arte medievale* 5 (1991): 71–95.

Brière, Pierre. "Une alliance familiale entre les Garlande, les Mauvoisin et les Mello au XIIe siècle." *Bulletin de la Société historique de Lagny* 1 (1961): 3–12.

Brown, Elizabeth A. R. "The Tyranny of a Construct: Feudalism and Historians of Medieval Europe." *American Historical Review* 79 (1974): 1063–88.

Brundage, James A. *Medieval Canon Law*. New York, 1995.

———. *Medieval Canon Law and the Crusader*. Madison, Wis., 1969.

Brunel, Ghislain. "The Knights Templar and Money." In *The Knights Templar: From the Days of Jerusalem to the Commanderies of Champagne*, ed. Arnaud Baudin, Ghislain Brunel, and Nicolas Dohrmann, 104–9. Paris, 2012.

———. "Les Rois de France et l'Orient." In *La Présence latine en Orient au Moyen Âge*, ed. Ghislain Brunel, 37–56. Paris, 2000.

Bruzelius, Caroline A. "Cistercian High Gothic: The Abbey Church of Longpont and the Architecture of the Cistercians in the Early Thirteenth Century." *Analecta Cisterciensia* 35 (1979): 3–204.

Buckland, W. W. *A Manual of Roman Private Law*. 2nd ed. Cambridge, 1947.

Buffum, Douglas L. "The Songs of the *Roman de la Violette*." In *Studies in Honor of A. Marshall Elliott*, 1:129–57. Baltimore, 1911.

Bugslag, James. "Ideology and Iconography in Chartres Cathedral: Jean Clément and the Oriflamme." *Zeitschrift für Kunstgeschichte* 61 (1998): 491–508.

———. "Pilgrimage to Chartres: The Visual Evidence." In *Art and Architecture of Late Medieval Pilgrimage in Northern Europe and the British Isles*, ed. Sarah Blick and Rita Tekippe, 1:135–83. Leiden, 2005.

Bur, Michel, ed. *La Maison forte au Moyen Âge: Actes de la table ronde de Nancy-Pont-à-Mousson des 31 mai– 3 juin 1984*. Paris, 1986.

Caillot, Isabelle, and Gaëlle André. "Vieux château, Lycée Turgot, Montmorency (95): Rapport final d'opération archéologique: fouille préventive." 3 vols. SRA Île-de-France, 2012.

Carolus-Barré, Louis. "Une arrière petite-fille de Hugues Capet, Aliénor de Vermandois, comtesse de Beaumont puis de Saint-Quentin, dame de Valois vers 1150, d. 19 juin 1213." In his *Études et documents sur l'Île-de-France et la Picardie au Moyen Âge*, 2:187–217. Compiègne, 1996. First published 1991.

Cartellieri, Alexander. *Philipp II. August, König von Frankreich*. 4 vols. Leipzig, 1899–1922.

Chapelot, Jean, and Robert Fossier. *Le Village et la maison au Moyen Âge*. Paris, 1980.

Châtelain, André. *Châteaux forts et féodalité en Île-de-France du XIe au XIIIe siècle*. Paris, 1983.

Chênerie, Marie-Luce. *Le Chevalier errant dans les romans arthuriens en vers des XIIe et XIIIe siècles*. Publications romanes et françaises 172. Geneva, 1986.

Civel, Nicolas. *La Fleur de France: Les Seigneurs d'Île-de-France au XIIe siècle*. Histoire de Famille, La Parenté au Moyen Âge 5. Turnhout, 2006.

Constable, Giles. *Monastic Tithes from Their Origins to the Twelfth Century*. Cambridge, 1964.

———. "Suger's Monastic Administration." In *Abbot Suger and Saint-Denis: A Symposium*, ed. Paula Gerson, 17–32. New York, 1986.

Cottineau, L.-H. *Répertoire topo-bibliographique des abbayes et prieurés*. 3 vols. Mâcon, 1936–39.

Coulson, Charles. "Fortress-Policy in Capetian Tradition and Angevin Practice: Aspects of the Conquest of Normandy by Philip II." *Anglo-Norman Studies* 6 (1983): 13–38.

Crouch, David. *The Birth of Nobility: Constructing Aristocracy in England and France, 900–1300*. London, 2005.

———. *William Marshal: Court, Career and Chivalry in the Angevin Empire, 1147–1219*. London, 1990.

Daon, Pierre. "Barthélemy de Roye, chambrier de France." *Positions des thèses, École des Chartes*, 1943, 49–53.

Darras, Eugène. *Les Seigneurs-châtelains de l'Île-Adam*. Pontoise, 1939.

de Curzon, Henri. *La Maison du Temple de Paris*. Paris, 1888.

Delisle, Léopold. "Chronologie des baillis et des sénéchaux royaux." In *RHF*, vol. 24, preface, pp. 15–385. Paris, 1904.

———. "Fragments de l'histoire de Gonesse principalement tirés des Archives hospitalières de cette commune." *Bibliothèque de l'École des Chartes* 20 (1859): 113–52, 247–77.

———. *Littérature latine et histoire du moyen âge*. Paris, 1890.

Depoin, Joseph. "Manuscrits funèbres de Saint-Léonor de Beaumont: Obituaire et martyrologe." *Mémoires de la Société historique et archéologique de Pontoise et du Vexin* 35 (1918): 1–60.

———. "Les Vicomtes de Corbeil et les chevaliers d'Étampes au XIIe siècle." *Bulletin de la Société historique et archéologique de Corbeil, d'Étampes et du Hurepoix* 5 (1899): 1–71, 159–65.

Deremble, Colette, and Jean-Paul Deremble. *Vitraux de Chartres*. Paris, 2003.

———. "Les Vitraux médiévaux, un patrimoine exceptionnel." In *La Grâce d'une cathédrale: Chartres*, ed. Michel Pansard, 147–210. Strasbourg, 2013.

Dimier, M.-Anselme. "Le Bienheureux Jean de Montmirail, moine de Longpont." *Mémoires de la Fédération des sociétés savantes de l'Aisne* 7 (1960–61): 182–91.

Dor, Marc-Antoine. "Seigneurs en Île-de-France occidentale et en Haute Normandie: Contributions à l'histoire des seigneurs de Montfort-l'Amaury, des comtes d'Évreux et de leur entourage, au XIIe siècle et au début du XIIIe siècle." 2 vols. Thèse de l'École Nationale des Chartes, 1992.

Douët d'Arcq, Louis. *Collection de sceaux*. 3 vols. Paris, 1863–68.

———. *Recherches historiques et critiques sur les anciens comtes de Beaumont-sur-Oise du XIe au XIIIe siècle*. Amiens, 1855.

Duby, Georges. *Guerriers et paysans, VIIe—XIIe siècle: Premier essor de l'économie européenne*. Paris, 1973.

———. *Guillaume le Maréchal, ou le Meilleur Chevalier du monde*. Paris, 1984.

———. *La Société aux XIe et XIIe siècles dans la région Mâconnaise*. Paris, 1953.

Duchesne, André. "Histoire de la maison des bouteillers de Senlis." *Revue historique, nobiliaire et biographique*, 3rd ser., vol. 3 (1878): 153–81.

———. *Histoire généalogique de la maison de Montmorency et de Laval*, and *Preuves de L'Histoire de la maison de Montmorency*. Paris, 1624.

———. *Histoire généalogique de la maison royale de Dreux* . . . . Paris, 1631.

Dufaÿ, Bruno. "Le Château de Beynes (Yvelines) du XIIe au XVIe siècle." *Revue archéologique du Centre de la France* 40 (2001): 243–85.

———. "Histoire du donjon de La Madeleine à Chevreuse." In *Rencontres archéologiques des Yvelines: Maisons des dieux, maisons des hommes; Colloque à Versailles, samedi 10 mars 1990*, 65–83. Versailles, 1990.

Dufour, Jean-Yves, ed. *Le Château de Roissy-en-France (Val d'Oise): Origine et développement d'une résidence seigneuriale du pays de France (XIIe–XIXe siècle)*. *Revue archéologique d'Île-de-France*, Supplément 2. Paris, 2014.

Duval-Arnould, Louis. "Les Aumônes d'Aliénor, dernière comtesse de Vermandois et dame de Valois." *Revue Mabillon* 60, nos. 295–96 (1984): 395–463.

———. "Quelques inscriptions funéraires de l'abbaye de Longpont." In *Mélanges à la mémoire du Père Anselme Dimier*, ed. Benoît Chauvin, tome 2, vol. 4, pp. 661–91. Arbois, 1984.

Evergates, Theodore. *The Aristocracy in the County of Champagne, 1100–1300*. Philadelphia, 2007.

———. *Feudal Society in the Bailliage of Troyes Under the Counts of Champagne, 1152–1284*. Baltimore, 1975.

Fassler, Margot. *The Virgin of Chartres: Making History Through Liturgy and the Arts*. New Haven, Conn., 2010.

Fawtier, Robert. "Un fragment du compte de l'hôtel du prince Louis de France pour le terme de la purification 1213." *Le Moyen Âge* 43 (1933): 225–50.

Flambard Héricher, Anne-Marie. "Le Château des comtes de Meulan à Vatteville-la-Rue: Approche comparative d'une demeure aristocratique normande." In *Aux marches du palais: Qu'est-ce qu'un palais médiéval?*, ed. A. Renoux, 213–21. Le Mans, 2001.

Flori, Jean. *L'Essor de la chevalerie, XIe–XIIe siècles*. Geneva, 1986.

Fourquin, Guy. *Les Campagnes de la région parisienne à la fin du moyen âge: Du milieu du XIIIe siècle au début du XVIe siècle*. Paris, 1964.

Fourrier, Anthime. "Raoul de Hodenc: Est-ce lui?" In *Mélanges de linguistique romane et de philologie médiévale offerts à M. Maurice Delbouille*, 2:165–93. Gembloux, 1964.

Friedmann, Adrien. *Paris, ses rues, ses paroisses du Moyen Âge à la Révolution: Origine et évolution des circonscriptions paroissiales*. Paris, 1959.

Gallia christiana in provincias ecclesiasticas distributa. 16 vols. Paris, 1739–1877.

Gentili, François, Sonia Bensaadoune, Jean-François Pastre, Isabelle Caillot, and Marc Viré. "Le Site du château d'Orville à Louvres (Val-d'Oise): Évolution d'une vallée, d'un habitat, d'un édifice; Trois manières d'appréhender la durée dans le cadre d'approches pluridisciplinaires." In *On the Road Again, l'Europe en mouvement: Medieval Europe, Paris 2007, 4th International Congress of Medieval and Modern Archaeology; Theme 2, Archaeology and Rural Landscape*, ed. Isabelle Catteddu, Paolo de Vingo, and Anne Nissen Jaubert, 75–99. Genoa, 2011.

Gentili, François, Isabelle Caillot, and Marc Viré. "Louvres (Val-d'Oise), château d'Orville, rapport d'activité 2005: Habitat rural du haut Moyen Âge et château médiéval." SRA Île-de-France, 2005.

Gorochov, Nathalie. *Naissance de l'université: Les écoles de Paris d'Innocent III à Thomas d'Aquin (v. 1200–v. 1245)*. Paris, 2012.

Gouget, Jean, and Thierry Le Hête. *Les Comtes de Blois et de Champagne et leur descendance agnatique: Généalogie et histoire d'une dynastie féodale*. Saint-Sébastien-de-Morsent, 2004.

Grant, Lindy. *Abbot Suger of St-Denis: Church and State in Early Twelfth-Century France*. London, 1998.

———. "Representing Dynasty: The Transept Windows at Chartres Cathedral." In *Representing History, 900–1300: Art, Music, History*, ed. Robert A. Maxwell, 109–14. University Park, Pa., 2010.

Gravelaine, Frédérique de. *Encyclopédie des prénoms: Symboles, étymologie, histoire et secrets de 6000 prénoms*. Paris, 1989.

Green, Judith A. *The Aristocracy of Norman England*. Cambridge, 1997.

Grosse, Rolf. "Remarques sur les cartulaires de Saint-Denis aux XIIIe et XIVe siècles." In *Les Cartulaires: Actes de la table ronde organisée par l'École nationale des chartes, 1991*, ed. Olivier Guyotjeannin, Laurent Morelle, and Michel Parisse, 279–89. Mémoires et documents de l'École des Chartes 39. Paris, 1993.

Grossel, Marie-Geneviève. *Le Milieu littéraire en Champagne sous les Thibaudiens (1200–1270)*. 2 vols. Orléans, 1997.

Guilhiermoz, Paul. "Une charte de Gace Brulé." *Romania* 22 (1893): 127–28.

Hallavant, Charlotte. "Étude carpologique du château de la Madeleine (Chevreuse, 78)." Unpublished report for the Service Archéologique Départemental des Yvelines, 2007.

Harmand, Jacques. "Le Donjon de Houdan: Études complémentaires." *Bulletin monumental* 130 (1972): 191–212, 347–48.

———. "Houdan et l'évolution des donjons au XIIe siècle." *Bulletin monumental* 127 (1969): 187–207.

Hasenohr, Geneviève. "Thibaut de Marly." In *Dictionnaire des lettres françaises: Le moyen âge*, ed. Geneviève Hasenohr and Michel Zink, 1425–26. Paris, 1992.

Helmholz, R. H. *Canon Law and the Law of England*. London, 1987.

Higounet, Charles. *La Grange de Vaulerent: Structure et exploitation d'un terroir cistercien de la plaine de France, XIIe–XVe siècle*. Les hommes et la terre 10. Paris, 1965.

Iogna-Prat, Dominique. "La Place idéale du laïc à Cluny (v. 930–v. 1150): D'une morale statuaire à une éthique absolue?" In *Guerriers et moines: Conversion et sainteté aristocratiques dans l'Occident médiéval (IXe–XIIe siècle)*, ed. Michel Lauwers, 291–316. Antibes, 2002.

Jeanroy, A. "Notes sur le tournoiement des dames." *Romania* 28 (1899): 232–44.

Jordan, William Chester. *The French Monarchy and the Jews: From Philip Augustus to the Last Capetians*. Philadelphia, 1989.

Kaeuper, Richard W. *Holy Warriors: The Religious Ideology of Chivalry*. Philadelphia, 2009.

Katzenellenbogen, Adolf. *The Sculptural Program of Chartres Cathedral: Christ, Mary, Ecclesia*. Baltimore, 1959.

Keyser, Richard. "La Transformation de l'échange des dons pieux: Montier-la-Celle, Champagne, 1100–1350." *Revue historique* 305, fasc. 628 (October 2003): 793–816.

Labie-Leurquin, Anne-Françoise, and Sara I. James. "Quinze signes du jugement dernier." In *Dictionnaire des lettres françaises: Le Moyen Âge*, ed. Geneviève Hasenohr and Michel Zink, 1217–18. Paris, 1992.

Lallau, Étienne, and Grégory Debout. *Le Château de Chevreuse: De l'an mil à nos jours*. Versailles, 2014.

Langdon, John. "Horse Hauling: A Revolution in Vehicle Transportation in Twelfth- and Thirteenth-Century England?" *Past and Present* 103 (1984): 37–66.

Langlois, Jean-Yves. "Beaumont-sur-Oise (Val-d'Oise), site du château: Rapport de fouille préliminaire." SRA Île-de-France, 1984.

Langlois, Marc. "Le Donjon de Montfort-l'Amaury." *Connaître les Yvelines: Histoire et archéologie*, 2e trim. 1990, 33–34.

Lautier, Claudine. "The Canons of Chartres: Their Patronage and Representation in the Stained Glass of the Cathedral." In *Patronage: Power and Agency in Medieval Art*, ed. Colum Hourihane, 99–118. Index of Christian Art Occasional Papers 15. University Park, Pa., 2013.

———. "Les Deux Galeries des rois." In *La Grâce d'une cathédrale: Chartres*, ed. Michel Pansard, 242–47. Strasbourg, 2013.

———. "La Diversité des ateliers de peintres-verriers du XIIIe siècle." In *La Grâce d'une cathédrale: Chartres*, ed. Pansard, 222–27. Strasbourg, 2013.

———. "Échos et correspondances iconographiques: Vitraux et reliques." In *La Grâce d'une cathédrale: Chartres*, ed. Pansard, 211–16. Strasbourg, 2013.

———. "Les Restaurations de vitraux du moyen âge à nos jours." In *La Grâce d'une cathédrale: Chartres*, ed. Pansard, 232–35. Strasbourg, 2013.

———. "Restaurations récentes à la cathédrale de Chartres et nouvelles recherches." *Bulletin monumental* 169, no. 1 (2011): 3–11.

———. "La Royauté française dans le décor de la cathédrale de Chartres." In "Dynastische Repräsentation in der Glasmalerei," special issue, *Österreichische Zeitschrift für Kunst und Denkmalpflege* 66, nos. 3–4 (2012): 236–47.

———. "The Sacred Topography of Chartres Cathedral: The Reliquary Chasse of the Virgin in the Liturgical Choir and Stained-Glass Decoration." In *The Four Modes of Seeing: Approaches to Medieval Imagery in Honor of Madeline Harrison Cavines*, ed. E. S. Lane, E. C. Pastan, and E. M. Shortell, 174–96. Burlington, Vt., 2009.

———. "Les Vitraux de la cathédrale de Chartres: Reliques et images." *Bulletin monumental* 161, no. 1 (2003): 3–97.

Lauwers, Michel. "Du pacte seigneurial à l'idéal de conversion: Les Légendes hagiographiques de Simon de Crépy (d. 1081–82)." In *Guerriers et moines*, ed. Lauwers, 559–88. Antibes, 2002.

———, ed. *Guerriers et moines: Conversion et sainteté aristocratiques dans l'Occident médiéval (IXe–XIIe siècle)*. Collection d'études médiévales de Nice 4. Antibes, 2002.

———. "La 'Vie du seigneur Bouchard, comte vénérable': Conflits d'avouerie, traditions carolingiennes et modèles de sainteté à l'abbaye des Fossés au XIe siècle." In *Guerriers et moines*, ed. Lauwers, 373–418. Antibes, 2002.

Lebeuf, L'Abbé. *Histoire de la ville et de tout le diocèse de Paris*. 6 vols. Paris: Féchoz et Letouzey, 1883–93. First published 1754–58.

Le Bras, Gabriel, Charles Lefebvre, and Jacqueline Rambaud. *L'Âge classique (1140–1378): Sources et théorie du droit*. Histoire du droit et des institutions de l'Église en Occident, vol. 7. Paris, 1965.

Lefebvre-Teillard, Anne. "L'École parisienne et la formation 'politique' des clercs au début du XIIIe siècle." In *Science politique et droit public dans les facultés de droit européennes (XIIIe–XVIIIe siècle)*, ed. Jacques Krynen and Michael Stolleis, 23–40. Frankfurt am Main, 2008.

———. "Petrus Brito, auteur de l'apparat 'Ecce vicit leo'?" In *Proceedings of the Thirteenth International Congress of Medieval Canon Law*, ed. Peter Erdö and S. Z. Anselm Szuromi, 117–35. Vatican City, 2010.

Lefèvre, Simone. "Les Dîmes novales dans la région parisienne du XIIe au XIIIe siècle." In *L'Encadrement religieux des fidèles au Moyen-âge et jusqu'au Concile de Trente*, 721–33. Actes du 109e Congrès National des Sociétés Savantes, Dijon, 1984. Paris, 1985.

Le Goff, Jacques. *La Naissance du purgatoire*. Paris, 1981.

Lemaître, Jean-Loup. *Répertoire des documents nécrologiques français*. Recueil des historiens de la France, Obituaires, vol. 7, nos. 1–5. Paris, 1980–92.

Lemesle, Bruno. *La Société aristocratique dans le Haut-Maine (XIe–XIIe siècles)*. Rennes, 1999.

Léonard, E.-G. *Introduction au cartulaire manuscrit du Temple (1150–1317) constitué par le marquis d'Albon et conservé à la Bibliothèque nationale*. Paris, 1930.

Leroy, Gabriel. "Le Refuge de Barbeau." *Bulletin de la Société d'archéologie, sciences, lettres et arts du département de Seine-et-Marne* 1 (1865): 193–97.

Leroy, Thierry. "Commanderies of Champagne and of Brie." In *The Knights Templar: From the Days of Jerusalem to the Commanderies of Champagne*, ed. Arnaud Baudin, Ghislain Brunel, and Nicolas Dohrmann, 188–203. Paris, 2012.

Lespinasse, René de. *Le Nivernais et les comtes de Nevers*. 3 vols. Paris, 1909–14.

Lewis, Andrew. *Royal Succession in Capetian France: Studies on Familial Order and the State*. Cambridge, Mass., 1981.

Livingstone, Amy. *Out of Love for My Kin: Aristocratic Family Life in the Lands of the Loire, 1000–1200*. Ithaca, N.Y., 2010.

Longnon, Jean. *Les Compagnons de Villehardouin: Recherches sur les croisés de la quatrième croisade*. Hautes études médiévales et modernes 30. Geneva, 1978.

Lynch, Joseph H. *Simoniacal Entry into Religious Life from 1000 to 1260: A Social, Economic, and Legal Study.* Columbus, Ohio, 1976.

Maddicott, J. R. *Simon de Montfort.* Cambridge, 1996.

Manhes-Deremble, Colette. *Les Vitraux narratifs de la cathédrale de Chartres: Étude iconographique.* Corpus vitrearum, France, Études, vol. 2. Paris, 1993.

Maquet, Adrien. *Les Seigneurs de Marly.* Paris, 1882.

Mathieu, Jean-Noël. "La Famille de Garlande à Possesse." *Mémoires de la Société d'agriculture, commerce, sciences et arts du département de la Marne* 108 (1993): 69–94

———. "Recherches sur les premiers comtes de Dammartin." *Paris et Ile-de-France, Mémoires* 47 (1996): 7–59.

———. *Recherches sur les premiers comtes de Dammartin: Un nouvel éclairage sur Renaud de Dammartin, comte de Boulogne.* 1995.

Mazel, Florien. "Pouvoirs locaux et acteurs du chantier." In *La Grâce d'une cathédrale: Chartres,* ed. Michel Pansard, 41–55. Strasbourg, 2013.

McLaughlin, Megan. *Consorting with Saints: Prayer for the Dead in Early Medieval France.* Ithaca, N.Y., 1994.

Mehl, Jean-Michel. *Les Jeux au royaume de France du XIIIe au début du XVIe siècle.* Paris, 1990.

Mesqui, Jean. *Les Demeures seigneuriales.* Vol. 2 of *Île-de-France gothique.* Paris, 1988.

———. *La Résidence et les éléments d'architecture.* Vol. 2 of *Châteaux et enceintes de la France médiévale: De la défense à la residence.* Paris, 1993.

Molinier, Auguste. "Catalogue des actes de Simon et d'Amauri de Montfort." *Bibliothèque de l'École des Chartes* 34 (1873): 153–203, 445–501.

Moutié, Auguste. *Chevreuse: Recherches historiques, archéologiques et généalogique.* Mémoires et documents de la Société archéologique de Rambouillet. 2 vols. Rambouillet, 1874–76.

Newman, William Mendel. *Les Seigneurs de Nesle en Picardie (XIIe–XIIIe siècle).* 2 vols. Memoirs of the American Philosophical Society 91. Philadelphia, 1971.

Nicholas, David. *Medieval Flanders.* New York, 1992.

Nieus, Jean-François. "Le Château au cœur du réseau vassalique: À propos des services de garde aux XIIe–XIIIe siècles." In *Lieu de pouvoir, lieu de gestion: Le Château aux XIIIe–XVIe siècles; Mâitres, terres et sujets,* ed. Jean-Marie Cauchies and Jacqueline Guisset, 93–108. Turnhout, 2011.

———. "Des seigneurs sans chancellerie? Pratiques de l'écrit documentaire chez les comtes et les barons du nord de la France aux XIIe–XIIIe siècles." In *Chancelleries princières et Scriptoria dans les anciens Pays-Bas, Xe–XVe siècles,* ed. Thérèse de Hemptinne and J.-M. Duvosquel, 285–311. Bulletin de la Commission royale d'histoire 176, no. 2. Brussels, 2010.

Painter, Sidney. *The Scourge of the Clergy: Peter of Dreux, Duke of Brittany.* Baltimore, 1937.

———. *William Marshal: Knight-Errant, Baron, and Regent of England.* Baltimore, 1933.

Pansard, Michel, ed. *La Grâce d'une cathédrale: Chartres.* Strasbourg, 2013.

Pastoureau, Michel. *L'Art héraldique au moyen âge.* Paris, 2009.

———. "Le Décor héraldique des clefs de voûte de la cathédrale de Chartres." *Bulletin monumental* 169, no. 1 (2011): 35–40.

———. "La Diffusion des armoiries et les débuts de l'héraldique." In *La France de Philippe Auguste: Le temps des mutations,* ed. Robert-Henri Bautier, 737–59. Paris, 1982.

———. *Les Emblèmes de la France.* Paris, 1998.

———. *Traité d'héraldique.* Paris, 1979.

Payen, Jean-Charles. *Le Motif du repentir dans la littérature française médiévale (des origines à 1230).* Publications romanes et françaises 98. Geneva, 1967.

Pegeon, Annick. "Le Château de Roissy-en-France et l'histoire: synthèse sur les occupations successives d'après les sources archivistiques et archéologiques." In *Le Château de Roissy-en-France (Val d'Oise): Origine et développement d'une résidence seigneuriale du pays de France (XIIe–XIXe siècle),* ed. Jean-Yves Dufour, 401–419. Paris, 2014.

Perrot, Françoise. "Le Vitrail, la croisade et la Champagne: Réflexion sur les fenêtres hautes du chœur à la cathédrale de Chartres." In *Les Champenois et la croisade*, ed. Yvonne Bellenger and Danielle Quéruel, 109–30. Paris, 1989.

Petit-Dutaillis, Charles. *Étude sur la vie et le règne de Louis VIII (1187–1226)*. Bibliothèque de l'École des Hautes Études, Sciences philologiques et historiques, no. 101. Paris, 1894.

Petot, Pierre. "L'Ordonnance du 1er mai 1209." In *Recueil de travaux offert à M. Clovis Brunel*, 2:371–80. Mémoires et documents de la Société de l'École des Chartes 12. Paris, 1955.

Piechaczyk, Michel. "Le Château de Brie-Comte-Robert, un château de Robert Ier de Dreux." In *Histoire de Dreux et du Drouais: État des connaissances et perspectives de recherche; Actes du colloque de Dreux des 4 et 5 juin 2010*, ed. Philippe Bujak, 141–53. Histoire médiévale et archéologie 26. Amiens, 2013.

Piechaczyk, Michel, Martine Piechaczyk, and Évelyne Coindre-Béon. *Le Château de Brie-Comte-Robert*. Moisenay, 2007.

Power, Daniel. *The Norman Frontier in the Twelfth and Early Thirteenth Centuries*. Cambridge, 2004.

Powicke, Maurice. *The Loss of Normandy, 1189–1204: Studies in the History of the Angevin Empire*. Manchester, 1961.

Quétif, Jacques, and Jacques Échard. *Scriptores ordinis praedicatorum*. 2 vols. Paris, 1719–21.

Rauch, Ivo. "Die Bundeslade und die wahren Israeliten: Anmerkungen zum mariologischen und politischen Programm der Hochchorfenster der Kathedrale von Chartres." In *Glas, Malerei, Forschung: Internationale Studien zu Ehren von Rüdiger Becksmann*, ed. Hartmut Scholz, Ivo Rauch, and Daniel Hess, 61–71. Berlin, 2004.

Reynolds, Susan. *Fiefs and Vassals: The Medieval Evidence Reinterpreted*. Oxford, 1994.

Rhein, André. "La Seigneurie de Montfort en Iveline." *Mémoires de la Société archéologique de Rambouillet* 21 (1910): 1–360.

Richemond, Émile-Louis. *Recherches généalogiques sur la famille des seigneurs de Nemours du XIIe au XVe siècle*. 2 vols. Fontainebleau, 1907–8.

Roach, Eleanor. "*Bruslez amis* and the Battle of Bouvines." *Zeitschrift für romanische Philologie* 95 (1979): 21–35.

Rosenwein, Barbara H. *To Be the Neighbor of Saint Peter: The Social Meaning of Cluny's Property, 909–1049*. Ithaca, N.Y., 1989.

Salch, Charles-Laurent. *L'Atlas des châteaux forts en France*. Strasbourg, 1977.

Sandauer, Pauline. *L'Élement scolastique dans l'œuvre de Raoul de Houdenc*. Travaux du Séminaire de philologie romane. Lwów, 1922.

Schenk, Jochen. *Templar Families: Landowning Families and the Order of the Temple in France, c. 1120–1307*. Cambridge, 2012.

Sheehan, Michael M. "The Influence of Canon Law on the Property Rights of Married Women in England." *Mediaeval Studies* 25 (1963): 109–24.

———. *The Will in Medieval England: From the Conversion of the Anglo-Saxons to the End of the Thirteenth Century*. Toronto, 1963.

Sirot, Élisabeth. *Noble et forte maison: L'Habitat seigneurial dans les compagnes médiévales du milieu du XIIe au début du XVIe siècle*. Paris, 2007.

Sivéry, Gérard. *L'Économie du royaume de France au siècle de Saint Louis (vers 1180–vers 1315)*. Lille, 1984.

Stein, Henri. "Le Mez-le-Maréchal." *Congrès archéologique de France*, 93rd session, 1930 (1931): 233–41.

———. "Un sénéchal du XIIIe siècle, Guillaume de Combreux." *Bibliothèque de l'École des Chartes* 94 (1933): 328–36.

Tabuteau, Emily Zack. *Transfers of Property in Eleventh-Century Norman Law*. Chapel Hill, N.C., 1988.

Thompson, Kathleen. *Power and Border Lordship in Medieval France: The County of Perche, 1000–1226*. Woodbridge, 2002.

Timbert, Arnaud. "La Construction de la cathédrale gothique: Formes, matériaux et techniques." In *La Grâce d'une cathédrale: Chartres*, ed. Michel Pansard, 57–104. Strasbourg, 2013.

Van Kerrebrouck, Patrick. *Les Capétiens, 987–1328*. Nouvelle histoire généalogique de l'auguste maison de France, vol. 2. Villeneuve d'Ascq, 2000.

Vic, Claude de, and Joseph Vaissette. *Histoire générale de Languedoc*. Ed. Auguste Molinier et al. 16 vols. Toulouse: Édouard Privat, 1872–1904.

Vincent, Nicholas. *Norman Charters from English Sources: Antiquaries, Archives and the Rediscovery of the Anglo-Norman Past*. Publications of the Pipe Roll Society. London, 2013.

Viré, Marc. "Rapport de synthèse sur le diagnostic archéologique entrepris dans le château de Blandy-les-Tours en 1995." Service départemental du Patrimoine de Seine-et-Marne, Dammarie-lès-Lys, 1995.

Les Vitraux du Centre et des Pays de la Loire. Introduction by Louis Grodecki and Françoise Perrot. Corpus vitrearum, France, Recensement des vitraux anciens de la France, vol. 2. Paris: CNRS, 1981.

White, Stephen D. *Custom, Kinship and Gifts to Saints: The* Laudatio parentum *in Western France, 1050–1150*. Chapel Hill, 1988.

Williams, Jane Welch. *Bread, Wine, and Money: The Windows of the Trades at Chartres Cathedral*. Chicago, 1993.

Woehl, Christine. *Volo vincere cum meis vel occumbere cum eisdem: Studien zu Simon von Montfort und seinen nordfranzösischen Gefolgsleuten während des Albigenserkreuzzugs (1209 bis 1218)*. Frankfurt am Main, 2001.

Zink, Michel. *Les Troubadours: Une histoire poétique*. Paris, 2013.

Index

Acknowledgments

The Baldwin family would like to acknowledge
the extraordinarily thorough and scholarly work of
Thomas Boeve in preparing this manuscript for publication.